Empire, Race and Global Justice

The status of boundaries and borders, questions of global poverty and inequality, criteria for the legitimate uses of force, the value of international law, human rights, nationality, sovereignty, migration, territory, and citizenship: debates over these critical issues are central to contemporary understandings of world politics. Bringing together an interdisciplinary range of contributors, including historians, political theorists, lawyers, and international relations scholars, this is the first volume of its kind to explore the racial and imperial dimensions of normative debates over global justice.

Duncan Bell is Reader in Political Thought and International Relations at the University of Cambridge, and a Fellow of Christ's College.

Empire, Race and Global Justice

Edited by

Duncan Bell
University of Cambridge

CAMBRIDGE
UNIVERSITY PRESS

University Printing House, Cambridge CB2 8BS, United Kingdom

One Liberty Plaza, 20th Floor, New York, NY 10006, USA

477 Williamstown Road, Port Melbourne, VIC 3207, Australia

314–321, 3rd Floor, Plot 3, Splendor Forum, Jasola District Centre,
New Delhi – 110025, India

79 Anson Road, #06–04/06, Singapore 079906

Cambridge University Press is part of the University of Cambridge.

It furthers the University's mission by disseminating knowledge in the pursuit of
education, learning, and research at the highest international levels of excellence.

www.cambridge.org
Information on this title: www.cambridge.org/9781108427791
DOI: 10.1017/9781108576307

© Duncan Bell 2019

First published 2019

A catalogue record for this publication is available from the British Library.

Library of Congress Cataloging-in-Publication Data
Names: Bell, Duncan, 1976– editor.
Title: Empire, race and global justice / edited by Duncan Bell.
Description: Cambridge, United Kingdom ; New York, NY : Cambridge
University Press, 2019. | Includes bibliographical references.
Identifiers: LCCN 2018038844 | ISBN 9781108427791 (hardback)
Subjects: LCSH: Globalization – Political aspects. | Globalization – Social
aspects. | International relations – Moral and ethical aspects. | Social justice. |
BISAC: POLITICAL SCIENCE / International Relations / General.
Classification: LCC JZ1318 .E519 2019 | DDC 327.1–dc23
LC record available at https://lccn.loc.gov/2018038844

ISBN 978-1-108-42779-1 Hardback

Contents

Contributors

DUNCAN BELL is Reader in Political Thought and International Relations, and a fellow of Christ's College, University of Cambridge.

KATRINA FORRESTER is Assistant Professor of Government at Harvard University.

KIMBERLEY HUTCHINGS is Professor of Politics and International Relations at Queen Mary University of London.

MARGARET KOHN is Professor of Political Science at the University of Toronto.

CATHERINE LU is Associate Professor of Political Science at McGill University.

CHARLES W. MILLS is Professor of Philosophy at the City University of New York.

JEANNE MOREFIELD is Professor of Politics at Whitman College.

SAMUEL MOYN is Professor of Law and History at Yale University.

ROBERT NICHOLS is Assistant Professor of Political Science at the University of Minnesota.

SUNDHYA PAHUJA is Professor of International Law, and Director of the Institute of Law and the Humanities, at the University of Melbourne Law School.

ANNE PHILLIPS FBA is the Graham Wallas Professor of Political Science, and Professor of Gender and Political Theory, at the London School of Economics.

INÉS VALDEZ is Assistant Professor of Political Science at the Ohio State University.

Acknowledgements

Many of the chapters in this book were first presented at a workshop in Cambridge in April 2016. I'd like to thank Or Rosenboim for her support in organising the event, Queens' College, Cambridge, for hosting it, and the Trevelyan Fund of the Faculty of History, the Department of Politics and International Studies, and the Leverhulme Trust, for generously funding it. I would also like to thank Taylor & Francis for permission to reprint, in modified form, an essay by Charles W. Mills. Thanks also to Randall Persuad and Jeanne Morefield for commenting on the introductory chapter. John Haslam at Cambridge University Press has been an exemplary editor. Above all, I would like to thank the contributors to the volume for their commitment to the project.

Introduction: Empire, Race and Global Justice

Duncan Bell

Abject poverty. Yawning inequality, political, economic, and social. Human rights and their systematic abuse. Nationality, sovereignty, citizenship. The identification of historical injustices and their possible rectification. Migration flows and border politics. The legitimation, conduct, and cessation of war. Terrorism, terror, territory. Democracy beyond and between states. All of these topics and more are addressed in contemporary debates over global justice. They have motivated activism, spawning social movements, political protest, and legal campaigns. They are debated across a range of academic disciplines and discourses: sociologists, International Relations (IR) scholars, geographers, anthropologists, economists, and historians have contributed important work on the subject. In political theory, global justice has been a core topic at least since the end of the Cold War, its meaning, scope, and policy implications contested by groups of egalitarian cosmopolitans, libertarians, liberal nationalists, and statists, among others.[1] The importance of the subject shows no sign of waning.

Despite the welcome attention paid to the topic, the debates on global justice among political theorists – at least in the so-called 'Anglo-American' (or 'analytical') tradition – are marked by some notable silences and omissions. This book addresses two of the most significant. First, there has been little detailed discussion of how the history of imperialism has shaped current patterns of global injustice, and the ethical and political consequences that follow from this troubling legacy. There is even less reflection on the thorny question of whether, and to what extent, that very history undermines or distorts the liberal theoretical frameworks typically employed to argue about global justice. The dominant approaches to the subject invoke ideas about justice,

---

[1] For useful surveys of the scholarly terrain, see Chris Brown and Robyn Eckersley (eds.), *The Oxford Handbook of International Political Theory* (Oxford: Oxford University Press, 2018), especially sections 3, 5, 6, and 7; Darrell Moellendorf and Heather Widdows (eds.), *The Routledge Handbook of Global Ethics* (Abingdon: Routledge, 2015).

1

liberty, democracy, and rights, while ignoring the ways in which the theories frameworks utilised as well as the institutions identified as possible agents of justice, were shaped by centuries of Western expansion and exploitation.

A second gap concerns the role of race. A growing body of scholarship has indicted the field of political theory for failing to pay sufficient attention to ideologies and practices of racial discrimination, domination, and white supremacism, past and present.[2] While imperialism and racism are not necessarily connected – imperialism antedates the development of modern conceptions of race by centuries, and many critics of empire held racist views – they have typically been fused together, especially during the nineteenth and twentieth centuries. Modern European empires were often justified through claims about racial inferiority and superiority, and white supremacism played a fundamental role in legitimating and structuring imperial formations. Racialized visions and practices, rooted in that history, continue to inflect global politics in myriad ways.

Empire, Race, and Global Justice engages these issues by bringing together an interdisciplinary group of scholars, working in departments of political science, philosophy, and law. Although they adopt different perspectives, and draw contrasting conclusions, all ask how empire and/or race figure (or should figure) in the way political theorists approach questions of global justice. The chapters explore the following types of question: Why have debates over global justice tended to downplay or ignore imperial history? What are the consequences of this gap for the construction of persuasive theoretical accounts of global order? Is global justice necessarily a racialized discourse? Are liberal accounts of global justice – and especially egalitarian cosmopolitanism – the latest iteration of liberal imperialism, or an effective antidote to it? Does work on the ethics of war reproduce or undermine traditional colonial accounts of legitimate political violence? How does settler colonialism challenge the conceptual assumptions of global justice scholarship? Should international law be seen as part of the solution, or part of the problem, in addressing global injustices? What resources do other traditions of political thought, and the practices of social movements, offer for theorising

---

[2] For valuable surveys of the literature, see Tommie Shelby, 'Race' in David Estlund (ed.), *The Oxford Handbook of Political Philosophy* (Oxford: Oxford University Press, 2014), 336–53; Charles W. Mills, 'Critical Philosophy of Race' in Herman Cappelen, Tamar Szabó Gendler, and John Hawthorne (eds.), *The Oxford Handbook of Philosophical Methodology* (New York: Oxford University Press, 2016), 709–32; Robert Bernasconi, 'Critical Philosophy of Race' in Sebastian Luft and Soren Overgaard (eds.), *The Routledge Companion to Phenomenology* (Abingdon: Routledge, 2012), 551–62; Naomi Zack (ed.), *The Oxford Handbook of the Philosophy of Race* (Oxford: Oxford University Press, 2016).

global justice? In addressing such questions, the following chapters seek to open up debate on the legacies of empire and racism.

The Burdens of History

In 1800 European states controlled 35 per cent of the landmass of the planet; by 1914 the figure had reached an extraordinary 84 per cent.[3] Empire was widely seen as a legitimate, even necessary, form of political order, capable of underwriting state power and prestige, maintaining geopolitical stability, and 'civilizing' purportedly backward peoples. The modern architecture of global governance – including international law and numerous international organisations – was forged in this imperial world system.[4] It was only with the process of decolonisation in the decades following the Second World War that empire ceased to be widely regarded as a justifiable political form. That process, often violent, left its imprint on the emergent world of states. Racist ideologies were developed, deployed, and reproduced in imperial contexts, often serving to justify the occupation and exploitation of distant lands. As with the territorial and institutional legacies of decolonisation, so the world-shaping power of racial ideologies outlasted the dissolution of the age of formal empire.

Historians of political thought have spent the last three decades excavating the multifarious ways in which the tradition of Western political thinking was interwoven with imperial legitimation.[5] The fraught relationship between liberalism and empire stands at the centre of this body of

---

[3] Paul Kennedy, *The Rise and Fall of the Great Powers* (New York: Random House, 1978), 148–9. For some macro-historical studies of empire in world history, see Dominic Lieven, *Empire: The Russian Empire and Its Rivals* (New Haven, CT: Yale University Press, 2002); Christopher Bayly, *The Birth of the Modern World* (Oxford: Blackwell, 2004); Jane Burbank and Frederick Cooper, *Empires in World History: Power and the Politics of Difference* (Princeton, NJ: Princeton University Press, 2010); Krishan Kumar, *Visions of Empire: How Five Imperial Regimes Shaped the World* (Princeton, NJ: Princeton University Press, 2017).

[4] See, among others, Susan Pedersen, *The Guardians: The League of Nations and the Crisis of Empire* (Oxford: Oxford University Press, 2015); Adom Getachew, *Worldmaking after Empire: The Rise and Fall of Self-Determination* (Princeton, NJ: Princeton University Press, 2018).

[5] Examples include: David Armitage, *The Ideological Origins of the British Empire* (Cambridge: Cambridge University Press, 2000); Andrew Fitzmaurice, *Sovereignty, Property and Empire, 1500–2000* (Cambridge: Cambridge University Press, 2013); Sankar Muthu (ed.), *Empire and Modern Political Thought* (Cambridge: Cambridge University Press, 2012); Jennifer Pitts, *A Turn to Empire: The Rise of Imperial Liberalism in Britain and France* (Princeton, NJ: Princeton University Press, 2005); Duncan Bell, *The Idea of Greater Britain: Empire and the Future of World Order, 1860–1900* (Princeton, NJ: Princeton University Press, 2007); Onur Ulas Ince, *Colonial Capitalism and the Dilemmas of Liberalism* (Oxford: Oxford University Press, 2018); Anthony Pagden, *Lords*

work.[6] Scholars disagree over whether the connection is *rejectionist, neces-sary,* or *contingent.* The *rejection thesis* posits that liberalism and imperial-ism are mutually exclusive, that authentic liberals cannot be imperialists. Few political theorists today adopt this position explicitly. The *necessity thesis* asserts that imperialism is an integral feature of liberal political thought; that to be a proper liberal is to be committed to the legitimacy of (liberal) empire. This is a common line of argument among critics of liberalism, though they often diverge over the particular features of liber-alism that are held responsible, and just how far they want to push the claim. In one of the most influential accounts, Uday Singh Mehta argues that liberalism and imperialism have been tightly braided together since the ideology emerged in the early modern era. Liberalism, he suggests, contains an 'urge' to eliminate difference and remake the world in its own image. In a discussion of British thinkers in the nineteenth century, centred on John Stuart Mill, he proclaimed: '[i]n the empire . . . liberalism had found the concrete place of its dreams'.[7] But not all advocates of the necessity thesis are critics of liberalism. Alan Ryan, for example, argues that liberal imperialism is the doctrine that 'a state with the capacity to force liberal political institutions and social aspirations upon nonliberal states and societies is justified in so doing', and he maintains that 'liberal-ism *is* intrinsically imperialist'. It is necessary to 'understand the attrac-tions of liberal imperialism and not flinch', he continues, before cautioning against 'succumbing to that attraction', chiefly on the prag-matic grounds that imperialism usually doesn't work in practice.[8]

---

of All the World: Ideologies of Empire in Spain, Britain, and France, c.1500–1800 (London: Yale University Press, 1995); Karuna Mantena, *Alibis of Empire: Henry Maine and the Ends of Liberal Imperialism* (Princeton, NJ: Princeton University Press, 2010); Burke Hendrix and Deborah Baumgold (eds.), *Colonial Exchanges: Political Theory and the Agency of the Colonized* (Manchester: Manchester University Press, 2017).

[6] I explore these debates, and offer my own argument about the relationship, in Duncan Bell, *Reordering the World: Essays on Liberalism and Empire* (Princeton, NJ: Princeton University Press, 2016), ch. 2. Prominent contributors to this debate include Richard Tuck, James Tully, Sankar Muthu, Jennifer Pitts, Karuna Mantena, Jeanne Morefield, Barbara Arneil, and Uday Singh Mehta. See also Jennifer Pitts, 'Political Theory of Empire and Imperialism', *Annual Review of Political Science*, 13 (2010), 211–35.

[7] Mehta, *Liberalism and Empire: A Study in Nineteenth-Century British Liberal Thought* (Chicago: University of Chicago Press, 1999), 37. 'Urges can of course be resisted, and liberals offer ample evidence of this ability, which is why I do not claim that liberalism must be imperialistic, only that the urge is internal to it' (20). See also Domenico Losurdo, *Liberalism: A Counter-History*, trans. Gregory Elliott (London: Verso, 2011).

[8] Ryan, 'Liberal Imperialism' [2004] in Ryan, *The Making of Modern Liberalism* (Princeton, NJ: Princeton University Press, 2012), 107, 122. Italics in original. For a conceptual discussion of liberal imperialism, see also Jedediah Purdy, 'Liberal Empire: Assessing the Arguments', *Ethics & International Affairs*, 17/2 (2003), 35–47.

On such a view, only practical constraints qualify the universalising imperative.

The *contingency thesis* posits that liberal normative commitments do not necessarily entail support for empire. Instead, the imperialism of liberal writers can be explained either through reference to superseded historical conditions or by disaggregating discrete strands of liberalism, some of which are more susceptible to imperial temptation than others. Thus Jennifer Pitts indicts the 'imperial liberalism' of John Stuart Mill and his followers, while insisting that other forms of liberal thought, including those advanced by Jeremy Bentham and Adam Smith, contained ample resources for imperial critique.[9] The relevance of these historical arguments for the global justice debates is obvious. Depending on the view one adopts of the history and scope of liberalism, it is possible to argue either that liberal accounts of global justice are but the latest iteration of an enduring tradition of liberal imperialism, or, alternatively, that while some forms of liberal argument for global justice are (potentially) imperialist, other anti-imperial forms can be fostered and developed. It is also possible to bite the bullet, as Michael Ignatieff has done, and acknowledge the imperial dimensions of contemporary liberal arguments about global order while endorsing them as the best available response to contemporary conditions. 'Nobody likes empires', he argued in *Empire Lite*, 'but there are some problems for which there are only imperial solutions'.[10] In this tragic register, empire is posited as the least worst option for responsible policy makers to adopt.

Identifying imperialism and its legacies, though, is not always a straightforward matter. This is because empire and imperialism come in different forms, and moreover, there is considerable dispute about how best to define them. There are also a range of thorny empirical problems concerning causality, of how to identify the relationship between past and present. Scholarly accounts of empire come in narrow and broad varieties.[11] On a narrow view, empire connotes

---

[9] Pitts, *A Turn to Empire*.

[10] Ignatieff, *Empire Lite: Nation-Building in Bosnia, Kosovo, and Afghanistan* (London: Penguin, 2003), 11. Niall Ferguson offers a more celebratory account of liberal imperialism. For a powerful attack on their arguments, see Jeanne Morefield, *Empires without Imperialism: Anglo-American Decline and the Politics of Deflection* (Oxford: Oxford University Press, 2014). In a different theoretical idiom, John Finnis has suggested that natural law arguments provide a compelling justification for British colonial occupation in Australia and Africa. Finnis, 'Natural Law and the Re-making of Boundaries' in Allen Buchanan and Margaret Moore (eds.), *States, Nations, and Borders: The Ethics of Making Boundaries* (Oxford: Oxford University Press, 2003), 171–8.

[11] Duncan Bell, 'Ideologies of Empire' in Michael Freeden, Marc Stears and Lyman Tower Sargent (eds.), *The Oxford Handbook of Political Ideologies* (Oxford: Oxford University Press, 2013), 562–83; James Tully, 'Lineages of Contemporary

the direct and comprehensive rule of one polity over another, 'a
relationship ... in which one state controls the effective political sovereignty of another political society'.[12] The British occupation of India in
the second half of the nineteenth century is a paradigmatic example.
Broad definitions characterise an empire as a polity that exerts decisive
or overwhelming power in a system of unequal political relations, thus
encompassing diverse forms of control and influence. Much contemporary discussion of American empire adopts this broader usage.[13]
Some IR scholars prefer 'hegemony' to 'empire', although the difference is often hard to specify with any precision. The concept of
imperialism is also utilised in various ways. On a narrow account,
imperialism is a strategy or policy that aims to consolidate or expand
an empire. According to broader definitions it a strategy or policy – or
even an attitude or disposition – that seeks to create, maintain, or
intensify relations of inequality between political communities. There
is also a debate over the connection between *formal* and *informal*
empire/imperialism. Some insist that 'empire' and 'imperialism' should
only designate direct intervention in, or sovereign control over,
a territorial space; others invoke them, and imperialism in particular,
to cover a plethora of formal and informal modes of influence, coercion, and control. Under conditions of informal imperialism, James
Tully explains, imperial states 'induce local rulers to keep their
resources, labour, and markets open to free trade dominated by western corporations and global markets'.[14] Thus during the nineteenth
century Britain integrated much of Latin America into its sphere of
influence through 'free trade imperialism'. During the second half of
the twentieth century, Tully contends, informal empire emerged as the
preferred mode of domination by the leading powers, chiefly the
United States. He argues that it is the predominant contemporary
manifestation of liberal civilising imperialism, though it has been called
a variety of (ideologically mystifying) names: modernisation, development, neoliberal globalisation. These constitute 'the continuation of

Imperialism' in Duncan Kelly (ed.), *Lineages of Empire: The Historical Roots of British Imperial Thought* (Oxford: Oxford University Press, 2009); Frederick Cooper, *Colonialism in Question: Theory, Knowledge, History* (Berkeley: University of California Press, 2005).
[12] Michael Doyle, *Empires* (Ithaca, NY: Cornell University Press, 1986), 45.
[13] For relevant discussion, see Paul MacDonald, 'Those who Forget Historiography Are Doomed to Repeat It: Empire, Imperialism, and Contemporary Debates about American Power', *Review of International Studies*, 35/1 (2009), 45–67; Miriam Prys and Stefan Robel, 'Hegemony, not Empire', *Journal of International Relations and Development*, 14/2 (2011), 247–79; Michael Cox, 'Empire, Imperialism and the Bush Doctrine', *Review of International Studies*, 30/4 (2003), 585–605.
[14] Tully, 'Lineages of Contemporary Imperialism', 13.

Western imperialism by informal means and through institutions of global governance'.[15] 'Humanitarian intervention' is often criticised in similar terms. Such claims are rejected by many (though not all) liberals, who maintain that current practices differ in vital respects from historical instances of imperialism, not least in the motivations driving them.

Settler colonialism constitutes a distinctive form of imperial domination. Settler colonies seek to establish new and permanent political communities, usually on land dispossessed from indigenous peoples. As Patrick Wolfe has argued, it is an 'inclusive, land-centred project that coordinates a comprehensive range of agencies, from the metropolitan centre to the frontier encampment, with a view to eliminating Indigenous societies'.[16] The paradigmatic modern example is the British settlement of North America, Australia, and New Zealand. These countries are, of course, the intellectual and institutional centres of 'Anglo-American' political theory – a fact that, as Robert Nichols explores in his chapter, is no coincidence.[17] The implications of settler colonialism for debates on global justice are profoundly complex, encompassing questions about both the styles of political theorising prevalent in settler states and the constitution of their dominant political ideologies. For many scholars of settler colonialism, the socio-political development and ideological armature of Anglo-American liberal democracy has been conditioned by the history of settler colonialism. Elsewhere, I have argued (contra Uday Singh Mehta) that it was in the settler colonies, rather than India and Africa, that nineteenth-century liberal thinkers found the concrete place of their dreams.[18] Other scholars argue that the political identities of settler states are indelibly shaped by their violent histories of conquest, dispossession, and violence. 'American democracy', as Joan Cocks puts it, 'did not simply emerge on the ground from which Indians

---

[15] Tully, *Public Philosophy in a New Key, Vol II: Imperialism and Civic Freedom* (Cambridge: Cambridge University Press, 2008), 7. For a parallel critique (though with a different conclusion), see Thomas McCarthy, *Race, Empire and the Idea of Human Development* (Cambridge: Cambridge University Press, 2009). I discuss Tully's account of empire in Duncan Bell, 'To Act Otherwise: Agonistic Republicanism and Global Citizenship' in David Owen (ed.), *On Global Citizenship: James Tully in Dialogue* (London: Bloomsbury, 2014), 181–205.

[16] Wolfe, 'Settler Colonialism and the Elimination of the Native', *Journal of Genocide Research*, 8/4 (2006), 393. Elimination need not include mass killing, but it often did. On settler violence, see Dirk Moses (ed.), *Genocide and Settler Society* (Oxford: Berghan, 2004).

[17] See also Carole Pateman, 'The Settler Contract' in Carole Pateman and Charles W. Mills, *Contract and Domination* (Cambridge: Polity, 2007), 35–78. For a pioneering discussion of domestic colonization, in Europe and North America, see Barbara Arneil, *Domestic Colonialism: The Turn Inward to Colony* (Oxford: Oxford University Press, 2017).

[18] Bell, *Reordering the World*.

and their life world was being cleared but owed its very existence as radical democracy to that clearance'.[19] Aziz Rana argues that American conceptions of freedom are derived from settler ideology. 'Settler freedom', he maintains, fuses 'ethnic nationalism, Protestant theology and republicanism to combine freedom as self-rule with a commitment to territorial empire'.[20] Mahmood Mamdani, meanwhile, suggests that '[t]he uncritical embrace of the settler experience explains the blind spot in the American imagination: an inability to coexist with difference, indeed a preoccupation with civilizing natives'.[21] Facing up to this situation is not only a matter of belatedly recognising an obligation to address past injustice, important as that is, but admitting that the current political order is founded on, and continues to be shaped by, colonialism. If settler ideologies permeate the political tradition(s) of the leading 'liberal democratic' states, what does this mean for our understanding of liberal theory in general, and global justice in particular?

Political theorists and historians of political thought have paid less attention to race. Yet explicit or implicit visions of racial hierarchy have animated, and helped to structure, ideologies of rule from the early modern era to the present.[22] The prevailing historical view is that race/racism is largely an invention of Western modernity, emerging simultaneously (and not coincidentally) with the Spanish conquest of the Americas, though some scholars seek to trace its proto-forms deep into the bedrock of European history.[23] The racial order was transcontinental in reach from the beginning, and subsequent centuries of imperialism both spread and consolidated it. By the nineteenth century it was a pervasive feature of the Western political imaginary. Critical philosophers of race have demonstrated that the canon of Western philosophy is

---

[19] Cocks, *On Sovereignty and Other Political Delusions* (London: Bloomsbury, 2015), 64.

[20] Rana, *The Two Faces of American Freedom* (Cambridge, MA: Harvard University Press, 2010), 12.

[21] Mamdani, 'Settler Colonialism', *Critical Inquiry*, 41 (2015), 598–9. See also Kevin Bruyneel, 'The American Liberal Colonial Tradition', *Settler Colonial Studies*, 3 (2013), 311–21.

[22] In the literature on postcolonial international law and IR, the centrality of race to questions of global order and justice has long been a vital theme. Examples would include: Siba N'Zatioula Grovougi, *Sovereigns, Quasi Sovereigns, and Africans: Race and Self-Determination in International Law* (Minneapolis: University of Minnesota Press, 1996); Roxanne Doty, *Imperial Encounters: The Politics of Representation in North-South Relations* (Minneapolis: University of Minnesota Press, 1996). Thanks to Randall Persuad for discussion of this point.

[23] See especially George Fredrickson, *Racism: A Short History* (Princeton, NJ: Princeton University Press, 2002). See also Francisco Bethencourt, *Racisms: From the Crusades to the Twentieth Century* (Princeton, NJ: Princeton University Press, 2013). On the debate about chronology, see Miriam Eliav-Feldon, Benjamin Isaac, and Joseph Ziegler (eds.), *The Origins of Racism in the West* (Cambridge: Cambridge University Press, 2009).

marked by persistent claims of racial superiority, where large parts of the world, and the peoples who lived there, were considered to be inferior to white Europeans in various ways.[24] Many suggest that philosophical scholarship (largely unwittingly) continues to perform this function. The modern social sciences have also acted as an important site for the incubation and dissemination of such ideas. Recent scholarship on the disciplinary histories of political science, IR, and sociology, for example, shows that from their emergence in the late nineteenth century they were preoccupied with the legitimation of white supremacism and (often) imperialism.[25] As Robert Vitalis has argued, until deep into the twentieth century IR was often regarded as a synonym for 'inter-racial relations'.[26] Du Bois uttered a commonplace in *The Souls of Black Folk* when he predicted that 'the problem of the twentieth century is the problem of the color-line'.[27] Half a century later, in *The Wretched of the Earth*, Frantz Fanon reiterated the point: 'It is evident that what parcels out the world is to begin with the fact of belonging to or not belonging to a given race.'[28] Racialized conceptions of politics and society continue to play a fundamental role in Western societies, shaping ideas, institutions, and public policies.

Despite its importance, race is largely absent from discussions of global justice in political theory. For Charles Mills, this means that theoretical

---

[24] See, for example, Zack (ed.), *The Oxford Handbook of the Philosophy of Race*, Sec. I & V; Justin E. H. Smith, *Nature, Human Nature, and Human Difference: Race in Early Modern Philosophy* (Princeton, NJ: Princeton University Press, 2015); Robert Bernasconi, 'The Philosophy of Race in the Nineteenth Century' in Dean Moyar (ed.), *Routledge Companion to Nineteenth Century Philosophy* (London: Routledge, 2010), 498–521; Charles Mills, 'Decolonizing Western Political Philosophy', *New Political Science*, 37/1 (2015), 1–24. See also Dipesh Chakrabarty, *Provincializing Europe: Postcolonial Thought and Historical Difference* (Princeton, NJ: Princeton University Press, 2000).

[25] Robert Vitalis, *White World Order, Black Power Politics: The Birth of American International Relations* (Ithaca, NY: Cornell University Press, 2015); Jessica Blatt, *Race and the Making of American Political Science* (Philadelphia: University of Pennsylvania Press, 2015); John Hobson, *The Eurocentric Conception of World Politics: Western International Theory, 1760–2010* (Cambridge: Cambridge University Press, 2010); Vineet Thakur, Alexander David, and Peter Vale, 'Imperial Missions, "Scientific" Method: An Alternative Account of the Origins of IR', *Millennium*, 46/1 (2017), 3–23; George Steinmetz (ed.), *Sociology and Empire: The Imperial Entanglements of a Discipline* (Durham, NC: Duke University Press, 2013).

[26] Vitalis, *White World Order, Black Power Politics*.

[27] Du Bois, *The Souls of Black Folk*, 2nd ed. (Chicago: McLurg, 1903), vii. This idea has been picked up in recent scholarship: Marilyn Lake and Henry Reynolds, *Drawing the Global Colour Line: White Men's Countries and the International Challenge of Racial Equality* (Cambridge: Cambridge University Press, 2008); Alexander Anievas, Nivi Manchanda, and Robbie Shilliam (eds.), *Race and Racism in International Relations: Confronting the Global Color Line* (Abingdon: Routledge, 2015).

[28] Fanon, *The Wretched of the Earth*, trans. Constance Farrington ([1961] New York: Grove Press, 1968), 40.

debates ignore or misunderstand some of the principal sources and sites of injustice.[29] 'Racial ideologies', he contends, 'circulate globally, assumptions of nonwhite inferiority and the legitimacy of white rule are taken for granted, a shared colonial history of pacts, treaties, international jurisprudence, and a racial-religious self-conception of being the bearers and preservers of civilization provide common norms and reference points.'[30] These assumptions have long been deeply ingrained in patterns of thought and behaviour. Several contributors to this volume suggests that the failure to address questions of race and empire is in part methodological – 'Anglo-American' political theorists have missed much of importance because of the way they approach the subject. For Mills, 'ideal theorizing' in a Rawlsian vein bears some of the blame.[31] It is no accident, he argues, that mainstream liberal political philosophy has routinely ignored or downplayed questions of racial domination, for this is a predictable result of generating theories divorced from, and even blind to, the historical processes and practices – imperialism, slavery, racism – that have helped structure the contemporary world. It is a feature not a bug. Political theory, then, often fails to adequately grasp the character of the injustices it purports to address. Such a worry animates many of the following chapters. A number of authors argue for the importance of recovering, and integrating into theoretical analysis, the views of those in the Global South usually presented as the passive 'recipients' of global justice. This highlights the promise of ethnographic work in political theory.[32] More generally, the following chapters emphasize the need for political theorists to engage more with social scientists and historians.[33]

[29] Mills, 'Race and Global Justice'.

[30] Mills, 'Race and Global Justice', Chapter 4 in this volume. For a relevant critique of human rights discourse, see Makua Mutua, *Human Rights: A Political and Cultural Critique* (Philadelphia: University of Pennsylvania Press, 2013).

[31] See especially Mills, 'Ideal Theory as Ideology' in Mills, *Black Rights/White Wrongs: The Critique of Racial Liberalism* (Oxford: Oxford University Press, 2017), ch. 5. For other relevant criticisms of ideal theorization, see Elizabeth Anderson, *The Imperative of Integration* (Princeton, NJ: Princeton University Press, 2010); Sarah Fine, 'Immigration and Discrimination' in Fine and Lea Ypi (eds.), *Migration and Political Theory: The Ethics of Movement and Membership* (Oxford: Oxford University Press, 2016), 125–50.

[32] *For a discussion of ethnography and political theory, see Lisa Herzog and Bernardo Zacka, 'Fieldwork in Political Theory: Five Argument for an Ethnographic Sensibility', British Journal of Political Science (2017, online first).*

[33] Michael Goodhart, *Injustice: Political Theory for the Real World* (Oxford: Oxford University Press, 2018). For an exploration of the ideas and practices of global justice movements in the Global South, focusing on the World Social Forum, see Manfred Stenger, James Goodman, and Erin K. Wilson, *Justice Globalism: Ideology, Crises, Policy* (Thousand Oaks, CA: Sage, 2013). See also Shari Stone-Mediatore, 'Global Ethics, Epistemic Colonialism, and Paths to More Democratic Knowledge',

Critical philosophers of race have tended not to engage in systematic discussion of global justice.[34] There is a historical-geographical reason for this distribution of attention. In the United States, questions of race loom large over contemporary life, casting a long shadow. 'All black people in the United States, irrespective of their class status or politics', bell hooks once wrote, 'live with the possibility that they will be terrorized by whiteness.'[35] This has come to a head with the emergence of the 'Black Lives Matter' movement. Since most critical philosophers of race are based in the United States, and since contemporary politics in that country is so heavily shaped by the grim legacy of slavery and Jim Crow, they have tended to concentrate on diagnosing and challenging domestic modes of domination.[36] While few have systematically explored the implications of this kind of work for global justice, the philosophical and sociological scholarship on race contains powerful insights for thinking about (in)justice on a global scale. It can be read profitably alongside material that deals with questions of indigenous politics and settler colonialism.[37] These rich bodies of scholarship constitute a vital resource for theorists of global justice.

Radical Philosophy Review (in press); Monique Deveaux, 'Poor-Led Social Movements and Global Justice', *Political Theory*, 46/5 (2018), 698-725.

[34] Notable examples of work on race and political theory include Mills, *The Racial Contract;* Tommie Shelby, *We Who Are Dark* (Cambridge, MA: Harvard University Press, 2005); Chris Lebron, *The Color of Our Shame: Race and Justice in Our Time* (Oxford: Oxford University Press, 2014); Lawrie Balfour, *Democracy's Reconstruction: Thinking Politically with W. E. B. Du Bois* (Oxford: Oxford University Press, 2011); Robert Gooding-Williams, *In the Shadow of Du Bois: Afro-Modern Political Thought in America* (Cambridge, MA: Harvard University Press, 2009).

[35] hooks, 'Representing Whiteness in the Black Imagination' in Lawrence Grossberg, Cary Nelson, and Paula A. Treichler (eds.), *Cultural Studies* (London: Routledge, 1992), 344–5. On whiteness, see, for example, Linda Martín Alcoff, *The Future of Whiteness* (Cambridge: Polity, 2015); Shannon Sullivan, 'White Privilege' in Zack (ed.), *The Oxford Handbook of the Philosophy of Race*; George Yancy, *Look, A White! Philosophical Essays on Whiteness* (Philadelphia: Temple University Press, 2012); Charles Mills, 'White Ignorance' in Shannon Sullivan and Nancy Tuana (eds.), *Race and Epistemologies of Ignorance* (Albany, NY: SUNY Press, 2007), 11–38. For historical examples of whiteness as world-ordering, see Duncan Bell, *Dreamworlds of Race: Empire, Utopia, and the Fate of Anglo-American* (Princeton, NJ: Princeton University Press, forth.); Lake and Reynolds, *Drawing the Global Colour Line*.

[36] Chris Lebron has sought to locate the movement in the history of Black social and political thought: *The Making of Black Lives Matter: A Brief History of an Idea* (Oxford: Oxford University Press, 2016). See also Keeanga-Yamahtta Taylor, *From #BlackLivesMatter to Black Liberation* (Boston: Haymarket, 2016), and the symposium on the Trayvon Martin killing, *Theory & Event*, 15/3 (2012).

[37] For valuable examples, see Kevin Bruyneel, *The Third Space of Sovereignty: The Postcolonial Politics of U.S.-Indigenous Relations* (Minneapolis: University of Minnesota Press, 2007); Audra Simpson, *Mohawk Interruptus: Political Life across the Borders of Settler States* (Durham, NC: Duke University Press, 2014); Glen Coulthard,

Throughout the chapters of this book, and in the wider literature on empire and its critics, we see the invocation of a counter-canon of global justice, a disparate range of thinkers who provide alternative ways of seeing the world and a repertoire of theoretical and conceptual resources to think through questions of global order. In IR, Vitalis argues that the thinkers of what he terms the 'Howard School' – including Alain Locke, Merze Tate, Ralph Bunche, and Du Bois – offered some of the most penetrating accounts of the dynamics of global politics written during the twentieth century, and that we would benefit from revisiting them for inspiration and ideas.[38] A wider list relevant for global justice would include Du Bois, Fanon, Locke, Tate, Bunche, Amilcar Cambral, Aimé Césaire, George Padmore, C. L. R. James, Marcus Garvey, Stuart Hall, Audre Lorde, Cedric Robinson, bell hooks, Edward Said, Chandra Mohanty, Achilee Mbembe, through to Mills and the lively debates among and between critical race, indigenous, and decolonial theorists.

None of this is to suggest that questions of empire and race have been completely ignored by those working on global justice. The burgeoning literature on historical injustice has engaged seriously with the legacy of imperialism, with a particular focus on the issue of reparations, both symbolic and material.[39] The last few years have also witnessed a burst

Red Skin, White Masks: Rejecting the Colonial Politics of Recognition (Minneapolis: University of Minnesota Press, 2014); Margaret Kohn and Keally McBride, *Political Theories of Decolonization: Postcolonialism and the Problem of Foundations* (Oxford: Oxford University Press, 2011); Nalini Persram (ed.), *Postcolonialism and Political Theory* (New York: Lexington, 2007); Paul Gilroy, 'Multiculturalism and Postcolonial Theory' in John Dryzek, Bonnie Honig, and Anne Phillips (eds.), *The Oxford Handbook of Political Theory* (Oxford: Oxford University Press, 2008), 656–76; Chandra Mohanty, *Feminism Without Borders: Decolonizing Theory, Practicing Solidarity* (Durham, NC: Duke University Press, 2003).

[38] Vitalis, *White World Order, Black Power Politics*. See also Errol Henderson, 'The Revolution Will Not Be Theorised: Du Bois, Locke, and the Howard School's Challenge to White Supremacist IR Theory', *Millennium*, 45/3 (2017), 492–510.

[39] For valuable (and varied) examples, see Daniel Butt, *Rectifying International Injustice: Principles of Compensation and Restitution between Nations* (Oxford: Oxford University Press, 2008); Butt, 'Repairing Historical Wrongs and the End of Empire', *Social & Legal Studies*, 21/2 (2012), 227–42; Kok-Chor Tan, 'Colonialism, Reparations, and Global Justice' in Jon Miller and Rahul Kumar (eds.), *Reparations: Interdisciplinary Inquiries* (Oxford: Oxford University Press, 2007), 280–306; Catherine Lu, 'Colonialism as Structural Injustice: Historical Responsibility and Contemporary Redress' in Robert Goodin and James Fishkin (eds.), *Political Theory without Borders* (Oxford: Blackwell, 2016), 237–59; David Scott, 'On the Moral Justification of Reparations for New World Slavery' in Robert Nichols and Jakeet Singh (eds.), *Freedom and Democracy in an Imperial Context* (New York: Routledge, 2014), 100–20; Lea Ypi, Christian Barry, and Robert Goodin, 'Associative Duties, Global Justice, and the Colonies', *Philosophy & Public Affairs*, 37/2 (2009), 103–35. There is an irony here. Arguments about the historical injustice of imperialism were once used to justify further imperial action: Bell, *Reordering the World*, ch. 2.

of writing seeking to identify the specific forms of injustice generated by imperial rule. A range of positions have been defended.[40] Lea Ypi and Anna Stilz have contended, albeit in different ways, that political domination is the principal wrong of imperialism. Thus Ypi argues that colonialism is a case of a more general injustice, 'the wrong exhibited by associations that deny their members equality and reciprocity in decision-making'.[41] Laura Valentini argues that there is no 'distinctive procedural wrong' in colonialism, but that its historical manifestations were characterised by numerous and overlapping forms of injustice.[42] Others, including Daniel Butt and Kok-Chor Tan, argue that imperialism is defined by a series of distinctive but interpenetrating injustices: exploitation, domination, and the coercive imposition of an alien culture.[43]

Important as it undoubtedly is, this literature is limited in scope and focus. First, as Margaret Moore notes, it often fails to distinguish between different types of imperial rule, and in particular it misses the distinctiveness of settler colonialism and the role played by the dispossession of land.[44] Second, it pays little attention to racial domination. Such arguments also presume that the (broadly liberal) theoretical framework being utilised is appropriate, a point that several chapters in this book challenge. Moore offers an internal critique, arguing that the individualism of much contemporary liberal theory means that scholars struggle to identify the relevant wrongs – especially as they are experienced by those subject to imperial imposition – given their deep ambivalence about group identifies and affiliations. Such liberals, she writes, 'are reluctant to get to the heart of the problem of political domination, because they are concerned that articulating the reason why communities should govern themselves as communities would confer on the community a problematic moral status'.[45] In particular, this raises the spectre of nationalism, an ideology central to many anti-colonial movements during the last century and

---

[40] I here follow the useful conceptual map in Margaret Moore, 'Justice and Colonialism', *Philosophy Compass*, 11/8 (2016), 447–61.

[41] Ypi, 'What's Wrong with Colonialism', *Philosophy & Public Affairs*, 41/2 (2013), 162. See also Stilz, 'Decolonization and Self-Determination', *Social Philosophy and Policy*, 32/1 (2015), 1–24.

[42] Valentini, 'On the Distinctive Procedural Wrong of Colonialism', *Philosophy & Public Affairs*, 43/4 (2015), 158–91.

[43] Butt, 'Colonialism and Postcolonialism' in Hugh LaFollette (ed.), *The International Encyclopaedia of Ethics* (Oxford: Blackwell, 2013), 892–98; Tan, 'Colonialism, Reparations, and Global Justice'.

[44] Moore, 'Justice and Colonialism', 455–6. Stilz has subsequently addressed this issue: Stilz, 'Settlement, Expulsion, and Return', *Politics, Philosophy & Economics*, 16/4 (2017), 351–74. See also Margaret Moore, 'The Taking of Territory and the Wrongs of Colonialism', *Journal of Political Philosophy* (2018, online first).

[45] Moore, 'Justice and Colonialism'.

14   *Duncan Bell*

a half, but usually denigrated by contemporary egalitarians.[46] It is little surprise that liberal nationalists (and other communitarians) often suggest that liberal cosmopolitanism is especially susceptible to imperial temptation.[47] Yet liberal nationalists are open to the charge that the identities and institutions of the 'nations' they privilege normatively have been constituted in part through forms of imperial and colonial injustice, and that rectifying those injustices leads to conclusions that they would otherwise reject. Drawing on insights from Edward Said, Sara Amighetti and Alasia Nuti, for example, argue that former colonies (e.g. India) represent 'a fundamental element' of the 'national identity of their colonizers' (e.g. Britain) and that as such, the latter have special obligations to the former, including granting a right to immigrate to the ex-imperial power.[48]

Structure of the Book

The role of history is a theme woven throughout *Empire, Race, and Global Justice*. All of the authors stress the imperative to take into account the conjoined histories of empire, colonialism, and race in thinking through current problems of global justice. However, each author responds to this challenge in a distinct manner. The result is a set of rich and challenging reflections on the relationship between past, present, and future, as well as on the nature of political theorising. For some, the intertwined histories of racism and empire have conditioned and contaminated the political vocabularies and theoretical frameworks which political thinkers – and often the wider public culture – utilise to make sense of the world. Consequently, existing theoretical frameworks need a fundamental overhaul, even rejection. Others, though, contend that flaws in global justice theorising can be addressed by modification and supplement rather than full-blown rejection. In combination, the contributors present a fruitful challenge to the shape and direction of contemporary debates about global justice.

---

[46] For an interesting critique of both cosmopolitanism and nationalism, see Rahul Rao, *Third World Protest: Between Home and the World* (Oxford: Oxford University Press, 2010). For critiques of (liberal) cosmopolitism as an articulation of imperialism, see Pratap Bhanu Mehta, 'Cosmopolitanism and the Circle of Reason', *Political Theory*, 28/5 (2000), 619–39; Jean Cohen, 'Whose Sovereignty? Empire versus International Law', *Ethics & International Affairs*, 18/3 (2004), 1–24; William Connolly, 'Speed, Concentric Circles, and Cosmopolitanism', *Political Theory*, 28 (2000), 596–618.

[47] See, for a prominent example, David Miller, *On Nationality* (Oxford: Oxford University Press, 1995), 77–8.

[48] Amighetti and Nuti, 'A Nation's Right to Exclude and the Colonies', *Political Theory*, 44/4 (2016), 543.

The opening three chapters probe the recent intellectual history of global justice, shedding light on how the debates assumed their focus and form. Katrina Forrester investigates the American legal and philosophical debates of the late 1960s and early 1970s about reparations for slavery, arguing that by the mid-1970s questions of racial injustice/reparations had been conceptually excised from mainstream liberal egalitarian political philosophy through the rejection of historically oriented conceptions of justice (especially those associated with Robert Nozick). Instead, and following Rawls in particular, theorists came to focus on current distributive patterns and how they could be assessed and potentially adjusted. The emphasis shifted, that is, from 'why certain parties had come to own more of the global social product' – an endeavour in which history played an integral role – to 'how it should now be shared'. This theoretical reorientation had significant consequences. 'Freeing justice theory from historical argument might have allowed for very demanding forms of domestic and global egalitarianism', she argues, 'but that egalitarianism in theory was bought at the cost of ignoring historical and structural injustice in practice.' In the following chapter, Samuel Moyn traces the emergence of the contemporary philosophy of human rights during the 1970s and early 1980s, focusing on the influential work of Henry Shue.[49] He argues that in formulating an individualist egalitarian approach Shue and other rights theorists 'abjured Southern agency' and 'embraced an antipolitical ethics of succor' incapable of grappling properly with the imperial and racial legacies that created many of the human rights abuses in the first place.

Both Forrester and Moyn suggest that the theoretical frameworks and normative focus of the subsequent global justice debates served (whether intentionally or not) to defuse more radical calls for economic and political transformation grounded in recognition of imperial and racial domination. Did a similar process occur in international law? The connections between empire, racism, and the development of international law have generated a substantial body of scholarship in recent years.[50] The third

[49] This chapter can be read profitably alongside Moyn's sharp account of the 1970s origins of arguments about global distributive justice: 'The Political Origins of Global Justice' in Joel Isaac, James T. Kloppenberg, Michael O'Brien, and Jennifer Ratner-Rosenhagen (eds.), *The Worlds of American Intellectual History* (Oxford: Oxford University Press, 2016), 133–54. See also Moyn, *Not Enough: Human Rights in an Unequal World* (Cambridge, MA: Harvard University Press, 2018).
[50] Anthony Anghie, *Imperialism, Sovereignty and the Making of International Law* (Cambridge: Cambridge University Press, 2004); Lauren Benton and Lisa Ford, *Rage for Order: The British Empire and the Origins of International Law, 1800–1850* (Cambridge, MA: Harvard University Press, 2016); Martti Koskenniemi, Walter Rech, and Manuel Jiménez Fonseca (eds.), *International Law and Empire* (Oxford: Oxford University Press,

chapter, by Sundhya Pahuja, steps back from the immediate philosophical debates to show how international law in the 1960s and 1970s became a site for clashing visions of global justice, and especially for conflict between an account common in the Global South (which identified the past and present of Western imperialism as the source of global injustice) and the dominant Western narrative (which was grounded in an a-historical moral universalism that regarded global poverty alleviation as an act of 'enlightened self-interest'). It was the latter that triumphed. Pahuja juxtaposes the arguments propounded by scholars and politicians from the Global South – including Frantz Fanon and Salvador Allende – with those from the Global North – including Henry Kissinger – over the proper role of international law in regulating capitalism (and in particular transnational corporations). For Pahuja, the old imperial hierarchies of race and civilisation were supplanted by new accounts of 'development' that encoded the existing patterns of stratification. The logic of hierarchy was rearticulated not rejected. Capitalism was presented as the solution to global poverty and 'backwardness', not one of its primary causes. Race was central to this rearticulation. 'Once a developmentalist ordering is taken up, what is forgotten is that the hierarchy reproduced is the same as the one generated by the imperial "science" grounded in (biological) race and racism.' As well as representing different visions of international legal authority and universalism, this was a clash between divergent accounts of time. Kissinger and others presented a 'ruptural' narrative, in which the past – including the past of imperial domination – was discontinuous with the present, and in which a new dawn beckoned, while for the Third World 'the present was historical, linked to what had gone before through the legacies of empire, and in emergent neo-imperialisms'.[51]

The remaining chapters in the book engage more directly in contemporary theoretical debates, while insisting on the vital importance of history. In Chapter 4, Charles Mills argues that the global justice debates have failed to take seriously the legacy of 'global white supremacy'.[52] This vision of hierarchical world order was once openly acknowledged, even celebrated, by social and political thinkers in the North Atlantic world, but since the Second World War it has been

2017); Koskenniemi, *The Gentle Civiliser of Nations: The Rise and Fall of International Law 1870–1960* (Cambridge: Cambridge University Press, 2001); Sundhya Pahuja, *Decolonizing International Law: Development, Economic Growth and the Politics of Universality* (Cambridge: Cambridge University Press, 2011); Jennifer Pitts, *Boundaries of the International: Law and Empire* (Cambridge, MA: Harvard University Press, 2018).

[51] Pahuja, 'Corporations, Universalism and the Domestication of Race in International Law', Chapter 3 in this volume.

[52] For his most sustained critique of white supremacism, see Mills, *The Racial Contract* (Ithaca, NY: Cornell University Press, 1997).

disavowed and sanitised, even as many of the underlying structures, norms, and beliefs have remained in place. Political theorists, including – and perhaps especially – theorists of global justice have not acknowledged it properly, despite its centrality in explaining the historical development and contemporary structures of global inequality, poverty, and violence. 'What is lacking', Mills writes, 'is the theoretical will to recognize [the] implications, the refusal to put them together into a composite picture.' Taking history seriously is a vital first step. '[T]he West has sought to white-out the multiple ways race and racial ideology underpinned its global domination. But we need to recover this past both so as better to understand it and to enable us to dismantle the legacy it has left behind.' Arguing against racial eliminativists, such as Anthony Appiah and Naomi Zack, Mills insists that race should remain a pivotal category, and site of investigation and reflection, for global justice scholars. He argues for a reformulated liberalism. '[W]e need to rethink and decolonize imperial liberalism, racial liberalism, so as to eliminate its distinctive *white* bias.'[53] Among other things, this demands the rejection of (Rawlsian) ideal theorising. It would also mean taking much more seriously the role of corrective justice, of seeking to compensate for the massive systemic injustices meted out through the structures of global white supremacy. This line of argument suggests that the demotion of history documented by Forrester led political philosophy badly astray.

The following three chapters delineate some of the problematic characteristics of contemporary accounts of global justice, including their inability to adequately theorize the historical and transnational sources of injustice (Inés Valdez), their reliance on developmental accounts of progress analogous to discredited forms of modernisation theory (Anne Phillips), and their Eurocentric character and questionable epistemology (Margaret Kohn). They also seek to identify viable alternatives. Drawing on the pioneering work of Du Bois, Valdez develops an innovative analysis of transnational politics. She calls for a demotion of the Western subject as the primary source of agency in accounts of global justice, while stressing the important emancipatory potential of coalition-building and collective action between marginalized groups in and across the North and South (she points to the civil rights and anti-colonial movements of the post-war years as valuable

---

[53] Mills, 'Race and Global Justice', Chapter 4 in this volume. Italics in original. See also Mills, 'Decolonizing Western Political Philosophy', *New Political Science*, 37/1 (2015), 1–24. For the need to save liberalism, rather than reject it, see Mills, 'Occupy Liberalism' in Mills, *Black Rights/White Wrongs*, ch. 2. For a different version of the argument, see Duncan Ivison, *Postcolonial Liberalism* (Cambridge: Cambridge University Press, 2002).

historical examples).[54] Valdez contends that we need to substitute a moral discourse centred on obligations and duties with a political framework centred on power, coalition-building, and contestation.[55] Phillips, meanwhile, suggests that arguments for global justice need to be (re)formulated to avoid inscribing some of the binary hierarchies – us/them, modernity/tradition, north/south – that they aim to overcome. As a first step, this involves being more sensitive to the power of local attachments and the historical (colonial) conditions that produced current forms of injustice. She turns to African history and politics to make her case. The language of global justice, Philips argues, 'neither speaks to nor offers much of a solution to the . . . institutionalisation of ethnic and community identity' produced by colonial rule in Africa. The challenge, as she puts it, is to find 'ways of mobilising the ethical imperative that underpins global justice theory without obscuring the history in which it is embedded: to find ways of pursuing justice that do not rebound on themselves by enacting a normative hierarchy'.[56]

Margaret Kohn agrees. She too argues that voices from the Global South need to have far more weight in deliberations and decision-making about global poverty and inequality, and in order to show how this might be accomplished she defends a modified version of feminist standpoint theory ('subaltern standpoint theory'). This does not result in a debilitating relativism, but rather in attentiveness to the voices and the claims of others. 'In order to decide whether something advances the public good, or whether there even is a public good', she argues, 'it is necessary to consider it from diverse perspectives. Since the perspectives of the subaltern tend to be ignored or dismissed, they must be privileged. By privileged I do not mean that they trump others, but rather that they should be given especially careful consideration.' Kohn utilises this 'sub-altern' standpoint approach, developed through an engagement with the work of Frantz Fanon, to discuss ideas about global justice emanating from the Global South (her examples include the Zapatistas and the

---

[54] For examples of such transnational connections, see John Munro, *The Anticolonial Front: The African-American Freedom Struggle and Global Decolonization* (Cambridge: Cambridge University Press, 2017); Robbie Shilliam, *The Black Pacific: Anti-Colonial Struggles and Oceanic Connections* (London: Bloomsbury, 2015); Nico Slate, *Colored Cosmopolitanism: The Shared Struggle for Freedom in the United States and India* (Cambridge, MA: Harvard University Press, 2012).

[55] For further reflections on Du Bois, see Valdez, 'Du Bois and the Fluid Subject: *Dark Princess* and the Splendid Subject' in Miriam Thaggert (ed.), *Expecting More: African American Literature in Transition, 1920–30* (Cambridge: Cambridge University Press, in press).

[56] Unusually for a political theorist, Phillips has done sustained empirical work on politics. See, for example, Phillips, *The Enigma of Colonialism: British Policy in West Africa* (London: Currey, 1989).

Global Social Forum). Such ideas, she suggests, present 'alternative ways of thinking about the content, grounds, and agents of global justice'.[57]

In Chapter 8 Jeanne Morefield turns to Edward Said's work to develop a critique of both liberal theories of global justice and of liberal internationalism in IR.[58] She argues that the lack of attention paid to imperial history by scholars in both fields makes it hard for them to recognize how they might unwittingly replicate imperial ideologies. In particular, she suggests, 'their amnesia regarding the historical and ongoing relationship between liberalism and imperial politics obscures alternative understandings of justice that might bubble up from sites of former and current colonial occupation and violence rather than trickle down from the heights of a perennially well intentioned liberal theory'. There are more productive options available. Said's recurrent interest in who is granted 'permission to narrate', when joined to his acute sensitivity to languages of domination and exclusion, Morefield argues, 'enabled him to develop counterpuntal readings of history that insistently dragged empire and exclusion back into our accounts of the present'. This is a lesson that should be heeded. Scholars interested in global justice, she concludes, would do well to 'think in a more Saidian fashion about the counternarratives of colonial violence and racial exclusion' rendered invisible by the institutions of the liberal international order that theorists often privilege as agents for implementing global justice. Ultimately, an approach indebted to Said 'requires intellectuals to slow down and actively reflect on that history even as it demands sustained political and scholarly engagement with the most pressing forms of injustice in the world today'.

While the first wave of work on global justice tended to concentrate on questions of poverty and economic inequality, recent years have seen the scope of the debates broaden to include a diverse array of other subjects. A relatively recent addition is the ethics of war. Cosmopolitan thinkers, in particular, have sought to challenge traditional forms of just war thinking, and bring the topic within the ambit of debates over liberal egalitarianism.[59] In Chapter 9, Kimberley Hutchings charges that

---

[57] For further reflections on the topic, see Kohn, 'Postcolonialism and Global Justice', *Journal of Global Ethics*, 9/2 (2013), 187–200.

[58] Morefield's previous work includes important analyses of liberal imperialism: Morefield, *Covenants without Swords: Idealist Liberalism and the Spirit of Empire* (Princeton, NJ: Princeton University Press, 2005); Morefield, *Empires without Imperialism: Anglo-American Decline and the Politics of Deflection* (Oxford: Oxford University Press, 2014).

[59] See, for example, Simon Caney, *Justice Beyond Borders: A Global Political Theory* (Oxford: Oxford University Press, 2005), who argues that a truly global political theory needs to engage systematically with questions of political violence, as well as socio-economic concerns. Influential contributions include Jeff McMahan, *Killing in War* (Oxford:

cosmopolitan just war theory inadvertently 'replays and reinforces the colonial and neo-colonial imaginary of war'. It does so through identifying a subset of Western actors as the most legitimate agents of political violence and adopting modified forms of 'civilizational' argument about who should be exposed to violence, and why. A potent combination of 'moral certainty and moral unilateralism', Hutchings argues, 'all too easily opens up the world to the righteous violence of righteous moral agents, whether the basis of this deep morality is the fundamental value of individuals or of states'. Neither cosmopolitan just war theory nor its more conventional Walzerian forms offer a sufficiently decolonial answer to the problems of political violence.[60] Hutchings concludes with some thoughts about where such an answer may be found.

Settler colonialism was one of the dominant forms of Western imperial expansion, and liberal political theory was intimately bound up with its legitimation. It presents a deep challenge to both the theoretical categories used to think about global justice and the legitimacy of many of the institutions that thinkers identify as agents of justice. The final two chapters, then, turn to settler colonialism and its legacies. Robert Nichols opens with the ongoing conflict over indigenous American land at Standing Rock, in order to reflect on what justice might mean in such contexts, and in particular whether it makes sense to think of indigenous struggles as instances of 'global' or 'domestic' justice. He argues that the conventional framing misses the historical creation of such distinctions through practices of settler colonialism. We cannot understand this situation without incorporating the history of dispossession and colonial violence in our interpretation of struggles for justice. Events such as Standing Rock are irreducibly historical, 'in the sense that we inherit the meaning and significance of such struggles from structures, systems and narratives that predate the present, which we cannot choose but must nevertheless own'. There is no interpretive framework that stands outside such histories, that is capable of adjudicating claims in a neutral manner. 'Rather, there is a recursive relation between historical struggles and the languages we draw upon to make sense of them.' For Nichols, conventional approaches to global justice are incapable of addressing this point.[61] Catherine Lu is not as pessimistic, though she agrees with some of

Oxford University Press, 2009); Cecile Fabre, *Cosmopolitan War* (Oxford: Oxford University Press, 2012). For an overview, see Seth Lazar and Helen Frowe (eds.), *The Oxford Handbook of the Ethics of War* (Oxford: Oxford University Press, 2016).

[60] The *locus classicus* of the modern just war tradition is Michael Walzer, *Just and Unjust Wars: A Moral Argument with Historical Illustrations* (New York: Basic, 1977).

[61] See also the discussion in Robert Nichols, 'Theft Is Property! The Recursive Logic of Dispossession', *Political Theory*, 46/1 (2018), 3–26; Nichols, 'Indigeneity and the Settler Contract Today', *Philosophy & Social Criticism*, 39/2 (2013), 165–86.

Nichols's diagnosis. She opens with a critique of the domestic/international binary, arguing that it is not 'normatively benign, but functions to entrench the structural indignity of indigenous peoples within settler colonial states as well as vis-à-vis the international order'. She then proceeds to develop an account of 'structural dignity' with which to address the current settler colonial order.[62] In combination, these chapters demonstrate the imperative to incorporate settler colonialism into accounts of (global) justice, and the profound conceptual, ethical, and political challenges that this involves.

---

[62] See also Catherine Lu, *Justice and Reconciliation in World Politics* (Cambridge: Cambridge University Press, 2017).

1   Reparations, History and the Origins of Global Justice

Katrina Forrester

In 2014, the writer Ta-Nehisi Coates revived an old debate about the reparations owed to African Americans for slavery.[1] The turn of the new century had seen an uptick in organizing around reparations claims: in the United States, the National Coalition of Blacks for Reparations in America (N'COBRA) lent its support to reparations bill HR40, claims were filed in state courts, the Reparations Coordinating Committee was set up to coordinate advocacy domestically and internationally and in 2010 the National Association for the Advancement of Colored People (NAACP) officially declared its support for reparations.[2] Yet Coates's was the most discussed intervention since Randall Robinson's *The Debt: What America Owes to Blacks* in 2000, and it ignited a fresh wave of debate.[3]

Criticized by many liberals as sympathetic in theory but unrealistic in practice, the case for reparations has long been opposed by the right on grounds of "reverse-racism": some claim reparations have already been made, in the form of white lives lost in the Civil War, or of welfare, the Civil Rights Act or the Great Society.[4] Reparations have also been challenged from the left. In 2016, Coates attacked Senator Bernie Sanders who, on his campaign trail for the Democratic Presidential nomination, restated a familiar leftist skepticism of reparation claims, defending "universal" welfarist policies that operate on class rather

For helpful discussion or comments on earlier drafts, thanks to Duncan Bell, Saul Dubow, Cecile Laborde, Jacob Levy, Jon Levy, Catherine Lu, Jamie Martin, Priya Menon, Charles Mills, Samuel Moyn, the participants of the Cambridge Empire, Race and Global Justice Workshop and audiences at the UCL Legal and Political Theory Seminar and the APSA Annual Meeting 2017.

[1] Ta-Nehisi Coates, "The Case for Reparations", *The Atlantic* (June 2014).

[2] http://naacp.3cdn.net/c1f7561993e5844143_4im6bn12c.pdf (accessed 10 March 2016).

[3] Randall Robinson, *The Debt: What America Owes to Blacks* (New York: E. P. Dutton, 2000).

[4] David Horowitz, "Ten Reasons Why Reparations Is a Bad Idea *for Blacks*, and Racist Too", *The Black Scholar: Journal of Black Studies and Research*, 32/1 (2001). On the racial divide in support for reparations see Michael C. Dawson and Rovana Popoff, "Reparations: Justice and Greed in Black and White", *Du Bois Review*, 1/1 (2004), 47–91.

than race lines.[5] The aim, he implied, of redistributive politics is to benefit the working class, regardless of race.[6] Political scientist Cedric Johnson made the argument explicit: African Americans are a significant proportion of the working class, and so benefit most from such universal policies; by contrast, reparations claims presuppose a unitary "black community", and in so doing, obfuscate class divisions and maintain the status quo.[7] Coates replied that existing racial disparities in poverty demand more than universalist solutions, and in any case, history shows that redistributive policies have often disadvantaged African Americans.[8] Many framed the debate as a dispute over identity versus class politics. On that framing, for Coates and his defenders, putting class over race was an old leftist mistake. For Johnson and his, putting race over class was a liberal strategy for distraction: Coates's case for reparations implied a tragic vision of politics that left market liberalism untouched.

There is, however, another way of stating the distinction between the two sides, which is more familiar to political philosophers and avoids false dichotomies of identity and class. For Coates, reparations are due for historic injustices faced by African Americans. For Johnson, reparative justice adds nothing of value to distributive justice; the demands of the former are weaponized in a way that hinders the latter.

American proponents of reparations for slavery disagree over what they would look like: pecuniary or non-pecuniary; one-off cash transfers to individuals, as in South Africa, or compensation in the form of transfers or pensions, like German reparations to the Jewish victims of Nazism; public investment; group-specific banks, trusts or funds; the return of land; job guarantees for black workers. They might be paid for by the federal government, the states, corporations unjustly enriched through their involvement in slavery, the "white community", white churches and

[5] Ta-Nehisi Coates, "Why Precisely Is Bernie Sanders Against Reparations?", *The Atlantic* (19 January 2016).
[6] http://fusion.net/video/255113/bernie-sanders-reparations-answer-iowa-forum/ (accessed 10 March 2016).
[7] Cedric Johnson, "An Open Letter to Ta-Nehisi Coates and the Liberals Who Love Him", *Jacobin* (3 February 2016); cf. Adolph Reed Jr., "The Case against Reparations", *The Progressive* (December 2000).
[8] Coates, "The Enduring Solidarity of Whiteness", *The Atlantic* (8 February 2016). For the history of institutional racism on which Coates draws see Jill Quadagno, *The Color of Welfare: How Racism Undermined the War on Poverty* (New York: Oxford University Press, 1994); Sean Farhang and Ira Katznelson, "The Southern Imposition: Congress and Labor in the New Deal and Fair Deal", *Studies in American Political Development*, 19 (2005), 1–30; Beryl Satter, *Family Properties: How the Struggle over Race and Real Estate Transformed Chicago and Urban America* (New York: Picador, 2011); Ira Katznelson, *When Affirmative Action Was White: An Untold History of Racial Inequality in Twentieth-Century America* (New York: W. W. Norton, 2005).

charities or the white descendants of slaveholders; and paid to the black community, descendants of enslaved peoples, African Americans living below a certain poverty line. There are disagreements over what reparations are for and how they should be calculated: whether they should compensate unpaid slave labor, unjust enrichment of slaveholders, wrongs suffered in the Jim Crow South or wrongs suffered because of institutional racism – in homebuying, segregated education and so on – in the North. When in 2017, the Democratic Socialists of America supported a resolution calling for reparations, they were reparations for "slave labor" and "economic exploitation" caused by "colonization", and as a means of wealth redistribution.[9] This array of practical choices suggests their ethical aim is up for grabs: are reparations a kind of reconciliation, a means of getting what was owed as a result of historic wrongs or an attack on the present disadvantages of African Americans – or postcolonial peoples in general?[10]

In twenty-first-century political philosophy, reparations have been debated less against a backdrop of debates about slavery, equality and structural racism in the USA, and more in terms of identity, cultural politics, global humanitarianism, transitional justice, and state power.[11] They tend to be part of a generalizable account of "reparative justice", often international in scope, which surfaced in liberal philosophy in the 1990s with the human rights movement, and the surge of internationalist attention to reconciliatory and "transitional" justice that followed the end of Apartheid in South Africa.[12] In this context, engaged political theorists have harbored a variety of worries: about the implications of reparations for perpetuating "victim and perpetrator" narratives, reinforcing state or

---

[9] Democratic Socialists of America Afro-Socialist Convention Proposal, August 2017, https://drive.google.com/file/d/0B5P0FbY9YTM-UlVwTzRSTGhQRG8/view (accessed 11 September 2018).

[10] For these views and more see Michael Martin and Marilyn Yaquinto (eds.), *Redress for Historical Injustices in the United States: On Reparations for Slavery, Jim Crow and their Legacies* (Durham, NC: Duke University Press, 2007); Jon Miller and Rahul Kumar, *Reparations: Interdisciplinary Inquiries* (Oxford: Oxford University Press, 2007).

[11] Many black political philosophers continue to explore problems of rectification and reparations for slavery in a US context, but their works are often neglected. See especially Howard McGary, *Race and Social Justice* (Oxford: Blackwell, 1999), 79–125 and Bernard Boxill, *Blacks and Social Justice* (Oxford: Rowman & Littlefield, 1984) whose original contribution to these debates is contextualized below. See also Rodney Roberts (ed.), *Injustice and Rectification* (New York: Peter Lang, 2002) and Rhonda Magee, "The Master's Tools, from the Bottom Up: Responses to African-American Reparations Theory in Mainstream and Outsider Remedies Discourse", *Virginia Law Review*, 79/4 (1993), 863–916. For other collections that focus on reparations for slavery in particular see Ronald Saltzburger and Mary Turk, *Reparations for Slavery: A Reader* (Oxford: Rowman & Littlefield, 2004).

[12] Paige Arthur, "How 'Transitions' Reshaped Human Rights: A Conceptual History of Transitional Justice", *Human Rights Quarterly*, 31/2 (2009), 321–67.

group power or individualism and, in its focus on the unpaid labor of slavery, ignoring Southern sexual slavery and problems of gender.[13] For liberal philosophers of domestic and global justice, reparations claims have largely been seen as at odds with egalitarian distributive claims (in a way that would suggest some shared conclusions, if not arguments, with Johnson, not Coates). Only recently have there been philosophical attempts to integrate reparative claims into theories of distributive justice. These have mostly been part of new theories of global justice, which try to take seriously the legacies of colonialism and empire, and weave claims about redress and repair into arguments about structural injustice that seem to cut across the reparative/ distributive divide.[14]

Yet this divide is itself a product of the history of reparation claims and its tangled relationship with Anglophone analytical liberal philosophy. The attempt to accommodate claims about historic injustice and reparations in global justice theory today are intended in part to address the relative philosophical silence about problems of racism and empire. But these correctives themselves do not explain the silence; nor do they explain the ideological underpinnings of the categories that have come to structure liberal philosophy in general, and global justice theory in particular. These were constructed during the late 1960s and 1970s – years which witnessed both the reinvention of political philosophy and the revival of the demand for reparations within African-American movements, particularly black nationalists with links to anti-colonial liberation groups.[15] Their demands spurred debate among a small number of lawyers, economists and philosophers, who for a brief time engaged with them, only to set them aside. This chapter charts these debates about reparations and explores why they matter for understanding the trajectory of philosophical debates about reparations and the place of race and empire in global justice theory. These debates did not last long

---

[13] John Torpey, "Paying for the Past? The Movement for Reparations for African-Americans", *Journal of Human Rights*, 3/2 (2004), 171–87; Lawrie Balfour, "Reparations after Identity Politics", *Political Theory*, 33/6 (2005), 786–811.

[14] Lea Ypi, Robert Goodin and Christian Barry, "Associative Duties, Global Justice, and the Colonies", *Philosophy and Public Affairs*, 37/2 (2009), 103–35; Catherine Lu, "Colonialism as Structural Injustice: Historical Responsibility and Contemporary Redress", *Journal of Political Philosophy*, 19/3 (2011), 261–81; Iris Marion Young, "Responsibility and Global Labor Justice", *Journal of Political Philosophy*, 12 (2004), 365–88; Cecile Fabre, *Justice in a Changing World* (Cambridge: Polity, 2007). For a non-international example see Chiara Cordelli, "Reparative Justice and the Moral Limits of Discretionary Philanthropy" in Rob Reich, Chiara Cordelli and Lucy Bernholz (eds.), *Philanthropy in Democratic Societies* (Chicago: University of Chicago Press, 2016).

[15] Robin Kelley, *Freedom Dreams: The Black Radical Imagination* (New York: Beacon Press, 2002), ch. 5; Thomas Sugrue, *Sweet Land of Liberty: The Forgotten Struggle for Civil Rights in the North* (New York: Random House, 2008), 434–6, 272.

within philosophy, and soon gave way to less radical remedies for injustice like preferential hiring and affirmative action. But they occurred at an important turning point in liberal philosophy's history. As such, they not only represent a road not taken, but shaped the ascendant global justice theory in crucial ways.

Though in the late 1960s, the demand for reparations was a demand of the black left, when it entered political philosophy it took on a different ideological valence. In this moment – bookended by black nationalists' reparations-demands and the uptake of reparations by international human rights movements – it was libertarians who were sympathetic to reparations.[16] And in the 1970s, tackling the libertarian challenge preoccupied egalitarian philosophers. This, as well as a number of other internalist theoretical concerns – with the nature of collective and corporate responsibility, and the presence of the past within theories of justice – led them to downplay demands for reparations for slavery. When they turned to theorize the international realm, they downgraded demands for reparations for colonial expropriation too. It was in these debates, however, that philosophers both developed the particular character of global justice theory, and secured the absence of race and empire within their theories for more than a generation. This chapter revisits them to show how the categories and divisions that characterize liberal philosophy today were constructed. By tracing the conceptual preoccupations that enabled the rebuttal of a particular kind of philosophical argument, it also illuminates the mechanisms by which a field of political concern was removed from domestic and global justice theory.

Black Reparations and Justice in the United States

The civil rights activists of the 1960s were famous for their demands for compensatory and distributive programs: from the "Marshall Plan for the Negro", the Black Panthers' demand for payment for the "overdue debt" owed by the federal government to black communities for their unpaid labor, to Audley "Queen Mother" Moore's broad, therapeutic vision of reparations advocated by her Reparations Committee for United States Slaves Descendants.[17] Many invoked nineteenth-century

---

[16] For recent statements see Janna Thompson, "Historical Injustice and Reparation: Justifying Claims of Descendants", *Ethics*, 112/1 (2001), 114–35; Daniel Butt, *Rectifying International Injustice: Principles of Compensation and Restitution between Nations* (Oxford: Oxford University Press, 2009).

[17] Sugrue, *Sweet Land of Liberty*, 434–6, 272.

precedents, when freed slaves, Radical Republicans and later the Ex-Slave Mutual Relief, Bounty and Pension Association had demanded compensatory measures for ex-slaves.[18] By 1968, group-specific demands for reparations increasingly stood alongside calls for universalizing welfarist plans like the Freedom Budget of October 1966,[19] sometimes within the same proposal. In April 1969, the Black Economic Development Conference adopted the "Black Manifesto".[20] The next month, the former executive secretary of the Student Nonviolent Coordinating Committee (SNCC) and Black Panther James Forman, then associated with the socialist League of Revolutionary Black Workers, interrupted a Sunday morning service at New York City's Riverside Church, attracting widespread controversy and bringing to national attention a demand for reparations based in a politics of liberation that was ultimately universal in its emancipatory aspirations.[21]

The Black Manifesto demanded reparations of $500 million to black Americans for the centuries of exploitation – of "resources", "minds", "bodies" and "labor" – which black people had suffered at the hands of "racist white America", and for their "role in developing the industrial base of the Western world through … slave labor".[22] Anti-capitalist and anti-imperialist in rhetoric, Forman described African Americans as living as "colonized people inside the United States". Unlike West German reparations to Nazi victims – that took the form of individual compensation for personal and professional damages to survivors and their immediate families – he demanded reparations in the form of race-specific public goods: a Southern land bank to establish cooperative farms, or compensate for lands expropriated; cooperative

---

[18] Eric Foner, *Reconstruction: America's Unfinished Revolution 1863–77* (New York: Harper, 1988); Mary Francis Berry, *My Face Is Black Is True: Callie House and the Struggle for Ex-Slave Reparations* (New York: Vintage, 2005).

[19] Foner, *Reconstruction*, 376.

[20] James Forman, "The Black Manifesto" reprinted in Boris I. Bittker, *The Case for Black Reparations* (New York: Beacon, 1973/2003), 161–75; Elaine Allen Lechtreck, "'We Are Demanding $500 Million for Reparations': The Black Manifesto, Mainline Religious Denominations, and Black Economic Development", *Journal of African American History*, 97/1–2 (2012), 39–71. The Black Manifesto was reprinted in multiple venues, notably (for the philosophical audience examined in this chapter) in *The New York Review of Books* (10 July 1969).

[21] Dan Georgakis and Marvin Surkin, *Detroit, I Do Mind Dying: A Study in Urban Revolution* (New York: South End Press Classics, 1998). Cf. Michael C. Dawson, *Blacks in and out of the Left* (Cambridge, MA: Harvard University Press, 2013), 4–6, 107–9. On Forman's class analysis in the context of black nationalism see Cedric Johnson, *Revolutionaries to Race Leaders: Black Power and the Making of African American Politics* (Minneapolis: University of Minnesota Press, 2007), 155.

[22] Forman, "Black Manifesto" in Bittker, *The Case for Black Reparations*, 167, 172.

investments in the black community in the form of publishing and printing industries, research skills centers and TV networks; a National Black Labor Strike and Defense Fund to protect black workers; investment in the International Black Appeal, a Black University, a Black Anti-Defamation League and more. Also unlike German reparations, Forman did not direct his demands at the US government but primarily at "the white Christian churches and the Jewish synagogues" that were "part and parcel of the system of capitalism". In keeping with radical black (and much New Left) politics, this reparations claim did not require a view of the state as legitimate.[23]

The demand for reparations pulled in different directions, and in the aftermath of the Manifesto its political valence remained ambiguous. Unlike its post-cold war iterations, reparations claims in the Black Power era were often as much associated with emancipation as they were with reconciliation, and were more liberationist than liberal.[24] While some Christian groups began to act on the demands, many of Forman's local and national audience were hostile to them. Critiques came from civil rights leaders, who saw Forman as "inflammatory", as well as the Democratic and labor left.[25] For them, despite Forman's revolutionary and liberationist rhetoric, the Manifesto was not one that a broad-based mass democratic movement could get behind. It was an appeal to private institutions, not the state. Bayard Rustin described reparations not only as unrealistic but as isolating blacks from whites with whom they shared economic interests.[26] Michael Harrington likewise condemned reparations as a distraction from redistributive campaigns.[27] It would not make sense to compensate only the descendants of slaves for past exploitation; all workers needed to be compensated. The demand for reparations was here not conceived as in itself redistributive, so it was not the right road to emancipation.

Black nationalists and church leaders, who continued to demand reparations as an acknowledgement of white guilt, emphasizing moral

---

[23] Forman, "Black Manifesto", 167–71.

[24] John Torpey, *On Making Whole What Has Been Smashed: On Reparations Politics* (Cambridge, MA: Harvard University Press, 2006), 5. On how to conceptualize the political thought of the Black Power era see Brandon M. Terry, "Requiem for a Dream: The Problem-Space of Black Power", in Tommie Shelby and Brandon M. Terry (eds.), *To Shape a New World* (Cambridge, MA: Harvard University Press, 2018), 293–5.

[25] Jerry Frye, "The 'Black Manifesto' and the Tactic of Objectification", *Journal of Black Studies*, 5/1 (1974), 65–76.

[26] Bayard Rustin, "The Failure of Black Separatism", in *Down the Line: The Collected Writings of Bayard Rustin* (Chicago: Quadrangle, 1971), 3–4.

[27] Arnold Kaufman and Michael Harrington, "Black Reparations – Two Views", *Dissent* (July–August 1969), 318–9.

repair and reconciliation, in part confirmed this perspective. Yet others stressed the economic dimension, advocating a monetary transfer, and were as much concerned with compensation as apology. Like Forman, saw slavery not only as the primary injustice facing African Americans but also a basis for an internationalist anti-colonial movement uniting descendants of slaves globally.[28] In 1972, economist Robert Browne argued that the objective of reparations was to "restore the black community to the economic position it would have had had it not been subjected to slavery and discrimination".[29] To make his case for material reparations, he appealed to a growing historical literature on the profitability of slavery and its contribution to America's economic growth.[30] He listed many feasible ways of calculating the cost of slavery to African Americans – the impact of slavery on the total economy; the market prices of slaves; their direct labor output; the value of unpaid black equity or the unpaid wage bill – and argued that reparations could not be a simple payment for unpaid labor, but needed to take seriously underpayment and the denial of opportunity since slavery. He suggested compiling "annual per capita earned income differential between the black and white community". Elsewhere, like Forman, he linked the issue to the need for land tenure, and the broader "land question" that then preoccupied black nationalist thinkers.[31] Reparations here were not just compensation but a means of redistribution.[32]

---

[28] James Forman, 'Control, Conflict and Change: The Underlying Concepts of the Black Manifesto' in Robert Lecky and H. Elliott Wright (eds.), *Black Manifesto: Religion, Racism and Reparations* (New York: Sheed & Ward, 1969), 47–50. For transnational and nationally differentiated demands for reparations (and their relationship to distinctive systems of slavery) see Ana Lucia Araujo, *Reparations for Slavery and the Slave Trade: A Transnational and Comparative History* (London: Bloomsbury, 2017).

[29] Robert Browne, 'The Economic Case for Reparations to Black America', *The American Economic Review*, 62/1–2 (1972), 43. Cf. Browne, 'Toward Making "Black Power" Real Power' in Lecky and Wright (eds.), *Black Manifesto*, 67–77.

[30] Alfred Conrad and John Meyer, *The Economics of Slavery* (Chicago: Aldine, 1964); Robert Starobin, *Industrial Slavery in the Old South* (Oxford: Oxford University Press, 1970); Jim Marketti, 'Black Equity in the Slave Industry', *Review of Black Political Economy*, 2/2 (1972), 43–66; Robert Fogel and Stanley Engerman, *Time on the Cross: The Economics of American Negro Slavery* (New York: Norton, 1974).

[31] Robert Browne, 'Black Land Loss: The Plight of Black Ownership', *Southern Exposure*, 2 (1974), 112–21; Browne, *Only Six Million Acres: The Decline of Black-Owned Land in the Rural South; A Report* (New York: Rockefeller, 1973). On the land question see Russell Rickford, '"We Can't Grow Food on All This Concrete": The Land Question, Agrarianism, and Black Nationalist Thought in the Late 1960s and 1970s', *Journal of American History*, 103/4 (2017), 956–80; and on land and reparations see Kelley, *Freedom Dreams*, 124–8.

[32] See also Graham Hughes, 'Reparations for Blacks?', *New York University Law Review*, 43 (1968), 1063–74.

In 1972, Hugo Bedau, an ethicist widely known for his account of civil disobedience, became the first white liberal philosopher to take up reparations. Bedau recognized the importance of black reparations for distributive justice in the USA. But he also saw a tension between reparations and the ascendant Rawlsian distributive justice theory: the Black Manifesto could be read as positing arguments for compensatory justice that were actually disguised arguments for distributive justice. Ostensibly an argument for repairing past wrongs, it was more concerned with redistributing resources to deal with the disadvantages suffered by contemporary African Americans.[33] Philosophers, Bedau suggested, might object to this confusion. He put it aside, because the distinction between compensatory and distributive justice was still under-theorized in available liberal theories of justice (he pointed here to Rawls, W. G. Runciman and Nicholas Rescher as among the most prominent).[34] It might well be the case that present disadvantages were sufficient justification for major redistribution, but this was in any case not Forman's point.

Yet Bedau defended the Manifesto's demands against many possible objections, three of which anticipated other ways in which reparations would pose a problem for liberal analytical philosophy. The first was their corporate nature: Bedau suggested that many would find unworkable the idea that it was to 'corporate black America' that reparations were owed, and that it was the corporate liability (rather than merely the collective guilt) of the white churches – understood as the conscience of a white America itself too disorganized to be viewed in corporate terms – that was at stake. After the Vietnam War raised the problem of war crimes, whether responsibility and guilt could be held individually, collectively or corporately had become a live issue.[35] For Bedau, writing just at the moment before corporate accounts of liability were replaced by individualistic accounts of responsibility, the corporate claims of the Manifesto were defensible. Just a few years later, a deep scepticism about ideas of corporate and collective responsibility, which Bedau anticipated, would make such a defense much more difficult.[36]

[33] Hugo Adam Bedau, "Compensatory Justice and the Black Manifesto", *The Monist*, 56/1 (1972), 22.
[34] Bedau, "Compensatory Justice", 23.
[35] Peter French (ed.), *Individual and Collective Responsibility: Massacre at My Lai* (Cambridge, MA: Harvard University Press, 1972); Joel Feinberg, "Collective Responsibility", *Journal of Philosophy*, 65 (1968), 674–88; D. Cooper, "Collective Responsibility", *Philosophy*, 43 (1968), 258–68; Virginia Held, "Can a Random Collection of Individuals Be Held Responsible?", *Journal of Philosophy*, 67 (1970), 471–81.
[36] Only recently has this philosophical aversion to theorizing corporate and collective responsibility been reversed. For discussion see Thomas McCarthy, "Coming to Terms with Our Past, Part II: On the Morality and Politics of Reparations for Slavery",

Another objection that Bedau briefly raised also reflected this turning point in the history of liberal philosophy. Given that the claims of the Manifesto turned on the concept of desert, liberals might view it as "anachronistic". As Brian Barry put it already in 1965, politics – with the rise of the welfare state and the move away from atomistic classical liberalism – had witnessed a "revolt against desert".[37] For Rawls, desert was likewise irrelevant to a theory of justice. For Bedau it was "a concept of declining relevance in the adjustment of social relations where inequalities suffered on the scale of those which burden American blacks are concerned".[38] But he put this aside, implying that the rejection of desert claims might be made compatible with openness to claims about the weight of the past. He was right to anticipate the objection. Yet he was overly optimistic about its implications. For the revolt against desert would not entail openness to the past, but the opposite. Soon, it was not simply desert claims that would be disputed by philosophers, but "historical" claims about how states of affairs had come about.

While Bedau dismissed the conflation of compensatory and distributive justice, he also predicted a third objection about Forman's combination of a Marxist critique of exploitation with a conventional liberal demand for "justifiable compensation". Bedau, like Arnold Kaufman in his response to Harrington, stressed that the justification for reparations for African Americans, unlike Nazi reparations, did not rely exclusively on an idea of past harm, but of "unjust enrichment". It was more a question of compensatory than corrective justice (and so not as reliant on proof of criminal harm in court). But it was nonetheless a familiar liberal, legalist demand. Set alongside exploitation, it pointed in the opposite direction. To be "workable" in practice, the Marxian component required evidence to establish that "current wealth in white institutions is the causal product of historic capitalist exploitation" (evidence of the kind that historians, and economists like Browne, were marshaling).[39] Claims about compensation, by contrast, need not rely on historical wrongs: it was sufficient to establish "only that blacks still suffer from uncompensated wrongs while others (whites) still enjoy the undeserved benefit of those historic wrongs". No historical argument about exploitation was necessary.

Political Theory, 32/6 (2004), 750–72. Only recently has the aversion among analytical philosophers to theorizing corporate and collective responsibility been reversed. For discussion see Avia Pasternak, "Limiting States Corporate Responsibility", *Journal of Political Philosophy*, 21/4 (2013), 361–81; Anna Stilz, "Collective Responsibility and the State", *Journal of Political Philosophy*, 19/2 (2011), 190–208.
[37] Brian Barry, *Political Argument* (London: Routledge, 1965), 112.
[38] Bedau, "Compensatory Justice", 41. See Barry, *Political Argument*, 113.
[39] Bedau, "Compensatory Justice", 29.

Bedau denied these aspects to Forman's argument were in tension, partly because of his ambiguous use of the terminology of exploitation and partly because he ignored the desert objection:

> The labor of generations of blacks has created surplus profits of slight or no benefit to them, and this labor was originally stolen and thenceforth made captive under conditions of structured injustice which a Hume, a Mill, or a Rawls would be able to recognize as such. The slave and Jim Crow heritage, therefore, constitutes both a moral and an economic exploitation. Blacks in America have been doubly exploited, so their argument for compensation is entitled to take this into account and it does. To put it another way, we might view The Black Manifesto as attempting to invoke not merely one or another version of conventional Liberal principles of justice, nor of Marxist justice – if there is such a thing – but what might be called *socialist justice*.[40]

The ideological ambiguity of reparations opened the possibility of a socialist justice theory, which could accommodate both redistribution and reparations.

But philosophical debate about reparations did not go in the direction Bedau hoped. For it was not a philosopher who took up reparations, but a lawyer. Boris Bittker at Yale was a tax lawyer, who had published influentially on segregation. Described as a "utopian technician", he was not interested in the philosophical case for reparations but their legal feasibility.[41] He did not attempt to explain Forman's slippages, between the liberal and Marxist, the compensatory and distributive, the legal and political. Instead he prised them apart. Bittker had no trouble with notions of corporate liability, and, not being concerned with ideal or institutional distributive theories, no qualms with the concept of desert. In *The Case for Black Reparations* (1973), reparations went from emancipatory to liberal: he made no claims about structural exploitation, and his argument turned on the existence of a legitimate state and legal system to redress wrongs. Demands for reparations, he argued, were no more complicated than any major social policy or civil damages claims: "a system of black reparations", not radical but in fact "familiar and conservative", had a statutory basis and "was actually secreted in existing laws".[42] Though this system would target discriminatory practices (rather than harmful acts), it was not distributive justice wearing the mask of compensatory justice. Reparations were not a "poverty program" but a "remedy for injustice".[43] They shared overlapping constituencies with non-racial welfare programs, but worked for

[40] Bedau, "Compensatory Justice", 29–30.
[41] Mark Tushnet, "The Utopian Technician", *Yale Law Journal*, 93/2 (1983), 208–10.
[42] Bittker, *The Case for Black Reparations*, 34, 68.
[43] Bittker, *The Case for Black Reparations*, 133.

different purposes, with different objectives and results. Reparative justice meant the correction of past injustice. It was historical in a way that distributive justice was not.

Precisely how historical was a concern. Bittker argued that black reparations should not be concerned with the "correction of ancient injustice", but righting the wrongs of segregation.[44] Slavery was a necessary but insufficient condition for compensatory proposals. An exclusive focus on slavery diminished the wrongs of segregation and let recent political actors off the hook. Reparations should redress injuries "caused by the system of legally imposed segregation", thus targeting the discriminatory practices of federal and state governments (and requiring federal funding).[45]

Bittker's shift from slavery to segregation anticipated the objection that long-past historical wrongs could not be taken legally seriously. Compensation for past injuries faced challenges. Statutes of limitation, and the fact that civil plaintiffs often had to have been injured themselves, made the damages claims of slave descendants unworkable – as did the assumption, implicit in the idea of rectification or restoration, of a status quo ante, a historical baseline for redress. As such, with ordinary damages claims and arguments for the pecuniary redress of government misconduct, the usual approach was to eliminate the conditions for future misconduct, rather than provide pecuniary solace for the past. Despite these barriers, Bittker was insistent on the historical nature of his argument, even as he limited its chronological scope: "Justice requires compensating past injuries rather than merely forbidding their repetition."[46] He sought to show that reparations were workable anyway, exploring different forms of liability and damage suits, and denying the effect of prior constitutionality of segregation on reparations claims. He focused on how section 1983 of the Civil Rights Act of 1871 – which allowed individuals to sue for damages and redress when federally protected rights were violated by persons acting under state authority – could be used to litigate black reparations suits. Section 1983 could encompass historical claims: it provided the potential for both a backward-looking and forward-looking dimension, opening the door to a distinction between remedying injustice by compensation for the past and by corrective action in the future – and allowed the former to play a central role.[47]

Bittker also thought section 1983 could be reinterpreted to provide a legal basis for the liability question – of whether public agencies or only

[44] Bittker, *The Case for Black Reparations*, 9.
[45] Bittker, *The Case for Black Reparations*, 19.
[46] Bittker, *The Case for Black Reparations*, 26.
[47] Bittker, *The Case for Black Reparations*, 36–7.

their members could be held responsible for discriminatory practices. It imposed "liability on 'every person' whose conduct under color of state law deprives another person of his federally protected rights". Did that mean, Bittker asked, that it reached "only natural persons, or does the phrase "every person" also embrace state governments and their political subdivisions and administrative agencies?".[48] It was conventionally interpreted as imposing liability only on individual officials, which would make it insufficient for any kind of real reparations claim. But in the Dictionary Act of the United States Code, the word "person", Bittker noted, was extended to "bodies politic and corporate", implying section 1983 – an act of the same year – could be similarly interpreted. The Supreme Court had held otherwise in *Monroe* v. *Pape*: section 1983 did not impose liability on municipalities, which were thence immune.[49] Against this, Bittker argued that government agencies could be held liable as corporate entities, and contested municipal immunity through this historical argument about the definition of personhood. Damage suits against the state or its agencies under section 1983 were thus possible.[50] Changes would be required: for one, the focus on official misconduct should be replaced by the recognition of "government sanctioned discrimination at the highest levels".[51]

Here Bittker showed the practical ways around the problems Bedau had recognized as facing the new justice theories – in particular, their neglect of corporate responsibility and its extension over time. In the early 1970s, philosophical concern with corporate responsibility was displaced by discussions of distributive justice: in Rawlsian theory, the state was part of the "basic structure", not primarily conceived as a corporate person or agent, as in older state personality theories (that dealt with claims about responsibility across time, not distribution in a static present). Corporate liability claims in law had, however, never gone away, and Bittker bypassed these philosophical difficulties, demonstrating that they could be viable in civil rights suits.[52]

Yet he acknowledged the political challenges. Like other social schemes, reparations would involve budgetary decisions, hard choices, implementation problems and conflicting interests. All forms of recompense had their downside: individual transfers might do little over the long term; public goods could be unequally accessed.[53] Whether

---

[48] Bittker, *The Case for Black Reparations*, 50.   [49] *Monroe* v. *Pape* 365 (1961).

[50] Bittker, *The Case for Black Reparations*, 51–8.

[51] Bittker, *The Case for Black Reparations*, 21.

[52] In fact, in 1978, municipal immunity would be dropped, and local governments deemed "persons" under section 1983 – as Bittker had proposed. *Monell* v. *Department of Social Services of the City of New York* (1978).

[53] Bittker, *The Case for Black Reparations*, 115–35.

reparations should be owed to groups or individuals, and who might speak for the "black community", raised familiar problems of representation and recognition. So did how its membership should be determined (racial classification being an obvious but controversial solution, and Bittker proposed eligibility determined by attendance at a segregated school instead). In charting these downsides, he portrayed reparations not as a problem of distributive justice, but as a technical problem of compensatory or corrective justice, understood purely in terms of damages claimed for harms suffered under a legal system of discriminatory practices. Bedau had tried to show that reparations could be easily taken up by "a Rawls, Hume or Mill". Bittker made it safe for lawyers (though very few, in fact, took reparations seriously). But he also made it philosophically unappealing. If reparations were a question of damages claimed through litigation, they had no place in an ideal theory of distributive justice. Or so it initially seemed.

Historical Injustice and Distributive Justice in Ideal Theory

As debates about distributive justice exploded onto the philosophical scene following the publication of Rawls's *A Theory of Justice* (1971), the reparations debate was pushed in new directions. Mostly this played out in discussions of employment practices. Problems of affirmative action, "reverse discrimination" and "preferential hiring" that had become national preoccupations during the previous decade soon preoccupied philosophers of justice, especially on their home turf, the universities.[54] Initially, some framed affirmative action as a form of reparation.[55] But they soon turned away from the question of how to repair the historical wrongs of slavery, and from "backward-looking principles" that justified preferential hiring as remedies for past harm or discrimination.[56] Historical arguments were highly flexible – and potentially suspect: they were used to justify inaction in desegregation cases (for instance, to justify segregated school districts so long as they had not been produced with intent).[57] Many defenders of affirmative action thus saw it not as reparation but compensation for current discrimination. Such

[54] Thomas Sugrue, "Affirmative Action from Below: Civil Rights, the Building Trades, and the Politics of Racial Equality in the Urban North, 1945–1969", *Journal of American History*, 91/1 (2004), 145–73.

[55] For the limits of this view see Albert Mosley, "Affirmative Action as a Form of Reparations", *University of Memphis Law Review*, 33/353 (2003).

[56] Owen Fiss, "School Desegregation: The Uncertain Path of theLaw", *Philosophy and Public Affairs*, 4/1 (1974), 3–39.

[57] *Milliken* v. *Bradley* (1974).

compensation was justifiable, often only temporarily, by "forward-looking principles" that aimed at future equality of opportunity. This move had its legal analogue in the *Bakke* decision of 1978, which took a further step away from backward-looking arguments, declaring affirmative action justifiable only for the sake of diversity (not even as compensation).[58] In debates about discriminatory practices in employment, then, claims to address historical injustice were often sidestepped or displaced by a focus on current inequities in the receipt of benefits. Bedau had made reparations a form of compensatory justice; soon they were detached from mainstream legal compensatory ideas altogether.

Those who did stress compensation tried to show that compensatory justice, despite its implicit reliance on an idea of desert, could be squeezed into a "Rawlsian" – as it was fast becoming known – theory of distributive justice.[59] Some argued that Rawls's principles themselves required compensation and remedy for the effects of discrimination; others that compensatory principles would be chosen in the original position alongside the principles of justice.[60] The problem of whether the beneficiaries of compensation should benefit as individuals or because of their membership in (historically or currently) disadvantaged groups was translated into Rawlsian terms.[61] Should "reparations for blacks" be understood solely as reparations for 'wronged individuals who happen to be black?"[62] The status of group identity continued to be vexed, though the case for individual compensation often won out (largely because of the perceived compatibility with Rawls's focus on persons). With a focus on "private" employment, the question of broader governmental responsibility and corporate public liability was dropped. Reparations for historical injustice were subsumed and domesticated into a theory of compensation for current disadvantage, amenable to a Rawlsian framework. This was largely for conceptual reasons. But the philosophical silences accompanied a political one: unlike the problems of civil rights in the South or civil disobedience against the Vietnam War, which had, just a few years earlier, mobilized numerous justifications and defences, very few philosophers – even among the many who wrote from Boston during the conflicts surrounding court-ordered

---

[58] Alan Goldman, "Affirmative Action", *Philosophy and Public Affairs*, 5/2 (1976), 178–95.
[59] Thomas Nagel, "Equal Treatment and Compensatory Discrimination", *Philosophy and Public Affairs*, 2/4 (1973), 348–63.
[60] James Nickel, "Discrimination and Morally Relevant Characteristics", *Analysis*, 32/4 (1972), 113–4.
[61] Alan Goldman, "Reparations to Individuals or Groups?", *Analysis*, 35/3 (1975), 168–70.
[62] James Nickel, 'Should Reparations be to Individuals or to Groups?', *Analysis*, 34/5 (1974), 154–60; J. L. Cowan, "Inverse Discrimination", *Analysis*, 33/1 (1972), 10–12; P. W. Taylor, "Reverse Discrimination and Compensatory Justice", *Analysis*, 33/6, 177–82; M. D. Bayles, "Reparations to Wronged Groups", *Analysis*, 33/6, 182–4.

school desegregation and the city's busing crisis – provided support for or explored the desegregation controversies they witnessed.[63]

Meanwhile, an alternative basis for reparations claims was being put forward, by Rawls's most influential early critic, that changed the terms of the reparations debate domestically and internationally. When libertarian Harvard philosopher Robert Nozick published his *Anarchy, State, and Utopia* (1974) he extended the anti-consequentialist strain of Rawls's theory into an account of individual rights that existed outside of any particular institutional arrangement, and in doing so shifted the basis of reparation or compensation claims from discriminatory practices to rights violations. Famously, he provided a critique of "patterned" theories of justice that controlled the goods of individuals by reference to an end-state theory, like a liberal, egalitarian or socialist theory of distribution. The justice of an individual's possessions and control over economic goods was not a function of their contribution to the general welfare, as might be claimed by an "end-state" theory. Instead, Nozick defended a backward-looking "entitlement" theory of justice in distribution that was 'historical', rather than 'structural', and according to which, "whether a distribution is just depends upon how it came about".[64]

For Nozick, a distribution was just only if it came about by a "just initial acquisition" or a "just transfer". But this did not account for all actual situations. People steal, enslave and exclude others, extract their product. When there is past injustice – when these principles have been violated – the principle of rectification kicks in.[65] Nozick opened the door to a theory that could accommodate rectification, restitution and reparation as crucial to distributive justice. Though an individualist harshly critical of more collectivist approaches, he agreed with socialists about the importance of "notions of earning, producing, entitlement, desert and so forth"; socialism's mistake lay in its "view of what entitlements arise out of what sort of productive processes".[66] It was not a question of whether your lot was deserved. It was about how it had come about – crucially, whether you had acquired it in accordance with his principles.

---

[63] The notable exceptions were legal philosophers, for instance Fiss, "School Desegregation" and the Harvard founder of critical race theory, Derrick Bell Jr, "Serving Two Masters: Integration Ideals and Client Interests in School Desegregation Litigation", *Yale Law Journal*, 86/470 (1976). On school desegregation see Jennifer Hochschild, *The New American Dilemma: Liberal Democracy and School Desegregation* (New Haven, CT: Yale University Press, 1984); Jason Sokol, *All Eyes Are Upon Us: Race and Politics from Boston to Brooklyn* (New York: Basic Books, 2012).

[64] Nozick, *Anarchy, State, and Utopia* (New York: Basic Books, 1974), 153. For another contemporary libertarian view of reparations see Julian Simon and Larry Neal, "A Calculation of the Black Reparations Bill", *Review of Black Political Economy*, 4/3 (1974), 75–86.

[65] Nozick, *Anarchy, State, and Utopia*, 152.   [66] Nozick, *Anarchy, State, and Utopia*, 55.

Opening the door to rectification raised a number of issues:

if past injustice has shaped present holdings in various ways, some identifiable and some not, what now, if anything ought to be done to rectify these injustices? What obligations do the performers of injustice have toward those whose position is worse than it would have been had the injustice not been done? Or, than it would have been had compensation been paid promptly? How, if at all, do things change if the beneficiaries and those made worse off are not the direct parties in the act of injustice, but, for example their descendants? Is an injustice done to someone whose holding was itself based upon an unrectified injustice? How far back must one go in wiping clean the historical slate of injustices? What may victims of injustice permissibly do in order to rectify the injustices being done to them, including the many injustices done by persons acting through their government?[67]

Nozick was likely thinking of reparations for slavery, both here – the footnote referenced Bittker – and when he wrote that it might be difficult to formulate the principle of rectification to apply to persons "who did not themselves violate the first two principles".[68] Yet he did not develop the principle of rectification, but merely stated that without one it was impossible "to condemn any particular scheme of transfer payments, unless it is clear that no considerations of rectification of injustice could apply to justify it". A fierce anti-statist, Nozick added that "although to introduce socialism as the punishment for our sins would be to go too far, past injustices might be so great as to make necessary in the short run a more extensive state in order to rectify them".[69]

What Nozick provided was a way of taking seriously historical argument. While his fellow-travelers in the "revolt against desert" eliminated history altogether, Nozick dug down. His theory accommodated injustices committed in the past, in ways Rawlsian theories did not. It built a basis for claims to rectify unjust holdings that did not rely on a set of agreed-upon social rules and practices, or existing institutions from which compensation need be demanded. In this respect, his theory cut against the trajectory of liberal philosophy, which, after Rawls, focused on justifying a set of social rules, but largely ignored moral relations outside of them. It was this that made Nozick attractive to those whom the existing social rules did not benefit, and for whom compensation for discrimination was not enough.

Bernard Boxill, one of the pioneers of African American political philosophy in this period, similarly moved reparations claims outside the social rules. Where Forman had attempted to integrate reparations into a Marxian liberationist framework, Boxill, in his response to Forman,

[67] Nozick, *Anarchy, State, and Utopia*, 152.
[68] Nozick, *Anarchy, State, and Utopia*, 172–3.
[69] Nozick, *Anarchy, State, and Utopia*, 230.

showed how reparations worked in a liberal one.[70] But his was not a Rawlsian framework that rested on contract, the acceptance of social rules or the "existence of a valid community". It depended, as Nozick's did, on rights – not entitlements in property, but of each person to "pursue and acquire what he values".[71] This distinction was crucial to Boxill's definition of reparation. He objected to Harrington's critique of reparations as non-egalitarian on grounds that Harrington had conflated compensation and reparations. Boxill argued that rights of compensation depended on the fact that individuals are "members of a single community which itself implies tacit agreement on the part of the whole to bear the costs of compensation". In cases where compensation is due, no prior injustice need have occurred: people can be compensated for their bad luck, for natural accidents and "acts of God". For Boxill, a vision of distributive justice (that rested on a view of society run in terms of fair competition and the protection of society's losers) required compensatory programmes (to keep competition fair and the losers protected). Such programmes were "forward-looking", concerned to keep society fair and running smoothly.[72] By contrast, the case for reparation was "more primitive". Unlike compensation cases, no "prior commitment" was required to "identify the parties who must bear the cost of reparation; it is simply and clearly the party who has acted unjustly". A social contract or agreement was unnecessary. The right to claim reparation derived "directly from self-preservation". Reparation was backward-looking: it "is due only when a breach of justice *has* occurred".[73]

Compensation from a community where some suffer from bad luck, need a leg up or safety net, was a different matter from reparations "to black and colonial people". This depended "precisely on the fact that such people have been reduced to their present condition by a history of injustice".[74] Slaves, for instance, had "an indisputable moral right to the products of their labor", a right they conferred to their descendants just as the slave masters passed the expropriated product to theirs, meaning that "the descendants of slave masters are in possession of wealth to which the descendants of slaves have rights". This possession extended to the "white community as a whole" – precisely not the federal government or states in

---

[70] George Yancy (ed.), *African American Philosophers: 17 Conversations* (Abingdon: Routledge, 1998), ch. 16. For other near-contemporary responses to Forman among African-American philosophers see Howard McGary Jr, "Reparations and Inverse Discrimination", *Dialogue*, 17/1 (1974), and "Justice and Reparations", *The Philosophical Forum*, 9/2–3 (1977–8).

[71] Bernard Boxill, 'The Morality of Reparation', *Social Theory and Practice*, 2/1 (1972), 113–23.

[72] Boxill, "The Morality of Reparation", 117.

[73] Boxill, "The Morality of Reparation", 116.

[74] Boxill, "The Morality of Reparation", 117.

its corporate capacity (that body, Boxill implied but did not argue, produced by a contract). It was the white community, construed socially rather than politically, who – whether considered as individuals receiving benefits to which others have rights, or as something like a corporation or company, the members of which have joint interests and access to benefits and shares of membership – owe "reparations to the sons of slaves".[75]

This was a neo-Lockean account, skeptical of the Rawlsian contract, and it provided an attractive theory for those who did not exist within a realm of social rules that benefitted them. But this reparations claim rested on an idea of inherited rights to ownership. Did it thus depend on the validity of inheritance? Boxill argued not, stating that even if the wealth of individuals were returned to the community on their death, the claim would remain. Yet even allowing for common ownership (and thus avoiding the libertarian interpretation of this argument) it still depended on an idea of inherited wealth. Like Nozick, Boxill took trans-historical rights for granted. His were more expansive (and later versions of his demand for repair reflected psychological harms suffered as well as material losses).[76] But both his and Nozick's accounts nonetheless supported the kind of reparative claims about unjust enrichment, extracted labor and land, that permeated the Black Manifesto.[77]

On the surface, there was nothing in these arguments – particularly on the common ownership interpretation – that made them unacceptable to socialists. While compensatory arguments had been subsumed into accounts of distributive justice, these historical, reparative arguments, intertwined with accounts of expropriation, seemed feasibly compatible with accounts of productive justice. The sticking point for socialists would not be the history of expropriation but the idea that a slave class had a distinct history, separable from that of all workers (or, more likely, the strategic argument Harrington suggested, that reparations claims were a distraction because they cut across class interests).[78] By contrast, for Rawlsians, such a neo-Lockean view could not be so easily integrated. It challenged the core of their theory, by positing a realm of historical

---

[75] Boxill, "The Morality of Reparation", 120–1.

[76] These would be important divisions in later debates, later brought back together in Janna Thompson, "Historical Injustice and Reparation: Justifying Claims of Descendants", *Ethics*, 112/1 (2001), 114–35. Many arguments about inheritance of possession run up against Waldron"s objection to historical injustice in the form of his "indeterminacy thesis" in Jeremy Waldron, "Superseding Historical Injustice", *Ethics*, 103/1 (1992), 4–28.

[77] David Scott, "On the Moral Justification for Reparations for New World Slavery" in Robert Nichols and Jakeet Singh (eds.), *Freedom and Democracy in an Imperial Context: Conversations with James Tully* (Abingdon: Routledge, 2014), 107–9.

[78] Kaufman and Harrington, "Black Reparations – Two Views", 318.

argument and transhistorical rights of ownership, property and inheritance that existed outside of social rules and agreements. With no theoretical support from Rawlsians and little practical from socialists, the philosophical case for reparations thus became associated not with the left, but with libertarianism, individualism, property rights and the kind of historical arguments antithetical to contractarian egalitarianism.

By the mid-1970s, Nozick had a near monopoly on historical arguments. The brief interest in squaring claims for black reparations with distributive justice theory had largely waned. One non-libertarian philosopher continued, however, to try to rescue historical argument – not by examining reparations for slavery but the campaign to return dispossessed land to Native Americans.[79] Unlike the expanding liberal-egalitarian mainstream, David Lyons welcomed Nozick's claim that historical factors were independently relevant to justice. But he thought Nozick went too far the other way when he claimed they were uniquely so, 'and that merit, desert, distribution of benefits and burdens in society are irrelevant'. For Lyons, Nozick exaggerated in this and in his claim that property rights, legitimately acquired, were unaffected by circumstance – both of which had consequences for the defence of reparation as rectification. The disadvantages facing Native Americans were, Lyons wrote, a "wrong it was incumbent on us to right"; their "dispossession may call for significant rectification". Simple rectification claims (whereby injustice corrected meant justice done) that restored land to its "original and rightful owners" were attractive propositions, particularly since they avoided difficulties of reparative and compensatory justice. But Nozick's rights could not give such claims the required support; rights to property and land were more flexible and variable than he assumed, and were not necessarily inheritable.[80] Inheritance, though not for Lyons always objectionable on egalitarian grounds, led to concentrations of wealth and power that could undermine justice in transfer by creating unfair social arrangements. It was not transhistorical, outside the social rules, but an economic institution that needed justification like any other.[81] Moreover, property rights were not stable even within a single generation – "they can be extinguished without being voluntarily transferred". Nozick's turn to history, while welcome, went wrong in assuming that changing social contexts had no effect on property claims.[82] This might enable the claim – not made by Nozick himself – that Native Americans had original land rights that were untouched by changing circumstances, but it was

[79] David Lyons, "The New Indian Claims and Original Rights to Land", *Social Theory and Practice*, 4/3 (1977), 249–72.
[80] Lyons, "The New Indian Claims", 253.   [81] Lyons, "The New Indian Claims", 258.
[82] Lyons, "The New Indian Claims", 268.

a mistake. Looking backwards should not be confused with identifying transhistorical moral claims.

Yet Lyons too ended up eliminating the historical, at least from a moral point of view. He argued that the force of Native American claims derived not from the returning of original land, dependent on inheritable property rights outside of institutional contexts, but from their current disadvantage. As would become a common argument in reparations debates, he used a thought experiment to show that if Native Americans were now rich, we would not think their dispossessed lands should be returned. They had claims to a fair share of resources, to compensation for wrongs done to them by the system that deprives them of that fair share. Their "deprivation and their claims are rooted, *causally and historically*, in the wrongs that ... their ancestors suffered". But their claims were not normatively derived from their original historical rights. Native Americans had faced systematic discrimination and had a "valid claim to fair share" of resources and opportunities:

> They also have a valid claim to compensation for unjust deprivation that the *current* generation has suffered from past injustices. But it is highly doubtful that they have any special claims based upon their distant ancestors' original occupation of the land. For circumstances have significantly changed. Most of the occupants of America today have had little, if anything, to do with dispossession of Native Americans. This does *not* mean that they have no complicity in a pattern of unjust deprivation of *current* Native Americans, for which compensation is required. I suggest, therefore, that the current Indian land claims be viewed, not as invoking an original right to the land, a right that has been passed down to current Native Americans and that now needs to be enforced, but rather as an occasion for rectifying current inequities (some of which, of course, may trace back causally to the dispossession of Native Americans and the aftermath).[83]

Lyons here crystallized the battle lines in debates about historic injustice. It was current wrongs that mattered, whether or not they were causally derived from past injustices.[84] Unless one insisted on transhistorical rights, the force of most claims about the injustices we think of as historical actually came from present inequality. To take seriously the wrongs of history here meant to give up on transhistorical claims and historical argument.

On the one hand, then, were theories that looked to history, reparation, rectification and rights outside of the social rules and institutions; on the other, those that looked to the present or future, compensation, and were dependent on social rules and institutions. The line between the two

---

[83] Lyons, "The New Indian Claims", 268.
[84] See also Marshall Cohen, Thomas Nagel and Thomas Scanlon (eds.), *Equality and Preferential Treatment* (Princeton, NJ: Princeton University Press, 1977), xii.

kinds of theory seemed now set.[85] The reluctance to admit backward-looking reasoning into accounts of justice was reinforced in subsequent years. While Bittker had dissociated slavery and ancient wrongs from backward-looking reasoning, yet still allowed for the latter within his account of reparations, now liberal egalitarian philosophers disconnected the two, looking only to forward-looking justifications, mostly for compensation. The focus shifted to the recent rather than distant past. Justifications focused on addressing current inequalities, or promoting future distributions and equality of opportunity.[86]

These debates were shaped by other changes in philosophy. Concern with environmental problems – declining resources, overpopulation and potential ecological catastrophe – led many to consider obligations to future generations. Relatedly, Derek Parfit's non-identity problem raised the question of whether we had obligations to future people at all (since the existence of those future people would themselves be determined by our actions in the present).[87] These concerns permeated debates about the past as well as the future. Reparations claims were faced not only with the problem of establishing a status quo ante but an additional one: given that current generations would not have been born if it were not for slavery, could it even be right to say there was such a thing as a status quo ante to be rectified, since the people alive today could not be said to be worse off than they would have been without slavery, because *these* people would not have been born?[88] These problems increasingly occupied a central place in debates about historic injustice.[89] The question of who should pay, and the particularities of the case of African Americans, dropped out of the picture. Liberal philosophy's fleeting encounter with radical black politics was over.

History and Global Justice

What was just beginning was liberal philosophers' explorations of the morality of international institutional arrangements, and what came to

---

[85] For this argument see Katrina Forrester, In the Shadow of Justice: Postwar Liberalism and the Remaking of Political Philosophy (Princeton, NJ: Princeton University Press, 2019), chapter 4.

[86] George Sher, "Ancient Wrongs and Modern Rights", *Philosophy and Public Affairs*, 10/1 (1981), 3–17.

[87] Katrina Forrester, "The Problem of the Future in Anglo-American Political Thought", *Climatic Change* (online first: August 2016).

[88] Lawrence Davis, "Comments on Nozick"s Entitlement Theory", *Journal of Philosophy*, 73/21 (1976); Michael Levin, "Reverse Discrimination, Shackled Runners, and Personal Identity", *Philosophical Studies*, 37/2 (1980), 139–49; George Sher, "Compensation and Transworld Personal Identity", *The Monist*, 62/3 (1979), 378–91.

[89] Leif Wenar, "Reparations for the Future", *Journal of Social Philosophy*, 37/2 (2006), 396–405.

be known as global justice theory. The case for black reparations had begun as a domestic question – so far as philosophers were concerned. In fact, activists had long connected the situation of African Americans to other colonized peoples, but these transnational solidarities and practical demands for internationally administered reparations were hard to square with the liberal and legalistic view of the civil rights movement prevalent among political philosophers.[90] So when Bedau and Bittker had examined the case for reparations, it was treated as a domestic, and a specifically American, problem. Yet when justice theory after Rawls went international, the problem of reparations shaped discussions of global justice in unexpected and crucial ways. For the Rawlsian reluctance to make historical claims relevant to normative arguments affected not only the philosophical fortunes of demands for black and Native American reparations in particular, but reparations for colonial injustice in general. In these years when international and global justice theory was first taking shape, this mattered. Indeed, it was in the first theories of international justice that the move to subsume arguments for rectification, reparation and compensation into liberal egalitarian theory, and to dull their ideological force, can most clearly be seen. In this international context, the demands from the left that liberal philosophers diffused were not for reparations for slavery, but colonialism. The vector that shaped their arguments from the right – those made by Nozick – remained the same.

In the early and mid-1970s, liberal philosophers turned their attention to international ethics – to the food crisis and world famine, and international inequality in an age of decolonization. One of the central problems they addressed was how Rawls's framework of distributive justice could be extended internationally. In his 1977 account of international order, Thomas Nagel observed two philosophical responses to the sense of growing international crisis. On the one hand was the humanitarian moralism of Peter Singer, which effectively called for rectification through charity, and did not challenge the legitimacy of existing distributions of wealth or property systems. On the other were those that identified the roots of global inequality in the colonial exploitation of trade, labor and development in poor countries.

---

[90] On internationalism, transnational solidarities and the black freedom struggle Nikhil Pal Singh, *Black Is a Country: Race and the Unfinished Struggle for Democracy* (Cambridge, MA: Harvard University Press, 2005); Penny von Eschen, *Race Against Empire: Black Americans and Anticolonialism 1937–57* (Ithaca, NY: Cornell University Press, 1997); Jonathan Rosenberg, *How Far the Promised Land? World Affairs and the American Civil Rights Movement from the First World War to Vietnam* (Princeton, NJ: Princeton University Press, 2006); Minkah Makalani, *In the Cause of Freedom: Radical Black Internationalism from Harlem to London, 1917–1939* (Chapel Hill: University of North Carolina Press, 2011); and the chapter by Inés Valdez in this volume (Chapter 5).

These latter arguments were historical, and Nagel objected to them by following Thomas Scanlon's response to Nozick (which shared some moves with Lyons's critique). They may have had historical accuracy, he wrote, but not philosophical or normative force.[91] Focusing solely on colonial exploitation lent all inequalities that were not caused by exploitation a veil of legitimacy. Exploitation could not be blamed for all international inequalities. There were other causes: resource distribution, technology, luck.[92] What mattered to Nagel was whether a system permitted inequalities, not whether people did bad things to bring about that system. Even if no one had cheated, coerced or exploited anyone else, inequality was still morally objectionable. The problem was the existing system of property under which claims of right and entitlement, defined by mechanisms of acquisition, exchange, inheritance and transfer, were made – the world economy that contributed to the production of radical inequality. It was the current system that should be challenged, not historical wrongs; the social rules, not claims made outside them. Distributive justice was not the same as the rectification of past wrongs.[93] At an international level, where the world economy did constitute a single system in the relevant sense (a claim about which Nagel would later become skeptical), it was distributive justice that mattered – a distributive justice that paid attention to the institutions of the present, not transhistorical rights from the past.

Charles Beitz and Brian Barry were among the first philosophers to go beyond Nagel's diagnosis to propose positive theories of international justice. They similarly shored up their theories by deploying the domestic egalitarian response to Nozick – not to rebut the case for black reparations, but to explore demands then being made by anti-colonial theorists, particularly the demands for a New International Economic Order (NIEO).[94] These were part of an anti-colonial effort to construct plans for a more egalitarian international order, in which autonomous states would get what they were owed. Here, demands for rectification and reparation were not yet associated with claims of reconciliation, human rights and retribution for past crimes – as they would be after the rise of "transitional justice" in the 1980s and

---

[91] T. M. Scanlon, "Liberty, Contract and Contribution" in G. Dworkin, G. Bermant and P. Brown (eds.), *Markets and Morals* (Washington, DC: Hemisphere Press, 1977).

[92] Nagel, "Poverty and Food: Why Charity Is Not Enough" in Peter Brown and Henry Shue (eds.), *Food Policy: U.S. Responsibility in the Life and Death Choices* (New York: Free Press, 1977), 54–62.

[93] Nagel, "Poverty and Food", 57.

[94] Nils Gilman, "The New International Order: A Reintroduction", *Humanity*, 6/1 (2015), 1–16.

1990s.[95] Where a language of reparation was used, it was still, like Forman's, associated with calls for economic justice and emancipation, now internationalized.

These anti-colonial demands took a number of forms. "The Declaration for the Establishment of the New International Economic Order" of 1974 itself had a reparation clause, stating the "right of all States, territories and peoples under foreign occupation, alien and colonial domination or apartheid to restitution and full compensation for the exploitation arid depletion of, and damages to, the natural resources and all other resources of those States, territories and peoples".[96] Many anti-colonial thinkers who called for a new order married historical argument and demands for redistribution, and posited rectification as remedy for both historic and present injustice and exploitation. Often Marxian in spirit, these ascribed historical, causal and moral responsibility for current inequalities to imperialism, colonial exploitation, capitalism or the affluence of rich countries.[97] Of these, perhaps the most important for the formation of global justice theory was dependency theory.[98] Dependency theory had its origins in the hypothesis, put forward by development economists Hans Singer and Raul Prebisch in the late 1940s, that the poverty of the developing world was the result of adverse terms of international trade. By the 1960s, its claim that there existed a causal relationship between poverty in poor countries and affluence in rich, and its remedy of restructuring the terms of global trade, was flourishing as an alternative to modernization theory.[99] In the 1970s, Andre Gunder Frank and others presented a dependency theory based on a vision of a world capitalist system in which development at the center generated underdevelopment in the peripheries.[100] It not only ascribed causal responsibility for global inequality to the development

---

[95] Nicolas Guilhot, "'The Transition to the Human World of Democracy': Notes for a History of the Concept of Transition, from Early Marxism to 1989", *European Journal of Social Theory*, 5/2 (2002), 219–42; Arthur, "How 'Transitions' Reshaped Human Rights".

[96] UN Resolution adopted by the General Assembly, 3201 (S-VI) Declaration on the Establishment of a New International Economic Order, 1 May 1974, 4f. www.un-documents.net/s6r3201.htm (accessed 11 September 2018).

[97] Cf. Adom Getachew, *Worldmaking after Empire* (Princeton, NJ: Princeton University Press, 2019).

[98] See the chapter by Anne Phillips in this volume (Chapter 6).

[99] Daniel Sargent, "North/South: The United States Responds to the New International Economic Order", *Humanity*, 6/1 (2015), 205–6.

[100] See e.g. Andre Gunder Frank and Samir Amin, "Self-Reliance and the New International Economic Order", *Monthly Review*, 29/3 (1977): 1–21; Arghiri Emmanuel, *Unequal Exchange: A Study of the Imperialism of Trade* (New York: Monthly Review, 1971); Tamas Szentes, *The Political Economy of Underdevelopment* (Budapest: Akadémiai Kiadó, 1976).

of rich countries under capitalism, but suggested that economic relations with rich countries actually worsened the plight of the poor countries. The solution was the rectification of historical expropriation by economic means.

When Beitz turned in the mid-1970s to explain why the distributive rules of the global economic scheme had to be transformed, he also looked to the economic realm but, by contrast, discounted historical arguments. He acknowledged the relevance of the historical description of the origins of global inequalities, and initially seemed sympathetic to certain theories that rested on historical claims for remedying colonial injustice and exploitation.[101] But his opposition to historical arguments would ultimately become central both to his own theory, and to the global justice theories that came to dominate philosophy in its wake. As he developed his argument for an international institutional justice theory, he challenged precisely those arguments based on the historical fact of colonialism that suggested that obligations owed from rich to poor countries should be understood as rectification or reparation.[102]

By 1979, Beitz made explicit his rejection of theories of reparation and economic dependency, which rested on the claim that relations between rich and poor countries are "exploitative": "the rich are said to prosper *because* of their relations with the poor, and the poor to suffer *because* of their relation with the rich". It was not that simple, Beitz claimed: rich countries do not always benefit from their relationships, poor countries may only be relatively (not absolutely) disadvantaged by their participation in the capitalist world economy and dependency does not always correlate with poverty. Nor was it clear, he wrote, why those who inherit colonial wealth have to bear the burden of the wrongs committed by their ancestors.[103] Beitz wanted to get away from the idea that dependency was the cause of inequality. History had to be left out of the equation. Distributive justice should not rest on past wrongs, original entitlements or an idea of desert. Rather, the point of distributive justice theories was to get its "grip on us as people who occupy positions in a social division of labor".[104] The question was not why certain parties had come to own more of the global social product, but how it should now be shared. Beitz took on the Rawlsian tools,

---

[101] Charles Beitz, "Justice and International Relations", *Philosophy and Public Affairs*, 4/4 (1975), 375. On Beitz and the NIEO see Samuel Moyn, "The Political Origins of Global Justice" in Joel Isaac et al. (eds.), *The Worlds of American Intellectual History* (Oxford: Oxford University Press, 2016), 133–54.

[102] Beitz, "Global Egalitarianism: Can We Make out a Case?", *Dissent*, 26/1 (1979), 59–68.

[103] Beitz, "Global Egalitarianism", 60.   [104] Beitz, "Global Egalitarianism", 62.

honed by the challenge of libertarianism, to domesticate the arguments of the anti-imperialist left.

In his 1980 Tanner Lectures, Brian Barry described his theory of international justice in precisely these terms, as an attempt to "domesticate" the idea of world distribution contained in the demands for the NIEO.[105] The trouble for liberal egalitarians remained how to squeeze historical reparations claims into distributive justice theories, with which they seemed ideologically incompatible. Barry took a different route to Beitz. He was not as uncomfortable with reparations claims as other liberal philosophers. It was, he suggested, citing Bittker, hard to argue that descendants of exploiters have no obligation to atone for the injustice of their ancestors – if they are themselves richer as a result of exploitation, and the descendants of the exploited poorer.[106] Yet what this qualifier showed was that the argumentative force derived again from current inequalities, not past injustice. Equality was what mattered, not rectification in itself – which Barry saw as basically "conservative".[107] This he made clear in his critique of the application of theories of justice as reciprocity to international politics. He conceded that one of the most plausible accounts of international justice rested on an idea of justice as requital or fair exchange. That idea he saw as underpinning the various Marxian and anti-colonial arguments that claimed reparations were owed by rich to poor countries, by the center to the periphery. He pointed to dependency economist Arghiri Emmanuel's account of unequal exchange; like Beitz, Barry looked to versions of dependency theory that focused on trade in commodities other than persons, rather than those that linked underdevelopment to slavery.[108]

Such ideas could not on their own generate a theory of international justice. Supplementary ideas were needed. Here Barry looked to theorists of fair exchange – from Locke to Robert Nozick to James Buchanan – who, by defending the need for an additional argument about the initial endowments and control of natural resources, got a handle on international justice in a way that non-historical Rawlsian arguments (which were silent on this question of initial access to

---

[105] Brian Barry, *Do Countries Have Moral Obligations?: The Case of World Poverty* (The Tanner Lectures on Human Values, 1980), 28. https://tannerlectures.utah.edu/_documents/a-to-z/b/barry81.pdf (accessed 11 September 2018).

[106] Brian Barry, "Justice as Reciprocity", in E. Kamenka and A. Erh-Soon Tay (eds.), *Justice* (New York: St Martins Press, 1980), 63.

[107] Barry, "Humanity and Justice in Global Perspective", in J. Pennock and J. Chapman (eds.), *NOMOS: Ethics, Economics and Law* (New York: Harvester, 1982), 227.

[108] See e.g. Walter Rodney, *How Europe Underdeveloped Africa* (London: Bogle-L'Ouverture Publications, 1972).

resources) did not.[109] Barry similarly attached an independent argument about initial control to his account of justice – not an individual right to property, but equality of opportunity in the sense of equal claims on the world's natural resources. This commons-style entitlement claim (which paralleled Boxill as much as Nozick) allowed Barry to argue for international distributive justice in a way that sidestepped historical reparation and rectification arguments, while acknowledging their force. The debt owed from rich to poor countries became not a question of compensating for what had been lost, but of transferring resources that belonged to one country but were in the possession of another. The idea of reparation had no stable place in his account of international distributive justice. Resources might be returned as a result of mistaken belonging, as a matter of justice in the present, but not because of a history of exploitation, expropriation or injustice.

Like Lyons, Barry recognized the force of historical arguments even as he deflected them. He also recognized the importance of an account of corporate liability and collective responsibility to reparations claims in a domestic context, and to any theory of international justice. Barry departed from Beitz, and subsequent theories of global justice, in stressing not only state autonomy but the autonomy and agency of collectivities in general. In his unpublished *Rich Countries and Poor Countries* (1980), he argued that an "individualistic ideology" was taking over liberal philosophy.[110] Philosophy had changed in precisely the ways Bedau had anticipated. The revolt against desert had continued, taking history with it. The attempt to reinterpret socialism had, for the most part, given way to its rejection. As Barry here confirmed, notions of corporate and collective responsibility had largely dropped out of liberal philosophy, replaced by a strict individualism. Even on Barry's model of international justice, where state autonomy remained vital, states were not bearers of historical responsibility but subjects of current distribution.

By the end of the 1970s, then, anti-historical arguments were widespread, and became fundamental to global justice theory. History dropped out of the egalitarian picture. Problems of corporate liability and responsibility were displaced. Reparations were absent from distributive justice, exploitation and colonialism cut off from global justice. Beitz's theory largely set the terms of the global justice that would develop in subsequent decades, most notably that of Thomas Pogge: it was an

---

[109] Barry, 'Justice as Reciprocity', 73; Barry, 'Humanity and Justice in Global Perspective', 247–50.
[110] Barry, *Rich Countries and Poor Countries* (unpublished ms, 1980), 13.

extension of Rawls's, institutional and egalitarian.[111] Viewed against what it was not – a theory of anti-colonial reparations – global justice theory's non-historical character, its relationship to social rules and practices in the present, was clear. Its presentist egalitarianism was an alternative to both historical anti-colonialism and libertarianism.

Freeing justice theory from historical argument might have allowed for a very demanding form of domestic and global egalitarianism, but that egalitarianism in theory was bought at the cost of ignoring historical and structural injustice in practice. For not only was the challenge of integrating reparations with egalitarian and emancipatory claims passed over by later liberal egalitarians, who domesticated elements of anti-colonial theories while rejecting the arguments on which they relied. In a context where liberal philosophers were not activist in their support for anti-racist politics, and with problems of racism and empire folded into the "cultural" politics of the 1980s, the rejection of reparations led to the concomitant neglect-by-association of other social and distributional problems categorized and conflated under the cover of "race".[112] That included those that might have been more readily conceptually accommodated within liberal egalitarianism – for instance, the racial wealth gap.

The demand for reparations did not disappear from mainstream liberal philosophy entirely. Decades later, it would be revived in the context of Australian and Canadian arguments about obligations to indigenous groups. In the interim years, where it survived, it was by and large not associated with African-American or anti-colonial politics but with libertarian and neo-Lockean arguments.[113] Continuing debates among African-American philosophers were were largely neglected. If the original object of reparations debates, black chattel slavery, made an appearance – other than as a slippery slope argument against utilitarianism – it was as a historical fact with little normative force. This did not mean, however, that the politics of reparations more broadly was moved out of a discourse of identity and unpaid labor, to one of property – an area where liberal philosophy was primed to offer solutions. Instead, the problem of reparations was transformed from one of anti-colonialism

---

[111] Samuel Scheffler, 'The Idea of Global Justice: A Progress Report', *Harvard Review of Philosophy*, 20 (2014), 17–35.

[112] On the substitution of 'culture' for 'race' see Thomas Holt, *The Problem of Race in the Twenty-First Century* (Cambridge, MA: Harvard University Press, 2002), 13–14; on the conflation of various concerns under the 'euphemism' of race see Karen Fields and Barbara Fields, *Racecraft: The Soul of Inequality in American Life* (London: Verso, 2012), 100.

[113] On the uses of the latter for the former see Bill Lawson, 'Locke and the Legal Obligations of Black Americans', *Public Affairs Quarterly*, 3 (1989). For reparations as treated by black philosophers outside the philosophical mainstream see n. 12.

and material compensation – bound to arguments about capitalist exploitation as much as liberal and legal compensation – to one of humanitarian transitional justice and reconciliation, synonymous with a sometimes depoliticized and often individualized repair. It was cut off from its emancipatory roots. And as the demand for reparations was left in the realm of humanity and identity, so were its original associations. Problems of racism and empire were relegated to these realms, and kept outside that of distributive justice, both domestic and global. The legacy of these early reparations debates was thus double. On the one hand, the logic of the arguments described here served to secure this absence; on the other, they contributed to the construction of an alternative form of argument and collection of categories that has dominated philosophy ever since. The recent efforts of justice theorists to find a compelling way out of these divisions, to reunite historical and distributive arguments, confirms how entrenched they have been for so long.

2   The Doctor's Plot
The Origins of the Philosophy of Human Rights

Samuel Moyn

Introduction

"Salvation is much too big a word for me." Albert Camus's doctor observes in the course of the classic novel *The Plague* (1947). "I don't aim so high; I'm concerned with man's health; and for me his health comes first." But, it also turns out that illness is permanent – and to try more than healing is to risk new harm. As a result, at the end of the novel, the doctor delivers what has long been taken to be the author's considered wisdom. After surveying the many reactions to sickness in Oran, the devastated city in French Algeria where the book's plot is set, Camus's protagonist understands that there can never be "a final victory" against the "relentless onslaughts" of disease. But, far from paralyzing him in the face of his powerlessness to realize ideals and enact solidarity, the plague made it even more important – as he concludes – to honor "all who, while unable to be saints but refusing to bow down to pestilences, strive their utmost to be healers." This moral credo is moving for many of Camus's readers, and it has proved influential in unexpected ways. For example, when he founded the contemporary philosophy of human rights in a study written decades later as part of the invention of global justice theory, ethicist Henry Shue self-consciously enrolled in Camus's way of thinking. As the epigraph for his field-defining study *Basic Rights: Subsistence, Affluence, and U.S. Foreign Policy* (1980), Shue chose the doctor's closing motto. In doing so, Shue was true to his source: global human rights, the philosopher insisted, should take up a healer's approach.[1]

It is surprising but true: before Shue published *Basic Rights*, there had never been an extended philosophical defense of human rights. To be sure, back to the tradition of early modern natural law, philosophers had argued for personal entitlements through appeals to "nature," and thus for rights that accrue to human beings in virtue of their

---

[1] Albert Camus, *La peste* (Paris: Gallimard, 1947), cited from *The Plague*, trans. Stuart Gilbert (New York: A. A. Knopf, 1948), 219, 308; Henry Shue, *Basic Rights: Subsistence, Affluence, and U.S. Foreign Policy* (Princeton, NJ: Princeton University Press, 1980).

humanity alone. But, no one had ever envisioned worldwide basic rights beyond extant borders that set up duties that fell on all in relation to all. John Locke, for instance, had instrumentalized human rights to buttress his support for violent revolutionary activity in England, and for centuries thereafter claims about human rights were connected with changing from one king to another or (later) from monarchical to democratic rule in one country. The content of rights changed over time, and there had been prior cases for subsistence rights at least as far back as the writings of Thomas Paine. But, they always accrued – whatever their basis in the human status – among fellow citizens in a boundaried territorial space. Shue removed such constraints, which to the best of my knowledge no philosopher had ever seriously done. As his friend and colleague Charles Beitz later recorded, "among the works of political philosophy stimulated by and contributing to" the rise of human rights to "the status of a *lingua franca* of global moral discourse," no other book to date "has proved more seminal" than Shue's. More than this, Shue's book anticipated a recent era of a human rights movement focused on a set of basic human entitlements that include socioeconomic or subsistence protection.[2]

It is highly interesting that the first philosophical theory of human rights engaged distributive justice, not merely freedom or security. But it did so in a particular way. As we shall see, first in Camus and then in Shue himself, such an ethic made sense for reasons that go to the heart of the nexus of race, empire, and global justice. Theories of "global justice" that arose in the United States starting in the mid-1970s and later elsewhere strove to provide an alternative approach to any vision that placed a history of racial and imperial domination across the globe at the heart of what a political response in the name of worldwide fairness might look like. The new theories did not champion corrective justice and, in Shue's case, turned away from specifically egalitarian justice in the name of subsistence instead. Most important, rather than welcoming anticolonial self-assertion, they abjured southern agency – although Shue warned that the threat of violence by the poor remained live if the rich did not act. Above all, his version of "global justice" embraced an antipolitical ethics of succor. But not only is it far from clear whether the human rights movement has since provided the sort of healing Shue envisioned, it is far from certain that healing is good enough.

---

[2] Charles Beitz and Robert Goodin, "Introduction: *Basic Rights* and Beyond" in Beitz and Goodin (eds.), *Global Basic Rights* (Oxford: Oxford University Press, 2009), 1.

The Healer's Ethic and Colonial Politics

It is useful to begin indirectly with the healer's ethic by which Shue was
inspired, and its own earlier relation to empire and race. In his brilliant
critical review of *The Plague* in 1955, literary critic Roland Barthes worried that a healer's ethic that might have made sense in relation to
a natural evil could never capture the different political response required
by a human evil. It was obvious to all that *The Plague* was an allegory of
sociohistorical evil – a representation of the occupation of metropolitan
France by the Germans during World War II. Camus's novel nevertheless
abstracts from that situation by converting human wrongdoing into
a natural disaster. For Barthes, such allegory offered a bad model of the
root political difficulty that resistance had to face down. Naturalization of
a human evil made it seem as if the enemy was not part of the history of
how human beings themselves have made immoral choices and set up
unjust structures. Even if his unintentional acts spread plague, no human
being would intentionally join in league with threat. The same, of course,
had hardly been true of the human instigators and collaborators of fascism
over its short time line, and it was not true of most structural domination,
often over centuries. In France's own history, the old regime had had to
be toppled, not "healed." As Barthes wrote, "Camus's world is one of
friends, not of fighters." And so Camus risked a morality in which humans
were called to join together as if no human beings were on the other side,
except perhaps inadvertently. The history of the structures they set up did
not matter either. This allegory did not clarify but obfuscated the nature
of human oppression.[3]

Worse, the medicalization of resistance made it fundamentally without
end or victory. The eradication of one disease in particular might indeed
occur through scientific advance; but human frailty and vulnerability, and
therefore the ravages of disease in general, can never disappear.
As a result, Camus's allegory offered a basically palliative ethics: keep
an eternal enemy at bay for as long as possible. It was not so much that the
evacuation of history in *The Plague* was bad allegory; it also took ethics in
a crucial sense out of history, into a realm of evanescent success against an
obdurate foe that would always win in the end. The expectations set for
Camus's healers' ethic were undoubtedly portrayed as high – the struggles
of the novel's characters would have been meaningless and undramatic
otherwise – but they could never achieve more than temporary respite
from horror. As Camus's doctor himself insisted, just as the plague had
hidden underground before invading the city, it would surely come back

---

[3] Roland Barthes, "*La peste*: Annales d'une épidémie ou roman de la solitude" in *Oeuvres
complètes*, 3 vols., ed. Eric Marty (Paris: Seuil, 1993), I, 544.

soon. In human terms, evil was postponed, but never vanquished, and the framework was not one built around the achievement of a *summum bonum* like institutionalized social justice. Just as evil human structures disappeared in the novel, so the need to replace them did too.

It is true that Barthes did not take very seriously what may have been Camus's core insight as a moralist all along in his spectacular career: that in taking up ethical activism against evil, one had to begin with precautions against making oneself its accomplice. It is all very well to insist – as Barthes wanted to do – that wrongdoing takes the form of past domination of humans by one another, and that, instead of stoicism in the face of nature, structural change to overcome a violent history is what counts. Camus's response was always that, unlike other actors who risked their own brutality, ethicists first did no harm. In the novel, this apparent truth is dramatized through the character who had once been a political militant until he realized he inevitably dirtied his hands along the way. "Such is the logic by which [we] live," he observes, that "we can't stir a finger in this world without the risk of bringing death to somebody." Horrified by this possibility, he pulls back, leaving it "to others to make history." The doctor sympathizes with this perspective, and the somewhat melodramatic desire to which it leads: to become a pure saint in a godless world. But he also rejects his interlocutor's simplistic withdrawal from action for the sake of a beautiful soul. Doggedly, the doctor goes on healing and, after the former militant's own death, understands that the only meaning of "winning" in the face of plague is extending people's lives as well as "witnessing" the horror and preserving memory of the dead. Anything more than evil abatement and victim commemoration, the doctor agrees, would fall prey to the danger that pursuing good could turn into its opposite. For Barthes, Camus preemptively ruled out the possibility that there are better options – that anything other than healing risked such perversion. And, even if such impurity was unavoidable, Barthes continued, Camus preemptively concluded that it is never worth it, all things considered. Through both preemptions, Barthes charged, the doctor's ethic itself took up an even greater risk: it "risked making man the accomplice of an evil whose effects alone he hopes to treat."[4]

---

[4] Camus, *The Plague*, 252–53; Barthes, *"La peste,"* 544. For emphasis on the witnessing ethic as even more important to Camus than the healing ethic, see Shoshana Felman's chapter on the book in Felman and Dori Laub (eds.), *Testimony: Crises of Witnessing in Literature, Psychoanalysis, and History* (New York: Routledge, 1992). Of course, the ethic of bearing witness to evil has been utterly central to the sensibility of human rights advocates, who have striven to witness themselves and provide fora for victims to do so. I do not pursue this here, but see, for example, James Dawes, *That the World May Know: Bearing Witness to Atrocity* (Cambridge, MA: Harvard University Press, 2007).

Finally, Barthes indicted the individualization of ethics that Camus associated with healing. Individuals in *The Plague* are fundamentally alone in a profane world that each faced in his own fashion, the threat of meaninglessness the deepest threat that no one could ever really evade. "Camus's men," Barthes wrote, were saved from complacency "only by accepting that they are as alone as they really are." It was on this point, in particular, that Camus dwelled in the letter of protest he sent to Barthes. In comparison to the absolute solitude of the protagonist of his prior novel *The Stranger*, Camus insisted in response, *The Plague* moves to "the recognition of a community and the necessity of sharing its struggles." Fellowship in a common situation, Camus now thought, could help, though it was tenuous. One character, after trying to flee the town, eventually realizes he must stay because the plague was "everybody's business" – a phrase repeated several times in the novel. But Barthes's point was that the nature of the sociability that Camus now proffered as the ethical response to the horror of existence took a certain form. True, it brought individuals out of utter existential solitude. Yet it was not militant or "political," or else it construed political solidarity in a narrow way:

To perform one's profession, to apply oneself conscientiously to keep a horrible, unjust, and even incomprehensible illness at bay, with the weapons of a doctor – modest, imperfect arms, but at least patient and uncontroversial ones, forged together and above all never themselves inflicting harm: such is the extent of a happiness that does not at all arise from overcoming suffering but simply from the agreement of men to reduce it, side by side, lacking hopelessness, but repudiating utopianism too.[5]

Since Camus's death, in spite of repeated attempts to revive his "Red Cross morality," he has often been tasked even more vociferously with avoiding history and neglecting solidarity. But now it is the history of European empire, and Camus's critique of other responses to it than the comparative quietism he subsequently took up, that have proved the largest blot on his reputation. Camus, after all, set his story not in metropolitan France but in the Algerian land of his birth, a fact that postcolonial critics have been quick to underscore. Irishman Conor Cruise O'Brien, in his Past Masters portrait published in 1970, mounted the attack first. As O'Brien noted, one character, a journalist, is on assignment in the city to report on health conditions among the indigenous population, but when the plague comes "the Arabs of Oran absolutely

---

[5] Barthes, "*La peste*," 543; Camus, *The Plague*, 209–10; Albert Camus, "Lettre d'Albert Camus à Roland Barthes" in Camus, *Théatre, récits, nouvelles*, ed. Roger Quilliot (Paris: Pléiade, 1962), 1973.

cease to exist." Writing near the conclusion of decolonization – and long after the Algerian war – O'Brien found it "extremely distasteful" that Camus, a self-appointed moralist, could never fathom that for Arabs European colonialism was not much different from Nazi domination Camus meant to dramatize. French Algeria was a strange place to set a parable about the latter without mentioning the former. Camus, O'Brien wrote, failed to register that, from the point of view of the colonized, his characters "were not devoted fighters against the plague: they were the plague itself."[6]

In the very years of writing the novel, it is only fair to note, Camus had also criticized the shortcomings of colonial rule, dramatizing how its shameful public health regime worsened repeated famine, inciting nationalist revolt and counterinsurgent killing in response. And David Carroll, a recent literary critic, may be right that, whatever Camus's own failings, there is no reason in principle that his allegory of evil should not cover colonial oppression, or any other example of wrongdoing past and future. It is "when no limits are placed on the means being used that the form of resistance to one form of the plague became in fact the carrier for the next form," Carroll observes, "with the means of resistance themselves rapidly spreading the disease they were meant to combat." Not only is Camus's meditation on acceptable forms of resistance in response to any oppression portable to the problem of colonial hierarchy, but it intuited in advance how emancipatory "structural justice" in postcolonial forms would so often lead to new horrors. Such a defense of Camus is powerful but also revealing: arguably the intelligibility of the healer's ethic depended on its colonial and, later, postcolonial setting of articulation, since it contrasted with a different and putatively dangerous alternative vision of justice. Those who can should heal, and it is all they can plausibly do.[7]

We can now turn to Shue's own version of that ethic and, perhaps a bit in the spirit of Barthes and O'Brien, worry about how controversial it ought to remain, especially as a vision of global distributive justice across a still hierarchical world. Is healing illness the right way to think about responding to a history of racialized empire that covered the world as the

---

[6] Conor Cruise O'Brien, *Camus* (London: Fontana, 1970), 46, 48. For the case that *The Plague* also meant to allegorize French colonial misrule in the era of the Sétif massacre, see Roger Quilliot, "Albert Camus's Algeria" in Germaine Brée (ed.), *Camus* (Englewood Cliffs, NJ: Prentice Hall, 1962). For the most hard-hitting postcolonial account, see Azzedine Haddour, *Colonial Myths: History and Narrative* (Manchester: Manchester University Press, 2000).

[7] See the series of articles in his newspaper, *Combat*, in May 1945, now in English in Albert Camus, *Algerian Chronicles*, trans. Arthur Goldhammer (Cambridge, MA: Harvard University Press, 2013). David Carroll, *Albert Camus the Algerian: Colonialism, Terrorism, Justice* (New York: Columbia University Press, 2007), 55–56.

central liberal project globally before its bankruptcy was revealed? Worse, does championing subsistence rights as part of a desire to heal, aside from opting for the distributive ideal of sufficiency rather than equality, risk concealing the structural sources of continuing global domination and turn away from a necessarily structural response? Whatever the case, I hope to suggest that Shue's ethics – like Camus's – are best understood in relation to an assertive and sometimes violent anticolonial nationalism, which had its own internationalist forms. In contrast to these once frightening alternatives, human rights as a theoretical proposal about global distributive justice came to prominence in Camus's spirit: as part of a desire to "do no harm," and potentially help a little, in a cruel postcolonial world, with higher ends out of sight.

Shue on Subsistence for the Global Poor

When Shue wrote, it was still new for Anglophone liberal ethicists to take up politics, let alone global distributive politics. By convention, John Rawls's epoch-making *A Theory of Justice* (1971) provided the single most important stimulus to do so, but historians are now piecing together a more detailed story. Theories of ethics had never been lacking but in the postwar era, as early global justice theorist Onora O'Neill mockingly commented in a laudatory review of Shue's book, they had been concerned with "genteel examples of the minor dilemmas of life (walking on forbidden grass, returning library books)" and failed to take up "the harshest of 'real world' moral problems." But after the founding of the Society for Philosophy and Public Affairs in 1969 and especially the launch of its eventually freestanding organ *Philosophy & Public Affairs* in 1971 (which itself gave rise to various spin-off publications), it became more and more mainstream to bring ethics to bear on burning themes of politics. A reading and discussion group involving Marshall Cohen, Ronald Dworkin, Owen Fiss, Charles Fried, Frank Michelman, Thomas Nagel, Robert Nozick, John Rawls, Thomas Scanlon, and Michael Walzer also became a generative context long before Shue developed his views.[8]

---

[8] Onora O'Neill, "In a Starving World, What's the Moral Minimum?," *Hastings Center Report*, 11/6 (December 1981), 42. For far more, see the relevant chapter of Katrina Forrester, *In the Shadow of Justice: Postwar Liberalism and the Remaking of Political Philosophy* (Princeton, NJ: Princeton University Press, 2019). The Society had originally been one for "philosophy and public policy" before changing its name. See the preface to Virginia Held et al. (eds.), *Philosophy and Political Action* (New York: Oxford University Press, 1972) as well as William Ruddick, "Philosophy and Public Affairs," *Social Research*, 47/4 (1980), 734–48. The most important spin-off collection was Virginia Held et al. (eds.), *Philosophy, Morality, and International Affairs* (New York: Oxford University Press, 1974). Scanlon provides the list of figures in an interview, referring to the group as "the most

But the characteristic themes of these circles, aside from those in Rawls's book itself in the exciting years of debate that led up to and followed its publication, concerned war specifically, notably atrocity abroad and civil disobedience at home. These intellectual events, which suddenly brought the world of war and massacre home to American philosophers, were undoubtedly departures, but mainly for them, who were hardly the first globally to understand the questionable morality of the American Cold War, or to criticize it on theoretical grounds. And the moral philosophizing unleashed by the collapse of consensus during the late Vietnam war really did not lead to the immediate invention of "global justice" – suggesting the need to search further into the era. It was an outgrowth not of the late 1960s and early 1970s on their own, but of the mid-1970s debate about world hunger and world distribution and then the quickly intervening human rights revolution of 1977 and after, not to mention an achievement of a younger generation. Rawls had not even used the phrase "human rights" in *A Theory of Justice*; after 1977 his followers immediately began to do so. It is in this context that Shue takes on all his importance.[9]

A courtly Southerner from the Shenandoah Valley in rural western Virginia and a pious Christian growing up, Shue (1940–) had attended Davidson College in North Carolina before winning a Rhodes Scholarship to Oxford University in 1961. He spent the 1960s there and at Princeton, where he earned his doctorate "a student deferment away from the Southeast Asian jungles" and writing about conscientious objection, slowly turning against a war he had initially supported on patriotic grounds. After time at Wellesley College, with his path to tenure blocked, philosopher Peter G. Brown invited him to join the Academy of Contemporary Problems, a short-lived public policy research center initially founded by Ohio State University earlier in the decade. Hoping to verse himself in public policy and possibly to enter politics, Shue worked to organize thinking concerning American food policy in an age of international hunger before he followed Brown to the University of Maryland, where he helped launch the Institute for Philosophy and Public Policy in the fall of 1976.[10]

---

important thing in my philosophical development." "An Interview with T. M. Scanlon," *The Utopian*, www.the-utopian.org/T.M.-Scanlon-Interview-6.

[9] Samuel Moyn, *The Last Utopia: Human Rights in History* (Cambridge, MA: Harvard University Press, 2010), esp. 214–16 on philosophers.

[10] Henry Shue, "Preface," in *Fighting Hurt: Rule and Exception in Torture and War* (Oxford: Oxford University Press, 2016), vi, where he also recalls that he was inspired to enter political theory by watching a then untenured Michael Walzer stand down senior colleagues at war teach-ins. Brown and Shue, eds., *Food Policy*; Brown and Douglas MacLean, eds., *Human Rights and U.S. Foreign Policy: Principles and Applications* (Lexington, MA: Lexington Books, 1979). On the Academy, see Mary McGarry, "Center to Help Solve Issues," *Columbus Dispatch*, February 10, 1974 and, on Brown's appointment, "Academy Appoints Nine Fellows," *Columbus Courier-Journal*, January 29, 1976.

This institute was the first of the ethics centers in the United States that followed the informal and later journal-based impulse to marry ethical theory to public affairs. It was the central site for the invention of global justice, holding pivotal events and publishing landmark volumes. Supported by the Ford Foundation and the Rockefeller Brothers Fund, Brown had founded the center with the explicit mission of informing public policy debate. Its location in Washington, DC and the coincidence of its founding with Jimmy Carter's 1977 annunciation of an American human rights policy affected Shue's project profoundly. As the institute started up, and with impeccable timing, Shue devised and organized a working group on human rights in American foreign policy that included leaders and staffers from prior congressional activism and nongovernmental advocates – the ragtag band that did the work that made human rights eligible for visibility thereafter – and was perfectly positioned to respond when Carter famously announced his administration's storied human rights policy in his January 1977 inaugural address. More than this, a basic needs revolution in development and US Secretary of State Cyrus Vance's May 1977 affirmation that vital needs to subsistence might become part of American policy also were clear incitements to Shue's thinking, as were his associations with activists urging a consolidation of the human rights movement with a focus on vital human necessities around the world. As with the rest of global justice in philosophy, for all its abstraction, *Basic Rights* was an artifact of an exceedingly specific time and place.[11]

Never publishing his dissertation, earlier in the 1970s Shue had written respectful interpretive essays on Rawls's achievement. In his new context, Shue embarked on *Basic Rights* in 1977, registering not an earlier moment of early to mid-1970s global distributive justice debates but a later one provided focus by the human rights revolution alone. Shue's project was to broaden an exclusionary focus on traditional civil liberties that had characterized the northern human rights movement back into the 1960s, and was amplified in Carter-era Washington, DC. Global subsistence, Shue contended in a pathbreaking development, was a matter of individual human rights. So-called "social rights" were not a creature of national

---

[11] For the Center's founding, see "Notes and News," *Journal of Philosophy*, 73/19 (1976), 768; Patricia Weiss Fagen, "The Link between Human Rights and Basic Needs," *Center for International Policy Background* (Spring 1978), 1–11 and personal communication. On the basic needs revolution, see my *Not Enough: Human Rights in an Unequal World* (Cambridge, MA: Harvard University Press, 2018), ch. 5.

welfare but a justification for international remedies for faraway indigence.[12]

Choosing the epigraph from Camus brilliantly encapsulated Shue's decision, in between conservatives rejecting supraterritorial obligation and leftists demanding global revolution, to seek not a full-scale theory of worldwide distribution, but to focus on "the moral minimum" – "the least," he explained in the book's first line, "that every person, every government, and every corporation may be made to do." "About the great aspiration and exalted ideals," he explained, "nothing appears here. They are not denied but simply deferred for another occasion." He contrasted his approach with Friedrich Nietzsche's interest in "how far some might soar," rising instead in defense of "a morality of the depths." The theory of basic rights was supposed to "specify the line beneath which no one is to be allowed to sink." Shue did not rule out the importance of excellence or equality alongside security and subsistence. But in the spirit of Camus's novel – which that Shue cited again in closing in exhorting an alliance of human rights activists to take up the imperative of healing – it would also be fair to say that *Basic Rights* was premised on a tragic moral outlook in which the permanence of evil required those who cared about good to seek a simple minimum of protection. After all, the bacillus of destitution would never die.[13]

Shue's gambit was to insist that alleviation of global misery was everyone's duty, correlated with the most basic rights of humans as such not simply to liberty or security but also to subsistence. In making it, he devised a number of novel arguments, several with quite lasting effects both within and far outside the precincts of professional philosophy. His central contributions in *Basic Rights* were two. One was to reconceive what a "human right" is. For Shue, it was always, among other things, a way of imposing a so-called positive duty. To that date, philosophical consensus had held that some rights merely imposed duties on the state (and possibly other actors) to *abstain* from violating them; and on this view it looked like subsistence rights were different, and possibly illegitimate, because they imposed duties to *act*. Free speech merely requires the state not to interfere with it, on this view, while health care demands a state program. But Shue contended that all rights imposed a complex set of duties to abstain and act, and while the set might differ from right to right, there was no categorical difference between "negative" and "positive" rights, as philosophers had frequently believed. Shue's trifurcation of the kinds of duties that every

---

[12] Henry Shue, "Liberty and Self-Respect," *Ethics*, 85/3 (1975), 195–203; Shue, "Justice, Rationality, and Desire: On the Logical Structure of Justice as Fairness," *Southern Journal of Philosophy*, 13 (1975–76), 89–97.

[13] Shue, *Basic Rights*, xi (and v, 173–74 for the Camus citations).

right involves – the duty to not violate it, the duty to keep third parties from violating it, and the duty to ensure its enjoyment – was later canonized in the United Nations as the command to "respect, protect, and fulfill" all human rights. More broadly, more than any other argument it ultimately swung the philosophical consensus from default skepticism toward economic and social rights to default belief in them.[14]

Shue's overriding desire – the reason he undertook the philosophical revision of the nature of rights and duties in the first place – was to reach the conclusion that there was a set of basic entitlements that included subsistence rights as fundamental. No one, Shue wanted to show, who said they cared about human rights – like many Americans suddenly in the years he wrote his book – could do so without treating subsistence rights as every bit as important as liberty rights such as freedom to speak or security rights such as the entitlement not to be tortured. "[T]he same considerations that establish that security rights are basic for everyone also support the conclusion that subsistence rights are basic for everyone," Shue insisted. In this regard, Shue was facing down a cold war philosophical consensus that, to the extent it took up the topic, had either refused to include or hierarchically downgraded the significance of "social rights." This very even much included John Rawls, who had claimed – outside historical or developmental states – that freedom of the person in particular, and the basic rights that protected it, were to be viewed as prior to and more important than the undertaking of distributive justice. After a transformative trip to Indonesia and the Philippines under the auspices of the United States Information Agency in 1978, Shue was weaned from his initial temptation of reversing Rawls's priorities in order to argue that subsistence was *more* fundamental than liberty or security; his brief encounter with authoritarian development, especially in Jakarta, convinced him that such claims could buttress right-wing rule as much as they appealed to leftists who feared that liberals insisted on freedom in order to postpone welfare indefinitely. Author of a classic philosophical essay on the immorality of torture that appeared in *Philosophy & Public Affairs*, also in 1978, Shue explained in his book that his point was not to "argue that liberty is secondary – only that liberty has no priority."[15]

---

[14] Shue, *Basic Rights*, ch. 2, as well as Shue, "Rights in the Light of Duties" in Brown and MacLean (eds.), *Human Rights*. Later, see Shue, "Mediating Duties," *Ethics*, 98/4 (1998), 687–704.

[15] Shue, *Basic Rights*, 25 and 192n and "Torture," *Philosophy & Public Affairs*, 7/2 (1978), 124–43. The information about Shue's trips and their impact is from personal communications. In the prior era, few had risen to defend the priority of civil and political rights within human rights explicitly, with the (for Beitz Shue and others, glaring) exception of Maurice Cranston, *Human Rights To-day* (London: Ampersand Books, 1955, 1962), published in the United States as *What Are Human Rights?* (New York: Basic Books,

There was more than a hint that Shue saw it as his task to translate dissident insight into global injustice into palatable terms, correcting regnant assumptions about what it exactly meant to embrace human rights in Washington, DC by reorienting concepts to which people there and elsewhere were already claiming allegiance in increasing numbers. "The original motivation for writing about basic rights," Shue openly commented in his preface, "was anger at lofty-sounding, but cheap and empty, promises of liberty in the absence of the essentials for people's actually exercising the promised liberty." His goal, he continued, was "to make some contribution to the gradual evolution of a conception of rights that is not distorted by the blind spots of any one intellectual tradition."[16]

However, the truth was that Shue considered himself not so much the philosophical translator of alternative philosophical traditions as the mouthpiece of dogged healers of the world suffering in the global south. A onetime candidate for the ministry, after his dissertation Shue had made an atypical and brief foray into Western Marxism in the early 1970s, but his reading for *Basic Rights* indicates that it was much more his exposure to literature on global immiseration – as well as the crucial trips to East Asia, where he met a nun healing and a lawyer defending the poor, to whom he then dedicated his book as healers in action – that mattered to his choices. Equally important, it would seem, was his exposure to the claim that the poor actually want subsistence and no more.

Shue's wife Vivienne, a China specialist, started teaching in the Yale political science department in the fall of 1976, and introduced him to her colleague James Scott and his just-published touchstone *The Moral Economy of the Peasant* (1976). According to Scott, no matter where in time and space, peasants want subsistence first and perhaps exclusively. It was a claim that played a key role in Shue's thinking. That they might want other things, like Christian redemption or secular revolution, had been entertained by Westerners before, but not now. Peasants in feudal Europe and colonial Asia, Scott claimed, organized their villages around providing enough to survive, and their attitude toward authority always stressed the need (in Scott's words) to "guarantee *minimal social rights*."

1963) and later revised heavily under the latter title (London: Bodley Head, 1973), echoed by Columbia University philosopher Charles Frankel in the midst of the human rights revolution in Frankel, *Human Rights and Foreign Policy* (New York: Foreign Policy Association, 1978), 36–49. But it is true that such prioritization fit well with liberal sensibility that Rawls had defended in his own terms. Shue's revolt against the priority of liberty in 1980 should be compared to his respectful reconstruction of it in his 1975 *Ethics* essay cited earlier. For the proviso concerning the allowable prioritization of development in certain cases (he clearly had postcolonial states in mind), see Rawls, *A Theory of Justice* (Cambridge, MA: Harvard University Press, 1971), 247–48; see also 62–63.

[16] Shue, *Basic Rights*, ix.

As capitalism and colonialism came to threaten their millennial strategies of provision, rebellion ensued: outsiders thwarting tried-and-true methods either by accident or through reform, as colonial and later new states often did, invited endless trouble for their rule. What mattered to the global poor, Shue stressed, was that "all should have a place, a living, *not that all should be equal*" – a pivotal claim from Scott that Shue revealingly cited twice in his short book. A philosophy of basic rights argued for entitlements to subsistence not just in view of right and wrong but also in view of what the global poor ostensibly wanted.[17]

Shue between Global Subsistence and Global Equality

One day in this period American graduate student Charles Beitz, who had arguably invented the post-Rawlsian theory of global justice in his own pathbreaking *Philosophy & Public Affairs* article in 1975, received a telephone call from Shue inviting him to take part in an early Maryland center conference. A friendship ensued but it is equally interesting to contrast the earliest global justice theories that the pair advanced.[18]

Beitz (1949–) had laid out, rather than a theory of global rights, a post-Rawlsian theory of global egalitarian distribution. Like Shue, who had preceded him in the program by a few years, Beitz and therefore global justice as he pioneered it were a product of Princeton's interdisciplinary program in political philosophy; for Shue this mattered because "few established philosophers ... could have known enough about politics, especially international politics," to get very far – and the same distinctive range that Beitz could boast characterized Shue's work as well.[19]

Developed before the full force of the human rights revolution and in the face of demands for global justice propounded by postcolonial states,

---

[17] Henry Shue, "Lukács: Notes on His Originality," *Journal of the History of Ideas*, 34/4 (1973), 645–50. Scott, *The Moral Economy of the Peasant: Rebellion and Subsistence in Southeast Asia* (New Haven, CT: Yale University Press, 1976), 40, emphasis added, cited by Shue, *Basic Rights*, pp. 28, 207–8n, and Scott, *Moral Economy*, 184, for social rights. Shue also registered the importance of Benedict Kerkvliet, *The Huk Rebellion: A Study of Peasant Revolt in the Philippines* (Berkeley: University of California Press, 1977), 252–55, a passage Shue cited for proving the "deep belief in a right of subsistence" of peasants (*Basic Rights*, 184n); the point of interest is what Shue found compelling in an examination of the communist revolutionary bid brutally put down in the 1940s with extensive US assistance.

[18] The first half of this section compresses my "The Political Origins of Global Justice" in Joel Isaac et al. (eds.), *The Worlds of American Intellectual History* (Oxford: Oxford University Press, 2016). Charles Beitz, "Justice and International Relations," *Philosophy & Public Affairs*, 4/4 (1975), 360–89.

[19] Henry Shue, "The Geography of Justice: Beitz's Critique of Skepticism and Statism," *Ethics*, 92/4 (1982), 710.

however, Beitz's vision in 1975 did not focus on rights and primarily took the form of scaling up Rawls's difference principle – allowing inequality only to the extent it serves the worst off – to the world stage. For all the innovative aspects of the book that provided the swansong of national welfarism in the United States, *A Theory of Justice* had taken up a surprisingly conventional picture of international affairs. Later, it seemed troubling that Rawls assumed that as its parties lost their classes, bodies (including genders), and cultures, the national units of the world persisted in the famous "original position" from which Rawls derived his principles of justice. In a brief discussion of international affairs, he postponed them to a second-stage contract undertaken by state parties resulting in conventional minimal principles of world order. Along with the fundamental treaty principle of *pacta sunt servanda*, these allowed the use of force for the sake of self-defense but prohibited aggression and constrained means of warfare. Human rights were unmentioned, and no distributive obligations. In short, it was an illuminating testament to the staying power of the post-World War II national framing of the welfarist aspiration.[20]

Nearly as soon as the ink was dry on *A Theory of Justice*, however, an alliance of states in the global south called for worldwide egalitarian distribution – in a once exciting (or frightening) set of proposals called the "New International Economic Order" (NIEO) that envisioned institutions of a global welfare structure. In other words, the global south invented a vision of global justice, while Beitz volunteered a Rawlsian rationale for it. Fully aware of and impelled by these proposals, in his 1975 article, Beitz elaborated a philosophical argument in their favor by scaling up the difference principle. Along the way, he offered a series of interesting claims about why Rawls had been wrong to restrict his social contract to modular territorial spaces, specifically contending that it was mistaken to regard these spaces as self-sufficient as well as that there was now enough global "interdependence" to make world affairs something like a basic structure for regulation by principles of distributive justice.

Having framed a case for a global difference principle, however, Beitz soon parted ways from its NIEO agent and inspiration as he himself experienced the human rights revolution of the immediate years that followed. The NIEO had made its case as a matter of collective ethics, not individual rights, appealed to a history of race and empire rather than merely present desert, and argued for the parity of nation-states and the ascendancy of a composite "Afro-Asian" ethical subject. In his complete dissertation, published as *Political Theory and International Relations* in

[20] Rawls, *A Theory of Justice*, 7–8, 115, 336, 378–79.

1979, Beitz launched a bitter critique of the third world state and, indirectly, the subaltern internationalism that first propounded a claim for global redistribution as a matter of justice. The high tide of the NIEO in the context of which Beitz first imagined a global social contract in 1973–75 passed. While faithful to his original arguments, Beitz worked to present them much more clearly as *an alternative to* rather than a regrounding of the NIEO's radical – and collectivist – claims. Beitz took a fateful turn against the very third-world nationalism and internationalism that originally prompted him to globalize the difference principle, as part of a repudiation of the third world that has defined the rise of human rights as much as anything else. States, in Beitz's view, were merely the technical intermediaries of a global difference principle entitling individuals to justice; the moral significance of collective identity defined by a common history of subjugation or the bonds of nationhood was nil. But Beitz maintained his case for global egalitarianism as a matter of justice, since individual persons certainly counted.[21]

Officially, Shue's philosophy of basic global rights merely postponed global social justice of the kind Beitz had cared most to harvest from the NIEO; but temperamentally, its healer's ethic assumed that there was no perfect or permanent health, only endless disease to succor. (Forty years later, Shue chose the phrase "fighting hurt" to encapsulate the goal of his career.) In focusing exclusively on a rights-based minimum, of course, Shue hardly abjured any argument that humans as such deserve *even more* than basic subsistence, whether as a matter of their rights or on some other ground. Yet as his reliance on Scott indicates, he did not appear to believe that, whatever they deserved, the global poor actually wanted equality.

This represented a certain shift of his own. In a late 1976 paper, written prior to commencing his book, Shue had been quite insistent (citing Beitz) that there was no avoiding the topic of global distributive justice overall for anyone interested in specific policy domains. To bracket it – for example to formulate a food aid or population control policy – endorsed existing injustice, given "our tendency to assume that we are entitled to all our wealth, however gained," as if it was incumbent on poor countries to reduce their population before deciding whether it was fair for them to be poor in the first place. How many human beings India could "carry" or sustain would differ drastically, Shue concluded, if the global south "benefitted from a 'new international economic order'." Conversely, Beitz, in a contribution to the Maryland center conference to which

---

[21] Charles Beitz, *Political Theory and International Relations* (Princeton, NJ: Princeton University Press, 1979).

Shue telephoned to invite him and the volume that followed on American human rights policy, argued – against the grain of the north Atlantic human rights revolution of the 1970s but in tune with basic needs rhetorics of the time – that the philosophical reasons often marshaled for favoring personal over socioeconomic rights were unconvincing; a theory like Rawls's, whatever its commitment the priority of liberty from coercion over distributive justice, showed more convincingly that human rights were best conceptualized within an overall theory of social justice that allowed the two commitments to be balanced rather than ranked in a simple hierarchy. And, as a matter of nonideal theory, Beitz's arguments were designed to support some of the same meliorist policies on the part of northern governments that Shue emphasized; the main difference between them was whether to argue for those policies on grounds of equality or subsistence. Yet Shue's subtle departure from egalitarianism by the time he finished his book was revealing.[22]

Beitz had been sufficiently undeterred by mounting objections to Rawls's difference principle in the era to make his task its straightforward elevation to the world stage. Shue rose in anger not so much in reaction to Rawls's failure to internationalize equality but rather to Rawls's failure to argue for an absolute social minimum even at the national level. In fact, Shue's commitment to a rights-based global social minimum broke rather fundamentally as much from Beitz's global egalitarianism as from Rawls's domestic egalitarianism – and he knew it. "Like someone committed to the fulfillment of subsistence rights, Rawls does focus his theory upon the fate of the worst-off," Shue acknowledged. "But instead of providing a floor, or, to change the metaphor, a life-preserver, Rawls provides only a rope, hitching the worst-off (in a rather loose way) to all of the better off." It was true, in other words, that any increase in wealth at the top, on Rawls's theory, was allowable only insofar as it helped at the bottom. "But Rawlsian theory contains no provision that everyone's head must, for a start, be held above the surface of the water," Shue continued. "The Rawlsian difference principle can be fulfilled while people continue to drown but with less and less water over their heads."[23]

Indeed, in a moment not very reminiscent of Camus, Shue surmised from this fact that people might well reserve the right to take the means of

---

[22] Henry Shue, "Food, Population, and Wealth" (paper delivered in September 1976 at the American Political Science Association), *Proceedings of the American Political Science Association* (1977), 14, 7. Charles Beitz, "Human Rights and Social Justice" in Brown and MacLean (eds.), *Human Rights*.

[23] Shue, *Basic Rights*, 128. The image of people who would drown without a minimum floor of protection came, this time unacknowledged, from Scott, who in turn owed it to R. H. Tawney, *Land and Labor in China* (Boston, MA: Beacon Press, 1966 [1932]), 77.

their subsistence violently (just as Scott had shown was actually occurring the world over) rather than abide by any social arrangement that did not provide them with it. "Is it clearly more rational," Shue wondered,

to agree that one's fortunes may permissibly be indefinitely low, provided only that when those who are already better-off than oneself become still better-off, one's own fortunes must improve at least slightly, rather than trying, at least where there is some prospect of success, to mobilize effective opposition to any system of institutions that does not redistribute available wealth until everyone has an adequate minimum?

The answer was not obvious: you might well bargain for your own subsistence – and equal social relations only past that threshold – and enter no agreement without it. If so, Rawls's egalitarian principles were wrongheaded domestically – and simply more graphically on the global scene, where millions could die from hunger every year and more lived in unending penury.[24]

In his distinctive contribution to the birth of theories of global justice, therefore, Shue bracketed equality in the name of sufficiency, most intent to show that nobody should accept a global justice that did not vindicate subsistence rights at the very least – and that foreign and global policy should focus resolutely on that vindication first and foremost. Indeed, in his otherwise enthusiastic published review of *Political Theory and International Relations*, Shue was actually quite critical of Beitz's respectful elevation of Rawls's difference principle to the world stage. The fact that *some* principle of global distributive justice existed, as Beitz may have shown in his own way, hardly meant that it was an egalitarian one. The arguments for the priority of subsistence Shue made for foreign policy applied equally well (or even in the first instance) at home, and it was not obvious that the two domains had to be treated the same in any case, even once it was clear that their empirical interdependence meant there had to be some principle of global justice that transcended local justice. Beitz had not demonstrated "that a difference principle would be chosen to guide international transfers, even if it would be chosen in the initial Rawlsian national case (as is doubtful)."[25]

In spite of his brief allusion to violence as what the global south might find acceptable if not provided subsistence, what Shue did not say was as significant as what he did. Unlike Beitz, he saw no respectable third-world agenda to register and engage, and no global distributive equality (whether of states or individuals) as its ultimate prize. Unlike Beitz, Shue did not attack a putative ethics rooted in third-world nationalism;

---

[24] Shue, *Basic Rights*, 128.   [25] Shue, "The Geography of Justice," 719.

he simply paid it no mind. Agency in Shue is that of northern healers. When it came to collective ethics, Shue's focus was, like so many others then and since, on whether claims of national compatriots might fully oust those of outside sufferers. Setting a minimum threshold based in rights, as least as a matter of initial or immediate obligation, allowed a way to limit or at least prioritize within the vast expansion of moral obligation that Beitz's approach implied. More important, Shue did not even see it as necessary to criticize third-world nationalism and its subaltern redistributive internationalism. In a sense, he marshaled Camus's critique of doing harm not against the third-world nationalism that insisted on emancipation and redistribution, through violence if necessary, but instead against the United States, a plausible agent of healing, if only the country could learn in its foreign policy after Vietnam to change its ways. Why it seemed more plausible for the American government to change its ways than for apparently now discredited third-world states to do so remains unclear. But Shue concluded his book by hoping that if America could not become, like Camus's doctor, a "true healer," that it could "at least try to take the victim's side."[26]

The Limits of Healing

The publication of Shue's book in 1980 was ironic. Oriented by the Maryland center's mandate, Shue ended his book with a series of recommendations for the policies of the United States government, starting with official recognition of subsistence rights. He did not address the United Nations or the international system – though his work was to have most impact there – but the American state alone. Doing so may not have been totally implausible.

For many northerners, the United Nations had become little more than a forum for apologetics for despotism, while the traction of international human rights law (especially concerning social rights) was barely imaginable. Shue was, however, able to cite the very minor assurances within Carter-era Washington, DC that the human rights revolution would not lop off economic and social rights from the era of national welfare and from the Universal Declaration of Human Rights (1948) as if they had never been – though it was precisely this that occurred in American foreign policy as well as in prestigious human rights non-governmental organizations until social rights were laboriously restored (and only to the

---

[26] Shue, *Basic Rights*, ch. 6 and 174. On the perceived need for limits, see James S. Fishkin, *The Limits of Obligation* (New Haven, CT: Yale University Press, 1982); Fishkin, "The Boundaries of Justice," *Journal of Conflict Resolution*, 27/2 (1983), 355–75; and Shue, "The Burdens of Justice," *Journal of Philosophy*, 80/10 (1983), 600–8.

latter) decades later. In a much noticed commencement address on the topic in the spring of 1977, Carter's secretary of state Cyrus Vance had affirmed "the right to the fulfillment of such basic needs as food, shelter, health care, and education." Shue further recommended regulating corporations operating abroad and, above all, conditioning American foreign assistance on insisting that beneficiary states not deprive their own citizens of their basis of subsistence.[27]

The truth, however, was that Carter's administration had generally rejected focus on such socioeconomic entitlements as rights in principle and ignored them in practice. And with Ronald Reagan's election the year *Basic Rights* appeared, any belief in the promotion of a global social minimum in the country's human rights policy must have seemed wholly premature. As one of the earliest of many enthusiastic reviews of Shue's book observed, "The Reagan administration's hostility to human rights activism promises a chilly reception for Shue's arguments for a right to subsistence." He would have to wait to the end of the cold war to see the shifting priorities of the human rights movement match them (and then only gingerly).[28]

Shue later dropped his policy recommendations when *Basic Rights* was republished, but they are critical to the moment in which even the most abstract philosophical interventions in the book were framed. It seemed believable, though unlikely, to turn the American rights revolution of the years during which the book was composed to take on distributive justice. But in Shue's hands, and that of the human rights movement that followed, it was an expansion that bracketed inequality as the political crisis to confront in the name of treating the most abject misery as the disease to heal.

"Whatever the other consequences of the demands by the Third World for a new, more egalitarian economic order, one thing is clear," an intelligent observer of 1970s ventures noted at the time. "[T]hose demands have given rise to an unprecedented debate on the subject of global distributive justice." Yet in retrospect it seems even clearer that the central development was the containment of egalitarian demands, alongside the rise of commitment to global subsistence as a matter of obligatory justice and not just optional charity for a vanguard of northern citizens. Nothing is more important about the rise of international ethics, put a different way, than how differentially its versions were realized in practice. Where the succor of faraway suffering (itself rooted in

[27] Shue, *Basic Rights*, ch. 7; Cyrus R. Vance, "Human Rights Policy," April 30, 1977, Bureau of Public Affairs, Office of Media Services, US Department of State.
[28] James Nickel and Lizbeth Hasse, "Book Review," *California Law Review*, 69 (1981), 1569.

longstanding humanitarian sentiment and practices) and the attempt to vindicate subsistence rights have enjoyed major practical support since, the philosophy of global egalitarianism remains a file in the archives of utopianism. And for all of its exciting contributions, and the moving passion of mainstream philosophers to take their discipline beyond its parochial and selective attention before, it is also critical to ask what features of the new international ethics fit with, rather than resisted, this containment.[29]

Three seem most pertinent. First, the consensus of the philosophers bypassed the history of northern exploitation of the global south as the best moral ground on which to argue for different outcomes in the future – with distributive justice defended in terms of corrective justice in the aftermath of a violent history of racialized empire. Barthes's criticism of an ahistorical ethics in Camus sounds powerfully against Shue thirty years later. Shue did not support widespread calls for reparations of the period, participating in the invention of global justice as a matter of present desert and need.[30]

Second, the consensus offered a brand of "ethics first" thinking that concluded that philosophers took up their most plausible role in determining right and wrong – for example, that feeding starving children is an obligation of justice – without worrying about the larger context of politics and power relations that would have to be shaken for morality to be honored. Even Shue's defense of a minimalist sufficiency rather than maximalist egalitarianism in the realm of principle, in this view, remained a matter of stating normative ideals divorced from a social theory of the realities that left those ideals persistently unrealized. Global justice became a moral theory of entitlement to change. But it was not a theory of why some enjoyed wealth and power others did not, nor a theory of why the former would never honor the entitlements of the latter on some philosopher's say-so.

The difficulty of viewing politics as applied ethics was indeed noted at the time (as it has been recently). Philosopher Kai Nielsen – himself original chairperson of the Society for Philosophy and Public Policy – acknowledged in an engagement with Beitz and Shue how normative ethicists typically responded to calls against a philosophical turn to politics that interpreted it as applied ethics. "[C]onsiderations of political sociology simply fail to take seriously the fact that normative political theory, in doing ideal theory, is concerned with abstract models of what

[29] Robert Amdur, "Global Distributive Justice: A Review Essay," *Journal of International Affairs*, 31/1 (1977), 81.
[30] For much more on this point, see Katrina Forrester, "Reparations, History and the Origins of Global Justice" in this volume (Chapter 1).

a well-ordered world should look like and thus can legitimately bypass such considerations." The trouble, Nielsen concluded, is that "this seemingly plausible response is actually an evasion" masking the need to seek social justice not so much or only in the distribution of goods and services but also and primarily in "relations of power, ... avoiding the kinds of social structures, including modes of production, which place some in positions of dominance and control and others in positions of submission and powerlessness." It was blindingly obvious, on this view, that there was no global justice (even if philosophers belatedly agreed), and the problem was not primarily the absence of a *philosophical theory* of it. Rather, the true intellectual difficulty was coming to grips with the sociohistorical creation of domination, just as the political one was mobilizing to end it: shades of Barthes once again.[31]

Finally, there was the individualization of ethics that so profoundly marked the invention of global justice. As important as its bypassing of history and interest in ethics as the template for politics, the birth of global justice, including Shue's work, involved a consensus about the individualization of the basis of social justice. Whether as a matter of their interests or rights, Shue and the others all argued in terms of the prerogatives of individual persons as the foundation of any transnational justice. In a remarkable aside in a footnote, Shue protested "the distorting atomism at the heart of liberalism," but he, too, erected his argument for the rights of subsistence firmly on individualistic grounds. Shue's project did have a collective agent: a new kind of international human rights movement, which slowly took up the cause of rights to subsistence that Shue had demanded and foreseen for it. The American state that Shue hoped to see pushed through that movement still treats international social rights dismissively, but the movement itself now honors social rights, in a spectacular reversal since its early priorities. Bands of healers beat back misery, now in the name of basic global rights to subsistence, alongside those to liberty and security. "This, and only this, can bring relief to men," in the words of Camus's character, "and, if not save them, at least do them the least harm possible and even, sometimes, a little good." But that is all. As Barthes might have worried, solidarity is available, but it proceeded from lonely and minimalist assumptions.[32]

Shue's participation in the human rights revolution of his and our time innovated tremendously but also recorded changing assumptions. The exclusionary moral individualism that marked the birth of global

[31] Kai Nielsen, "Global Justice and the Imperatives of Capitalism," *Journal of Philosophy*, 80/10 (1983), 608–9. See also Nielsen, "Global Justice, Power, and the Logic of Capitalism," *Crítica*, 16/48 (1984), 35–51.

[32] Shue, *Basic Rights*, 192n; Camus, *The Plague*, 252.

justice so profoundly positioned it poles apart from the nationalist premises of the construction of the welfare state, zealous attempts to transplant it to developing nations, and to elevate it to the worldwide stage in the name of the anti-imperialism and antiracism of the prior era (or since). Skeptics have doubted that the movement for basic subsistence rights has provided results in the domain of global distribution since then, even as worldwide market fundamentalism took off across the same decades. But perhaps that does not matter: human rights have done no harm.[33]

[33] Stephen Hopgood et al. (eds.), *Human Rights Futures* (Cambridge: Cambridge University Press, 2017), pits optimists versus pessimists about how big a dent in evil human rights law and movements have made.

3 Corporations, Universalism, and the Domestication of Race in International Law

Sundhya Pahuja

International law does not recognize any distinctions ... based on religious, geographical or cultural differences.

(*Oppenheim's International Law*)[1]

Introduction

In 1960, Frantz Fanon, a Martiniquan, French trained psychiatrist, wrote not long before his death that when '[l]ooking at the immediacies of the colonial context, it is clear that what divides this world is first and foremost what species, what race one belongs to. In the colonies the economic infrastructure is also a superstructure. The cause is effect: You are rich because you are white, you are white because you are rich.'[2] Some forty years later, in a seminal article about 'global justice', philosopher Thomas Pogge wrote, '[w]e are quite tolerant of the persistence of massive and severe poverty abroad even though it would not cost us much to reduce such poverty dramatically. How well does this tolerance really fit with our commitment to moral universalism?'[3]

The juxtaposition of these two texts is intriguing. It invites us to consider how we can understand the difference – and relationship – between them. Although in different poetic registers, they each centre on the question of material distribution beyond the bounds of the nation-state. Each gestures towards an account of a relation with those outside one's community, Fanon in a critical register, Pogge in a normative one. For

---

[1] Robert Jennings and Arthur Watts (eds.), *Oppenheim's International Law: Volume 1* (London: Oxford University Press, 1997), 4.
[2] Fanon, *The Wretched of the Earth*, trans. Richard Philcox (New York: Grove Press, 1963), 5. Fanon died on the 6th of December 1961 in Bethesda, Maryland, where he was undergoing treatment for leukaemia. He was writing in the context of the ongoing colonial status of Algeria, two years before Algeria became independent. (Algeria became independent in July 1962.)
[3] Pogge, 'Moral Universalism and Global Economic Justice', *Politics, Philosophy and Economics*, 1/1 (2002), 30.

74

Fanon, the question of economic inequality can be separated neither from history in general, and the history of colonialism in particular, nor from the question of race. In other words, race, history and economics are intertwined. This is not because race is 'real' as a biological or genetic fact – quite the contrary. Instead, it is because race was – and remains – an operative (historical) category in the constitution of the 'human'. For Fanon, race is 'sociogenic' – a socially co-produced fact[4] through which a skin tone becomes a status. This socio-genesis is linked centrally to economic structures. In asserting that 'you are rich because you are white', as well as its inverse, 'you are white because you are rich', Fanon is both pointing to the centrality of capitalism in the socio-genesis of 'race', and more radically, asserting that capitalist accumulation is grounded in racial differentiation itself. This grounding endures even after biological racism is discredited scientifically, at which point cultural racism, or Eurocentrism, performs its work. As Adam Shatz puts it, for Fanon, 'the defence of "Western values" had superseded biological racism in the arsenal of imperialism'.[5]

For Pogge, on the other hand – speaking from the dawn of the twenty-first century – the question of 'global justice' is a new one; '[e]arlier generations of European civilization were not committed to moral universalism'.[6] The causes too, of the unequal distribution of wealth are proximate, and race belongs in a separate category to economics. 'Skin color, or ancestry' is relevant to his argument insofar as it is 'disqualified' as a basis for the unequal assignment of 'fundamental moral benefits'. In other words, the ethical position of this approach is a colour-blind universalism. It's no coincidence that the register is normative. This is an orientation which directs the reader toward an horizon of futurity, and away from historical causes.[7]

In one sense, Fanon and Pogge can be read heuristically as avatars for two distinct approaches to the question of material deprivation, as both a world, and worldly concern. Each approach has a different view about how to understand the problem, what its causes might be, where the authority to decide how to tackle it might be located and where the responsibility to address it may lie. These approaches take international institutional form in the encounters between the three 'worlds' –

---

[4] Lewis Gordon et al., *What Fanon Said: A Philosophical Introduction to His Life and Thought* (New York: Fordham University Press, 2015), esp. 2, 138. On 'co-production' see Sheila Jasanoff, 'The Idiom of Co-Production' in Jasanoff (ed.), *States of Knowledge: The Co-Production of Science and the Social Order* (London: Routledge, 2004), 1–12.

[5] Shatz, 'Where Life Is Seized', *London Review of Books*, 39/2 (2017), 19–27.

[6] Pogge, 'Moral Universalism and Global Economic Justice'.

[7] Thomas Pogge, 'Recognized and Violated by International Law: The Human Rights of the Global Poor'. *Leiden Journal of International Law*, 18 (2005), 723.

First, Second and Third – in the emergent years of what we might call bureaucratic multilateralism, and track the development and expansion of international institutions. But in another sense, the texts bookend a particular period during which we see race gradually disappear as an axis of analysis from international legal and institutional accounts of inequality. This erasure happens precisely through the 'supercession' of biological race by culture, and the production of a developmental scale which contains cultures within the territorial bounds of nation-states, and places them in a hierarchy, organised according to their 'stage of development'. Once a developmentalist ordering is taken up, what is forgotten is that the hierarchy reproduced is the same as the one generated by the imperial 'science' grounded in (biological) race and racism. When domesticated as a concern of the national sphere, race is no longer understood to be a global practice of ordering; neither global nor economic structures are understood to play a generative role in its socio-genesis.[8]

In this chapter, I will draw out what is at stake in the differences between the two approaches – as well as in the convergences between them – by focusing on one episode in the ongoing series of encounters between them in the first fifty years of bureaucratic multilateralism. This version of the international was inaugurated with the establishment of the contemporary institutions of international law after the Second World War. Our time frame here ends with the end of the Cold War. The writings of Fanon and Pogge bookend this period in an uncanny, if not tragic, way.[9] The episode centres on the attempt starting in the late 1960s, by the Third World to assert international institutional control over transnational corporations, and the response to that assertion by a key group of powerful Western states, particularly the United States. To sharpen the account for our purposes here, I close in on an 'exchange' between Salvador Allende, then president of Chile, and Henry Kissinger, then US Secretary of State, conducted indirectly through institutional speeches. Although the relationship between the institutional debates about the multinational corporation, and the question of 'global justice', race and international law may at first seem oblique, the battle turns out to be revelatory of the way that embedded hierarchies of race (still) order the global economy, and helps us to understand the relationship between

---

[8] Siba Grovogui, 'Deferring Difference: A Postcolonial Critique of the "Race Problem" in Moral Thought' in Sanjay Seth (ed.), *Postcolonial Theory and International Relations: A Critical Introduction* (London: Routledge, 2012), 106–23; John Agnew, 'The Territorial Trap: The Geographical Assumptions of International Relations Theory', *Review of International Political Economy*, 1/1 (1994), 53–80.

[9] For an account of the 'narrative arc of tragedy' see Simon Critchley, 'Tragedy's Philosophy and Philosophy's Tragedy' (Humanities Center Annual Lecture, Brigham Young University, 2014).

such hierarchies, and the patterns of the distribution of authority, responsibility – and wealth – in the world today.

Duelling Speeches – Allende v. Kissinger

Allende

In 1972, the Third Session of the newly formed United Nations
Conference on Trade and Development (UNCTAD) was held in
Santiago, Chile.[10] As president of the country hosting the event, Allende
gave the opening speech.[11] In a clarion call to action, Salvador Allende
outlined the mission of the Third Session as continuing the work begun
with decolonization, and institutional initiatives to reform international
economic structures of replacing the 'outdated and essentially unjust economic and trade order'.[12] Even after the demise of formal colonialism in
many parts of the world, it was clear to Allende that many countries
'exist[ed] under unbearable conditions ... their economy [being] dominated by foreign powers; outsiders hold[ing] all or part of their territory;
still endur[ing] the yoke of colonialism ... deep social disparities [were]
oppress[ing] the masses and benefit[ing] only the privileged few'.[13] Like
Fanon, Allende understood that poverty is produced by economic arrangements, and is not a natural state of being. Similarly, for Allende, like Fanon,
the generation of wealth and the production of poverty exist in 'a clear-cut
dialectical relationship': 'imperialism exists because under-development
exists; under-development exists because imperialism exists'.[14]

For Allende, transnational corporations were central to the problem.
In his account, their further expansion would be fatal to the new worlds
being made through Third World solidarity, inaugurated in institutional
terms at the Bandung Conference in 1955[15] and made manifest in calls
for a New International Economic Order[16] and the possibility of

---

[10] Diego Cordovez, 'The Making of UNCTAD: Institutional Background and Legislative
History', *Journal of World Trade Law*, 1/3 (1967), 272.

[11] Salvador Allende (Republic of Chile), 'Address Delivered at the Inaugural Ceremony',
Proceedings of the United Nations Conference on Trade and Development (13 April 1972,
Santiago, Chile); Salvador Allende (Republic of Chile), 'Address Delivered at 2096th
Plenary Meeting', *Official Records of the United Nations General Assembly*
(4 December 1972, New York).

[12] Allende, 'Address Delivered at the Inaugural Ceremony', 9.

[13] Allende, 'Address Delivered at the Inaugural Ceremony', 12.

[14] Allende, 'Address Delivered at 2096th Plenary Meeting', 65.

[15] Luis Eslava et al. (eds.), *Bandung, Global History, and International Law: Critical Pasts and
Pending Futures* (Cambridge: Cambridge University Press, 2017).

[16] Jennifer Bair, 'Taking Aim at the New International Economic Order' in Philip Mirowski
and Dieter Plehwe (eds.), *The Road from Mont Pèlerin: The Making of the Neoliberal*

remaining 'non-aligned' in the struggle between the nominally anti-imperial, American and Soviet empires.[17] In Allende's view, the unchecked power of ever-expanding corporations would also scuttle the possibility of cooperation, and diplomatic exchange, between the 'industrialised' countries and what had already become known by then as the 'developing countries'.[18] With this speech, the question of the large multinational corporation was thrust onto the stage of international institutionalism.

Allende's speech must have been electrifying given the context. A contemporaneous report from 1972 in *The Observer* reads:

Western delegates, expecting a platitudinous inauguration, writhed in their seats as the Chilean leader, conscious that he was speaking for virtually the whole of the Third World, tore into the trade and aid practices of rich countries. ... Few orators could successfully have followed that speech ... As Allende left the rostrum [covered symbolically in copper] ... the atmosphere was electric. One Western European Cabinet Minister looked almost apoplectic. A Scandinavian delegate chuckled quietly that one could have expected nothing less from a country which was being squeezed in a vice by the US.[19]

The speech is often remembered for its strong critique of interference by corporations in the political and economic sovereignty of Chile. It turns out Allende was right to be concerned. The companies he mentioned in 1972 as being intent on destabilizing the democratically elected government because it pursued a socialist agenda (including nationalizing the copper and telecommunications industries), had, by 1973, with the complicity of the Central Intelligence Agency (CIA), fomented the coup which toppled the elected government, led to Allende's death and installed General Augusto Pinochet as president of Chile.[20]

Thought Collective (Cambridge, MA: Harvard University Press, 2009), 347–85; Mohammed Bedjaoui, *Towards a New International Economic Order* (New York: Holmes and Meier Publishers, 1979).

[17] Natasa Miskovic et al. (eds.), *The Non-Aligned Movement and the Cold War: Delhi-Bandung-Belgrade* (New York: Routledge, 2014); Hani Sayed, 'The Humanization of the Third World' in Eslava et al. (eds.), *Bandung, Global History, and International Law*, 431–49; William Louis and Ronald Robinson, 'The Imperialism of Decolonization' in James Le Sueur (ed.), *The Decolonization Reader* (London: Routledge, 2003), 49–79.

[18] Allende, 'Address Delivered at 2096th Plenary Meeting', 60.

[19] Hugh O'Shaughnessy, 'Poor Nations Warn: Give Us a Better Deal or else', *The Observer*, 16 April 1972.

[20] Anthony Sampson, *The Sovereign State: The Secret History of ITT* (London: Hodder and Stoughton, 1973); United States Senate, 'First Session, Volume 7: Covert Action', *Hearings before the Select Committee to Study Governmental Operations with Respect to Intelligence Activities* (Ninety Fourth Congress, 1975). Available at: www.intelligence .senate.gov/resources/intelligence-related-commissions [website last visited 5 June 2018].

Although that is how it is primarily remembered, Allende himself was concerned not just with the question of the present interference in Chile's sovereignty. Instead, he drew a longer historical arc, referring to colonialism as well as to the Monroe doctrine of 1823,[21] and the Roosevelt Corollary of 1904, which ostensibly protected Latin America from recolonization by European states, but asserted a US right to intervene in the continent to prevent 'flagrant and chronic wrongdoing by a Latin American Nation'.[22] The gesture is part of a pattern of that time (and beyond), in which Western states, and the institutions in which they were dominant, repeatedly inaugurated the world anew, describing the decolonised nations as 'new', or 'emerging' states, 'entering' the world for the first time.[23] For the Third World, on the other hand, the present was historical, linked to what had gone before through the legacies of empire, and in emergent neo-imperialisms.[24] For them, diplomacy after empire was in large part an historiographical enterprise, involving a need to assert a continuity between pre- and post-colonial civilizations in the non-West, and to reclaim a 'rightful place' in history for those civilizations.[25]

As well as making an historiographical assertion in general, Allende was also concerned, in particular, with how to understand the modern corporation in its historical context. In his account, that entity too was historically grounded, the transnational corporation existing on a continuum with colonial companies. Unlike the 'private' entities they were said to be in the American jurisprudence flexing its muscle through

[21] Mark Gilderhus, 'The Monroe Doctrine: Meanings and Implications', *Presidential Studies Quarterly*, 36/1 (2006), 5–16; Juan Pablo Scarfi, 'In the Name of the Americas: The Pan-American Redefinition of the Monroe Doctrine and the Emerging Language of American International Law in The Western Hemisphere, 1898–1922', *Diplomatic History*, 40/2 (2016), 189–218.

[22] There is a version of this doctrine on the website of the Office of the Historian of the United States: Department of State, United States of America, 'New Policies for Latin American, Asia', *Office of the Historian* (n.d.). Available at: https://history.state.gov/dep artmenthistory/short-history/newpolicies [website last visited 13 June 2018]. For analysis, see Gilderhus, 'The Monroe Doctrine'.

[23] Sundhya Pahuja, 'Letters from Bandung' in Eslava et al. (eds.), *Bandung, Global History, and International Law*, 552–73.

[24] On the 'durability' of imperial modes of thought and a challenge to the idea of the 'post' colonial, see generally, Ann Laura Stoler, *Duress: Imperial Durabilities in our Times* (Durham, NC: Duke University Press, 2016).

[25] For one example of this gesture at the level of the state, see Jawaharlal Nehru, 'Meeting Ground of East and West' (Speech given in the Constituent Assembly (Legislative) of India, 8 March 1949, New Delhi, India). Reproduced in Ministry of Information and Broadcasting, *Jawaharlal Nehru's Speeches, Volume I: September 1946–May 1949* (Coimbatore: Government of India Press, 1967). See also Upendra Baxi, 'Some Remarks on Eurocentrism and the Law of Nations' in R. P. Anand (ed.), *Asian States and the Development of Universal International Law* (New Delhi: Vikas Publications, 1972), 3–9.

Marshall plan interventions at the time,[26] transnational corporations were better understood as political entities, for they had long been experienced in the Third World as both carrying out political functions and exercising public authority.[27] For Allende, this experience produced two axes of concern. The first was how to manage the conduct and activities of transnational corporations; the second was the question of how corporations came to acquire assets, and how they were protected. We can think of these two axes as the 'conduct' and 'property' axes respectively.

In terms of the first axis, the conduct question, Allende was concerned to ensure that all states should have the ability to assess for themselves whether transnational corporations doing business in their territories were making a contribution to the economic development of the country as a whole. Like many in the Second and Third Worlds, Allende understood that the devil of 'foreign investment' is in the detail,[28] including the density of linkages between the company's operations and the local economy and society as a whole, the extent of the repatriation of profits, the use of 'restrictive business practices', such as invoking intellectual property regimes to prevent technology transfer to the state 'hosting' the investment, the issue of environmental degradation and the conditions of work promoted by the corporation.

In terms of the second axis, how companies had acquired investments and how they were protected, Allende was mindful of the way that during the nineteenth century the major European powers had 'propagate[d] Western standards of individual ownership around the world and secure[d] these standards in the face of considerable social, cultural, [legal] and political diversity' in order to facilitate the security of foreign investment.[29] In the process, they displaced or radically transformed collective forms of ownership and systems of use rights (or confined them to 'native' sectors of dual economies), and created regimes of private property as part of a politically guaranteed 'order' for European states through a variety of means 'ranging from [direct] colonialism to extraterritorial laws to informal commercial empire'.[30] Although the

---

[26] Terence Gourvish and Nick Tiratsoo (eds.), *Missionaries and Managers: American Influences on European Management Education, 1945–60* (New York: Manchester University Press, 1998), 3; Paddy Ireland, 'Defending the Rentier: Corporate Theory and the Reprivatization of the Public Company' in John Parkinson et al. (eds.), *The Political Economy of the Company* (Oxford: Hart, 2001), 141–74.

[27] Bedjaoui, *Towards a New International Economic Order*, 36–7: 'The present situation, with the multinational companies, is even more alienating for the under-developed countries than it was in the colonization period with the chartered companies.'

[28] David Fieldhouse, *The West and the Third World: Trade, Colonialism, Dependence and Development* (Oxford: Wiley-Blackwell Publishing, 1999), 254–86.

[29] Charles Lipson, *Standing Guard: Protecting Foreign Capital in the Nineteenth and Twentieth Centuries* (Berkeley: University of California Press, 1985), 20.

[30] Lipson, *Standing Guard*, 21.

language of law was used by some to justify these actions, these practices were highly contested, and not accepted at the time as anything like the 'international legal order' they are now often retrospectively described as having reflected.

From the perspective of the West, this 'order' was asserted as something like an 'international law governing expropriation of foreign investments', imposing strict 'minimum standards' on all states, and requiring full compensation for expropriation.[31] In keeping with the assertion of legality, these particular values were cast as universal, and enforcement of this 'standard' was closely intertwined with empire and intervention. As Detlav Vagts put it, 'at the high tide of this version of international law, breaches by host countries might be avenged by any number of plagues ranging from gunboats to arbitration'.[32] But even from the inside of this 'system', such as it was, there was uncertainty over the status of 'foreign property' as a question of international law. Imperial states had, in any case, jurisdiction over their own colonies, as well as their colonies' foreign affairs.[33] And the force of the Russian revolution and Mexican nationalizations of the early twentieth century meant that there was no legal or institutional resolution at the League of Nations over the question of whether foreign-owned private property should be granted international protection.[34]

But as the post-war period went on and agitation for decolonization increased, tremors began to shake the 'system'. The most notable example is perhaps the nationalization of the Anglo-Iranian Oil company by the democratically elected prime minister Mohamed Mossadeq in Iran in 1951.[35] As decolonization proceeded, the quakes became more frequent, as both the substance of the asserted 'rules' protecting foreign-owned private property and the preferred modes of 'enforcement' were subject to radical challenge. From the perspective of the West, this was perceived as a crisis of 'legitimacy'.[36] But from the perspective of the Second and

---

[31] Lipson, *Standing Guard*, 24.

[32] Detlev Vagts, 'The Global Corporation and International Law', *Journal of International Law and Economics*, 6 (1972), 254.

[33] John Grant and Craig Barker, *Encyclopaedic Dictionary of International Law* (Oxford: Oxford University Press, 2009): 'Colonial Clause' citing Lord McNair, *The Law of Treaties* (Oxford: Oxford University Press, 1986), 118–19. (Similar clauses are now commonly styled territorial application clauses, see Anthony Aust, *Modern Treaty Law and Practice* (Cambridge: Cambridge University Press, 2000), ch. 11.)

[34] Arghyrios Fatouros, 'An International Code to Protect Private Investment: Proposals and Perspectives', *University of Toronto Law Journal*, 14 (1961), 79.

[35] Sundhya Pahuja and Cait Storr, 'Rethinking Iran and International Law: The Anglo-Iranian Oil Company Case Revisited' in James Crawford et al. (eds.), *The International Legal Order: Current Needs and Possible Responses, Essays in Honour of Djamchid Momtaz* (Leiden: Brill, 2017), 53.

[36] See generally, Lipson, *Standing Guard*.

Third Worlds, it represented the beginning of another struggle, this time to remake the international economic order after empire, and to offer a wholesale challenge to the political-economic legacies of colonialism.

The response of the West in the face of this challenge was to experiment with a new mode of post-colonial enforcement to protect foreign-owned private property: intervention by the CIA, underpinning corporate/state alliances.[37] This was not the sole province of the United States. Recently declassified documents have revealed that Cold War paranoia was actively mobilised by weakened imperial powers, such as Britain, to persuade the United States to help protect the property of their investors.[38] Again, the Iranian example is a case in point as Mossadeq's nationalizations prompted a coup, assisted by the CIA, which reinstalled the Shah.[39] But as this new mode of protecting foreign property began to surface – in Chile certainly, and people suspected even then in Iran – the 'legitimacy' of the imperial regime was eroded further still, and resistance to it, even from inside the United States, increased.[40] This erosion of legitimacy, combined with the existence of the different imaginary offered by communism(s),[41] the political ballast of inter-world rivalry and the visible manifestations of Third World solidarity, created the space for the assertion of the Third World as a *juridical*, and not simply political, project. The particular terms of the juridical assertion now being forcefully made related to the distribution of legal authority. Specifically, the Third World asserted that the conduct of foreign corporations should be regulated by international law, and that authority to admit, restrict or expropriate foreign investment, should rest with the nation-state. An international approach was needed to address the conduct question because of the collective action problem engendered by the hypermobility of the elements of production. National authority was needed over the foreign ownership of property question as a response to imperialism.

In asserting that international law should govern the (corporate) conduct question, and that national law should govern the (foreign) property question, Allende's conception of the corporation becomes important. He shared with those in both colonial and semi-colonial places an

[37] For a list of instances, see William Blum, *Killing Hope: U.S. Military and C.I.A. Interventions Since World War II* (Monroe, ME: Common Courage Press, 2008).
[38] This was done through the Information Research Division, a secret division of the British Foreign Office. Andrew Rubin, *Archives of Authority: Empire, Culture and the Cold War* (Princeton, NJ: Princeton University Press, 2012), 20, 34.
[39] Pahuja and Storr, 'Rethinking Iran and International Law', 53, 74.
[40] United States Senate, 'First Session, Volume 7: Covert Action'.
[41] In both its Chinese and Soviet versions. See Jeremy Friedman, *Shadow Cold War: The Sino-Soviet Competition for the Third World* (Chapel Hill: University of North Carolina Press, 2015).

enduring experience of the corporation as a 'real' entity.[42] It was neither a child of the state,[43] nor a mere 'nexus of contracts'.[44] Instead, for Allende, the corporation was an organic entity which exists regardless of the state. For him, it was an associational form adjacent to the state, asserting a distinct form of authority, and acting according to a rival form of law.[45] In Allende's assessment, the secret of the corporation's power was its rootlessness in both effective and affective terms; '[m]erchants have no country of their own. Wherever they may be they have no ties with the soil. All they are interested in is the source of their profits.'[46]

But if he understood that mobility gave corporations power, then he also understood that the justifications for, or 'rightfulness' of that power, lay in the relationship that corporations claimed to bear to 'development'. In his speech at UNCTAD III, Allende reminded the assembled crowd that foreign corporations invariably represented their actions as being in the interests of those whose resources they exploit, and that transnational corporations 'arrogate to themselves the role of agents promoting the progress of the poorer countries'.[47] Through this arrogation, such corporations 'have become a supranational force that is threatening to get completely out of control'.[48] In other words, this rhetorical merger between self-interest and altruism[49] – a contemporary repurposing of Fredrick Lugard's 'dual mandate' for the present day – was the secret of the corporation's asserted *authority* to do business in the Third World. In this, corporations were key actors in the self-proclaimed duty of the West to develop the rest as an exogenous exercise of authority, and the alleviation of poverty as a gesture of enlightened self-interest. Allende makes clear that this idea of development provided (juridical) *authority* for the activities of transnational corporations.

[42] See generally, Otto von Gierke, *Political Theories of the Middle Ages*, trans. F. W. Maitland (Cambridge: Cambridge University Press, 1902; reprint 1951), xxvi.
[43] John Dewey, 'The Historic Background of Corporate Legal Personality', *Yale Law Journal*, 35/6 (1926), 655–73. Some will recognise Von Savigny's 'fiction theory' here. For one example of the reception of that theory, see Martin Petrin, 'Reconceptualizing the Theory of the Firm – from Nature to Function', *Penn State Law Review*, 118/1 (2013), 4–6.
[44] The seminal article here is Michael Jensen and William Meckling, 'Theory of the Firm: Managerial Behaviour, Agency Costs and Ownership Structure', *Journal of Financial Economics*, 3/4 (1976), 305–60.
[45] Von Gierke, *Political Theories of the Middle Age*. See also David Ciepley, 'Beyond Public and Private: Toward a Political Theory of the Corporation', *American Political Science Review*, 107/1 (2013), 139–58.
[46] Allende, 'Address Delivered at 2096th Plenary Meeting', 59.
[47] Allende, 'Address Delivered at 2096th Plenary Meeting', 58.
[48] Allende, 'Address Delivered at 2096th Plenary Meeting', 58.
[49] Gilbert Rist, *The History of Development: From Western Origins to Global Faith* (London: Zed Books, 2014).

In Allende's account, the better concept of development was an endogenous one, 'self-determined and independent',[50] rather than the exogenous conception of the industrialised states, which, he knew all too well, was grounded in a hierarchy that would condemn the 'underdeveloped countries' to a 'second-class, eternally subordinate status'.[51] This conception of development, ideally determined by each state according to its needs, and shaped through their own political authority, was nonetheless a response to the shared condition of 'underdevelopment', an economic state arising from the depredations of imperialism.[52] What was happening in Chile was 'opening up a new stage in the battle between imperialism and the weaker countries of the Third World'.[53] This shared history was giving rise to collective action between Asia, Africa and Latin America. Allende describes with gratitude the expression of 'complete solidarity' with Chile offered by the 'spokesman of the African group of States in the Trade and Development Board' over the issue which 'represented a potential threat to the entire developing world'.[54]

But if Allende, like Fanon, understands the present as history, is aware of the centrality of historiography to international legal and diplomatic encounters between the 'Worlds' and has a keen awareness that the generation of wealth and the production of poverty are two sides of the same process, he is less attentive to the persistence of racialised thinking in these same practices of world ordering. The hierarchical arrangement of 'sovereign' states in a developmental scale, after all, looks very like the imperial, race-based, hierarchy. And Allende falls back into those racialised hierarchies of imperialism, mapping developmental grids onto (global) lines drawn by colour, drawing attention to the 'thousands of people living in shanty towns' in the 'much-admired cities of Latin America', 'whose nutrition and health standards are no higher than in Africa'.[55] And although 'dramatic deficiencies in housing, work, food and health' are visible in Latin America, 'the situation is even worse in Asia and Africa, with their lower *per capita* income and weaker development process'.[56]

[50] Allende, 'Address Delivered at 2096th Plenary Meeting', 6.
[51] Allende, 'Address Delivered at 2096th Plenary Meeting', 6; Joseph Hodge, 'Writing the History of Development (Part 1: The First Wave)', *Humanity*, 6/3 (2015), 429–63; Hodge, 'Writing the History of Development (Part 2: Longer, Deeper, Wider)', *Humanity*, 7/1 (2016), 125–74; Sundhya Pahuja, *Decolonising International Law: Development, Economic Growth and the Politics of Universality* (Cambridge: Cambridge University Press, 2011).
[52] Allende, 'Address Delivered at 2096th Plenary Meeting', 65.
[53] Allende, 'Address Delivered at 2096th Plenary Meeting', 64.
[54] Allende, 'Address Delivered at 2096th Plenary Meeting', 64.
[55] Allende, 'Address Delivered at 2096th Plenary Meeting', 73.
[56] Allende, 'Address Delivered at 2096th Plenary Meeting', 75.

Once a developmentalist ordering is taken up, it becomes 'common sense in the creation of a normative regime that [is at its core, a] technolog[y] of power, legitimation and affect', giving rise to 'a tendency to conceal the mechanisms of subordination ... that operate through time and space through scientific method'.[57] What is forgotten is that the hierarchy reproduced is the same one generated by the imperial 'science' grounded in (biological) race and racism. And so we see that already by the time of Allende's attempt to wrest legal authority from the First World over the regulation of foreign property ownership, and to assert over corporate conduct, a version of international law 'not subordinated to capital interests',[58] the global dimensions of 'race' had already begun to become less visible in the international institutional setting. Race was being superseded by culture, and conceptually confined to the national sphere through the discourse of development.

Kissinger

At around the same time that the first session of the newly established UN Commission on Transnational Corporations (UNCTC) took place in March of 1975, on the 1st of September of the same year the General Assembly of the UN held a Special Session on Development and Economic Co-operation. The session was planned as part of the ongoing institutional efforts to establish the principles of a New International Economic Order.[59] And although the question of a binding treaty to hold transnational corporations to international legal standards of behaviour had already fallen off the new UNCTC's programme of work (and despite Allende's death during the Chilean coup on 11 September 1973), the question of corporations was very much alive at the General Assembly session.

The purpose of the gathering was to consider 'new concepts and options with a view to promoting effectively the solution of world economic problems, especially those of developing countries'.[60] At the very

[57] Grovogui, 'Deterring Difference', 121.
[58] Allende, 'Address Delivered at 2096th Plenary Meeting', 49.
[59] This was in the wake of the Declaration establishing a New International Economic Order at the UN General Assembly in 1974: United Nations General Assembly, 'Declaration on the Establishment of a New International Economic Order', GA Res 3201 (S-VI), 1 May 1974, UN Doc A/RES/S-6/3201.
[60] Azeredo Da Silverira (Brazil), 'Address Delivered at 2327th Plenary Meeting', *Official Records of the United Nations General Assembly* (1 September 1975, New York), [3], citing United Nations General Assembly, 'Resolution adopted by the General Assembly: 3172 (XXVIII) Holding of a Special Session of the General Assembly Devoted to Development and International Economic Co-operation', GA Res 3172 (XXVIII), 17 December 1963, UN Doc A/RES/28/3172.

forefront of the session was the United States.[61] Then US Secretary of State, Henry Kissinger, was due to deliver a speech at the beginning of the proceedings. As it turned out, he was drawn away by the conclusion of the Sinai Pact between Egypt and Israel,[62] but his speech was read in his absence by Daniel Moynihan, US Representative to the UN. The speech, called 'Global Consensus and Economic Development', announced the moment as 'an opportunity to improve the condition of mankind'. The United States, Kissinger announced, was committed to 'a pro- gramme of practical steps' to address the concerns of the developing world.[63] The impelling circumstances were twofold. First, the availability of 'technical capacity' to 'provide a tolerable standard of life for the world's 4 billion people', and second, a 'point of moral choice' precipi- tated by the availability of the technical means to bring about 'the ancient dream of mankind – a world without poverty'. When such means make fulfilment of the 'ancient dream' possible, says Kissinger, 'our profound moral convictions make it also our duty'. Like Truman before him, the content of the duty was not to transfer material resources, but to share American knowledge.[64] Recall that for Truman in 1947, '[t]he United States is pre-eminent among nations in the development of industrial and scientific techniques. The material resources which we can afford to use for assistance of other peoples are limited. But our imponderable resources in technical knowledge are constantly growing and are inexhaustible.'[65] For Truman then and Kissinger after him, the existence of human suffering, and superior technical know-how, authorises, as Grovogui puts it, 'a Western [and here, specifically American] claim to moral authority as a provider of rules and models to the rest'.[66]

The claim to moral authority grounded in scientific knowledge is the flip side of the way Pogge's account in 2002, of the moral responsibility of the 'developed West', has the effect of authorizing its actions vis-à-vis 'the

---

[61] Daniel Moynihan (United States of America), 'Address Delivered at 2327th Plenary Meeting', *Official Records of the United Nations General Assembly* (1 September 1975, New York), [33]–[203].

[62] Bernard Gwertzman, 'Kissinger Seeks Approval Today of Mideast Pact', *The New York Times* (1 September 1975). Available at: www.nytimes.com/1975/09/01/archives/kis singer-seeks-approval-today-of-mideast-pact-works-with-israelis.html [website last vis- ited 5 June 2018].

[63] Moynihan, 'Address Delivered at 2327th Plenary Meeting', 35–6. Kissinger served as US Secretary of State from 1973 to 1977.

[64] Harry Truman, 'Truman's Inaugural Address', *Harry S. Truman Presidential Library and Museum* (20 January 1949). Available at: www.trumanlibrary.org/whistlestop/50yr_arc hive/inagural20jan1949.htm [website last visited 11 June 2018].

[65] Truman, 'Inaugural Address'.

[66] Siba Grovogui, 'Come to Africa: A Hermeneutics of Race in International Theory', *Alternatives: Global, Local, Political*, 26/4 (2001), 427.

poor'. The 'poor', for Pogge, 'can cause little harm or benefit to the politicians and officials who rule them' because of the afflictions of poverty: they are 'often physically and mentally stunted due to malnutrition in infancy, illiterate due to lack of school, and much pre-occupied with their family's survival'.[67] Their abjection and political disenfranchisement means 'the poor' must be both helped and spoken for now by 'those who live in protected affluence' in the 'developed West'.[68] Newly enlightened, today's generations of 'European civilization' now 'widely accept' 'the equal moral status of all human beings' and must therefore take up the salvific responsibility that 'equal moral status' confers upon the fortunate, not to 'tolerate' extreme poverty. This moral obligation, in Pogge's view, should operate as a constraint on 'the kinds of global economic order persons may impose on others'.[69] In this acknowledged capacity to 'impose' a global economic order on others, a power differential is acknowledged, but agency to act – and to authorise law – still inures only in the fortunate, not in 'the poor'.

The role of history in producing the capacity to 'impose' economic order is also attenuated in both Pogge and Kissinger's accounts. In contrast to the Third World's insistence on the continued presence of history, and the active impoverishment by the West of the rest, for Kissinger the moment from which he spoke was ruptural, representing a radical break with the past: the 'global order of colonial power that lasted through centuries has now disappeared'.[70] In contrast to Kissinger, Pogge in a later article does 'recall briefly that existing peoples have arrived at their present levels of social, economic and cultural development through an historical process that was pervaded by enslavement, colonialism, even genocide', but like Kissinger, Pogge announces a definitive break, as 'these monumental crimes are now in the past'.[71] For him, the importance of the 'legacy' they have left does not reside in the dominance of the particular forms of (international) law or knowledge that those practices were crucial in actualizing, but 'a legacy of great inequalities'. Pogge draws a line in the mid-twentieth century, under the moment when 'Europe released Africa from the colonial yoke'. This line then becomes the point of departure for the universalist argument that 'we' have a moral responsibility to 'the global poor', because of the '*initial* economic inequality' which tends to benefit 'the stronger party'.[72]

[67] Pogge, 'Moral Universalism and Global Economic Justice', 29.
[68] Pogge, 'Moral Universalism and Global Economic Justice', 30.
[69] Pogge, 'Moral Universalism and Global Economic Justice', 32.
[70] Moynihan, 'Address delivered at 2327th Plenary Meeting', 38.
[71] Pogge, 'Recognized and Violated by International Law', 723.
[72] Pogge, 'Recognized and Violated by International Law', 723. Emphasis added.

For Kissinger, the present was so new that, by 1972, even 'the cold war division of the world into two rigid blocs ha[d] now also broken down', and there remained, he said, only states united in the common endeavour of development.[73] But because of its obvious under-development, action taken by the Third World at the international institutional level could not be read as the assertion of a different account of (international) law. Instead, Third World solidarity was positioned in opposition to the inauguration of what could be a new era of 'human progress'. The threat lay in the formation of the Non-Aligned Movement, a 'new bloc' which was counterproductive to this endeavour, engaging 'in a kind of solidarity that often clearly sacrifices practical interests'.[74] What was required to address the economic problems faced by all states was not division, said Kissinger, but 'consensus, first and foremost, on the prin- ciple that our common development goals can be achieved only by co- operation, not by the politics of confrontation'.[75]

The 'transnational enterprise' was amongst the most contentious of these lines of 'political division'. The ongoing 'controversy over their role and conduct' which had continued in various forms and fora since Allende's speech was 'itself an obstacle to economic development'. In his view, 'if the world community [was] committed to economic development, it [could] not afford to treat transnational enterprises as objects of economic warfare'.[76] Nevertheless, Kissinger conceded that 'the time [had] come for the international community to articulate stan- dards of conduct' for corporations, and acknowledged that the UNCTC 'had begun such an effort'. But for Kissinger, 'transnational enterprises ha[d] been powerful instruments of modernization' and 'may well be one of the most effective engines of development'. As Allende had fore- showed, 'foreign investment' was imputed with a tutelary dimension, and tied closely to an exogenous, salvific project of developing the under- developed. For Kissinger, given that only 'transnational enterprises' and the private capital they provided could facilitate the solution to the problem of under-development, standards should be formulated which applied both to the behaviour of corporations *and* to the governments that hosted them.[77]

The principles that Kissinger laid out underpinning these standards were extensive, but two elements were key to the question of the transna- tional corporation. First was an insistence that corporate conduct should

[73] Moynihan, 'Address Delivered at 2327th Plenary Meeting', 38.
[74] Moynihan, 'Address Delivered at 2327th Plenary Meeting', 44.
[75] Moynihan, 'Address Delivered at 2327th Plenary Meeting', 47.
[76] Moynihan, 'Address Delivered at 2327th Plenary Meeting', 105, 119.
[77] Moynihan, 'Address Delivered at 2327th Plenary Meeting', 103, 108.

be governed by local, not international law. Transnational corporations were of course 'obliged to obey local law' and should 'refrain from unlawful interference in the domestic affairs of the host country' and 'respect local customs and employ qualified local personnel'. But second, in return, those corporations must receive a stable, apolitical environment in which to operate, characterised by equitable and non-discriminatory treatment. And unlike corporate conduct governed by local law, 'host states' must accord transnational enterprises protection 'in accordance with *international law*'.[78] In Kissinger's account, these protections would be supported by a suite of international endeavours, including the harmonization of tax treatment, the promotion of arbitral procedures for the settlement of investment disputes, the reduction of restrictive business practices and the multilateralization of the insurance of foreign investment.[79] These would be underpinned by the 'development of agricultural technologies' for food production, 'assistance to improve productivity and competitiveness' in relation to non-agricultural food production, and the assurance of future access to 'borrowing in the [international] capital market', which was already relied upon heavily in the Latin American countries. In essence, what Kissinger was mapping was a different kind of 'new international economic order', one which drew for its authority on 'development' and the needs of the poorest 'one billion people', but which precisely contradicted in its every element the other 'New International Economic Order' being proposed by the Global South at the same moment.[80]

As we know now, Kissinger's map was prefigurative of what was to come. What looked like a victory of sorts in the creation of the UNCTC failed to produce the collective state action sought by the Third World to regulate the conduct of multinational corporations. The UNCTC was quietly put to rest in 1993, folded into the United Nations Development Programme (UNDP) as part of the 'Division on Investment and Enterprise'. But more than portending a simple failure, Kissinger's detailed plan foreshadowed the eventual inversion of what was being attempted by the Third World, and the preclusion of the exercise by the Third World, of juridical authority. Today that particular attempt to establish a conversation at the United Nations about multinational corporations is almost invariably forgotten.[81] When it is remembered at all, it is usually characterised as an ill-fated attempt to assert a Third World

[78] Moynihan, 'Address Delivered at 2327th Plenary Meeting', 110, 111. Emphasis added.
[79] Moynihan, 'Address Delivered at 2327th Plenary Meeting', 112, 118.
[80] Moynihan, 'Address Delivered at 2327th Plenary Meeting', 84, 165.
[81] For one notable exception to this, see Jennifer Bair, 'Corporations at the United Nations: Echoes of the New International Economic Order', *Humanity*, 6/1 (2015), 159–71.

sovereign jurisdiction against an international jurisdiction, with all the hierarchies of value that characterization implies. The story is now largely retold (for better or worse) as 'sovereignty' versus international 'community'.

But slowing the story down reveals that what was being asserted was not the simple 'domestic' versus 'international' story, but the authority to decide which matters should be put into the basket of 'domestic', which should be 'international' and with what consequences. As it emerged from formal empire, the Third World sought to assert authority over private property in the national realm as a way to address the economic legacies of imperialism, and to internationalise the capacity to regulate corporate conduct as a response to the essential rootlessness of the multinational corporation.

This manifests precisely with respect to 'global' corporations and their operations at large. What we have seen during the period from the end of the Cold War to the present is the *internationalization* of the protection of private property through an emerging regime of 'international investment law'[82] and the relegation to the national sphere of the regulation over corporate conduct, along with the vulnerabilities and collective action problems that brings. This has been accompanied by a turn to 'business and human rights' which pushes responsibility for enforcing the standards downwards into the (Third World) nation-state, but invests authority over setting the standards themselves upwards, into the international community through its jurisdiction over the universal 'human'.[83]

Conclusion

To those who believe that Europe and North America have already invented a universal civilization and all the rest of us have to do is hurry up and enrol, what I am proposing will appear un-necessary if not downright foolish. But for others, who may believe with me that

---

[82] Sundhya Pahuja, 'Part 3: Contemporary Patterns of Ordering: Business and Human Rights and International Investment Law', *Hersch Lauterpacht Memorial Lectures* (March 2018, University of Cambridge). Available at: www.lcil.cam.ac.uk/hersch-lauterpacht-memorial-lectures [website last visited 15 June 2018]. See Muthucumaraswamy Sornarajah, 'The Myth of International Contract Law', *Journal of World Trade Law*, 15/3 (1981), 187–217. On the 'levitation' out of the sphere of domestic law into that of international law, see Muthucumaraswamy Sornarajah, *Law of International Joint Ventures* (Spore: Longman, 1992), 298.

[83] United Nations Human Rights Office of the High Commissioner, 'Guiding Principles on Business and Human Rights: Implementing the United Nations "Protect, Respect and Remedy" Framework' (Geneva: United Nations, 2011); Erika George, 'Incorporating Rights: Empire, Global Enterprise and Global Justice', *University of St. Thomas Law Journal*, 10 (2013), 917.

a universal civilisation is nowhere yet in sight, the task will be how to enter the preliminary conversations.[84]

This chapter is not an (intellectual) history in the sense of tracing an idea of 'Global Justice' as it emerges, travels from one place to another and touches down in academic or institutional contexts. Instead, it is an approach which considers particular articulations of the kinds of arguments about justice and distribution, and inequality and material deprivation, made at the level of international law and institutions over time, and the practices such arguments authorise. Thinking of law as practice and technique, rather than concept and norm, helps us to see the ways such authorization happens through specific actors, and groups of actors authoring particular accounts of the world which include a story about how particular kinds of relationships should be understood, what counts as problems and what should be done about them. In this it shares the intuition that normative and descriptive accounts of the world – the 'is' and the 'ought' – are thought, performed and actualised together, or in Jasanoff's idiom, 'co-produced'.[85]

In the example given here, contestations over how to hold the corporation to account at the end of European imperialism reveal three things. The first is that at least two rivalrous accounts were explicitly doing battle at the institutional level during the 1970s and 1980s. The second is that each account carried with it an explanation for the causes of material deprivation, which invited different normative approaches to what should be done about it. The third is that these accounts can be understood as 'rival' accounts in the formal sense that each generated – and was generated from within – a different understanding of the whole world. They are not two poles on one scale between which a 'balance' can be struck. Instead, they exist in a relation of what we might call 'radical plurality' insofar as no single set of institutions can accommodate – or actualise – both world views.[86]

The central point of differentiation between the two approaches is the question of authority. It plays out explicitly with respect to the global

[84] Chinua Achebe, 'Today, the Balance of Stories', in Achebe, *Home and Exile* (New York: Oxford University Press, 2000), 104.
[85] Jasanoff, 'The Idiom of Co-Production', 1–6.
[86] Paul Voice, 'Global Justice and the Challenge of Radical Pluralism', *Theoria: A Journal of Social and Political Theory*, 104 (2004), 15–37. I am borrowing Voice's definition of what he calls 'radical plural*ism*', but adapting it to an account of plurality. An 'ism' suggests an orientation toward a thing, whereas an 'ity' denotes a state, not an attitude. People often use the word 'legal pluralism' (for example) to describe both a theoretical orientation toward being attentive toward multiple laws and the fact of that plurality itself. This is to confuse two elements, the fact of legal plurality, which exists regardless of one's attitude (for example, indigenous law and colonial law), and what kind of response scholars and institutions may have to that fact.

corporation, in the way that the Third World sought national control over the property question, and international agreement over the conduct question, and the inversion of that demand by a suite of US-led initiatives. But the prior question is the question of who has the authority to decide. This extends to the question of who may decide what counts as law. It is fairly clear that since the end of formal empire, Third World states have consistently sought a capacity to determine their own affairs. ('The notion of justice is not complicated. It is universally accepted that a dominance of one people by another, or one group by another, must be ended so that equality is restored.')[87] They have put forward a corollary account of international law and institutions as an agonistic space of meeting.[88]

It is similarly clear that Western states have asserted the authority to decide not only for themselves, but for everyone ('humanity') and everything ('global economy'), on the basis of a claim to the universality of their asserted law.[89] ('International law does not recognise any distinctions . . . based on religious, geographical or cultural differences.')[90] The 'First World' put forward a corollary account of international law and institutions as directed toward 'governing'. Because of its asserted universality, this law positions itself above, rather than between, plural entities. Once a law is asserted as inclusive regardless of difference, the inclusive, universally oriented law authors the jurisdictional forms which give shape to life, and authorises the governance of the other. And so although this claim to universality is asserted as a virtue which carries the promise of inclusion and universal access to moral rights, when combined with power, it has the effect of dominating those who are included within it.

The mechanisms, stories, practices and arrangements which permit this assertion, and its actualization, are many. Developmentalism, or the scalar organization of states according to putatively economic criteria, has done much of the work in recent years to sustain the claim to universality made by the West. Notwithstanding the fact that many understand this, 'the languages of post-Enlightenment constitutional

---

[87] Muthucumaraswamy Sornarajah, 'On Fighting for Global Justice: The Role of a Third World International Lawyer', *Third World Quarterly*, 37/11 (2016), 1972.

[88] On an agonistic conception of democratic politics, see Chantal Mouffe, 'Agonistic Democracy and Radical Politics', *Pavilion Journal for Politics and Culture* (n.d.). Available at: http://pavilionmagazine.org/chantal-mouffe-agonistic-democracy-and-radical-politics/ [website last visited 15 June 2018]; William Connolly, *Pluralism* (Durham, NC: Duke University Press, 2005). On laws of encounter, see Pahuja, 'Letters from Bandung' and Pahuja, 'Laws of Encounter: A Jurisdictional Account of International Law', *London Review of International Law*, 1/1 (2013), 63–98.

[89] The claim to universality arguably extends to existence as a whole, not just law. There are many books devoted to this idea. For one recent example, see Hamid Dabashi, *Can Non-Europeans Think?* (London: Zed Books, 2015).

[90] Jennings and Watts, *Oppenheim's International Law: Volume 1.*

arrangements' are still assumed to be sufficient in international institutions, and in almost all official centres of international law-making and foreign policy. This is perhaps unsurprising given that the 'axiomatics of imperialism' have always been intended to 'reproduce the systems, values, norms and institutions ... that preserve vested interests under the guise of truth'.[91]

Perhaps more surprising is the way that those engaged critically with the developmental scale, and those who have tried to redefine development in a legal and institutional context, have forgotten that the origins of the scale lie in a racialised understanding of theories of history, justice and science.[92] The forgetting of race means the concealment of its persistence as an organising idea. And so by the end of the Cold War, at the level of international law and institutions race had been contained by the 'territorial trap' of the nation-state, and transformed into a domestic issue, both institutionally and phenomenologically.[93] With this, the roots of contemporary economic structures in 'scientific' theories of biological racial inferiority are both erased and the political and moral theories which flow from them are 'exonerated' of their racism.[94]

---

[91] Grovogui, 'Deferring Difference', 107. Grovogui is taking 'axiomatics of imperialism' from Gayatri Spivak, *A Critique of Postcolonial Reason: Toward a History of the Vanishing Present* (Cambridge, MA: Harvard University Press, 1999).

[92] Grovogui, 'Deferring Difference', 107.

[93] Agnew, 'The Territorial Trap'; Gordon et al., *What Fanon Said*, 2.

[94] Grovogui, 'Deferring Difference'. See, generally, Joel Modiri, 'The Colour of Law, Power and Knowledge: Introducing Critical Race Theory in (Post-)Apartheid South Africa', *South African Journal on Human Rights*, 28 (2012), 405–36. For a recent example of the way a cultural account of difference exonerates the racialized underpinnings of that account, see Martti Koskenniemi, 'Race, Hierarchy and International Law: Lorimer's Legal Science', *European Journal of International Law*, 27/2 (2016), 415–29. By distinguishing Lorimer's explicitly race-based account from other international lawyers of the time, Koskenniemi is missing the racialized underpinnings of those putatively 'cultural' accounts.

4   Race and Global Justice

Charles W. Mills

Introduction

The theme of this volume is empire, race, and global justice. So I want to begin with a striking global analysis from less than a century ago, from the 1920s. I will conceal for the moment the author's identity, except to say that he is a well-known historical figure. See if you can guess who it is before you turn the page:

Of the billion and a half people in the world, the most powerful are the 400 million whites on the European and American continents; from this base the white races have started out to swallow up other races. The American red aborigines are gone, the African blacks will soon be exterminated, the brown race of India is in the process of dissolution, the yellow races of Asia are now being subjected to the white man's oppression and may, before long, be wiped out. But the 150 million Russians, when their revolution succeeded, broke with the other white races and condemned the white man's imperialistic behaviour; now they are thinking of throwing in their lot with the weaker, smaller peoples of Asia in a struggle against the tyrannical races. So only 250 million of the tyrannical races are left, but they are still trying by inhuman methods and military force to subjugate the other 1,250 million. So hereafter mankind will be divided into two camps: on one hand will be the 1,250 million; on the other side, the 250 million. ... Now we want to revive [—'s] lost nationalism and use the strength of our [—] millions to fight for mankind against injustice; this is our divine mission. The Powers are afraid that we will have such thoughts and are setting forth a specious doctrine. They are now advocating cosmopolitanism to inflame us, declaring that, as the civilization of the world advances and as mankind's vision enlarges, nationalism becomes too narrow, unsuited to the present age, and hence that we should espouse cosmo-politanism. In recent years some of [— 's] youth, devotees of the new culture, have been opposing nationalism, led astray by this doctrine. But it is not a doctrine which wronged races should talk about. We, the wronged races, must first recover our position of national freedom and equality before we are fit to discuss cosmopolitanism.

For a contemporary readership, especially one unfamiliar with the history of colonialism and anti-colonial struggles, this passage will, I suggest, be

94

quite startling in its matter-of-factly *racialist* framework of analysis. The author takes for granted, in a way that clearly indicates he does not see it as likely to be controversial for his audience, that he and his readers are living in a world characterized by white racial hegemony and exterminist policy. Whites dominate the planet and are seeking to extend their rule indefinitely, if necessary through the genocide of the remaining races. (The reference to Africa is probably to the depredations of King Leopold II in the Belgian Congo from the late nineteenth to the early twentieth centuries, largely forgotten in the West until Adam Hochschild's *King Leopold's Ghost* refreshed official memory two decades ago. Hochschild estimates the death toll under the regime at about 10 million people.)[1] So white supremacy is global and a united transnational struggle of the nonwhite races against it is necessary for their survival. Races are not at all merely abstract sociological categories, but active social agents.

The editor of the collection from which I took this excerpt characterizes the author's views as "Social Darwinist." But, if Social Darwinism is committed to natural racial hierarchy, unavoidable interracial struggle, a biologistic dynamic, and the evolutionary goal of the triumph of the "superior" races, this judgment (at least on the basis of the passage here) seems to me to be questionable.[2] The author's interpretation of the Bolshevik Revolution as constituting a massive white defection from the ranks of the "tyrannical races" – politically naïve as it may appear to us a century later – shows that what is presumed to be at work is not an ineluctable, biologically driven racial determinism. Options are open and moral choice is possible. A class-based Marxism is clearly not taken to be incongruent with a "racial" struggle against global white supremacy; whites may change sides (becoming, in a contemporary vocabulary, "race traitors") and adopt a politics of anti-imperialism instead of a politics of conquest. Note also that this resistance is not being represented as the struggle to achieve a racial dictatorship of nonwhites over their oppressors, nor to prosecute a retaliatory exterminism. Rather, what is being sought is global justice for the "wronged races" of "mankind," a mission with divine sanction. In the writer's opinion, however, it would be a mistake at this stage to endorse a cosmopolitan ideal. Instead, a racial nationalism to restore the "freedom and equality" of the author's oppressed conationals is what is called for. Only after that has been achieved will it be appropriate to discuss the issue of cosmopolitanism.

[1] Hochschild, *King Leopold's Ghost: A Story of Greed, Terror, and Heroism in Colonial Africa* (New York: Houghton Mifflin, 1998).
[2] For a general discussion, see Mike Hawkins, *Social Darwinism in European and American Thought, 1860–1945: Nature as Model and Nature as Threat* (New York: Cambridge University Press, 1997), esp. ch. 8.

I want to use this passage, with all its obvious problems, as a stalking horse to challenge the conventional frameworks in which global domination and global justice are discussed. (The author, I will now reveal, is Sun Yat-sen, standardly viewed as "the father of modern China"; the population figure, which I omitted since it would have given the game away, was 400 million.[3] You might have guessed Marcus Garvey, though imminent African extinction would certainly not have been so offhandedly mentioned by him.) For what it does is bring home both how routinely racial categories were employed in the analysis of European colonial domination only a few decades ago, and how absent they are today from contemporary debates on the problems of globalization.

The philosophical literature on global justice has dramatically expanded in recent years, a manifestation both of the contraction of the planet through ease of communication and travel (so that the longtime cliché of the global village is on the verge of literal realization) and the worsening in many respects of issues of poverty and relative underdevelopment. What might once have been the subject of an occasional article in the conscientious editor's ethics anthology is now routinely the exclusive topic of entire courses. But, though a wide range of normative approaches (modified Rawlsian, egalitarian, sufficientarian, cosmopolitan) will typically be canvassed in such readings, a commonality of this literature is the virtual absence of any discussion of race and racism. For those from the former Third World (such as myself) familiar with any of the anti-colonial writings of the nineteenth and twentieth centuries, this silence is remarkable, since the global injustice of imperialism and colonialism was classically seen (as the Sun Yat-sen excerpt makes clear) precisely *as* a matter of white domination over people of color. This racial dimension was not at all taken to be a merely contingent correlation, accidental and theoretically irrelevant, but causally central and deeply consequential.

Consider the black radical political tradition, which, though it has sometimes degenerated into chauvinism and racism, has at its best been both internationalist and anti-racist, seeking racial equality rather than racial revenge, and advocating a global elimination of racial hierarchy and privilege.[4] Here we can find former slave Quobna Cugoano condemning in 1787 the "Christian nations" not merely for their enslavement of

[3] Sun Yat-sen, "*San Min Chu I (The Three Principles of the People)*," selections from Lecture 4, trans. Frank W. Price [1927], excerpted in Prasenjit Duara (ed.), *Decolonization: Perspectives from Now and Then* (New York: Routledge, 2004), 25.
[4] See Anthony Bogues, *Black Heretics, Black Prophets: Radical Political Intellectuals* (New York: Routledge, 2003), for an illuminating overview of some key figures from this international tradition.

Africans but also for their treatment of "the various Indian nations," thereby violating "the universal natural rights and privileges of all men," among whom "there are no inferior species, but all of one blood and of one nature"; David Walker directing his 1829 *Appeal* not just to his fellow black Americans but to "the coloured citizens of the world"; Pan-Africanist Martin Delany complaining in 1852 that though "there are two colored persons for each White man in the world ... the White race dominates the colored"; W. E. B. Du Bois describing at the 1900 Pan-African Conference the global problem of "the color line, the question as to how far differences of race ... are going to be made, hereafter, the basis of denying to over half the world the right of sharing to their utmost ability the opportunities and privileges of modern civilization," and in his famous 1903 *The Souls of Black Folk* predicting that "The problem of the twentieth century is the problem of the color-line, the relation of the darker to the lighter races of men in Asia and Africa, in America and the islands of the sea"; a judgment still being echoed more than half a century later by Frantz Fanon's 1961 *The Wretched of the Earth*: "It is evident that what parcels out the world is to begin with the fact of belonging to or not belonging to a given race."[5]

Admittedly, because blacks had to suffer racial slavery and its stig-matizing legacy as well as colonization, and because anti-black racism has historically been more virulent and more systematically and elabo-rately developed than any of the other varieties of colonial white racism (as against anti-Semitism), racial theorization has been more salient here than in any other anti-colonial/anti-imperialist tradition. A forced black diaspora, largely to the Americas but also to Europe, generated an oppositional body of political theory – recently denominated "Afro-modern political thought"[6] – for which race was the central organizing prism. But, it was not at all unique for the period, which is why I made a point of beginning with the Chinese nationalist rather than a black writer. The question then is whether it is worth trying to recuperate the insights of such a racially informed internationalism in a contemporary

---

[5] Quobna Ottobah Cugoano, *Thoughts and Sentiments on the Evil of Slavery and Other Writings*, ed. Vincent Carretta (New York: Penguin, 1999), 22, 28–29, 61; David Walker, *David Walker's Appeal: To the Colored Citizens of the World*, ed. Peter P. Hinks (University Park: Pennsylvania State University Press, 2000); Martin Robinson Delany, *The Condition, Elevation, Emigration and Destiny of the Colored People of the United States, Politically Considered* (Philadelphia, 1852); W. E. B. Du Bois, "To the Nations of the World" [1900], in David Levering Lewis (ed.), *W. E. B. Du Bois: A Reader* (New York: Henry Holt, 1995), 639; Du Bois, *The Souls of Black Folk* ([1903] New York: Penguin, 1996), 13; Frantz Fanon, *The Wretched of the Earth*, trans. Constance Farrington ([1961] New York: Grove Press, 1968), 40.
[6] Robert Gooding-Williams, *In the Shadow of Du Bois: Afro-Modern Political Thought in America* (Cambridge, MA: Harvard University Press, 2009).

context.[7] Would the formal thematic introduction of race add anything of value to the current debate, if so how, and by what means do we successfully negotiate the various conceptual and methodological hurdles on such a path?

Race (and Whiteness) as a Global Institution

The natural starting point is a clarification of the racial metaphysics presupposed by this framework. While skeptics may concede that racism was central to the ideological rationale for imperialism and colonialism, this concession will not generally be intended to imply the same for race. One is ideational, the other material. The understandable fear is that this vocabulary, this kind of discourse, cannot in fact be retrieved without a resurrection of Social Darwinist assumptions, or something similarly dubious. After all, it will be pointed out, it is no accident that these terms have disappeared from mainstream theory. Why try to revive a language that is surely no more than an "oppositional" version of classic racial theory, an "anti-racist racism" in Sartre's famous characterization of Negritude – motivationally perhaps perfectly understandable, but theoretically obviously problematic, a stage to be sublated and transcended? Moreover, how in any case could this vocabulary be applied on a global scale? So a series of refutations is constructed, what could be seen as concentric fallback positions: either race does not exist at all, or it does not exist globally, or it does not exist in the way necessary to sustain any generalizations and theorizations, descriptive and normative, of the desired kind.

Consider the first claim. In the philosophical circles where race is discussed, the key umbrella metaphysical positions are eliminativism and anti-eliminativism. Eliminativists, as the word implies, want to eliminate "race" from our vocabulary, as a nonreferring term like "witch" or "phlogiston."[8] They argue that science has disproved the reality of race and we should stop using a concept that is not only evidentially discredited, but one that has caused great harm historically. Anti-eliminativists disagree. Some contend that there is by no means a scientific consensus

---

[7] Ifeoma Kiddoe Nwankwo, *Black Cosmopolitanism: Racial Consciousness and Transnational Identity in the Nineteenth-Century Americas* (Philadelphia: University of Pennsylvania Press, 2005); Nico Slate, *Colored Cosmopolitanism: The Shared Struggle for Freedom in the United States and India* (Cambridge, MA: Harvard University Press, 2012); Babacar M'Baye, *Black Cosmopolitanism and Anticolonialism: Pivotal Moments* (New York: Routledge, 2018).

[8] The most prominent eliminativist among philosophers who have worked on race is Kwame Anthony Appiah (from whom the comparison to witches comes). See, for example, *In My Father's House: Africa in the Philosophy of Culture* (New York: Oxford University Press, 1992): "The truth is that there are no races" (40).

yet, and that recent research in population genetics and genetic clustering shows that we need to retain the concept, even if we reject the idea of racial hierarchy that is, of course, its most infamous and pernicious accompaniment. So for them reports of the demise of biological race are greatly exaggerated; racial realism (though without racial "superiority" and "inferiority") turns out to have been correct after all. However, the most important version of anti-eliminativism agrees with eliminativism that race does not exist biologically, but insists that it exists as a social construct. So, from this perspective, we need to retain the term to track social realities, both descriptive/explanatory (how particular social groups, "races," come into being and how a racialized society then works) and normative (issues of racial injustice).

In this framework, to say that race is constructed means that it is brought into existence as a social convention established by social mores, legal decisions, opportunity structures, discriminatory practices, the internalization by people of the racial norms and concepts accompanying these institutions and processes, and the corresponding habits of "self" and "other" categorization developed in everyday cognition and everyday interaction.[9] As this listing should have made clear, such a reconceptualization of race is quite anti-biologistic in its assumptions, so that it would be denied that the specter of classic racial theory is necessarily invoked by it. Indeed, the point of the "critical" in "critical philosophy of race" and "critical race theory" – apart from linking them with "critical theory" in the left tradition – is in part precisely to distinguish them from classic "[*uncritical*] race theory," which usually just meant racist theory. So, critical philosophy of race and critical race theory are explicitly anti-racist in their assumptions and their mission, and should not at all be seen as potentially assimilable to a nonwhite version of *Rassenwissenschaft*.[10]

Now, for the past few hundred years, whiteness has been the central racial category – the normative reference point, the default mode.[11] This is illustrated by the simple fact that it comes "naturally" to us (a social naturalness, to be sure) to speak of whites and nonwhites, and not, say, of

[9] Sally Haslanger, *Resisting Reality: Social Construction and Social Critique* (New York: Oxford University Press, 2012); Paul Taylor, *Race: A Philosophical Introduction*, 2nd edn. (Malden, MA: Polity, 2013).

[10] Charles W. Mills, "Critical Philosophy of Race," in Herman Cappelen, Tamar Szabó Gendler, and John Hawthorne (eds.), *The Oxford Handbook of Philosophical Methodology* (New York: Oxford University Press, 2016), 709–32. For critical race theory in legal theory specifically, see Kimberlé Crenshaw, Neil Gotanda, Gary Peller, and Kendall Thomas (eds.), *Critical Race Theory: The Key Writings That Formed the Movement* (New York: The New Press, 1995).

[11] Richard Dyer, *White*, 20th anniversary edition (New York: Routledge, 2017).

blacks and nonblacks, or to speak of whites and people of color, and not, say, of people of color and people of noncolor. But, whiteness is not natural, but, as with race in general, a social construct: hence such literature of recent years as *The History of White People, The Invention of the White Race, Whiteness of a Different Color, How the Irish Became White, How Jews Became White Folks and What That Says about Race in America, White on Arrival, White by Law, The Future of Whiteness,* and many others.[12] These books make it clear that whiteness as a social category is invented (it did not exist in the premodern world) and its boundaries and content are conventionally determined. But, this invention does not mean that it is *not* real; it is quite real in its social effects of privileging whites, disadvantaging people of color, shaping social opportunities, affecting public policy, determining life chances, impacting how nominally inclusive rights and freedoms are actually differentially operationalized, structuring moral consciousness and one's sense of identity, and so forth. As such, race could be seen not merely as *an* institution, but as an institution so important that it would arguably count as part of John Rawls's "basic structure" in its multidimensional social impact on the modern state.[13] The modern state in general, as David Theo Goldberg contends – and certainly the US state – is in fact a racial state.[14]

So, that would be the first hurdle cleared. The second is the objection that even if race is real, it could not be global in the appropriate way. After all, the texts cited above are all American, written by Americans and referring primarily to the United States. Michael Root has famously said that "Race does not travel." If race is a social construct, an artifact of convention, then surely there is going to be variation in the construction and the conventions from nation to nation, including the possibility that

[12] Nell Irvin Painter, *The History of White People* (New York: Norton, 2010); Theodore W. Allen, *The Invention of the White Race*, 2 vols., 2nd edn. (New York: Verso, 2012); Matthew Frye Jacobson, *Whiteness of a Different Color: European Immigrants and the Alchemy of Race* (Cambridge, MA: Harvard University Press, 1998); Noel Ignatiev, *How the Irish Became White* (New York: Routledge, 2008); Karen Brodkin, *How Jews Became White Folks and What That Says about Race in America* (New Brunswick, NJ: Rutgers University Press, 1998); Thomas Guglielmo, *White on Arrival: Italians, Race, Color, and Power in Chicago, 1890–1945* (New York: Oxford University Press, 2003); Ian F. Haney López, *White by Law: The Legal Construction of Race*, rev. 10th anniversary edn. (New York: New York University Press, 2006); Linda Martín Alcoff, *The Future of Whiteness* (Malden, MA: Polity, 2015).
[13] Rawls, *A Theory of Justice*, rev. edn. (Cambridge, MA: Harvard University Press, 1999).
[14] David Theo Goldberg, *The Racial State* (Malden, MA: Blackwell, 2002); Anthony W. Marx, *Making Race and Nation: A Comparison of the United States, South Africa, and Brazil* (New York: Cambridge University Press, 1998); Desmond King, *Separate and Unequal: African Americans and the U.S. Federal Government*, rev. edn. (New York: Oxford University Press, 2007); Moon-Kie Jung, João H. Costa Vargas, and Eduardo Bonilla-Silva (eds.), *State of White Supremacy* (Palo Alto, CA: Stanford University Press, 2011).

in some countries race will not exist at all. I am classified as black in the United States, for example, and duly fill in the appropriate box on bureaucratic forms, thereby counting as "African-American" for the census and the CUNY Graduate Center's faculty statistics. But, in my native Jamaica, I count as "brown" rather than black, not being dark enough, and as such I am fitted into the middle stratum of what was once, post-Emancipation, a three-tiered pyramid (white/brown/black).[15] So, could it not be argued that even if race is global (and there might be exceptions), it is a global patchwork of diverse and competing local systems rather than a planetarily uniform set of norms? And, as such, it would be claimed, it cannot play the kind of role this analysis is trying to impute to it.

But, though Root's aphorism does capture a constructionist truth, the reality of national variation, it is misleading insofar as it implies that there are *no* overarching commonalities. In both Jamaica and the United States, I will still be categorized as a person of color, someone not white, and as such on the "wrong" side of what is the central and most important global racial divide. And, though the borders of whiteness vary, white is a transnational category for the simple reason that it is established by European expansionism – European imperialism and European colonialism. As Howard Winant writes, the result of this process is an "immense planetary metamorphosis" that leads to the creation of a "world racial system."[16] So, while some people counted as white in some countries will not count as (fully?) white in others, it is generally the case across the planet that Europeans and their descendants are dominant, and that there is a "core" (roughly, northwestern Europeans) whiteness of people who are counted as whites pretty well everywhere.[17] Recently, theorists have begun trying to extend critical race theory and critical whiteness studies beyond US borders, with work being done on the Caribbean, Latin America, Canada, the UK, Europe, South Africa, and Australia, and as the body of such literature expands, we can expect more detailed and fine-grained case studies of race and

---

[15] M. G. Smith, *The Plural Society in the British West Indies* ([1965] Berkeley: University of California Press, 1984).
[16] Howard Winant, *The World Is a Ghetto: Race and Democracy Since World War II* (New York: Basic Books, 2001), 21, 3.
[17] However, with specific reference to the United States, though perhaps with more general applicability, Thomas Guglielmo has argued that the "ethnic" European immigrants (Jews, Irish, Italians) some have claimed to be originally (late nineteenth century/early twentieth century) nonwhite in the USA *were* actually categorized as whites, but inferior ones. In other words, "whiteness" in the period was not a monolith but itself a hierarchically structured category. Nonetheless, even inferior whites were superior to people of color: Guglielmo, *White on Arrival*.

whiteness across the world that both address such variations and point out the commonalities.[18]

Finally, to the objection that a global whiteness, even if it existed, could have no explanatory power, bear in mind that in the modern period this category becomes, as emphasized, one of the most central markers of social privilege. It is a matter neither of an accidental and causally otiose correlation, like foot size, nor of a biologically driven *Rassenkampf*, with all the unhappy historical associations such a term will evoke. It is a matter of people being categorized in a certain way, internalizing that categorization, growing up in a world structured around such categories, *and leading lives in the light of that ascribed empowering identity* (with its distinctive motivational and belief sets).

In my own work over the past twenty-plus years, I have used the phrase "global white supremacy," which to many will seem like a clearly extremist and indefensible concept.[19] But, imagine we jump in the time machine and set the controls for a trip of a century backward. Emerging in 1919, what will we find? We will find a world recovering from the horrors of World War I, which is completely dominated by the colonial empires: British, French, Dutch, Belgian, German, Portuguese, Russian. By Edward Said's estimate, 85 percent of the earth at the time is under some kind of control by the European powers, white European nations ruling over nonwhite nations.[20] (China is not formally colonized, but – recall the opening passage from Sun Yat-sen – it is under European hegemony.) Moreover, in independent countries like the Anglo white settler states – the USA, Canada, South Africa, Australia, and New Zealand – it is again whites who are the dominant group, with widespread formal and informal discrimination against aboriginal peoples and (where they exist) the descendants of black slaves being the norm. In the Latin American nations that gained their independence in the nineteenth century, whites and the light-skinned are, contra the myths of "racial

---

[18] See, for example: Steve Garner, *Whiteness: An Introduction* (New York: Routledge, 2007); Jane Carey and Claire McLisky (eds.), *Creating White Australia* (Sydney: Sydney University Press, 2009); Rachel Sarah O'Toole, *Bound Lives: Africans, Indians, and the Making of Race in Colonial Peru* (Pittsburgh: University of Pittsburgh Press, 2012); Michael McEachran (ed.), *Afro-Nordic Landscapes: Equality and Race in Northern Europe* (New York: Routledge, 2014); Veronica Watson, Deirdre Howard-Wagner, and Lisa Spanierman (eds.), *Unveiling Whiteness in the Twenty-First Century: Global Manifestations, Transdisciplinary Interventions* (Lanham, MD: Rowman & Littlefield, 2015); Crystal Marie Fleming, *Resurrecting Slavery: Racial Legacies and White Supremacy in France* (Philadelphia: Temple University Press, 2017); Jennifer Roth-Gordon, *Race and the Brazilian Body: Blackness, Whiteness, and Everyday Language in Rio de Janeiro* (Oakland: University of California Press, 2017).

[19] Mills, *The Racial Contract* (Ithaca, NY: Cornell University Press, 1997).

[20] Said, *Culture and Imperialism* (New York: Knopf, 1993), 8.

democracy" and an all-inclusive *mestizaje*, economically, socially, politically, and culturally privileged over the darker and the indigenous: political *pigmentocracy* in the classic formulation.[21] In sum, across most of the globe, whites are the rulers, both internationally and nationally. The few independent nations of color – black nations like Haiti and Ethiopia, the Asian nation of Japan – all have to operate within a white-dominated world and are all constrained by its norms and power relationships.

None of these facts is novel; they can be found in any objective history book. What is lacking is the theoretical will to recognize their implications, the refusal to put them together into a composite picture. It might also be objected that "global white supremacy" implies a single coordinating and governing body, say a White House that is not American but globally empowered and authoritative. But, a planet dominated by sub-planetary political entities that are themselves white-ruled is still, though polycentric, white-ruled overall, even if there is no white world state as such. So, even if these nations and colonial systems were largely siloed from one another, the characterization of a global white supremacy would still be accurate. But, in fact, the case for the concept is made even stronger once one takes into account the actual patterns of international relations and communications. For, though there is no centralized planetary seat of formal white governing power, though whites the world over are divided by national membership, citizens of countries and empires sometimes in conflict with each other, and internally divided by class and gender, there are nonetheless binding transoceanic and transsocietal links. Racial ideologies circulate globally, assumptions of nonwhite inferiority and the legitimacy of white rule are taken for granted, a shared colonial history of pacts, treaties, international jurisprudence, and a racial-religious self-conception of being the bearers and preservers of civilization provide common norms and reference points. Across the world, white elites coordinate and share information on particular racial issues and follow prescriptions of international law predicated on differential white entitlements. Indeed, had our time-travelling educational mission taken us to Paris, to the post-World War I 1919 Versailles Conference, we would have been able to witness a dramatic illustration of this coordination: the vetoing by the six "Anglo-Saxon" nations, as they were then called – the UK, the USA, Canada, South Africa, Australia, and New Zealand – of the Japanese delegation's proposal to insert

---

[21] George Reid Andrews, *Afro-Latin America, 1800–2000* (New York: Oxford University Press, 2004); Edward E. Telles, *Pigmentocracies: Ethnicity, Race, and Color in Latin America* (Chapel Hill: University of North Carolina Press, 2014); Juliet Hooker, *Theorizing Race in the Americas: Douglass, Sarmiento, Du Bois, and Vasconcelos* (New York: Oxford University Press, 2017).

a "racial equality" clause into the League of Nations Covenant.[22] In a world structured by material and normative racial inequality, by white-over-nonwhite domination, such an idea was clearly unthinkable. So, the "whiteness" of Europeans in Europe and their Euro-created world is not at all causally irrelevant, but shapes their conception of themselves and others, their view of their group interests, their collective and individual identities, and the political and moral framework within which they understand the world. As Branwen Gruffydd Jones comments: "The belief in a hierarchy of peoples – in the superiority of Europeans or people with European ancestry and the inferiority of non-Europeans or 'people of color' – was widespread and routine, a generally unquestioned assumption embedded both in the public and personal European imagination and in the formal institutions of European and international order."[23]

So, I would suggest that the concept implicit or explicit in the excerpts cited at the start from Sun Yat-sen, Walker, Delany, Du Bois, and Fanon – the concept of a white supremacy that is global – that when first encountered may seem obviously problematic, is actually theoretically quite defensible. And, in fact it *is* now being used by some historians and "radical" International Relations (IR) theorists to characterize the period. Thus, historian Martin Borstelmann refers to "the era of global white supremacy," "the international character of white rule over people of color": "Continuing differences in the racial distribution of power and wealth confirm the ongoing relevance of this theme to contemporary international history."[24] Similarly, two Australian historians, Marilyn Lake and Henry Reynolds, have published a book whose title pays tribute to Du Bois: *Drawing the Global Colour Line: White Men's Countries and the International Challenge of Racial Equality.* They describe "the spread of 'whiteness' as a transnational form of racial identification," "the basis of geo-political alliances and a subjective sense of self," and comment critically on Benedict Anderson's well-known *Imagined Communities*: "Paradoxically, one outcome of Anderson's argument has been to naturalize the nation as *the* imagined community of modern times, an effect that has obscured the ascendancy of transnational racial identifications and their potency in shaping both personal identity and global politics."[25]

---

[22] Marilyn Lake and Henry Reynolds, *Drawing the Global Colour Line: White Men's Countries and the International Challenge of Racial Equality* (New York: Cambridge University Press, 2008), ch. 12.

[23] Gruffydd Jones, "Introduction," in Gruffydd Jones (ed.), *Decolonizing International Relations* (Lanham, MD: Rowman & Littlefield, 2006).

[24] Borstelmann, *The Cold War and the Color Line: American Race Relations in the Global Arena* (Cambridge, MA: Harvard University Press, 2001), 15, 6.

[25] Lake and Reynolds, *Drawing the Global Colour Line*, 3, 6.

Likewise, one chapter of the Italian philosopher Domenico Losurdo's *Liberalism: A Counter-History* is titled "The West and the Barbarians: A 'Master-Race Democracy' on a Planetary Scale."[26] And, Robert Vitalis's recent *White World Order, Black Power Politics* begins, as his title declares, with the judgment that in the time period in question "international relations meant race relations," on a planet characterized by "the world hegemony of whites."[27]

In effect, then, these contemporary scholars are *recovering* a concept that was quite obvious and uncontroversial to theorists and activists of color of the period, but that seems strange to us *now* because of the efficiency of the postwar West's erasure of the centrality of race to its rule. Writing specifically about the "Anglosphere" (that for me would be a subsystem, even if the most important one, of the larger global racial system), Srdjan Vucetic points out that "[i]n an effort to forget its racist past, IR turned race into a 'taboo'."[28] But, the reality is that "the origins of [the] Anglosphere are racial," "a hierarchy made up of the core and mostly white Self on the one hand and on the other the peripheral and overwhelmingly nonwhite Other."[29] Similarly, Sankaran Krishna argues that "the discipline of International Relations (IR) was and is predicated on a systematic politics of forgetting, a willful amnesia, on the question of race."[30] Embarrassed both by the death camps' demonstration of where the logic of racism leads – even Europeans could be subjected to mass murder – and by a colonial discourse no longer appropriate for a postcolonial world (if only nominally), the West has sought to white-out the multiple ways race and racial ideology underpinned its global domination. But, we need to recover this past both so as better to understand it and to enable us to dismantle the legacy it has left behind. Suitably reconceptualized, race is necessary for such a revisionist theorization and intended egalitarian transformation.

Liberalism and Race

Facing rather than evading this history thus requires that we confront how liberalism has been shaped by race. For, with the seeming demise of

---

[26] Losurdo, *Liberalism: A Counter-History*, trans. Gregory Elliott (New York: Verso, 2011), ch. 7.
[27] Vitalis, *White World Order, Black Power Politics: The Birth of American International Relations* (Ithaca, NY: Cornell University Press, 2015), 1.
[28] Vucetic, *The Anglosphere: A Genealogy of a Racialized Identity in International Relations* (Palo Alto, CA: Stanford University Press, 2011), 7.
[29] Vucetic, *The Anglosphere*, 3, 6.
[30] Krishna, "Race, Amnesia, and the Education of International Relations," in Gruffydd Jones (ed.), *Decolonizing International Relations*, 89.

Marxism, liberalism – though admittedly now under challenge by authoritarian ethno-nationalism – is now, or at least has been until recently, the
globally dominant political ideology. As such, it constitutes an ethico-
juridical set of concepts, norms and principles, underlying assumptions
and overarching narratives, which will necessarily be a central reference
point for debate, whether as an accepted framework or one to be challenged, modified, and built upon. And, at least until recent decades,
liberalism has sanitized its racial past. Even now, the accounts standardly
given in political philosophy textbooks and encyclopedia summaries are
whitewashed versions of the reality. (I emphasize political *philosophy*
because far greater progress has been made in political theory.) These
accounts usually center on Europe and focus on the white male population, telling an inspirational Whig narrative of the triumph of moral
egalitarianism over ascriptive hierarchy, of John Locke's victory over Sir
Robert Filmer. But, once this tale is set in a global context, and the focus
broadened to include white women and people of color (i.e., the majority
of the world's population), it will be appreciated that the actual story is
very different. As Duncan Ivison, Paul Patton, and Will Sanders pointed
out two decades ago:

Contemporary political theory has much to learn from the encounter with its
colonial past. ... [D]ifferent strands of western political thought have not only
been complicit with, but helped to justify, colonial expansion and imperial control
over indigenous peoples and their territories. As much as modern political theory,
especially in its liberal and social democratic variants, has emphasized universal
human rights, equality before the law and individual and collective freedom, it has
also explicitly denied such entitlements to indigenous peoples. ... As a result,
egalitarian political theory has often ended up justifying explicitly inegalitarian
institutions and practices.[31]

And, race has provided the theoretical and normative rationale for reconciling egalitarianism and inegalitarianism, differentiating the human
population into those deserving and those undeserving of equal treat-
ment. In such works as Barbara Arneil's *John Locke and America*, Uday
Singh Mehta's *Liberalism and Empire*, Duncan Ivison's *Postcolonial
Liberalism*, Jennifer Pitts's *A Turn to Empire*, James Tully's *Imperialism
and Civic Freedom*, Thomas McCarthy's *Race, Empire, and the Idea of
Human Development*, John Hobson's *The Eurocentric Conception of World
Politics*, Alexander Anievas et al.'s *Race and Racism in International
Relations*, Duncan Bell's *Reordering the World: Essays on Liberalism and*

---

[31] Ivison, Patton, and Sanders, "Introduction," in Ivison, Patton, and Sanders (eds.),
Political Theory and the Rights of Indigenous Peoples (New York: Cambridge University
Press, 2000), 1–2.

Empire, and others, we have traced for us the contours of what Pitts usefully calls an "imperial liberalism," in which it is not merely that pejorative characterizations of Native Americans and Native Australians, Africans and Asians, are routine, but in which the key concepts of liberalism *as a theory* are shaped by this imperial logic.[32] The latter is, of course, the really interesting theoretical point, since obviously contemporary white liberals will be emphatic about their repudiation of any demeaning representations of non-European peoples to be found in the tradition's classic writings. But, the question is whether such excisions are sufficient to address possibly deeper structural biases in terms of crucial assumptions, framings, norms, and narratives. If liberalism is to be salvaged, if we want to develop an anti-imperial liberalism, such as Pitts claims can be found in many theorists in the tradition before the development of empire, an *Enlightenment against Empire,*[33] in Sankar Muthu's titular phrase, or a "decolonial liberalism" (Ivison), how can this best be done? In political theory, as noted above, there is already a significant body of work seeking to address this question by engaging nuts-and-bolts issues of constitutional reform and indigenous autonomy. But, what might the distinctive contribution at the more abstract level of political philosophy be, in terms of the kind of descriptive and normative theory that is its specialization?

I suggest that the feminist example on gender could be illuminating as a model to be followed for race. Second-wave feminist philosophers, faced with the task of advancing a feminist agenda in a theoretical and conceptual universe dominated by male frameworks, took various approaches. One was to repudiate liberalism (and Marxism, at a time when Marxism was still seen as a viable contender) in the name of a distinctive, radically new theory that (putatively) owed nothing to "masculinist" thought in any form. But, another approach was to argue that liberalism's key assumptions and values were not intrinsically

---

[32] Arneil, *John Locke and America: The Defence of English Colonialism* (Oxford: Clarendon Press, 1996); Mehta, *Liberalism and Empire: A Study in Nineteenth-Century British Liberal Thought* (Chicago: University of Chicago Press, 1999); Ivison, *Postcolonial Liberalism* (New York: Cambridge University Press, 2002); Pitts, *A Turn to Empire: The Rise of Imperial Liberalism in Britain and France* (Princeton, NJ: Princeton University Press, 2005); Tully, *Public Philosophy in a New Key, vol. II: Imperialism and Civic Freedom* (New York: Cambridge University Press, 2008); McCarthy, *Race, Empire, and the Idea of Human Development* (New York: Cambridge University Press, 2009); Hobson, *The Eurocentric Conception of World Politics: Western International Theory, 1760–2010* (New York: Cambridge University Press, 2012); Anievas, Nivi Manchanda, and Robbie Shilliam (eds.), *Race and Racism in International Relations: Confronting the Global Colour Line* (New York: Routledge, 2015); Bell, *Reordering the World: Essays on Liberalism and Empire* (Princeton, NJ: Princeton University Press, 2016).

[33] Muthu, *Enlightenment against Empire* (Princeton, NJ: Princeton University Press, 2003).

problematic, but needed to be rethought in the light of its sexist exclusions. So, as Susan Moller Okin pointed out long ago, it was not just a matter of conscientiously using "person" or sometimes even "woman" as the generic human representative, but of reconceptualizing the theory from the ground up.[34] One asked oneself the question: how, counterfactually, would liberalism have developed had its leading thinkers not taken female subordination for granted? What kind of liberalism would one get if the public/private divide had not been drawn in such a way as to exclude women from political life and social justice? How would a theory nominally predicated on the need to safeguard the rights and freedoms of all individuals have to be reconstructed if half of those individuals had not been positioned, by virtue of their sex, as superior to the other half, and had this not been embedded in conceptual framings, normative orientation, and value development?

So, rather than regarding this body of thought as *liberalism* simpliciter, one framed it self-consciously as *patriarchal liberalism*, and then tried to go beyond its epistemic horizon, in keeping with the critical theory tradition (originally applied just to class society) that the ideological effects of systems of domination are best analyzed and corrected for by reconstructing how the material functioning of the system produces and reproduces them. Thomas McCarthy writes in general of critical theory's strategy that it

contains elements of immanent, transcendent, and genealogical critique: "immanent" in that it starts from values, ideas, and principles embedded in the cultures and societies it analyzes; (context-) "transcendent" in that it reconstructs these values, ideals, and principles in terms of a general, discourse-ethical account of practical reasoning; and "genealogical" in that it is self-reflectively metacritical of the historical and contemporary forms of existing reason that it seeks to reconstruct as critical resources.[35]

The key point, then, is that one examines hegemonic concepts and norms from a critical perspective predicated on the assumption that they will have been shaped by social domination, and so need either to be reconstructed in more acceptable forms, or rejected outright, by the standards of the superior social mapping and egalitarian norms of an order without such domination. Class society and class theory historically played this role for Marxism and subsequent critical theory; patriarchy and gender theory have more recently played this role for feminism. And, what I am suggesting is that global white supremacy and critical race theory can and should play a similar role for anti-racism. Pitts's "imperial liberalism"

---

[34] Okin, *Justice, Gender, and the Family* (New York: Basic Books, 1989).
[35] McCarthy, *Race, Empire*, 14 n.26.

can, I propose, be more broadly formulated as "racial liberalism" (thereby conceptually uniting inter- and intra-national racial domination).[36] Reconceptualizing liberalism this way would, I believe, have several virtues:

(i) It would make clear what I have suggested has tended to be buried in postwar political philosophy, the intimate historical connection between liberalism and race. The study of the racial shaping of the thought of many, if not most, of the central figures of the modern Western canon could thus become a legitimate research area within the field rather than an offhand concession marginalized to the realm (if that much) of occasional footnotes. We would then have a more comprehensive and holistic picture of the tradition, one not sanitized for reasons of political expediency. In addition, it would highlight the link between imperial expansion and the creation of racial polities both in the former First World and the former Third World nations, preempting the psychologizing of racism which has been the liberal norm since the aftermath of World War II. Continuing racial subordination would be conceptualized, as it should be, as a matter of political economy, with racism as its ideology. Whether as one strain of (in Rogers Smith's formulation) "multiple traditions" in American national political culture (and elsewhere too, I would claim) or as "symbiotic" with liberalism (my own preferred analysis), racial discourse would be given the theoretical centrality to moral and political philosophy it deserves.[37]

(ii) Correspondingly, it would open the conceptual door for the admission to the canon of thinkers in the black, anti-colonial, and Third World traditions of political philosophy, whose central focus historically was, of course, white racism and European domination. In other words, the construction of "Western" political philosophy as raceless has the ideological consequence not merely of misrepresenting its own actual past, but of erecting a convenient *cordon sanitaire* between it and the oppositional anti-racist tradition of people of color. A political theorist of the stature of W. E. B. Du Bois, for example, can be excluded from the canon because his work is preoccupied with the issue of racial subordination and how to overcome it. And, since racial subordination is not recognized *as* political (or even as existent), his writings – "Afro-modern political

---

[36] Charles W. Mills, *Black Rights/White Wrongs: The Critique of Racial Liberalism* (New York: Oxford University Press, 2017).

[37] Smith, *Civic Ideals: Conflicting Visions of Citizenship in US History* (New Haven, CT: Yale University Press, 1997); Mills, *Black Rights/White Wrongs*.

thought" – cannot be political philosophy.[38] Thus, we get the absurd situation of a white tradition representing itself as colorless and separate from the black tradition when it is *precisely because of its historically exclusionary racist whiteness* that the oppositional black tradition has had to come into existence in the first place! And, given the planetary reach of the West, a case can obviously be made that globalization *avant la lettre* suggests the need for a redrawing of how the political thought of the nationals of non-Western nations should be categorized also, when we seek to demarcate the boundaries of "Western" political philosophy.

(iii) Finally, it would help to end the ghettoization of contemporary political philosophers who work on race, who are currently regarded as pursuing an idiosyncratic agenda, marginal to the mainstream of the profession. Critical philosophy of race would not be viewed as a field unto itself, a self-created intellectual ghetto sharply conceptually separated from both the (by implication raceless) mainstream political philosophy literature and the global justice literature, but as offering a distinct perspective on that subject matter that needs to be engaged with. Through such a desegregation of intellectual worlds – a desegregation of both key thinkers and key themes – the conceptual space would then be opened up for a rethinking of descriptive and normative political philosophy in the light of this unacknowledged history: Locke's self-owning appropriators confronted with the non-self-owning Frederick Douglass; Kant's cosmopolitanism in critical dialogue with Edward Said's; Hegel's World-Spirit challenged by Du Bois's indictment of global whiteness. Personhood, rights, freedoms, democracy, recognition, autonomy, property, self-ownership, respect for self and others, civilization, the nation-state, the social contract, the ambit of justice – how might all of these have to be rethought once the history of imperialism and colonialism is taken into account, and its influence on the shaping of all of these concepts made the subject of philosophical investigation?

Race and the Rethinking of Justice

Let us turn now to justice, and racial justice. There is a remarkable disjuncture – indeed a chasm – between the *professional* literature on justice produced by philosophers and the *popular* discussions of the subject, both in the United States, and – at least historically (as pointed out in

---

[38] Gooding-Williams, *Shadow of Du Bois*, and, more recently, Nick Bromell (ed.), *A Political Companion to W. E. B. Du Bois* (Lexington: University Press of Kentucky, 2018).

my opening pages) – globally. *Racial justice* is one of the main banners under which the American civil rights movement and to a significant extent the global anti-colonial movement (that Martin Borstelmann characterizes as "the international civil rights movement") marched.[39] Yet, in the tremendous revival of Anglo-American political philosophy over the past fifty years stimulated by John Rawls's 1971 *A Theory of Justice*, it is a phrase and a topic that is virtually completely absent (see Katrina Forrester's chapter in this book for further discussion). Whether directed at national or planetary justice, this huge body of work has almost nothing to say about racial justice. In such authoritative reference works of the last decade and a half as Samuel Freeman's edited *Cambridge Companion to Rawls* (2003), his own exhaustively expository *Rawls* (2007), Jon Mandle's *Rawls's* A Theory of Justice: *An Introduction* (2009), Percy B. Lehning's *John Rawls: An Introduction* (2009), Sebastiano Maffetone's *Rawls: An Introduction* (2010), and Jon Mandle and David Reidy's huge, nearly 600-page coedited *Companion to Rawls* (2014), for example, one finds at best isolated sentences or paragraphs referring to racial discrimination, never any detailed exploration of its implications for racial justice.[40]

What explains this silence? In my opinion, a confluence of factors is at work. First, there is the demographic whiteness of the profession: about 97 percent in the United States, almost 100 percent in the United Kingdom. Insofar as, even within a subject as abstract as philosophy, group experience and group privilege play a role in influencing concerns and interests, we would expect that those who have historically been the beneficiaries of racial injustice would tend to have less interest in exploring the topic than those who have been its victims. (Again, the feminist analogy is illuminating: compare the nondiscussion of gender justice as a topic in philosophy over the 2,500-year period before the gradual influx of women into the profession from the 1970s onward.) Second, there is the whiteness of the tradition itself – the fact that race has not until recent decades generally been an issue critically examined within white philosophy (as against uncritically endorsed in racist statements by white philosophers).[41] Third, as mentioned at the start, it might be felt (now)

[39] Borstelmann, *Cold War*, 46.
[40] Freeman (ed.), *The Cambridge Companion to Rawls* (New York: Cambridge University Press, 2003); Freeman, *Rawls* (New York: Routledge, 2007); Mandle, *Rawls's* A Theory of Justice: *An Introduction* (New York: Cambridge University Press, 2009); Lehning, *John Rawls: An Introduction* (New York: Cambridge University Press, 2009); Maffetone, *Rawls: An Introduction* (Malden, MA: Polity, 2010); Mandle and Reidy (eds.), *A Companion to Rawls* (Malden, MA: Wiley Blackwell, 2014).
[41] Andrew Valls (ed.), *Race and Racism in Modern Philosophy* (Ithaca, NY: Cornell University Press, 2005).

that race is not really a respectable category, and that racial justice can be subsumed into other kinds of justice, so that in any case it is really redundant. Fourth, we have the problem – not peculiar to philosophy, but exacerbated here because of its disciplinary abstraction away from the empirical – of the general sanitization of the racist historical record, again at least until comparatively recently, by the academies of the European colonial powers and their offshoots, such as the United States. With a few honorable exceptions, it has been a history of whitewash – a past of racial atrocity now embarrassing, that needs to be denied or downplayed. Finally, I would suggest that the overwhelming orientation of the field toward what Rawls famously called "ideal theory," the theory of distributive justice appropriate for a "perfectly just society," has itself been a major contributor to this outcome. Not only did it postpone matters of nonideal theory, preeminently matters of compensatory justice, to such time (ever-receding over the horizon) as ideal theory would have been properly worked out, but – as a number of chapters in this volume emphasize – it marginalized as a peripheral concern the historically accurate mapping of the past with which compensatory justice is definitionally concerned. Ideal theory would turn out to have deleterious effects not merely normatively but, as Onora O'Neill has pointed out, descriptively, in terms of the conceptualizations typically deployed of society and the polity, which have generally abstracted away from real-life, nonideal structures of oppression.[42]

How do we redress this situation? In her *Scales of Justice*, Nancy Fraser argues that the "framing" of justice needs to be self-consciously rethought in a world where "transnational social movements contest the national frame within which justice conflicts have historically been situated and seek to re-map the bounds of justice on a broader scale," one that challenges "the Westphalian mapping of political space," that is, "political communities as geographically bounded units, demarcated by sharply drawn borders and arrayed side by side."[43] As indicated at the start of the chapter, such a mapping was always put into question by the international anti-colonial movement, which saw European domination and white racial hegemony as global. More recently, the question of what justice demands to repair the legacy of the colonial history has explicitly been raised by nations of the Global South. The marginality of such concerns in the mainstream justice literature can illuminatingly be thought of as manifestations of a particular frame, what Joe Feagin calls

[42] O'Neill, "Justice, Gender, and International Boundaries," in Martha C. Nussbaum and Amartya Sen (eds.), *The Quality of Life* (New York: The Clarendon Press, 1993).
[43] Fraser, *Scales of Justice: Reimagining Political Space in a Globalizing World* (New York: Columbia University Press, 2009), 1, 4.

the "white racial frame," which has been so influential in shaping white cognition over the past few hundred years that even – or should I say *especially* – normative theory has been affected by it.[44] As feminist liberals trying to reclaim rather than repudiate liberalism have sought to rethink patriarchal liberalism so as to purge it of a masculinist bias that runs far deeper than overtly stigmatizing representations of women, so too, I would suggest, we need to rethink and decolonize imperial liberalism, racial liberalism, so as to eliminate its distinctive *white* bias.[45]

(i) The first step, in my opinion, should be explicitly to shift from ideal to nonideal theory. While a growing body of recent work has questioned the utility of Rawlsian ideal theory, the specific problems posed by race have still not been addressed.[46] But, racial justice is, almost by definition, a matter of nonideal theory. This follows because – if social constructionism is correct – *races would not even exist in an ideal society.*[47] We would still have human beings of different skin colors, hair textures, and facial morphologies, but in the absence of racially discriminatory (nonideal) social practices and institutions they would not constitute significant social existents. (Arguably, this is true even if the biologically realist position is vindicated.) So the "whiteness" of ideal theory is manifest not merely in an epistemology that draws a curtain over the past and focuses instead on the depiction of an ideally just order that supposedly has the potential for addressing everybody's concerns, transracially, but in its very metaphysics, in that a Rawlsian well-ordered society would be raceless. Either races would not exist at all or even if they had a "minimal" biological existence, they would have no significant socially shaping presence.[48] And, even if racelessness can arguably constitute a normative target for us, an ideal to be aimed at, a society where race has been created and then dismantled through the appropriate public policy measures is not the moral equivalent of a society where

---

[44] Feagin, *The White Racial Frame: Centuries of Racial Framing and Counter-Framing*, 2nd edn. (New York: Routledge, 2013).

[45] Charles W. Mills, "Decolonizing Western Political Philosophy," *New Political Science* 37/ 1 (2015), 1–24.

[46] Ingrid Robeyns and Adam Swift (eds.), *Social Theory and Practice* 34/3 (2008), Special Issue: Social Justice: Ideal Theory, Nonideal Circumstances; A. John Simmons, "Ideal and Nonideal Theory," *Philosophy & Public Affairs* 38/1 (2010), 5–36; Zofia Stemplowska and Adam Swift, "Rawls on Ideal and Nonideal Theory," in Mandle and Reidy (ed.), *Companion to Rawls*.

[47] But, for a challenging critique of my line of argument here, see D. C. Matthew, "Rawls and Racial Justice," *Politics, Philosophy & Economics*, 16/3 (2017), 235–58.

[48] Michael O. Hardimon's recent book, for example, distinguishes between "minimal" race (biological) and "social" race: *Rethinking Race: The Case for Deflationary Realism* (Cambridge, MA: Harvard University Press, 2017).

race never came into existence in the first place. So, the principles of justice necessary for bringing about the former will in key respects be different from Rawlsian principles, since they will be predicated on the need to correct past oppression, whereas Rawls's principles are not.[49]

Racial justice should then be thought of as a concept for the realm of nonideal theory, meant to complement rather than substitute for work such as Thomas Pogge's moral indictment of past Western colonialism and imperialism, and present Western global institutional domination.[50] *Racial justice* is a heuristically useful category because, to a high degree, it tracks the legacy of the unfair global racial structure, established by colonialism and imperialism, white settlement and African slavery, that tendentially privileges whites globally, and that needs to be "repaired." As Thomas McCarthy writes:

[S]ince the most developed countries are disproportionately former colonial powers, and the least developed are former colonies, the neoimperial system of domination and exploitation appears to be, in some considerable measure, a legacy of the five preceding centuries of colonialism and imperialism in their classical modern forms. If this is so, the present requirements of global justice include not only establishing relations of non-domination and fair terms of exchange but also, and interdependently, repairing the harmful effects of past injustice. ... Coming to terms with this past of racial and imperial injustice, and seeking to remedy the continuing harms that resulted from it are demands of reparative justice.[51]

"Race," in other words, tracks unfair advantage and disadvantage. Whites as a group have more wealth, more status, more political and cultural influence. This edge is not the result of differential innate ability, or a greater degree of industriousness, but is the outcome of several hundred years of transnational as well as intra-national (in the white settler states, for example) exploitation, manifest both in greater resources for whites as a racial group (that would advantage them in itself) and national and transnational structures that favor whites locally and the European and Euro-settler states globally. This is not a claim about individual racism, though it would also be naïve to think we are living in a post-racial epoch. Rather, it is a claim about *the social-systemic reproduction of unfair white advantage.* Race cannot subsume other categories of justice because other metrics of social oppression exist also (class, gender). But,

[49] Mills, *Black Rights/White Wrongs*, epilogue, and also "Racial Equality," in George Hull (ed.), *The Equal Society: Essays on Equality in Theory and Practice* (Lanham, MD: Rowman & Littlefield, 2015).
[50] Pogge, *World Poverty and Human Rights: Cosmopolitan Responsibilities and Reforms*, 2nd edn. (Malden, MA: Polity, 2008).
[51] McCarthy, *Race, Empire, and the Idea of Human Development*, 4, 17.

neither is it the case that these other metrics can subsume race without theoretical residue, because of racial differentiation in the causal chains accounting for poverty among whites and nonwhites, distinct dimensions to racial injustice that are absent from class injustice, and a radically divergent history that violates the norms even of right-wing liberalism, thus making possible a normative strategy that need not rely on social-democratic values.

(ii) The conceptual shift from distributive to corrective justice, from the distributive norms of a well-ordered society to the rectificatory norms appropriate for an ill-ordered society, is thus crucial, and can, in my opinion, be seen as roughly the equivalent for race theory of the feminist challenge to the drawing of the public/private demarcation for gender theory. The key insight of second-wave feminism was that the way the private sphere was demarcated from the public sphere was theoretically pivotal, since gender justice as a normative issue was then conceptually obfuscated. Injustice happened in the public sphere, the state, and the marketplace, not in the family and the household, which were beyond justice.[52] Here the approximate homologue is the realization that what Rawls calls "compensatory justice" cannot, for race, be achieved within his conceptual framework, and that ideal theory, rather than providing the best theoretical foundation upon which to do nonideal theory adequately, as Rawls claimed, actually obstructs its mission. So, the very orientation towards ideal theory has not merely left these issues *contingently* unaddressed (that is, white philosophers have not as a matter of fact chosen to address them), but *structurally unaddressable* (that is, the apparatus itself, unmodified and unsupplemented, is inimical to carrying out this normative agenda). If we are directed by Rawls to think of society as "a cooperative venture for mutual advantage," whose rules are "designed to advance the good of those taking part in it,"[53] and never offered any complementary theorization of "noncooperative," oppressive societies (aka, "the world"), how can systemic structural injustice even be understood, let alone theorized and remedied?

The introduction of racial justice as a theme and imperative in both the domestic and the global justice literature would thus have the virtue of making clear that what is demanded is a correction of past wrongs, thereby forcing on to the table an accounting of those wrongs. Moreover, a reparative normative project has traditionally been seen as more urgent in ethical theory, since it is obligatory for all liberals to

---

[52] Okin, *Justice, Gender, and the Family*.   [53] Rawls, *Theory of Justice*, 4.

correct violations of negative rights, whereas poverty relief is too easily pushed over the moral border into the realm of the supererogatory, praiseworthy but not (for right-wing liberals) required of us. Rectificatory justice might thus generate a higher degree of convergence between rival theoretical positions than distributive justice – think of the huge differences between egalitarians, modified Rawlsians, libertarians, adequacy theorists, and cosmopolitans on what the latter requires of us. As Daniel Butt points out in his book, *Rectifying International Injustice*:

> It is hard to maintain that there is a great deal of real world support for redistributive cosmopolitanism. ... Given the apparent lack of public support for global egalitarianism ... it may well be that the best political strategy for those who support extensive redistribution is not to seek to challenge the deeply held foundational principles of real world political actors, but to maintain that these very principles, if properly understood, call for a substantial [global] redistribution of resources. ... [Accordingly, the] account of harm given in this book ... draws upon paradigm cases of unjust international interaction.[54]

More recently, Göran Collste's *Global Rectificatory Justice* begins similarly by pointing out that although "[t]he discussion on global justice is vibrant and expanding," it has completely ignored rectificatory justice, despite the fact that "[t]he present global order ... mirrors colonialism in many respects."[55] Insofar as even right-wing liberals presumably oppose (as good liberals) racism and unjust enrichment, they should be able to agree that the victims of racial injustice deserve compensation for the past. (Admittedly, the picture is more complicated than I am representing it here, since there can be value-convergence across the spectrum of views on anti-discrimination principles, but radical *factual* divergence on what that history is, and whether it can truly be claimed that the situation of the less developed nations today, or of, say, blacks in the United States, results from this history. The political right will have competing narratives of their own to offer.)[56]

But, apart from this strategic point, there is also, more importantly, a principled point. Simply put, justice, and morality in general, requires that moral actions be carried out under a certain description for them to

---

[54] Butt, *Rectifying International Injustice: Principles of Compensation and Restitution Between Nations* (New York: Oxford University Press, 2009), 13, 14, 16.

[55] Collste, *Global Rectificatory Justice* (New York: Palgrave, 2015), 1. See also Federico Lenzerini (ed.), *Reparations for Indigenous Peoples: International and Comparative Perspectives* (New York: Oxford University Press, 2008) and Fernne Brennan and John Packer (eds.), *Colonialism, Slavery, Reparations and Trade: Remedying the Past?* (New York: Routledge, 2012).

[56] See, for example, the controversy over Bruce Gilley's "The Case for Colonialism," originally published online on September 8, 2017 in *Third World Quarterly*, but subsequently withdrawn.

have the appropriate identity. This is not, of course, peculiar to ethics but a general feature of all actions. In this context, the relevant point is that all redistribution is not the same. If I give you twenty dollars because I am feeling sorry for you, it is not the same as if I give you twenty dollars to repay the money I borrowed from you last month. In both cases, twenty dollars have gone from me to you, but the first is an act of charity while the second is the repayment of a debt. So, the answer to the question of what the nature of the transaction is depends not merely on the ("objective") material transfer of a twenty-dollar bill between us but the ("subjective"/"intersubjective") description under which it is carried out, and our respective understandings of what is going on.

More seriously, and on a global scale, suppose that governments or international bodies were won over by egalitarian arguments or a Rawlsian commitment to remedying the situation of the worst-off, and transferred resources to black Americans who are the descendants of slaves, or to Australian Aborigines suffering from their ancestors' expropriation, or to Third World peoples impoverished because of the historic colonization of their country. Still, they would have arguably not gotten their due. For reparations to be made, for the wrong against them and their ancestors to be corrected – repaired, made good, rectified – what is required is not merely a physical transfer of resources but a transfer taking place under a description and on a normative foundation that make it a certain kind of action and not another kind of action. If the narrative that philosophers such as McCarthy and myself believe is roughly true (and obviously this is a hugely controversial and contested topic), then distributive justice approaches, Rawlsian or otherwise, are failing to target the actual wrong involved.[57]

Relatedly, rectificatory justice, resting on a different normative justification than distributive justice, has additional prerequisites for it to be fully achieved. There are symbolic aspects to rectification – an official apology, moral condemnation of perpetrators, rewriting of governing narratives, memorialization – that simply do not arise if it is just a matter of redistributing assets and resources. The ideal of rectification is healing, and the recognition of the wrongs of the past *as* wrongs. If the wrong has involved the systematic denial of personhood to the group in question, as racial wrongs typically do, then correction requires that this denial be retracted through a reaffirmation of racial personhood (or an affirmation, if personhood was never conceded in the first place). Moreover, this applies not just to the living but the dead also. The dead

---

[57] Pablo de Greiff (ed.), *The Handbook of Reparations* (New York: Oxford University Press, 2006).

cannot be brought back, but one can choose to respect or continue to disrespect them. This is, of course, one of the central aims of memoria-lization, which justified the postwar creation of Holocaust Memorial Museums. But, the question to be asked is: where are the memorials for all of Europe's other dead? The Third Reich is universally condemned, but what about the Weiss Reich? Where are the memorials for Spain's Amerindian Holocaust, or the South Asian victims of avoidable famines under British rule, or the Congolese who died under Belgium's King Leopold II, or the Nama and Herero people exterminated by the *Vernichtungsbefehl* in German Southwest Africa, or the Ethiopians and Libyans gassed in Italy's colonial wars, or the Kikuyu slaughtered in the British counterinsurgency campaign in Kenya, or the Algerians subjected to torture and massacre by French troops, or the millions of Africans who perished in the Atlantic Slave Trade? What is required is a global Truth and Reconciliation Commission that would bring to light these sup-pressed histories, and pay the appropriate respect to this huge unmarked and unacknowledged nonwhite necropolis.

Conclusion

I want to close by returning to the issue raised at the start of this chapter. Against this background, we should now better be able to appreciate Sun Yat-sen's wariness about what could be termed a premature cosmopoli-tanism, and understand why a racially informed cosmopolitanism is neither a contradiction in terms nor incompatible with liberal universalism.[58] In the final chapter of her book on Du Bois, *Democracy's Reconstruction*, Lawrie Balfour warns that in "a modern world order begotten through racial slavery and colonial conquest," a putatively color-blind and race-transcendent cosmopolitanism is likely to be bogus, evad-ing rather than confronting "the racialized forms of power that have defined modern experience."[59] In the context of the times – and even today, nearly a century later – the cosmopolitanism being excoriated by Sun Yat-sen was, I would suggest, the global conceptual equivalent of a supposed "color-blindness" and "post-raciality" – a verbal, rather than substantive, dissolving of continuing hierarchies of white racial privilege in a spuriously attractive ideal that, by its failure to name, confront, and address the past will only guarantee its perpetuation. Race can only be transcended by facing and working through it, not by evading and

---

[58] Nwankwo, *Black Cosmopolitanism*; Slate, *Colored Cosmopolitanism*; M'Baye, *Black Cosmopolitanism and Anticolonialism*.

[59] Balfour, *Democracy's Reconstruction: Thinking Politically with W.E.B. Du Bois* (New York: Oxford University Press, 2011), 116, 129.

pretending to have sublated it. A liberalism and a cosmopolitanism that fail to deal with race will continue to be a racial liberalism and cosmopolitanism, incapable of prescribing the measures of rectificatory racial justice necessary not just for dismantling the long-established structures of racial domination, but also for transforming white moral psychology and consciousness, thereby laying the foundations for a new, genuinely post-racial world.[60]

[60] An earlier version of this chapter was presented at the conference, "Domination Across Borders," in Bad Homburg, Germany, on July 4–5, 2011, and subsequently published in Barbara Buckinx, Jonathan Trejo-Mathys, and Timothy Waligore, eds., *Domination and Global Political Justice: Conceptual, Historical, and Institutional Perspectives* (New York: Routledge, 2015).

5 Association, Reciprocity, and Emancipation
A Transnational Account of the Politics of Global Justice

Inés Valdez

> Let's simply look at the world across time and space and see how people
> have thought and acted beyond the local.
>
> (Sheldon Pollock et al., 2000)[1]

> Even our American brothers, as a result of racial discrimination, find
> themselves within a great modern nation in an artificial situation that can
> only be understood in reference to colonialism.
>
> (Aimé Cesaire, 1956)[2]

Introduction

Historians have recently provided detailed accounts of the strong
connections between the civil rights and Black Power movements in
the United States and the anti-colonial movement worldwide after
World War II.[3] These connections resulted in important transformations of the perceived nature of injustice that American blacks
struggled against and also transformed the political subjectivity of
the actors involved in these coalitions. Other accounts have noted
the connection between the struggles of African-Americans, Asian
immigrants, and Indian anti-colonialism in the early twentieth

I'm indebted to excellent research assistance by Rahel Admasu, Jada Earl, and Alex Konicki.
For comments and feedback I would like to thank Duncan Bell, Patti Lenard, Srdjan
Vucetic, the seminar audience at the University of Ottawa, and the other participants at
the workshop on "Race, Empire, and Global Justice" at Cambridge University.
[1] Sheldon Pollock, Homi K. Bhabha, Carol A. Breckenridge, and Dipesh Chakrabarty,
"Cosmopolitanisms," *Public Culture*, 12/3 (2000), 586.
[2] Aimé Cesaire, "Culture and Colonization," *Presence Africaine: Cultural Journal of the Negro
World*, 8–10 (June–November, 1956), 13.
[3] Carol Anderson, *Bourgeois Radicals. The NAACP and the Struggle for Colonial Liberation,
1941–1960* (New York: Cambridge University Press, 2015); Joshua Bloom and
Waldo Martin, *Black against Empire: The History and Politics of the Black Panther Party*
(Berkeley: University of California Press, 2014); Nico Slate, *Black Power Beyond Borders:
The Global Dimensions of the Black Power Movement* (Basingstoke: Palgrave, 2012);
Penny M. Von Eschen, *Race against Empire: Black Americans and Anticolonialism,
1937–1957* (Ithaca, NY: Cornell University Press, 1997).

century.[4] These accounts suggest that even during the Cold War – an era in which the USA was known for its anti-internationalism – marginalized groups were willing and able to find grounds for cooperation with actors abroad. While the United States stood with Europe when it sought to maintain the colonial status quo in the founding of the United Nations, this did not prevent groups experiencing domestic oppression from finding political affinities with actors that stood opposed to the Western imperial consensus.

I take to these accounts as an impulse to explore a cosmopolitan orientation that contrasts with that which characterizes frameworks of global justice, in which the privileged West considers its faults and extends a helping or reparatory hand toward the Global South. In the countercyclical internationalisms referenced above the cosmopolitan subjects are the subject of oppression in the West and those struggling against colonialism abroad, who enter into coalitions out of the commonality of the injustice they experience in order to think and act together politically against oppression. This alternative configuration results in important implications for (a) the implicit global (rather than transnational) historiography of the global justice literature, (b) the conceptualization of association that grounds obligation for both camps in the global justice debate, and (c) the normative character of the theorization of transnational (rather than global) justice.

This alternative cosmopolitan orientation has not been noted by the literature on global justice, which relies upon two contestable notions of history. On the one hand, this literature disavows the transnational character of past and present injustice. On the other hand, it does not engage with recent instances of political coalition that brought together marginalized groups in the West and the non-West. These groups put forward particular definitions of their grievances and attempted to pursue justice beyond the nation. In contrast, mainstream internationalisms, like that of the peace movement at the turn of the century, were – with few exceptions – devoted to the discussion and celebration of peace among imperial Western states. This background remains relevant to explain the coexistence of the League of Nations and the United Nations with imperialism. Throughout this period, and before, however, blacks and Asian-Americans were at the center of efforts to establish transnational alliances built upon the commonality of their struggles and those in the colonial world and the joint commitment to counter transnational forms

---

[4] Robeson Taj Frazier, *The East Is Black: Cold War China in the Black Radical Imagination* (Durham, NC: Duke University Press, 2014); Nico Slate, *Colored Cosmopolitanism: The Shared Struggle for Freedom in the United States and India* (Cambridge, MA: Harvard University Press, 2012).

of race-based domination. These alliances could provide a roadmap to chart projects of global justice that recognize the transnational character of injustice and its complex contemporary instantiations. Despite this potential, they currently have no place in a literature that privileges unilateral humanitarian or duty-based projects of redistribution with a focus on the West as both the culprit of injustice and the agent in the task of global justice.

In order to trace these historical erasures and clarify my normative claims I focus on the concept of associations – one of the grounding constructs of the debate on global justice. I argue that this construct is used in a very limited way, despite the fact that critical race theory accounts – prominently among them Charles Mills's work on the racial contract – have used it to conceptualize associations of domination. Additionally, I propose that this concept can be used critically to theorize coalition-making emerging from shared oppression and put forward a political notion of transnational justice. I propose the concept of "association for emancipation" as productive for tracking the currents of transnational politics that rightly belong in the project of global justice.

Normatively, my approach provides a critical lens to complement the contemporary literature on global justice. First, it urges scholars of global justice to decenter the elite Western subject as the implicit cosmopolitan subject. Second, it proposes to incorporate associations for emancipation into the theorization of global justice, i.e., the realms of politics inaugurated by coalition-making among marginalized Western actors and other transnational movements. Finally, it argues that a shift of emphasis from morality (duty, obligation) to politics (power, coalition-making, contestation) is necessary to consider the question of political feasibility of transnational justice.

In the rest of this chapter I develop these claims. In the next section I review the global justice literature and discuss the absent treatment of domination within Western societies. I then rely on the notions of special relationship and associations to illuminate the world of transnational alliances between the West and the non-West. Finally, I engage with W. E. B. Du Bois's transnational writings and political practice to develop the normative implications of the transnational approach to (in)justice I put forward.

The Genealogy of Global Justice

The "discovery" of global justice in Western academia can be traced to the publication in 1979 of Charles Beitz's *Political Theory and International*

Relations (followed closely by Henry Shue's *Basic Rights* in 1980).[5] This particular chronology is no doubt connected to the lively debate on justice brought about by the publication of John Rawls's *Theory of Justice*, but also carries with it a particular historiography.[6] In particular, the turn to the global in the discussion of justice came during the renaissance of human rights in the post-colonial 1970s, when the West recuperates its moral authority in the international sphere.[7] The turn to delineate Western economic responsibilities for global ills is undoubtedly a welcome contrast with the otherwise one-sided use of human rights discourse during the Carter administration to condemn authoritarian excesses in Latin America and Eastern Europe. Yet, the inauguration of the global justice debate in this period and within the field of analytical philosophy contains – in Koselleck's terms – a specific temporality of history that assimilates experience in particular ways.[8]

Two significant historical erasures of consequence come with contemporary thinking about global justice. First, the global justice literature focuses on the present shape of injustice, which it sometimes identifies with Western capitalist dominance. This structure, however, does not explore the historical genealogy of global inequality and assumes a tidy division between the prosperous West and the desperately poor South. In particular, the global justice literature does not concern itself with how the complex interweaving of the institutions of colonialism, settler colonialism, the slave trade, slavery, and indentured work, among others, shaped the globe in ways that preclude us from separating structures of domination neatly between geographical and political units and assuming their internal homogeneity.[9] Second, and despite its historical proximity, this literature does not engage with the abundant transnational connections between the American civil rights movement and the anti-colonial movement, one of a series of transnational coalition-making instances in

---

[5] Samuel Scheffler, "The Idea of Global Justice: A Progress Report," The Harvard Review of Philosophy, 20 (2014), 17–35. See also the chapters by Moyn and Forrester in this volume.

[6] David Miller, *Justice for Earthlings: Essays in Political Philosophy* (Cambridge: Cambridge University Press, 2013), 165–6.

[7] Samuel Moyn, *The Last Utopia: Human Rights in History* (Cambridge, MA: Harvard University Press, 2010).

[8] Reinhart Koselleck, *Futures Past: On the Semantics of Historical Time* (New York: Columbia University Press, 1985), 4.

[9] Opponents of global justice within this literature "forget" imperialism and the anti-colonial movement to such an extent that – as Lea Ypi and coauthors note – they do not consider the possibility that some of its associative justifications to *not* extend assistance beyond borders actually imply substantial obligations toward former colonies. Lea Ypi, Robert Goodin, and Christian Barry, "Associative Duties, Global Justice, and the Colonies," *Philosophy & Public Affairs*, 37/2 (2009), 103–35.

that era that pursued justice but cannot be simply categorized as national or international.

These twin erasures are partly explained by the literature's investment in the "global" as opposed to the "transnational." The global – even when critical – concentrates on processes of globalization that move from the West to the non-West and that are seen as homogenizing.[10] Transnationalism, in contrast, is an approach that captures how multiple sets of dynamically overlapping and interacting social fields that exceed the national "create and shape seemingly bordered and bounded structures, actors, and processes."[11] A transnational approach does not imply that the domestic or the local are irrelevant, as Ranjoo Herr notes, as it must also account for the particular ways in which these social fields become grounded and particularized in local sites by paying attention to the situation and standpoint of the oppressed, which serves to demystify the very forces that envelop them.[12] A transnational approach offers a grounded and particularized analysis of localized forms of domination in a way that illuminates the common links with larger, even global, economic and political structures.[13]

Transnationalism is useful to conceptualize how the encounter of distinct forms of political and economic structures such as colonialism, slavery, and migration result in instances of domination that do not track neatly the division between the West and the non-West. Accordingly, when proponents of global justice rely on a binary division between the West and the rest and a global view of injustice, whereby the unjust actions of Western countries result in a normative obligation for redistribution, they are less responsive to the heterogeneity of domination and its multiple locations (in the West, as well as the developing world) and cannot pay attention to dissonant forms of politics (like instances of transnational politics inaugurated by coalition-making between

---

[10] Gurminder Bhambra, "Multiple Modernities or Global Interconnections: Understanding the Global Post the Colonial," in Nathalie Karagiannis and Peter Wagner (eds.), *Varieties of World-making: Beyond Globalization* (Liverpool: Liverpool University Press, 2007), 60; Inderpal Grewal and Caren Kaplan, "Global Identities: Theorizing Transnational Studies of Sexuality," *GLQ: A Journal of Lesbian and Gay Studies*, 7/4 (2001), 663.

[11] Sanjeev Khagram and Peggy Levitt, "Constructing Transnational Studies," in L. Pries (ed.), *Rethinking Transnationalism: The Meso-Link of Organizations* (New York: Routledge, 2008), 26.

[12] Ranjoo Seodu Herr, "Reclaiming Third World Feminism: Or Why Transnational Feminism Needs Third World Feminism," *Meridians: Feminism, Race, Transnationalism*, 12/1 (2014), 24–5; Chandra Talpade Mohanty, "'Under Western Eyes' Revisited: Feminist Solidarity through Anticapitalist Struggles," *Signs*, 28/2 (2002), 501, 511, 514.

[13] Mohanty, "'Under Western Eyes' Revisited," 501, 505.

marginalized groups in the West and non-West).[14] In other words, the "global" is underspecified, and the goal of successfully tracking oppression and chains of responsibility – that concerns the discussion on global justice – could be furthered by abandoning West/non-West geographical binaries and attempting to track politics where it happens, even if "where" is not the realm of the nation-state or the international.

As I show below, rescuing experiences of transnational politics problematizes the domestic sphere and highlights the persisting injustices around race – among other difference markers – that characterize Western societies. Incorporating this dimension of oppression to the literature on global justice also shows that marginalized actors within the West are particularly well positioned to illuminate the shape of transnational injustice and contribute to addressing the question of the political feasibility of global justice (see also Kohn, in this volume). This examination also reveals promising political dimensions of notions that are commonly used in the global justice literature, including that of associations and special relationships.

The Wealthy West

While the assumption that the West is homogeneously prosperous and the rest of the world homogeneously poor is rarely acknowledged, a piece by Jonathan Seglow makes this explicit: "For the sake of simplicity, I assume throughout that rich states consist of fairly rich (i.e. not poor) people and that poor states are home to poor (i.e. not rich) people. Though false, I do not believe this assumption affects the central argument."[15] Within the global justice debate, Seglow advocates the coexistence of domestic and global duties, but cosmopolitans, who privilege global redistribution, are equally committed to this assumption. This is clear, for example, in Arash Abizadeh and Pablo Gilabert's argument – against Samuel Scheffler – that special responsibilities are secondary to cosmopolitan obligations. In their argument the authors assume that Westerners' special relationships are with other Westerners who – like them – are "quite rich," as opposed to individuals with whom Westerners do not hold relationships, who face "life-threatening poverty."[16]

---

[14] This claim is indebted to Joseph Winters's interpretation of Adorno's negative dialectics and his suggestion that past and present suffering can serve as the occasion for hope. Winters, "Theodor Adorno and the Unhopeless Work of the Negative," *Journal of Culture and Religious Theory*, 14/1 (2014), 184–7.

[15] Jonathan Seglow, "Associative Duties and Global Justice," *Journal of Moral Philosophy*, 7/1 (2010), 59n.

[16] Arash Abizadeh and Pablo Gilabert, "Is there a Genuine Tension between Cosmopolitan Egalitarianism and Special Responsibilities?" *Philosophical Studies*, 138/3 (2008), 361.

What explains the common assumption by both sides of the debate on global justice that the West is homogeneously wealthy? This assumption may be a legacy of the ideal approach privileged by Rawls's theory of justice. Social liberals who object to the extension of obligations beyond domestic boundaries, do so based on a variety of Rawlsian arguments that ground obligations of justice on notions of cooperation, reciprocity, special obligations, and/or accountably coercive relations among conationals.[17] Cosmopolitans either replicate Rawls's original position and conclude that obligations of justice can be logically extended to the world or criticize the particular conceptualizations used to defend the primacy of domestic obligations.[18] By extending the scope to the globe, however, proponents of global justice are more invested in highlighting the vast differences in well-being between the West and the non-West rather than in delving into domestic inequalities.

Yet, many social liberals, despite defending the priority of domestic justice, also do without an examination of domestic inequalities. This is despite the fact that a defense of limiting the scope of justice to the domestic realm could be predicated on the persistence of pervasive inequalities at home that must be addressed before considering inequalities beyond borders. Instead, the associations that these scholars privilege above the global seem to be stable and cooperatives ventures among equally prosperous members of a well-ordered society. This is reminiscent of Rawls's international theory, which assumes that well-ordered societies with no egregious inequalities are characteristic of the West; societies that can be understood as cooperative ventures for mutual advantage.[19]

For further other examples of this assumption see Thomas Pogge, *World Poverty and Human Rights* (New York: Polity, 2008); Richard Child, "The Global Justice Gap," *Critical Review of International Social and Political Philosophy*, 19/5 (2016), 574–90.

[17] Samuel Scheffler, *Boundaries and Allegiances: Problems of Justice and Responsibility in Liberal Thought* (New York: Oxford University Press, 2002); Michael Blake, "Distributive Justice, State Coercion, and Autonomy," *Philosophy & Public Affairs*, 30/3 (2005), 257–95; Andrea Sangiovanni, "Global Justice, Reciprocity, and the State," *Philosophy & Public Affairs*, 35/1 (2007), 4–39.

[18] Charles Beitz, *Political Theory and International Relations* (Princeton, NY: Princeton University Press, 1999); Thomas Pogge, *Realizing Rawls* (Ithaca, NY: Cornell University Press, 1989). For the latter, see Arash Abizadeh, "Cooperation, Pervasive Impact, and Coercion: On the Scope (Not Site) of Distributive Justice," *Philosophy & Public Affairs*, 35/4 (2007), 318–58; Ypi et al., "Associative Duties, Global Justice, and the Colonies."

[19] Charles W. Mills, *The Racial Contract* (Ithaca, NY: Cornell University Press, 1997); Mills, "Realizing (Through Racializing) Pogge," in Alison Jaggar (ed.), *Thomas Pogge and His Critics* (Cambridge: Polity, 2010); John Rawls, *The Law of Peoples with "The Idea of Public Reason Revisited"* (Cambridge, MA: Harvard University Press, 1997).

As Charles Mills has argued, however, this claim is evidently absurd since a brief look at history shows that most societies in history have had as their central goal "domination and exploitation," rather than mutual advantage.[20] Even if the notion that societies are ventures for mutual advantage is simply a feature of ideal theorizing, it has nonetheless limited the range of questions that philosophers of justice ask and thus has practical consequences. In the absence of nonideal theorizing, the linkage between legitimate association and obligations of justice grants normative value to associations per se, which then perversely grant legitimacy to status quo institutions and conflate the current site of justice with the proper scope that could result from an examination of broader principles and actual responsibility.[21]

There are two disavowals at play. On the one hand, instances of domination within the West are disowned, as noted by Mills. On the other hand, the lack of examination of domestic inequality also prevents questions about the potentially transnational sources of domestic inequality from being raised. The second disavowal is present even in works that consider the question of inequality (not domination) within the West, like those of David Miller, who focuses on the tension between the interests of the needy in the domestic sphere and those abroad.[22] In this approach the fate of the domestic poor is considered independent from that of the global poor and there is no effort to consider the political ramifications of such commonality (as I do below). Instead, domestic and global obligations are considered to be in tension with each other.[23] In cosmopolitan approaches to global justice, it is sometimes argued that domestic and global obligations are compatible.[24] However, in these cases, the compatibility of domestic and global obligations is derived at the level of principle, rather than in relation to a common origin of injustice or its political potential.

[20] Mills, "Realizing (Through Racializing) Pogge," 155–6.
[21] Abizadeh, "Cooperation, Pervasive Impact, and Coercion," 330, 352.
[22] David Miller, *On Nationality* (Oxford: Oxford University Press, 1995). See also Michael Blake, "Distributive Justice, State Coercion, and Autonomy," *Philosophy & Public Affairs* 30/3 (2005), 257–95.
[23] Miller, *Justice for Earthlings: Essays in Political Philosophy* (Cambridge: Cambridge University Press, 2013); Scheffler, *Boundaries and Allegiances*. This is also the case of the literature that cites "special obligations" toward the domestic poor as a justification for limiting migration. For a recent survey of this literature see Arash Abizadeh, "The Special Obligations Challenge to More Open Borders," in Sarah Fine and Lea Ypi (eds.), *Migration in Political Theory: The Ethics of Movement and Membership* (Oxford: Oxford University Press, 2016).
[24] Arash Abizadeh and Pablo Gilabert, "Is There a Genuine Tension between Cosmopolitan Egalitarianism and Special Responsibilities?," *Philosophical Studies*, 138/3 (2008); Richard W Miller, "Cosmopolitan Respect and Patriotic Concern," *Philosophy & Public Affairs*, 27/3 (1998).

In sum, the literature on global justice seldom considers question of domestic injustice within the West. When they do consider domestic injustice, they do it in order to preempt global obligations, rather than to interrogate their normative and political connection. By so doing, these scholars disallow the consideration of forms of domestic injustice within the West whose redress might be empirically, normatively, and politically connected to causes we tend to identify with cosmopolitan justice.[25]

These omissions are connected to the particular uses to which the global justice literature puts the related notions of association, cooperation, reciprocity, and special relationships, all of which serve conceptually to ground obligations of justice in the domestic realm. These notions therefore deserve closer scrutiny. The next subsection expands on the way in which cooperative associations may underwrite domination. The section after that, based on the transnational experiences of exchange between black activists and the anti-colonial movement, examines how cooperative associations built upon special relationships can be rethought as elements of emancipatory politics that must be considered in theory and practice as an important element of transnational justice.

Association for Domination

Thomas Nagel's classic 2005 article on global justice proposes a notion of accountably coercive association as the basis to his claim that obligations of justice only apply within national borders. According to his argument, sovereign power sustains the institutions required for citizens to comply with the duties of justice that they owe to fellow citizens.[26] These are "associative obligations" to the extent that we only owe justice *through* our shared institutions and to those *with whom* we hold a strong political relation.[27] Associative obligations emerge because the state and fellow citizens make "exceptional demands" on the will of citizens and those demands "bring with them obligations" that reach no further than the

---

[25] These two disavowals are at the center of Rawls's account of global politics in *The Law of Peoples*, which posits Western societies as having only mild inequalities and confines hierarchy to non-Western societies ("decent hierarchical," "burdened," "benevolent authoritarian," or "outlaw"; John Rawls, "The Law of Peoples," in *The Law of Peoples with "The Idea of Public Reason Revisited"* (Cambridge, MA: Harvard University Press, 1999), 4). He then claims that beyond a duty of assistance differential wealth does not result in obligations because it is due to different preferences (for industrialization versus a "more pastoral and leisurely society") and thus requires no redistribution. The well-ordered and substantially equal character of the West is ultimately a crucial element in his rewriting of Enlightenment Eurocentric developmentalism.

[26] Nagel, "The Problem of Global Justice," *Philosophy & Public Affairs*, 33/2 (2005), 121.

[27] Nagel, "The Problem of Global Justice," 121.

demands, which roots the obligations strictly in a political association.[28] Nagel's position is typical of a broader set of arguments that seek to ground obligations in existing political association, whether based on reciprocity, state coercive power, or cooperation.[29]

Critics argue that these approaches conflate two roles of association (or coordination, or coercion) in attaining justice. Associations, as Arash Abizadeh notes, may be constitutive of justice or simply instrumental for its attainment.[30] In the latter case, the range of association does not tell us much about the scope of the obligations of justice, unlike what associationist accounts claim. Beyond this question, the assumption that institutions serve mutual advantage, characteristic of ideal theorizing, does not lend itself to the task of considering how associations are also instrumental in domination. Feminist and critical race theorists are clear on this point, which translates into forms of theorization focused on naming and understanding institutions of patriarchy and white supremacy, respectively. In these systems, political agreements among white males entail the exclusion of women and nonwhites from cooperative ventures, the denial of reciprocal treatment toward them, and the exclusion from participation in their association. In Charles Mills's conceptualization, white supremacist organizations are based on the Racial Contract, which creates: "A partitioned social ontology ... a universe divided between persons and racial subpersons, *Untermenschen*, ... who are collectively and appropriately known as 'subject races'."[31] The "Racial Contract" includes "an agreement to *mis*interpret the world" supported by white epistemic authority; the political association is centrally defined by the entitlement of whites and the subordination of nonwhites.[32] In the same vein, Nikhil Singh offers the following definition of racism as a social and institutional fact in the United States: "the construction of black people as subjects proscribed from participating in the social state in which they live, and that part of the public whose relation to the public is always in radical doubt."[33]

In other words, injustice *requires* association in order to establish regimes of unaccountable coercion that enforce/legitimize a generalized refusal by dominant groups to extend cooperation and reciprocity toward the oppressed. Moreover, domestic exclusionary associations in the West

---

[28] Nagel, "The Problem of Global Justice," 130.
[29] Sangiovanni, "Global Justice, Reciprocity, and the State"; Blake, "Distributive Justice, State Coercion, and Autonomy."
[30] Abizadeh, "Cooperation, Pervasive Impact, and Coercion."
[31] Mills, *The Racial Contract*, 16–17.　[32] Mills, *The Racial Contract*, 18, 57.
[33] Nikhil Pal Singh, *Black Is a Country: Race and the Unfinished Struggle for Democracy* (Cambridge, MA: Harvard University Press, 2004), 30–1.

are not independent from unjust international arrangements and their persistence. For example, historians have noted that the inclusion of principles of self-determination, minority rights, and race equality in the League of Nations and the UN Declaration of Human Rights was blocked by the great powers, who were eager to protect their colonial holdings or prevent external involvement in their domestic race problems.[34] Thus, the consideration of domestic instances of domination within the West is central to correct existing accounts of global justice not because they preempt global obligations but because they sit at the intersection of power relations that founded and maintain injustice domestically and globally.

The lack of engagement with these instances by proponents of global justice thus implies a loss for this literature's capacity to reconstruct the shape of injustice and – as the next section explores – consider potential political paths of emancipation. Before turning to that, however, it is worth noting that cosmopolitans within this scholarship also do not engage with domestic injustice or its interconnections with forms of injustice that exceed the domestic. This is perhaps due to their loyalty to the Rawlsian notion of cooperation, which – at the outset – Charles Beitz took up and extended to argue for a global original position. According to Beitz, a global original position follows because the global system of trade and investment and the international institutions that organize it constitute a "scheme of social cooperation."[35] Thomas Pogge also supports a global original position and in later work he even adopts assumptions that are more stringent than the ones Rawls imposes in *The Law of Peoples* in order to defend an egalitarian law of peoples despite "a self-imposed triple handicap."[36]

In sum, working within a Rawlsian framework – dominant in the field of analytical philosophy – brings significant blind spots with it. When applied to global justice, theories start from the assumption that there is global inequality but devote the bulk of the theorization to devise the kind of system that would realize equality, rather than to delve into the forms of domination that underlie inequality and the way in which these relations result in pockets of domination within the West. Relatedly, there is little exploration of the shape of injustice in the international sphere, including

[34] Mark Mazower, "The Strange Triumph of Human Rights, 1933–1950," *Historical Journal*, 47/2 (2004), 379–98; Moyn, *The Last Utopia*.
[35] Beitz, *Political Theory and International Relations*, 126–36, 43–53; Beitz, "Cosmopolitan Ideals and National Sentiment," *Journal of Philosophy*, 80/10 (1983), 595.
[36] Pogge, "An Egalitarian Law of Peoples," *Philosophy & Public Affairs*, 23/3 (1994), 199.

the role of Western elites in enforcing it and its connection with forms of domination within Western countries.[37]

Association for Emancipation

In this section I offer a broader reconsideration of associations as instruments that may not only work for the mutual advantage of its members – in the ideal world – or serve to administer domination – in the real world – but also serve emancipatory roles. In particular, I suggest we consider a set of alternative associations that emerge based on commonalities and in order to struggle against domination.

The "associations for emancipation" I have in mind are not equivalent to the society-wide associations that the global justice literature focuses on, which are formally coextensive with a bounded society. This is partly because – as argued in the previous section – these associations are in fact not society-wide and do not work to the advantage of certain subgroups, whose cooperation is not rewarded reciprocally. The associations I have in mind are those that bring together groups that have been excluded domestically and oppressed groups abroad in order to contest associations for domination. A concept in the literature on global justice that is used in overlapping ways to that of association – special relationships – is helpful in this task. The notion of special relationships has been predominantly used to contest the weight of global obligations. According to Samuel Scheffler's definition, the normative character of special relationships refers to the noninstrumental value that these relationships hold, which translates into: "[the disposition] to see that person's needs, interests and desires as, in themselves, providing me with presumptively decisive reasons for action, reasons that I would not have had in the absence of that relationship."[38]

Neither side of the global justice literature considers the possibility that special relationships may exist among people that do not share national affiliation, presumably because these connections are deemed nonexistent, marginal, or politically irrelevant. This seems to be the case in Scheffler's rebuttal of Martha Nussbaum's notion of cosmopolitanism, which posits "special relationships" as unproblematically opposed to cosmopolitan loyalties.[39] Despite this, the language in the definition above is suggestive of just the kinds of relationships that motivated the

---

[37] Thomas Pogge's effort to trace chains of responsibility is a partial exception, although it is still the case that these connections presume a homogeneous West and a global – rather than transnational – notion of injustice. I address Pogge in the sections below.

[38] Scheffler, *Boundaries and Allegiances*, 101.

[39] Scheffler, *Boundaries and Allegiances*, ch. 7.

transnational connections among marginalized groups and nonnationals, or what Du Bois calls "the badge of color":

But one thing is sure and that is the fact that since the fifteenth century these ancestors of mine and their other descendants … have suffered a common disaster and have a long memory. … But the physical bond is least and the badge of color relatively unimportant save as a badge; the real essence of this kinship is its social heritage of slavery; the discrimination and insult; and this heritage … extends through yellow Asia and into the South Seas. It is this unity that draws me to Africa.[40]

This claim suggests that the search for alliances abroad may be partly associated to exclusion at home and the need for alternative associations for those excluded. As Scheffler argues: "[T]he relationships that generate responsibilities for an individual are those relationships that the individual has reason to value. *No claims at all arise from relationships that are degrading or demeaning,* or which serve to undermine rather than to enhance human flourishing."[41] Associationist accounts thus open the door for challenging the legitimacy of domestic arrangements based on the degrading character of relationships or the lack of consideration of the will of some societal members, but do not spend time conceptualizing this possibility. By so doing, the literature leaves untheorized not only the character of domination but also the political response to such domination, including the normative importance of association among those demeaned by existing associations and the possibility that this association is with groups beyond the nation.

In principle, one could expect reflection on these issues by democratic theorists, given their focus on domestic injustice, difference, and exclusion. This literature refers to deliberation, the establishment of counterpublics, and/or fugitive moments of radical democracy through which we (attempt to) approximate a *demos* that is worthy of its name.[42] Yet, these theories are limited by their methodological nationalism and fail to consider the transnational origins of oppression and the way in which those joint origins create transnational affinities that failed democratic

---

[40] Du Bois, *Dusk of Dawn: An Essay toward an Autobiography of a Race Concept* (New Brunswick, NJ: Transaction, 1997), 117.

[41] Scheffler, *Boundaries and Allegiances*, 108 (my emphasis). The possibility that relationships are not normatively valuable is also present in Nagel's account, which finds associations legitimate when they engage "the will of each member of the society in its operation," and illegitimate if they function on "pure coercion": Nagel, "The Problem of Global Justice," 129.

[42] Jürgen Habermas, "Three Normative Models of Democracy," *Constellations*, 1/1 (1994), 1–10; Michael Warner, *Publics and Counterpublics* (New York: Zone Books, 2005); Sheldon Wolin, "Fugitive Democracy," *Constellations*, 1/1 (1994), 11–25.

processes may heighten, leading excluded actors to enter into schemes of cooperation with other actors beyond borders.[43]

Thus, the efforts to establish transnational connections between the American civil rights movement and anti-colonial advocates, the enthusiasm elicited by Bandung in Malcolm X,[44] and the vocal opposition to the Vietnam war by Martin Luther King Jr. and other African-American leaders, are all important traces of transnational political feeling that often led to action but get lost in subdisciplinary divisions that characterize contemporary political theory in ways that impoverish the concepts of global justice and democracy.

Transnational Politics of Justice

The historical documentation of instances of transnational connections between marginalized groups in the West and the non-West provides a starting point for the theorization of a more nuanced notion of global justice that decenters the West, acknowledges forms of association beyond the nation that have the goal of furthering justice, and incorporates those into a theorization that is more political than moral. The writings of Du Bois, a central figure in the interwar and postwar flurry of transnational activity, provide an excellent resource for conceptualizing these dimensions. These writings – on the topics of imperialism, African history, and international politics – have so far received little attention from political theorists. However, starting in the second decade

---

[43] For a consideration of a transnational democratic *ethos* in the thought of Frederick Douglass and Du Bois see Juliet Hooker, "'A Black Sister to Massachusetts': Latin America and the Fugitive Democratic Ethos of Frederick Douglass," *American Political Science Review*, 109/4 (2015), 690–702, and Lawrie Balfour, *Democracy's Reconstruction. Thinking Politically with W.E.B. Du Bois* (New York: Oxford University Press, 2011), ch. 6, who, however, are mostly concerned with considering the effect of the transnational *on* American democracy. Other scholars invested in transnational democracy, like James Bohman, tend to see this as a solution to the mismatched publics that result from globalization as opposed to a question that follows from the nature of injustice: Bohman, "Democratization through Transnational Publics: Deliberative Inclusion Across Borders," in *Does Truth Matter? Democracy and Public Space* (Leuven: Springer, 2009). Seyla Benhabib's work theorizes the connection between democratic theory and the cosmopolitan realm but tends to limit attention to the effects of a cosmopolitan public sphere on domestic polities, rather than on the politically more contentious transnational coalitions analyzed in this chapter: Benhabib, *The Rights of Others: Aliens, Residents, and Citizens* (Cambridge: Cambridge University Press, 2004); Benhabib, "Claiming Rights across Borders: International Human Rights and Democratic Sovereignty," *American Political Science Review*, 103/4 (2009), 691–704.

[44] Arif Dirlik, *The Postcolonial Aura: Third World Criticism in the Age of Global Capitalism* (New York: Westview Press, 1998), 169; James Tyner, "Territoriality, Social Justice and Gendered Revolutions in the Speeches of Malcolm X," *Transactions of the Institute of British Geographers*, 29/3 (2004), 334.

of the twentieth century, and following his relocation to New York as the founder and editor of the NAACP magazine *The Crisis*, Du Bois wrote extensively on these topics in ways that augmented and revised his earlier thoughts on the race question.[45]

The immediate context for Du Bois's writings was World War I, which raised the hopes of racial progress for African-Americans, who expected to see their service rewarded through social advancement. During the war, African-American soldiers also became exposed to the different racial formations characteristic of European societies, which changed their outlook in more cosmopolitan directions.[46] While these hopes were not fulfilled, this juncture gave Du Bois the impetus to rethink the quest for racial justice as transnational, a kernel that had been present since the original iteration of the concept of the "color line" in 1900, but whose political dimensions are theorized more carefully only after *The Souls of Black Folk*.[47] World War II – and the migration of Africans to the Western hemisphere – heightens the viability of Du Bois's coalitional project by expanding radically the base of the Pan-African movement and bringing into relief the affinities of the struggles taking place in the colonies and the metropoles.[48] At this juncture, according to Nikhil Singh, black intellectuals locate a "disjuncture between the global promise of American universalism, the domestic realities of racial exclusion, and the problems of colonial empires."[49]

In the United States, Du Bois was a central voice in reconfiguring the character of racial injustice as transnational and a central actor in spearheading the organizations that would activate politically those affinities, including the Pan-African Congress and the Council on

[45] See, however, Juliet Hooker's recent consideration of racial mixture in Du Bois's transnational writings: Juliet Hooker, *Theorizing Race in the Americas: Douglass, Sarmiento, Du Bois, and Vasconcelos* (New York: Oxford University Press, 2017), ch. 3.
[46] Mark Whalan, "Not only War: The First World War and African American Literature," in S. Das (ed.), *Race, Empire, and First World War Writing* (New York: Cambridge University Press, 2011).
[47] I examine the trajectory of Du Bois's thought in greater detail in my forthcoming book, Transnational, *Cosmopolitanism* : Kant, Du Bois, and Justice as a Political Craft (New York: Cambridge University Press).
[48] Du Bois, "India," in *W. E. B. Du Bois on Asia: Crossing the World Color Line*, ed. B. Mullen and C. Watson (Jackson: University Press of Mississippi, 2005), 7; Valdez, "Du Bois and the Fluid Subject: *Dark Princess* and the Splendid Transnational," in M. Thaggert (ed.), *Expecting More: African American Literature in Transition, 1920–30* (New York: Cambridge University Press, in press); Von Eschen, *Race Against Empire*, ch. 1.
[49] Singh, *Black Is a Country*, 126–7. While my examples focus on one particular kind of transnational politics – the alliances between the anti-colonial movement and the US civil rights movement – these alliances are just one example in a long list of instances that would fit the same outlines of transnational coalition-making across the West/non-West divide in other locations or time periods: Michael West, William G. Martin, and Fanon Che Wilkins (eds.), *From Toussaint to Tupac: The Black International Since the Age of Revolution* (Chapel Hill: University of North Carolina Press, 2014).

African Affairs.[50] Du Bois's writings during this period offer a notion of transnational justice that problematizes the West-centric notion of global justice, activate awareness of instances of politics that operate at the margins of national and international politics, and put forward a political – rather than moral – understanding of justice. Based on Du Bois's thought and political practice, I develop three normative dimensions of transnational associations for emancipation.

Decentering the West

As an intervention in the then-current debates about peace, war, and imperialism, Du Bois's writings have the effect of decentering the West. In 1915 he published his book *The Negro* and an article in *The Atlantic Monthly* entitled "The African Roots of War." These works offer a pioneering account of the role of African people in world history and a discussion of the central role of Africa and colonialism in explaining the Great War, respectively. By centering Africa in world history and the Great War, Du Bois criticizes Western pseudo-universalism and suggests a political vision for its democratization. Already in 1911, Du Bois writes enthusiastically about the United Races Congress (URC), which took place in London that year and brought together the people of the world "not as master and slave, ... conqueror and conquered – but as men and equals in the *center of the world*."[51]

In anticipation of the Congress, Du Bois drew a contrast between the Western peace movement and the URC, noting the partial character of the former. Du Bois assiduously attended the meetings of various American peace societies and was publicly critical of the narrow notions of humanity and peace espoused by this movement. This movement, he noted, excluded from its realm of concern the majority of the world, made up of colored men, and refused to bring up the topic of race and colonialism in its meetings.[52]

---

[50] Von Eschen, *Race Against Empire*, 17. As Carol Anderson notes, there is a risk that centering on Du Bois – and his own narrative of the era – leads us away from considering other actors and organizations that were committed to transnational coalition-making and advocacy on behalf of the colonies, including the post-Du Bois NAACP. Anderson, *Bourgeois Radicals: The NAACP and the Struggle for Colonial Liberation, 1941–1960* (New York: Cambridge University Press, 2015). My interest in Du Bois's writings and actions during this period is not to claim their centrality but rather to, first, start the process of countering the lack of reflection within political theory of *any* of these actors/ intellectuals, and, second, engage with the substance of Du Bois's conception of transnational politics and justice he puts forward.

[51] Du Bois, "London," *The Crisis*, 2/4 (1911), 159 (my emphasis).

[52] Du Bois, "Editorial," *The Crisis*, 1/2 (1910), 17, 20; Du Bois, "The African Roots of War," *The Atlantic Monthly*, 115/5 (1915), 712.

136   *Inés Valdez*

While we cannot think of current multilateral fora as equally exclusionary as in the first half of the twentieth century, Du Bois's insights still
point to the lack of thematization in the global justice literature of issues of
colonialism and racialized inequality. Moreover, Du Bois's political
action and his emphasis on an egalitarian sphere of encounter contrast
with the dominant voice within the global justice literature, that of the
Western theorists diagnosing the problem of injustice and devising the
terms for overcoming it. His description of the URC suggests the need to
carve out a *central* space that is not affected by hierarchies, which is the
task that occupies Du Bois in the decades that follow. The process of
decentering also opens the view to other realms of politics that exist at the
margins (or even the center) of Europe.

Inaugurating Transnational Publics

While Western peace activists at the time were concerned with "arbitration and international law" ruling the interaction between Western
powers, the URC was invested in an epoch-changing project of
equality.[53] "London," the column he writes for *The Crisis* about his
experience in the city that hosted the Congress, conveys a fascination
with the "capital of the world" in which "endless interests, worldwide
ramifications, tremendous power" meet. Du Bois sees in London the site
of tradition, memory ("clothed in living flesh and word") and power, the
expression of the "empire on which the sun never sets."[54] Despite this
commanding picture, Du Bois notes that during his stay the unrest in
Egypt and India and the situation in South Africa is making London
"uneasy" and apprehensive about the future.

The prose in this essay is powerful; it conveys the feeling of London as
the center of the world, as a site in which history, power, and interests
converge in a formidable mixture. Yet, this city is not invulnerable to the
prospect of colonial rebellion and the possibility of emancipation of the
colonial masses, i.e., to politics. It is this site that Du Bois finds the most
fitting "center" for the coming together of a congress of the races and the
peoples of the world. His enthusiasm for the URC results from the
inauguration of a public that – in contrast to the West-centric peace
movement – includes blacks and other peoples of color and foregrounds
the question of race injustice as both domestic and international.

This spatialized view of politics and its focus on disruption informs the
political praxis and Pan-African activism in which Du Bois is involved in

[53] Du Bois, "Editorial," *The Crisis*, 6/1 (1913), 26.
[54] Du Bois, "London," *The Crisis*, 2/4 (1911), 159.

the coming decades. In particular, in 1919 he finds himself in Paris as a correspondent at the Peace Council meeting, where the powers would discuss the postwar. *The Crisis* announces Du Bois's trip and its goal of putting "all pressure possible" on the delegates at the Peace Table on behalf of the colored peoples of the United States and the world.[55] His concern with "colored people of the United States and the world" highlights the diverse forms of exclusion from the international sphere of politics.[56] Domestic and overseas domination are weaved together to the extent that the government officials appearing at international summits represent neither group. Du Bois creates a space for this public by summoning a Pan-African congress to take place in Paris. This congress is explicitly opposed by the United States and colonial countries (that did not grant visas for those who attempted to attend) and only takes place after Du Bois strikes a backroom deal with Premier Clemenceau through the General Commissary in charge of the recruitment of African native troops.[57]

Du Bois's comments on the URC and his travails organizing the Pan-African Congress are acts of founding of transnational spaces of politics that stand in opposition to the dominant (and dominating) forms of association prevalent in the international sphere. Their political marginality – at least at their inception – does not mean that these spaces did not serve the important goals of articulating shared goals and setting up agendas, resulting in novel forms of consciousness among political actors that fueled progress against colonialism and racial oppression.[58]

These transnational arenas have not vanished, as research in history and the humanities reveals, yet, from the perspective of global justice theory it would seem that the task of global justice is one that is exclusively in the hands of Western theorists, professionals in nongovernmental organizations, and international technocrats. The lack of awareness of these spaces of politics is not due to the lack of agents in these theories,

---

[55] Du Bois, "Editorial," *The Crisis*, 17/3 (1919), 111.

[56] It also highlights the fact that after the URC, Du Bois turns to forms of coalition that privilege bringing together African and Asian activists. This is not just out of the necessity, as Du Bois's writings provide a rationale for nurturing a common consciousness separately from whites.

[57] Manning Marable, *W. E. B. Du Bois: Black Radical Democrat* (Boulder, CO: Paradigm Publishers, 1986), 101; Du Bois, "The Pan-African Movement," in George Padmore (ed.), *History of the Pan-African Congress* (London: The Hammersmith Bookshop, 1945), 15; Clarence Contee, "Du Bois, the NAACP, and the Pan-African Congress of 1919," *The Journal of Negro History*, 57/1 (1972), 16.

[58] Valdez, *Toward Transnational Cosmopolitanism*, Chapters 4 and 5.

but to their primarily economic and moral, rather than political, character, an issue that I address next.

Du Bois and the Political

Looking back at his first published monograph, *The Origins of the Suppression of the African Slave Trade in the United States of America, 1638–1870*, Du Bois regretted its predominant moral narrative so much that he included an "Apologia" in the 1954 edition of that work. In it, he lamented not having studied Marx and Freud and having understood slavery simply as a "matter ... of morals." He also regretted his "pat and simple" understanding of men's psyches and motivations when it came to explaining action on the question of slavery.[59] Du Bois's work between his first publication (1896) and the 1950s undoubtedly makes up for this failing. His writings on political propaganda, consciousness, and transnationalism as well as his move from academia to the editorship of *The Crisis* show a rethinking of the problem of racial prejudice and the shape of the struggle to contest it.

It is worthwhile to return to the organization of the 1919 Pan-African Congress in Paris and the superimposition of a black public on the heart of Western power to reflect on the emerging Duboisian notion of politics. These actions address directly the question of politics and exclusion by underlining that without the representation of colonial subjects and US Blacks, the gathering in Paris is an agreement for domination. This point is made powerfully by Du Bois's understanding of "European concord," which he defines as "satisfaction, or acquiescence, in a given division of the spoils of world-dominion." After all, European disarmament cannot go below the "necessity of defending the aggressions of the whites against the blacks and browns and yellows."[60]

Given the goal of domination served by Western association, the mere gesture of organizing such a gathering was potentially destabilizing. Further, this critique is accompanied by a positive plan – sent by Du Bois to President Woodrow Wilson ahead of the meeting – requesting that the fate of former German colonies be decided by a public including "chiefs and intelligent Negroes natives of the German colonies in Africa," the "twelve millions civilized Negroes of the United States," the "educated persons of Negro descent in South America and the West Indies," and the educated classes among the Negroes of French and

[59] Du Bois, "Apologia," in *The Suppression of the African Slave-Trade to the United States of America 1638–1870* (New York: Russell & Russell, 1965), 327, 9.
[60] Du Bois, "The African Roots of War," 713.

British colonies.[61] What is notable in this plan – which did not progress – is the broad notion of representation/self-determination it contains. Du Bois's claim suggests an affinity among transnationally located blacks that makes any decision on the fate of the colonies simply illegitimate without this group.

The centering of non-Western subjects in the postwar era contrasts with the absence of non-Western subjects in the global justice literature. This issue has been taken up by Thomas Pogge in a response to critics, where he argues that his work addresses the world's affluent not because he sees the poor as passive subjects instead of agents but because he does not have any standing to advise them.[62] This response illuminates the role of agents in global justice theory: they are individuals who are economically wealthy to whom we can assign responsibility and duties to fulfill. This contrasts with a notion of transnational justice whose shape is defined not by a calculation of income, responsibility, and duty but by a consideration of the relations of power that establish domination, an awareness of the spaces of politics opened by those oppressed, and a reconstruction of their particular understanding of the character and shape of injustice and the structural transformations that they see necessary for the achievement of justice.

In this sense, including Western subjects in the global justice literature does not require "speaking for them," but giving normative importance to the participation of non-Western publics in the definition of the shape of injustice and the form of reparation. In this sense, Pogge's assertion in the same text that he believes that "minor modifications to the global economic and political order would suffice to eradicate most present human rights deficits" engages in precisely the "speaking for others" that he rebuffs a few paragraphs below.[63] The political subject who engages in political action even in the presence of human rights deficits (or precisely because of them) and attempts to conceptualize her grievances in concert with others is being spoken for when the shape of injustice and the form of reparation are determined prior or in parallel to their political engagement.[64] The normative orientation to include these sites of politics and these political actors is thus not speaking for others but rather theorizing novel international and transnational institutional forms so

---

[61] NAACP, "The Future of Africa," *The Crisis*, 17/3 (1919), 119.

[62] Pogge, "Responses to the Critics," in Jaggar (ed.), *Thomas Pogge and His Critics*, 209.

[63] Pogge, "Responses to the Critics," 208.

[64] I discuss the question of freedom in the presence of power and attempts at domination in Valdez, "Non-Domination or Practices of Freedom? French Muslim Women, Foucault, and the Full Veil Ban," American Political Science Review, 110/1 (2016), 18–30.

that these speaking subjects can access them and their own notions of power, responsibility and duty can be heard.

Conceptualizing politics complements an otherwise simplified understanding of human psychology prevalent in the global justice literature, which assumes that a rational derivation of responsibilities and duties will be enough to persuade wealthy individuals of their responsibilities. By examining politics, power, and resistance we learn of the structural character of injustice, the way in which it is supported by particular constructions of subjectivity and specific institutional practices, and the sources of resistance to acknowledge such injustice among the privileged. Racial constructions, updated through governance and development discourses after the lost currency of scientific racism,[65] and neoliberal justifications for free trade, deregulation, and privatization, underlie the daily practices that today maintain and reinforce transnational injustice.

Colonialism in the Global Justice Literature

Before concluding, it is important to acknowledge that several global justice scholars do address the question of the history of colonialism in their theorization of global justice and/or seek to conceptualize the form of political relationship that colonialism entailed. In this section I engage with a few of these scholars to further illustrate the particular points about history and politics that I put forward in this chapter.

Among these scholars, Thomas Pogge has most clearly acknowledged that a "dramatic period of conquest and colonization" shaped the contemporary situation of the global poor as well as that of the better-off.[66] He recognizes that a "single historical process that was pervaded by massive, grievous wrongs" gave rise to the "misery" of the global poor and continues to dramatically affect them through "[t]he presence and relevance of shared institutions."[67] Pogge's incorporation of the question of colonialism and the continued effects of shared institutions over the situation of the global poor is an important step in historicizing global (in) justice. However, this acknowledgment does not lead him to consider the question transnationally or politically. He does not consider the question transnationally because instead of attending to the variegated topography of domination that results from the trends he narrates, he remains committed to a model of injustice in which the West owes redistribution to the

---

[65] Anthony Anghie, "Decolonizing the Concept of 'Good Governance'," in B. G. Jones (ed.), *Decolonizing International Relations* (Lanham, MD: Rowman & Littlefield, 2006).

[66] Pogge, *World Poverty and Human Rights* (Cambridge: Polity, 2008), 203.

[67] Pogge, *World Poverty and Human Rights*, 203.

poor in the non-West, rather than examining how the past of slavery and the present of migration contribute to racialized structures of domination within Western democracies.

Pogge does not consider the question politically because his analysis is not concerned with denaturalizing the realms of politics where the question of justice is raised. In this sense, the task of persuading Western individuals and motivating Western states to action prevail as the orienting political questions. This is in contrast to what this chapter proposes: to track the political claims of those affected by injustice, and incorporate into our theorization the kind of redress they request, which may substantially differ from that engineered by Western intellectuals and international organizations. The lack of examination of the transnational and political dimensions of colonial injustice is not surprising, given that Pogge's historical engagement does not occupy a central space in his theory. Instead – at least in *World Poverty and Human Rights* – it is a step of the proof that there is a negative duty toward the world's poor. As a consequence, the task remains to draw lessons about the character of injustice, incorporate the instances of politics into theories of global justice, and rethink the central subject of cosmopolitanism, as this chapter proposes.

Emerging approaches to colonialism within the global justice literature differ somewhat from Pogge's in that they take colonialism to be the central question of their analysis. In particular, Lea Ypi, Robert Goodin, and Christian Barry note that the "associative relations" account, based as it is on the reach of "coercive power with pervasive impact," undoubtedly covers colonial relations because of the binding and common legal system that covered colonizer and colonized.[68] This approach, however, maintains the focus on the reciprocity that is owed due to the ties of association and argues for its extension, rather than exploring the character of domination and rescuing the way in which those oppressed articulated alternative associations that engaged precisely in the task of defining the wrongs of colonialism and politically organizing to seek redress.

Still working within the associative framework, Ypi's more recent work defines the "distinctive wrong" of colonialism and argues that it resides in the "creation and upholding of a political association that denies its members equal and reciprocal terms of cooperation."[69] This account is

[68] Ypi, Goodin, and Barry, "Associative Duties, Global Justice, and the Colonies," 109.
[69] Ypi, "What's Wrong with Colonialism," *Philosophy & Public Affairs*, 41/2 (2013), 158. Laura Valentini argues – contra Ypi – that while there is a distinctive procedural wrong in the unilateral takeover of political collectives, she does not believe it is distinctive of colonialism. Valentini, "On the Distinctive Procedural Wrong of Colonialism," *Philosophy & Public Affairs*, 43/4 (2015), 312–31.

promising because it moves away from the benign notion of association to conceptualize the question of domination, but its departure from the ideal framework could be more substantial in at least two ways. First, this examination could consider the character colonial injustice beyond non-reciprocal dyadic relations in order to explore the systemic and transnational character of colonial injustice, as this chapter suggests. Second, this examination could be complemented by an exploration of the also transnational politics of emancipation that emerged in response to colonialism. Second, and related, this exploration could also consider the political relevance of race to the denial of reciprocity within associations, which figures prominently in the writings of colonial and US black intellectuals,[70] as well as the role of racial identity in organizing associations for emancipation.

Conclusion

In this chapter I advocate a transnational critique of the global justice literature. I propose the notion of "association for emancipation" to theorize transnational political linkages between marginalized groups in the West and the non-West. This concept allows us to historicize how frustrated attempts at domestic justice by oppressed minorities in the West motivated instances of transnational politics in coalition with other groups fighting race-based injustice. These events were proximate in time to the period in which the global justice literature was inaugurated.

Thinking about associations for emancipation complements the use of associations by the global justice literature, which has so far devoted little attention to domination within the West and its joint origin with transnational forms of domination that preoccupy this literature. This results from the lack of consideration of the way in which associations may work for domination, or the fact that alternative associations may be constructed to contest this situation politically. As a consequence, the global justice literature misses the possibility that the excluded may seek association with groups beyond the nation. This possibility is relevant to cosmopolitan approaches because it speaks to the shape of injustice and the chains of responsibility they are interested in tracing and addressing. This possibility, however, also affects social liberals' claim that obligations toward the domestic poor should take precedence over global obligations This move would be relativized if the origins of domestic injustice

---

[70] Mills, "Realizing (through Racializing) Pogge"; Césaire, "Culture and Colonization"; Du Bois, *Color and Democracy: Colonies and Peace* (New York: Harcourt, Brace and Company, 1945).

are transnational, and there is political will among domestic oppressed groups to act beyond the nation.

Relying on Du Bois's writings on peace, war, and colonialism I suggest that global justice approaches (a) should displace the elite Western subject from its privileged position as the agent working toward cosmopolitan justice, (b) should incorporate into their theorization the transnational spaces of politics inaugurated by the coalitions of the oppressed in the West and non-West, and (c) should reframe the conversation about global justice in political rather than moral terms. Writing on the context established by the Western peace movement, the wars, and their aftermath, Du Bois, in alliance with anti-colonial activists, contests the legitimacy of Western powers to decide on behalf of the colonies and recenters Africa and its diaspora by inaugurating transnational sites of political contestation. Du Bois puts forward an inherently political view of internationalism and a project – as much theoretical as practical – to rewrite Western cosmopolitanism that – even when charitable – privileges its own voice and location in determining the shape and content of justice.

In closing, it is worth clarifying that by focusing on transnational coalitions between marginalized groups in the West and the non-West my goal is not to demote normatively the weight of Western obligations toward the non-West, but to properly conceptualize how the forces of oppression result in a more complex topography of domination and resistance, whose shape we must grapple with to understand the politics of transnational justice. Moreover, my goal is to argue that the political work of justice might be well served by building upon existing networks of solidarity whose aim is emancipatory, rather than relying on global institutions dominated by Western elites with considerable institutional legacies weighing against emancipation. This suggests that it might be productive to move away from a critique that counters the focus on associations with a more historically accurate and politically astute consideration of the way in which associations for emancipation have emerged throughout history and continue to do so. This project has affinities with Chandra Talpade Mohanty's notion of transnationalism, which combines attention to "local contradictions or contexts of struggle" and "solidarities across borders" with an awareness of the systemic character of power.[71] Within political theory, my project echoes Joshua Cohen and Charles Sabel's effort to consider "[a] transnational politics of movements and organizations – beyond the intergovernmental politics of between states" that "contests and aims to reshape the

---

[71] Chandra Talpade Mohanty, "Transnational Feminist Crossings: On Neoliberalism and Radical Critique," *Signs*, 38/4 (2013), 969–70.

activities of supranational rulemaking" as a dimension of what they call "global democracy."[72]

The benefit of the proposed exploration is ultimately to recover forgotten political connections that speak to the viability of politics beyond the national and international frame so that they can inform and orient contemporary political thinking on global justice. The hope is that they also make us more attentive to contemporary instances of politics that contain emancipatory scripts overlooked by political theorists and encourage a transnational reconsideration of the issue of (in)justice.

---

[72] See Joshua Cohen and Charles Sabel, "Global Democracy," *NYU Journal of International Law and Politics*, 37/4 (2004), 764.

6   Global Justice: Just Another Modernisation Theory?

Anne Phillips

Introduction

Debates about global justice find little resonance amongst scholars in the post-colonial world.[1] At one level, the reason is obvious: this is not their problem. The literature on global justice primarily concerns itself with the obligations of citizens and governments in the richer countries towards those in poorer ones. To put it more historically, it asks what those who are beneficiaries of colonialism and imperialism owe to those who were subjected to imperial power. The addressees are not those located in the post-colonies; nor are they the many millions who used to live there, but later migrated (or fled) to the imperial centres. It is, indeed, one of the oddities of the literature that it poses questions about global responsibility without always taking on board the nature of contemporary globalisation. In its pursuit of what 'we' owe to 'distant others',[2] it treats the global north and south as relatively discrete and distant entities, overlooking the many ways in which the empire has come home.[3] In asking whether principles of domestic egalitarian justice can or should be applied to the global realm,[4] it presumes a separation that is already challenged by patterns of global migration.

The lack of resonance is substantive as well as perspectival, for it also reflects a mismatch between the post-national, post-communal, post-ethnic framework of much global justice debate and the institutional

---

[1] See, for example, Katrin Flikschuh, 'The Idea of Philosophical Fieldwork: Global Justice, Moral Ignorance, and Intellectual Attitudes', *Journal of Political Philosophy*, 22 (2014), 1–26; Neera Chandhoke, 'How Much Is Enough, Mr Thomas? How Much Will Ever Be Enough?' in Alison M. Jaggar (ed.), *Thomas Pogge and His Critics* (Cambridge: Polity, 2010).

[2] As reflected in Leif Wenar's title, 'What Do We Owe to Distant Others?' *Politics, Philosophy and Economics*, 2/3 (2003), 283–304.

[3] As Stuart Hall put it in 'The Local and the Global' in Anthony King (ed.), *Culture, Globalisation, and the World System: Contemporary Conditions for the Representation of Identity* (Albany: SUNY Press, 1989).

[4] This is the question, for example, that underpins Laura Valentini's exploration of the challenges of global justice in *Justice in a Globalized World: A Normative Account* (Oxford: Oxford University Press, 2011).

legacies of colonial power. Global justice typically speaks to us as individuals, stressing our rights and obligations as human beings rather than as
members of a community or citizens of a nation. As Margaret Kohn
notes, it is embedded within an analytic framework, usually either
Kantian or utilitarian, that takes the moral obligations of the individual
as its primary concern.[5] States will of course figure in this: if the obligations are discharged, it will be mainly through state action, not as a result
of individual citizens increasing their donations to development charities.
But especially for the more cosmopolitan inclined theorists, the nation-
state is not the moral centre. They take issue, to the contrary, with state-
centric understandings of responsibility and loyalty, elevating a normative
universalism that conceives of us as in our persona as individual human
beings over the (by implication) parochialism of the national community.
In *World Poverty and Human Rights*, Thomas Pogge characterises cosmopolitanism as composed of three elements, the first of which is the view
that 'the ultimate units of concern are *human beings*, or *persons* – rather
than, say, family lines, tribes, ethnic, cultural, or religious communities,
nations, or states. The latter may be units of concern only indirectly, in
virtue of their individual members or citizens.'[6] In *Justice Beyond Borders*,
Simon Caney identifies three main challenges to global conceptions of
justice – realism, nationalism, and 'the society of states' – and sees all of
these as characterised by the excess significance they attach to either state
or nation.[7] Most global justice theorists will attach primary normative
weight to the individual.

There *are* global justice theorists who regard nation-states as ethically
significant: Daniel Butt, for one, contrasts his approach to that of cosmopolitanism, and sees his work on *Rectifying International Injustice* as identifying the rectificatory duties of beneficiary states towards those they
colonised or otherwise treated unjustly.[8] Methodologically, however,

[5] Margaret Kohn, 'Postcolonialism and Global Justice', *Journal of Global Ethics*, 9/2 (2013),
187–200.

[6] Thomas Pogge, *World Poverty and Human Rights: Cosmopolitan Responsibilities and Reforms*
(Cambridge: Polity Press, 2002), 169. The second element is '*universality*: the status of
ultimate unit of concern attaches to *every* living human being *equally* – not merely to some
subset, such as men, aristocrats, Aryans, whites, or Muslims. Third, *generality*: this special
status has global force. Persons are ultimate units of concern – not only for their compatriots, fellow religionists, or suchlike.'

[7] Realism thinks it both appropriate and inevitable that states will pursue their own national
interests; nationalism that people have special obligations to their fellow nationals; and
'the society of states' regards international justice as best conceived in terms of what states
might owe to other states, rather than what individuals might owe to the poor.
Simon Caney, *Justice Beyond Borders: A Global Political Theory* (Oxford: Oxford
University Press, 2005).

[8] Daniel Butt, *Rectifying International Injustice: Principles of Compensation and Restitution
between Nations* (Oxford: Oxford University Press, 2008). Butt is then closer to Caney's

Butt's approach is strikingly similar to that of the more cosmopolitan theorists. In particular, he extrapolates the principles of justice that ought to regulate relations between nations from principles that ought to regulate relations between individuals;[9] and he represents nations very much as agglomerations of individuals, referring to 'modern-day populations' or 'present day generations' or 'overlapping generations', as if there were no significant stratifications intervening between the individual and the state.[10] Even, that is, where national boundaries are taken as ethically significant, and the post-national impetus is explicitly rejected, the framework remains fundamentally individualist.

Other chapters in this collection also draw attention to the methodological and normative individualism of much global justice theory. Samuel Moyn goes so far as to argue that the commitment to normative individualism was forged *in resistance* to the focus on state action and national self-determination that characterised the anti-colonial and immediately post-colonial movements.[11] He argues that the global justice literature shares with the subsequent neo-liberal order an indifference to state autonomy, as did the human rights revolution, which focuses on the individual regardless of citizenship or location and tends, if anything, to consider nation-states as the enemy. States then figure mainly as the abusers of human rights, and corrupt state officials are seen as contributing significantly (as indeed they do) to continuing inequalities. Kimberley Hutchings similarly draws attention to the methodological and normative individualism that pervades global justice theory, focusing, in her chapter, on the subset of this that addresses the ethics of war. Here, the methodological individualism is especially striking. Hutchings argues that the abstraction and individualism that characterises much writing on the ethics of war tends towards a colonial imaginary that locates moral intelligence and moral agency in the West.

My own argument shares much common ground with these, and in particular with the implications of normative and methodological individualism. I focus on two aspects. The first is the mismatch between the

---

'society of states' category, but it would be odd not to include him in the general camp of global justice theory.

[9] Butt argues, for example, that the principles that ought to govern international interaction are 'strikingly similar to the principles which libertarian theorists, such as Robert Nozick, believe govern interaction between individuals at a domestic level': *Rectifying International Injustice*, 8–9.

[10] This is part of what Catherine Lu then challenges in her structural account of injustice. Lu, 'Colonialism as Structural Injustice: Historical Responsibility and Contemporary Redress', *Journal of Political Philosophy*, 19/3 (2011), 261–81.

[11] See also Samuel Moyn, 'The Political Origins of Global Justice' in Joel Isaac et al. (eds.), *The Worlds of American Intellectual History* (Oxford: Oxford University Press, 2016).

assumptions and methodologies of global justice theory and what has been the typical experience of countries subjected to colonial rule: the absence, one might say, of a historical grounding. Colonialism destroyed communities and established historically arbitrary national boundaries, but it did not do so in order to usher in a world of abstract human beings. To the contrary, it largely secured and strengthened ethnic and religious boundaries, laying the basis for what Mahmood Mamdani has described as a 'decentralized despotism'.[12] The language of global justice neither speaks to nor offers much of a solution to the resulting institutionalisation of ethnic and community identity, for it operates within a post-national individualism that calls on us to go *beyond* the local towards the global, *beyond* the national towards the universal. Speaking, as it does, to readers in the global north, it calls on them 'to disregard their private and local, including national, commitments and loyalties to give equal consideration to the needs and interests of every human being on this planet'.[13] But other than reparations (and I do not dismiss the significance of these), it is unclear what this has to offer to readers in the global south.

The first part of my argument addresses what might be described as sins of omission: a tendency to concentrate on some problems to the exclusion of others; to speak to some audiences but not others; a failure adequately to address the more burning issues for the global south. The global justice theorist might reasonably respond that no-one can do everything. My second claim is that this is not just something left undone, but a tendency that helps reproduce relations of power. When we are encouraged to think of what we owe to others as fellow humans, rather than as fellow citizens or fellow Europeans or fellow Igbo, this carries with it, however inadvertently, the suggestion that those who fail to make this normative move remain trapped within an older paradigm. The focus on a person-to-person morality can then be said to reflect a modernist stance, in which the highest form of morality is the one that transcends the specificities of difference. Especially in its more cosmopolitan versions, global justice theory encourages us to view the power of local, ethnic, and community identification as an as-yet-untransformed traditional, something that holds us back from what justice really demands. In doing so, it suggests a trajectory from tradition to modernity of the kind more commonly associated with modernisation theory and its unthinking identification of modernity with the West.

---

[12] Mahmood Mamdani, *Citizen and Subject: Contemporary Africa and the Legacy of Late Colonialism* (Princeton, NJ: Princeton University Press, 1996), 48.
[13] Thomas Pogge, 'Concluding Reflections' in Gillian Brock (ed.), *Cosmopolitanism versus non-Cosmopolitanism* (Oxford: Oxford University Press, 2013), 298.

In what follows, I first draw on some of the literature on modernisation and modernity to clarify pitfalls in conceptions of the modern, and more specifically, to illuminate the role commonly allocated
to the individual as emblem of modernity. I then turn to the legacy of
colonialism, drawing particularly on sub-Saharan Africa, and use
some of that legacy to challenge the traditional/modern dichotomy
that suffuses modernisation theory. I then return to global justice
theory. I am not, in this chapter, claiming an intellectual lineage
that stretches from modernisation theory to contemporary work on
global justice – though the genealogy Katrina Forrester excavates in
her contribution to this collection might provide some support for
this. My main point is less about historical influences and more about
contemporary effects. I suggest that global justice expresses
a modernist bias that mirrors some of the now discredited assumptions of modernisation theory.

Modernity and Modernisation

What is modernisation theory? I use the term to refer to a branch of
development theory that thinks of societies as positioned along
a continuum stretching from traditional to modern; defines the modern
by reference to an (often idealised) version of Western society; and sees
the 'problem' of development as a matter of overcoming the obstacles that
tradition has set in its path. What counts as an obstacle varies from one
version to another, as does the precise specification of traditional and
modern, and few modernisation theorists today would endorse Walt
Rostow's over-formalised 'five stages' of economic and political
growth.[14] In most cases, however, there will be some variant of the
distinction between ascription and achievement: some claim to the effect
that 'traditional' societies attribute status on the basis of family, kinship
group, or caste, whilst 'modern' societies attribute status on the basis of
achievement. In traditional societies, the story goes, the community is
likely to take precedence over the individual; in modern societies, the
individual takes precedence over the community. In traditional societies,
there is no clear demarcation between economic, political, and social
power; in modern societies, there is a separation between these spheres.
In early modernisation theory there was limited nostalgia for the traditions that must be jettisoned in order to move along the route to

---

[14] Walt Rostow, 'The Stages of Economic Growth', *Economic History Review*, 12/1 (1959),
1–16; Rostow, *Politics and the Stages of Growth* (Cambridge: Cambridge University Press,
1971); Rostow, *The Stages of Economic Growth: A Non-communist Manifesto* (Cambridge:
Cambridge University Press, 1990).

development.[15] Later writers, perhaps less confident about the virtues of modernity, have been more ambivalent, worrying that something valuable is lost in the process. The general character of the approach remains: a relatively un-self-conscious differentiation between traditional and modern, with the latter modelled on the self-image (rather than reality) of Western societies; and a belief that all societies must eventually make their way along this path if they are to achieve economic growth, development, and democracy. Modernisation theory operates, that is, with what Dipesh Chakrabarty describes as a 'transition narrative': a 'first in Europe, then elsewhere' understanding of history that takes Europe and America as the model of all that is progressive and advanced, and presumes (at its more optimistic) that other countries must eventually arrive at the same destination, even if they get there by different routes.[16]

This way of viewing historical change is self-evidently vulnerable to criticism, and the death of modernisation theory has been repeatedly announced, from as early as 1976.[17] In its fundamentals, however, it remains a major paradigm within the social sciences, and a number of commentators have noted its recent revival and reinvention.[18] In 2005, to give one example, Ronald Inglehart and Christian Welzel published *Modernization, Cultural Change, and Democracy: The Human Development Sequence*, presenting a body of evidence to support what they took to be the central insight of modernisation theory: the claim that 'socioeconomic development brings systemic changes in political, social, and cultural life'.[19] While they represent themselves as offering a revised modernisation theory, the revisions they propose are mainly concerned with challenging the excess determinism of earlier models. 'Other things being equal', they argue, 'socioeconomic development tends to make people more secular, tolerant, and trusting and to place more emphasis on self-expression, participation, and the quality of life. But socioeconomic factors are not the only significant influences.'[20]

[15] For example, Gabriel Almond and Sidney Verba, *The Civic Culture: Political Attitudes and Democracy in Five Nations* (New York: Little, Brown, 1963); David Apter, *The Politics of Modernization* (Chicago: University of Chicago Press, 1967). For an overview of early modernisation theory see Henry Bernstein, 'Modernization Theory and the Sociological Study of Development', *Journal of Development Studies*, 7/2 (1971), 141–60.

[16] Dipesh Chakrabarty *Provincializing Europe: Postcolonial Thought and Historical Difference* (Princeton, NJ: Princeton University Press, 2000).

[17] Immanuel Wallerstein, 'Modernization: Requiescat in Pace' in L. Coser and O. Larsen (eds.), *The Uses of Controversy in Sociology* (New York: Free Press, 1976).

[18] Including Robert Marsh, 'Modernization Theory, Then and Now', *Comparative Sociology*, 13 (2014), 261–83.

[19] Ronald Inglehart and Christian Welzel, *Modernization, Cultural Change, and Democracy: The Human Development Sequence* (Cambridge: Cambridge University Press, 2005), 46.

[20] Inglehart and Welzel, *Modernization, Cultural Change, and Democracy*, 46.

So religion will not necessarily die out; cultural convergence is by no means guaranteed; and change is not unilinear. The revised version shares, however, with the classics a contrast between the communalism of traditional societies and individualism of modern ones, and differs mainly in insisting on the resilience and robustness of belief systems, even in periods of rapid socio-economic change. It remains vulnerable to the same kind of criticism that has been levelled at earlier versions.

One objection to modernisation theory is that it is bad history and bad sociology. It represents 'traditional' societies as if they have existed for centuries in splendid isolation, carrying on in their distinctively traditional ways, until propelled by the interventions of international agencies or processes of socio-economic development along the path towards modernity. In doing so, it treats social forms that were in large part *produced* by global interaction as if they were original conditions, understating the impact of centuries of global commerce, including the slave trade, and of colonialism and neocolonialism. As critics have argued, societies at the raw end of global interactions are not so much *un*developed as actively *under*developed, through the loss of their people and raw materials, the destruction of often thriving industries that were unable to compete with new imports, and the creation of new 'traditions' of hierarchy and authority that block further change.[21] The binary of traditional and modern also misses the interweaving of the alleged alternatives in pretty much every known society. In the ascription/achievement dichotomy, for example, it is supposed to be traditional societies that position people according to the group they are born into while modern societies judge us by what we have managed to do. This ignores both the importance of inherited privilege in so-called modern societies (think of Thomas Piketty's analysis of the way inheritance patterns propel contemporary capitalism into deeper and deeper inequality), and the continuing power of gender and race.[22] The sex we are born into remains an enormously powerful determinant of status in so-called 'modern' societies, in ways that cannot be plausibly represented as an unfortunate hangover from a more disreputable past. The power of gender is better understood as constitutive of all known societies and something that is being continually reproduced.

The further point is that adopting a binary of traditional and modern conveys a normative hierarchy that asserts the superiority of the latter. Though modernity is, at one level, a descriptive term, something we can

---

[21] Andre Gunder Frank, *The Development of Underdevelopment* (Boston, MA: New England Free Press, 1966).
[22] Thomas Piketty, *Capital in the Twenty-First Century* (Cambridge, MA: Harvard University Press, 2013).

attach to particular periods in history whilst leaving open for future examination its precise characteristics, it is most commonly normative as well, with the modern as what we aspire to and the traditional as what we seek to leave behind. The binary then performs a hierarchy, and it has proved difficult to dislodge this even in a growing literature that detaches modernity from its more exclusively Euro-American form. Thomas McCarthy, for example, provides a careful critique of the racial hierarchies that have underpinned ideas of human development. He nonetheless ends with certain 'practically unavoidable presuppositions of contemporary discourse', some of which hover uncomfortably close to presuppositions of modernisation theory.[23] In his analysis, the 'facts of cultural and societal modernity' bring with them the necessity of questioning received beliefs, inherited norms, and ascribed identities; encourage reflexivity and toleration of difference; and promote awareness of the possibilities for reasonable disagreement. Even when stripped of the presumption in favour of a European model, and moderated by explicit recognition of social and cultural diversity, this still recalls elements of the traditional/modern divide.[24]

There are similar strains even in Chakrabarty's account of Hindu reformers in late-nineteenth/early-twentieth-century Bengal, reformers who had a strong sense of themselves as modern, drew in many ways on European narratives of modernity, but developed what he identifies as a distinctively Bengali version. In the European narratives, he argues, modernity came to be associated with the capacity to conceptualise individuals as abstracted from specific social context, and in their generalised and disembodied rationality, sustaining the emerging ideas of equality, autonomy, democracy, and nation. The history of Bengali nationalism, by contrast, offers 'a colonial modernity that was intimately tied to European modernity but that did not reproduce the autonomous "individual" of European political thought as a figure of its own desire'.[25]

Chakrabarty contrasts Lockean conceptions of the nation, in which an absolutist, paternally derived, power is replaced by a social contract between equal (male) individuals, with the early Bengali understanding of national unity as an expression of 'natural brotherhood'. (He is well aware that both versions exclude women.) The power of the Bengali

---

[23] Thomas McCarthy, *Race, Empire and the Idea of Human Development* (Cambridge: Cambridge University Press, 2009), 156.

[24] McCarthy works broadly within the tradition of critical theory. As Amy Allen argues in *The End of Progress: Decolonizing the Normative Foundations of Critical Theory* (New York: Columbia University Press, 2016), critical theory has faced particular difficulties in rescuing what is positive in ideas of progress, development, and modernity from what is problematic in progressivist theories of history.

[25] Chakrabarty, *Provincializing Europe*, 218.

patriarch did not, he argues, have to be jettisoned in the same symbolic way in order to enter modernity, partly because his authority was not seen as exercised through command but via the devotion of his sons. Familial bonds could then continue to play a part in the theorisation of the 'modern' nation. So when, for example, Lord Curzon announced, in 1905, the first partition of Bengal to divide the largely Muslim areas in the east from the largely Hindu areas in the west, the movement protesting this 'was rich in the symbolism of the country imagined as Mother and national unity as fraternal bond'.[26] It was through the cultivation and widening of what was in some ways a very 'traditional' sentiment – the feeling of attachment to one's brother – that a national sentiment could emerge. This makes an illuminating contrast between different conceptions of modernity, but one point in Chakrabarty's account troubles me, as indeed it troubled him. As he notes, the invocation of a national unity framed in terms of brotherhood was inadequate when faced with the central issue of Indian nationalism, which was how to achieve unity across the Hindu-Muslim divide. Not surprisingly, 'Muslims did not buy this largely Hindu, upper-caste rhetoric of natural brotherhood. Nor did the lower castes, as the twentieth century progressed.'[27] He does not press this point, but one might well argue that the more abstract individual of Lockean modernity, however marked and constrained by exclusions of class, gender, and race, at least contained the potential to think beyond difference: to think of a unity in which it genuinely did not matter whether one was male or female, Hindu or Muslim, upper or lower caste. The figure of the abstract, autonomous individual continues to haunt notions of modernity even among those critical of its European focus.

Legacies of Colonialism

Yet colonialism did little to promote this supposedly modern figure. To the contrary, one of its most cited legacies – at least in sub-Saharan Africa – is that it rigidified what was previously more fluid, especially as regards ethnic and communal identities.[28] There were moments, particularly in the early years, when advocates of colonial expansion imagined the newly acquired territories as a tabula rasa on which they could inscribe whatever they chose. In particular, they expected to be able to introduce the private markets in land and 'free' wage labour that provide the

[26] Chakrabarty, *Provincializing Europe*, 234.
[27] Chakrabarty, *Provincializing Europe*, 234.
[28] Terence Ranger, 'The Invention of Tradition in Colonial Africa' in Eric Hobsbawn and Terence Ranger (eds.), *The Invention of Tradition* (Cambridge: Cambridge University Press, 1983), 211–62; Mamdani, *Citizen and Subject*.

economic underpinning of (what they deemed to be) modernity. But while the colonial states enjoyed a monopoly of military force and deployed this with frequent brutality, they were nonetheless dependent on a layer of local notables to mobilise labour, collect taxes, and settle disputes. Whatever their ideological preferences, whether they formally espoused direct or indirect rule, administrators everywhere had to respond to what Mamdani describes as the 'central and overriding dilemma: the native question. Briefly put, how can a tiny and foreign minority rule over an indigenous majority?'[29] The answer, typically, was some version of indirect rule that selectively legitimised 'customary law' and 'traditional authority', picking out those elements that best served colonial imperatives and setting aside others. In British-controlled West Africa, for example, the recalcitrance of local conditions, or all-too-fast uptake of new possibilities for private accumulation, soon encouraged a retreat to less ambitiously transformative plans. Faced with processes they could not easily control, colonial administrators came to comfort themselves with a romanticised scenario of independent smallholders, cultivating their lands under conditions of customary land tenure, and protected by a combination of chiefly and colonial power against the rise of freehold land and its counterpart, free wage labour.[30] For those who still toyed with more ambitious dreams of capitalist accumulation, reports of the horrific killings in the Belgian Congo provided a sharp reminder of the disruptions associated with plantation agriculture. It need hardly be added that the romanticised vision of the colonial settlement was not the full story, but it conveys something of the ways in which colonialism sustained its power.

In most parts of Africa, the administration of the colonies then came to depend on the delegation of authority to selected 'tribal' leaders (the uncooperative ones were quickly removed), who were secured in their power through their role as now state-endorsed custodians of the land, and enabled through this to determine who had access and under what conditions. In return, they ensured a steady supply of forced labour, taxes, military recruits, and agricultural commodities. Their role as custodians was commonly referred to as reflecting a system of customary land tenure, as if it simply formalised practices from before the colonial conquest, but the authority granted to the newly recognised tribal authorities usually exceeded that of their predecessors. As Mamdani puts it,

---

[29] Mamdani, *Citizen and Subject*, 16.

[30] I explore this story in Phillips, *The Enigma of Colonialism: British Policy in West Africa* (London: James Currey, 1989). For a parallel account of Kenya, see John Lonsdale and Bruce Berman, 'Coping with the Contradictions: The Development of the Colonial State in Kenya, 1895–1914', *Journal of African History*, 20 (1979), 487–505.

'from African tradition, colonial powers salvaged a widespread and time-honored practice, one of a decentralized exercise of power, but freed that power of restraint, of peers or people. Thus they laid the basis for a decentralized despotism.'[31] The chiefs and local notables became more unrestrained in their authority, but also the fixing of boundaries between one community and another, and attachment of these to what was seen as tribal difference, made it harder for those not deemed to share the same ethnicity to move across the territories and gain access to new land.[32] The winning of independence made less of a difference here than might have been hoped, for postcolonial rulers faced much the same constraints as regards their administrative capacity and the reach of their authority, and frequently incorporated these neocustomary authorities into their structures of governance. In Catherine Boone's analysis, 'chiefs and other neocustomary leaders often remained the gatekeepers, political brokers, and local strongmen they had been under colonial rule, mediating local citizens' access to land and local justice, and brokering access to opportunities (and exposure to risks) posed by government'.[33]

One important consequence was the ethnicisation of land conflict. 'Across much of rural Africa, the definition of "who is a stranger" and the second-class status of strangers tended to harden over time',[34] and this has proved particularly damaging at a time of increasing population pressure on the land. A further important consequence has been the strengthening of traditional authorities who then resist the rights of women to inherit the land or exercise power. Pre-colonial Africa was no matriarchal haven, but women had assumed important positions of leadership in some of the ancient empires of the continent, and as the example of the Queen Mothers of West Africa illustrates, had continued to exercise significant authority well into the colonial period. At a more decentralised level, 'most African societies had women's organisations which controlled or organised agricultural work, trade, the markets, and women's culture and its relevant ideology';[35] again, the market women of West Africa are a significant illustration. But while the colonial regimes employed, and in many instances magnified, the authority of male chiefs, they had no place in their conception of colonial rule for these forms of

---

[31] Mamdani, *Citizen and Subject*, 48.
[32] For an account of the ethnicisation of land entitlements, see Catherine Boone, *Property and Political Order in Africa: Land Rights and the Structure of Politics* (Cambridge: Cambridge University Press, 2014).
[33] Boone, *Property and Political Order in Africa*, 26.
[34] Boone, *Property and Political Order in Africa*, 33.
[35] Ifi Amadiume, 'Gender, Political Systems and Social Movements: A West African Experience' in Mahmood Mamdani and Ernest Wamba-dia-Wamba (eds.), *African Studies in Social Movement and Democracy* (Senegal: CODESRIA, 1995), 36.

female power. Colonialism did little for women's rights, and nothing of significance as regards their rights to the land: again, this was not the world of private property and individual rights that some earlier exponents of imperialism's transformative power had anticipated.

Karuna Mantena has traced the ways these developments played out in imperial thinking within the metropolis – in her study, particularly within Britain – and identifies the Indian Mutiny of 1857 and Governor Eyre's brutal suppression of the Morant Bay rebellion in Jamaica in 1865 as key moments in the shift.[36] What was once justified by reference to the 'civilising mission' and the capacity to bring 'backward' natives to a higher stage of civilization, came to be thought of more as a matter of maintaining order over peoples who were fundamentally different. 'In the transition from universalist civilizing justification to culturalist alibis for the maintenance of empire, social order and stability supplanted agendas of reform as the motivating ground of imperial rule.'[37] Or as Mamdani similarly puts it, there was a 'midstream shift in perspective: from the zeal of a civilizing mission to a calculated preoccupation with holding power; from being the torchbearers of individual freedom to being custodians protecting the customary integrity of dominated tribes'.[38] With the 'turn to culture', those colonial subjects who had too willingly imbibed the lessons of Western civilization now became objects of disdain. The colonial administrators who most explicitly positioned themselves as defenders of what they conceived to be custom and tradition much preferred the dignified difference of traditional rulers to the now despised products of the missionary schools, with their ties and their umbrellas. Mantena cites Lord Lugard's disdain for the 'unstable', 'untrustworthy', Europeanised African as one example of this.[39] Joyce Cary provides another in his description of a District Officer in the novel *Mister Johnson*.

His expression is mild and benign, but the truth is that he dislikes all Negro clerks and especially Johnson. He is a deeply sentimental man, a conservative nature. He likes all old things in their old places and he dreads all change, all innovation. To his mind, a messenger in a white gown, even if he speaks and writes English, is a gentleman; but a clerk in trousers, even if he can barely do either, is an upstart, dangerous to the established order of things.[40]

---

[36] Mantena, *Alibis of Empire: Henry Maine and the Ends of Liberal Imperialism* (Princeton, NJ: Princeton University Press, 2010).

[37] Mantena, *Alibis of Empire*, 160.   [38] Mamdani, *Citizen and Subject*, 286.

[39] Mantena, *Alibis of Empire*, 174. Lugard was the architect – or at least exponent – of principles of indirect rule, as derived from his experience in Nigeria. Lugard, *The Dual Mandate in British Tropical Africa* (London: William Blackwood, 1922).

[40] Joyce Cary, *Mister Johnson* (London: Penguin, 1962 [1939]), 25.

In colonial ideology, racial hierarchy often appeared in the guise of racial difference, with each regarded as worthy so long as he remained in his own place. But of course both the English-speaking messenger in the white gown and the upstart Christianised clerk in trousers were alike products of the colonial conquest; the former was no more representative of the old ways than the latter was representative of the new ones.

Global Justice Theory

How might any of this relate to questions of global justice? First, a caveat: it would not be entirely fair to say of global justice theory that it ignores historical causation. This might be a reasonable criticism as regards Peter Singer's drowning child scenario, which explicitly sets to one side whether the person under a moral obligation to rescue the child had any causal role in her ending up in the pond, and by extension, sets to one side whether those now called upon to address global poverty had any role in creating it.[41] It would be less convincing as applied, say, to Pogge, who argues that 'existing peoples have arrived at their present levels of social, economic, and cultural development through a historical process that was pervaded by enslavement, colonialism, even genocide', and that 'the global economic order plays a major role in the persistence of severe poverty worldwide'.[42] Here, the case for global redistribution is directly linked to an account of richer countries as historically responsible for the poverty of poorer ones. Environmental degradation, malnutrition, and starvation are traced to a global economy that continues to channel resources to people elsewhere.

One could not say, of this, that it treats what was produced by colonialism as if it were an original state. The perspective, however, remains very much that of the richer countries, and the references to colonialism work primarily to put pressure on the citizens and governments of these countries to recognise their responsibilities for global injustice and take remedial action. The key message is that justice cannot be contained within the narrow confines of the nation-state, and one effect of this is to render the specificities of each national context – including the specificities of each post-colonial context – as of lesser significance. Consider the two standard objections to global justice. These are, first, that people have compelling local attachments to their fellow citizens; second, that the problems of global poverty stem more from domestic failings, like corrupt

---

[41] Peter Singer, 'Famine, Affluence, and Morality', *Philosophy & Public Affairs*, 1/3 (1971), 229–43.

[42] Thomas Pogge, '"Assisting" the Global Poor', in Deen K Chatterjee (ed.) *The Ethics of Assistance : Morality and the Distant Needy* (Cambridge : Cambridge University Press 2004), 262, 265.

elites, than from the workings of the global economy. Answering the first typically involves challenging the normative priority given to the nation-state by citizens in the rich countries. Answering the second involves challenging the analytic priority given to the nation-state within the post-colonial ones. On the first argument, we should not think the obligation to deliver justice stops at the border of the rich countries. On the second, we should not think the *causes* of injustice arise within the borders of the poor ones. Both responses push in the post-national, post-communal, post-ethnic direction that modernisation theory identifies as at the 'modern' rather than 'traditional' end of the spectrum.

The paradigm encourages us to bracket what goes on inside each country and treat it as both normatively and analytically of lesser importance. The history of colonialism then figures mainly as confirming the case for reparations, as demonstrating the responsibility of the richer countries and their obligations to the poorer ones. This is an important message: I am not arguing against reparations. But an exclusive focus on colonial wrongs is not always the most productive message for those living in the post-colonies. As the example of Zimbabwe under (the later) Mugabe suggests, the story of colonial depredations can become an alibi for governments unwilling to address the impact of their own policies, and refusing to acknowledge their own plundering of their citizens. Because it concentrates on *global* responsibility, global justice theory is inclined to gloss over more local causes of injustice. Because it focuses on person-to-person relations, it is inclined to ignore what happens at the level of the state. The normative framing encourages us to think primarily in terms of the global rich and global poor, abstract conglomerates of abstract individuals, identifiable mainly by location (global north or global south) and resources. This is not a particularly illuminating framework for addressing the political and economic structures that sustain inequality. Among other things, it means that those who continue to devote their energies to critical analysis of the aid relationship or the failings of post-colonial elites may be left feeling they are undermining the normative case for global justice, and providing too easy an escape route for those seeking to evade their responsibilities. Yet for those living in the post-colonies, analysis of these political and economic structures, local as well as global, might seem the most pressing task.

This is one potential failing of the global justice approach, but does not yet link it decisively to modernisation theory. The latter, after all, tends to focus quite closely on local structures and the obstacles these present to further development, and on that score is better understood as the target of much global justice theory rather than its ally. The two approaches nonetheless have a shared investment in a modernist mentality that regards the transcendence of difference as representing morality's highest stage. For modernisation theorists, including of the revised kind, development involves a transition from the closed communities of traditional society to the open-ended individualism of modern society: modernity is then understood as post-national, post-communal, post-ethnic. Global justice theorists do not talk in the same way about development, but they operate with an understanding of normative maturity that involves a similar trajectory: we move beyond the local attachments that conceive of obligation as ending at the boundary of community or nation, and come to appreciate that justice is a global affair. There is no explicit theory of transition in this, and no endorsement of the language of tradition and modernity, but there *is* a related confidence about what counts as the higher stage. 'We' (in the richer countries) are not only represented as those with the obligations. We are also implicitly represented as those more capable of responding to the normative call to deliver global justice, because the centrality we already attach to the individual enables us to get beyond the limitations of either a statist or localist perspective.

In a critique of Pogge, Neera Chandhoke has argued that tying the obligation to remedy to the causal role one has played in creating the problem can limit rather than expand the scope of the obligation, and that those who can alleviate global poverty have an obligation to do so even if they are not institutionally connected in a causal chain.[43] Her argument is not just that the rich in the rich countries should not be able to get themselves off the hook by showing that they were not responsible for all the poverty in the world. She wants also to stress the obligations of the rich in the poorer countries, and argues that in failing to emphasise or include these, global justice theorists implicitly rate the inhabitants of poorer countries as of lesser moral status, as recipients of other people's actions rather than actors themselves. 'Are we', she asks,

who live and work in the developing world, fated to remain consumers of acts, whether these are acts of harm or of duty, performed by the West? Do those of us who live in India have any kind of duty to the poor in other countries? And if we do not, do we lack status as moral beings who count?[44]

The worry, that is, is that in addressing itself so exclusively to the citizens of rich countries, global justice theory not only treats them as causally responsible and richer in resources, but perceives them as richer in agency too. My suggestion is that this is not just a perverse consequence of first

---

[43] This suggests a position closer to that of Singer, though her critique of the causal model also resonates with some of the arguments developed by Iris Marion Young in *Responsibility for Justice* (Oxford: Oxford University Press, 2011).
[44] Chandhoke, 'How Much Is Enough, Mr Thomas?', 80.

world guilt. Insofar as the capacity for ethical action is being associated with the capacity to think beyond the local to the global, or beyond the national to the rights and obligations of the individual, it both blocks analysis of the structures sustaining inequality and conveys a normative hierarchy.

One element of this is that appealing 'beyond' difference to what then becomes an excessively abstract humanity threatens to deprive us of the collective resources on which mobilisations against injustice often depend. When people defend a local community against the power of global corporations (think of the Movement for the Survival of the Ogoni People against the power of Shell and the Nigerian National Petroleum Corporation), they rarely do so in a post-national, post-communal, post-ethnic framework. To the contrary, they often appeal to the values of their community, to principles of fairness or mutual concern they see as being swept aside by the juggernauts of modernity. There is typically some romanticisation of the past in this: the past, like the present, is always a mixture of good and bad, and nostalgia for tradition commonly obscures its less attractive aspects. But as a mobilising force, references to earlier but now threatened values are often more powerful than the abstract invocation of a common humanity. And there are good reasons for this, for one of the risks in invoking our common humanity is that this can encourage us to think of our humanness as *distinct from* the specificities that characterise us: to think of it as a kind of transcendence, an ability to set aside the particularities, those supposedly less essential aspects of ourselves. We do, indeed, need to make connections with those we perceive as different from ourselves – this is the important truth in appeals to our common humanity – but this does not (and cannot) require transcendence of all difference. When connecting across difference is presented as a matter of refusing to attach significance to that difference, this discourages analysis of the structures that continue to turn that difference into inequality. It also encourages the view that difference per se is a problem, something we need mentally to erase in order to embrace that commonality. Against this view, it is important to stress that we are not human *instead of* but *as* ... women, men, black, white, gay, lesbian, heterosexual, Fante, Hausa, Igbo. These are not exclusive alternatives, though they are too often presented as such within the framework of a methodological or normative individualism.

There is a particularly compelling articulation of this point in a speech Hannah Arendt gave on the occasion of receiving the Lessing Prize in 1959. This was her first return to Germany since being obliged to leave the country in 1933, and she used the occasion to reflect critically on the notion of the human and invocations of our common humanity, and how little these supposedly inclusive ideals had been able to achieve in those 'dark times'. When Jewishness carried such life and death significance, she saw it as evasion simply to insist on a shared humanity.

> [I]n the case of a friendship between a German and a Jew under the conditions of the Third Reich it would scarcely have been a sign of humanness for the friends to have said: Are we not both human beings? It would have been mere evasion of reality and of the world common to both at that time; they would not have been resisting the world as it was. A law that prohibited the intercourse of Jews and Germans could be evaded but could not be defied by people who denied the reality of the distinction. In keeping with a humanness that had not lost the solid ground of reality, a humanness in the midst of the reality of persecution, they would have had to say to each other: A German and a Jew, and friends.[45]

The parallel context, for much of the previously colonised world, is an institutionalisation of ethnic and community identity that cannot be defied by people who simply deny the reality of the distinctions. In Africa today, it is of course possible to refuse the identifications, to espouse a cosmopolitan humanism that attaches no significance to them. But this would be a matter of individual stance or attitude, and of itself hardly begins the work of dismantling the structures that can make those ethnic and community identifications so lethal. The effect, moreover, is very often to institute a new kind of hierarchy, through which the progressive-minded and usually urban dweller marks his distance from the benighted rural population.[46] The modern, again, becomes associated with the capacity to think of oneself as abstracted from social context, to question received beliefs, inherited norms, or ascribed identities; and the capacity to do this becomes elevated into the mark of normative maturity.

To clarify, I am *not* arguing against attaching normative weight to individuals; I am *not* seeking to defend tradition against modernity; I am not even arguing for a more communitarian understanding of the individual, though I will happily settle for a more relational one. As I hope has become clear, I see contrasts between traditional and modern, revolving as they so often do around further contrasts between particularity and universality, or embeddedness in one's social relations and the capacity for abstracting oneself from these, as obscuring the interweaving of the so-called traditional and so-called modern in pretty much every known society. More specifically, my comments on the legacies of colonialism are intended to convey scepticism about what gets named as 'tradition' in

---

[45] Hannah Arendt, 'On Humanity in Dark Times: Thoughts about Lessing' (1959), in Arendt, *Men in Dark Times* (New York: Harcourt Brace, 1983), 23.

[46] One of the arguments Mamdani makes in *Citizen and Subject* is that strategies of top-down modernisation, aimed at detribalising power, may just replace a decentralised despotism by a centralised one, in ways that exacerbate the urban/rural divide.

societies that were subjected to the upheavals of colonial rule. I am not then endorsing the kind of cultural revivalism that uncritically reclaims those past traditions as alternatives for the future.[47] My claim, more simply, is that a normative theory that revolves around the abstraction of the individual – and the capacity of that individual to abstract herself from her surroundings – participates, however inadvertently, in a binary of traditional and modern.

Global justice theory enacts its modernity by refusing the significance of substantive characteristics beyond location (X lives in the global north not south) or resources (X is rich rather than poor). This simultaneously obscures the structures that sustain inequality – structures that are local as well as global – and endorses an ethical framework that calls on us to set aside local and national loyalties. This is not particularly meant for those living in the post-colonies, on the (often reasonable) grounds that they are the ones who were wronged, not the ones with the duties of justice. My point is that it *could not* be addressed to them, for an exhortation to set aside the private, local, and communal, and disregard national commitments and concerns is too patently at odds with the challenges people face in the worlds created through the colonial encounters. Global justice claims to address us all in our shared humanity, but in reality speaks only to some, and in doing so becomes vulnerable to the charge of dividing the world into an 'us' and 'them'. The 'us' are figured as having arrived at the stage where they can at last set aside local loyalties while the 'them' are not really figured at all.

One might, of course, argue that it is precisely in contexts where there is an excess of attachment to the ethnic or local that global justice theory comes into its own: that its great strength lies in the resources it offers for challenging ethnic, gender, and national exclusions. There is something in this, but not enough. As critics of race-blind and gender-blind approaches to inequality have repeatedly argued (including, in this volume, Charles Mills), while the high-minded refusal to regard differences of gender, ethnicity, or nationality can, in some contexts, alleviate discrimination, it can also close down analysis of the structures that reproduce the inequalities and discrimination, and block initiatives for change. The challenge is to find ways of mobilising the ethical imperative that underpins global justice theory without obscuring the history in which it is embedded: to find ways of pursuing justice that do not rebound on themselves by enacting a normative hierarchy.

---

[47] I am sceptical, for example, about some of the ways in which *ubuntu* is invoked in some current discourses about the individual and community in Africa: for example, in Drucilla Cornell, *Law and Revolution in South Africa: uBuntu, Dignity, and the Struggle for Constitutional Transformation* (New York: Fordham University Press, 2014).

7   Globalizing Global Justice

Margaret Kohn

In this chapter I argue that scholars who are concerned about global justice should draw on perspectives from the global south. This claim rests on a modified version of standpoint theory, which I explain and defend. The term "global justice" describes normative theories about the sources and extent of obligations to combat economic inequality, human rights abuses, and poverty in poor countries. The title of one influential article captures the core concern of this approach succinctly: what do we owe to the global poor?[1] Drawing on Kantian or utilitarian frameworks, this literature urges people living in wealthy countries to examine their obligations to distant others.

Before explaining the limitations of this approach, I want to emphasize its value. This way of posing the question forces students and scholars to consider themselves as agents who are at least partially responsible for the unfair distribution of burdens and benefits in the world. There are different ways of construing this responsibility. Some writers describe the source of this responsibility as the wealthy world's failure to meet the basic needs of the poor, and others emphasize that inequalities are actually produced by economic and political structures that benefit the privileged.[2] These philosophical arguments about responsibility call on the reader to respond, to think about global poverty, and to think about it in a way that gives it a sense of urgency and proximity. Furthermore, while early contributions such as Peter Singer's may have relied on problematic analogies and may have overlooked political and economic analysis, this is much less true of recent debates, which have focused

---

[1] Leif Wenar, "What We Owe to Distant Others," *Politics, Philosophy & Economics*, 2/3 (2003), 283–304; Matthias Risse, "Do We Owe the Global Poor Assistance or Rectification?" *Ethics & International Affairs*, 19/1 (2005), 9–18.
[2] Thomas Pogge and Darrel Moellendorf (eds.), *Global Justice: Seminal Essays* (St. Paul, MN: Paragon House, 2008).

on international institutions, structures, and the legacy of colonialism.[3]

Given the considerable strengths of the literature on global justice, why are other perspectives important? One reason is that at least some analyses of global justice fit into what Makau Mutua called the narrative of "victims, savages, and saviors," a narrative that dehumanizes the poor, obscures their agency, and legitimizes global institutions.[4] It legitimizes global institutions by depicting them as instruments of global justice and overlooking the way they have secured rather than dismantled global inequalities.[5] According to Nancy Fraser, the dominant theories of global justice are not adequate because they do not tell us how to proceed when we encounter conflicting views on moral standing, social cleavages, and the means of redressing injustices.[6] My chapter also builds on recent work calling for greater pluralism in discussions of global justice.[7] Attending to the perspectives from the global south is one specific way to foster greater pluralism by incorporating distinctive arguments about the grounds, agents, and content of global justice.

The term global south is not simply a geographical designation. It is often used as an alternative to "lesser developed countries," because that latter term rests on a strong notion of historical progress that scholars have come to question. "Postcolonial" would be a possible alternative because it signals that global inequalities were produced by a shared history of military, political, and economic domination, but this term is limited by two weaknesses. First, the prefix "post" implies that the legacy of colonialism is superseded; second, postcolonialism is often associated with a specific set of theoretical arguments about power and representation. In order to avoid these sources of confusion, I use the terms "global south" and "subaltern perspectives" to identify theories that emerge from or focus on countries with minimal economic and political power.

---

[3] Peter Singer, "Famine, Affluence, and Morality," *Philosophy & Public Affairs*, 1/3 (1972), 229–243. For work discussing colonialism, see Lea Ypi, Robert Goodin, and Christian Barry, "Associative Duties, Global Justice, and the Colonies," *Philosophy & Public Affairs*, 37/2 (2009), 103–135; Thomas Pogge, *World Poverty and Human Rights*, 2nd edn. (Cambridge: Polity, 2008); Leif Wenar, *Blood Oil: Tyrants, Violence, and the Rules That Run the World* (Oxford: Oxford University Press, 2015).
[4] Makau Mutua, *Human Rights: A Political and Cultural Critique* (Philadelphia: University of Pennsylvania Press, 2002).
[5] Martha Nussbaum, *Frontiers of Justice: Disability, Nationality, Species Membership* (Cambridge, MA: Harvard University Press, 2007).
[6] Nancy Fraser, "Abnormal Justice," *Critical Inquiry*, 34/3 (2008), 393–422.
[7] Helena De Bres, "The Many, Not the Few: Pluralism about Global Distributive Justice," *Journal of Political Philosophy*, 20/3 (2012), 314–340; Lea Ypi, *Global Justice and Avant-Garde Political Agency* (Oxford: Oxford University Press, 2012).

Standpoint theory is a methodological approach that is opposed to abstraction, and highlights the importance of history, context, perspective, and power.[8] The first two sections of this chapter clarify this methodology by responding to two very different objections: the essentialist critique and the objectivity/impartiality critique. Elements of these critiques are persuasive, but a modified version of standpoint theory is both defensible and necessary to explain why we need to globalize theories of global justice. The final section provides a preliminary sketch of some distinctive ideas from the global south about how to address global injustice and inequality. These include alternative ways of thinking about the content, grounds, and agents of global justice. For example, global justice could focus on the redistribution of wealth or on the regulation of production. It could emphasize the individual moral responsibility of wealthy people, the power of corporations, or global solidaristic networks.[9]

The more abstract discussions of global justice explain why agents have a duty to aid disadvantaged people from other countries, but they tell us less about what mechanisms are effective at alleviating poverty. This argument is similar to the Hegelian critique of Kantian morality. Abstract reason indicates that we should act according to duty, but it cannot specify the determinate content of that duty. Standpoint theory explains why the content of this duty cannot be discerned without considering the causes and solutions from the perspective of those most directly affected. If you want to help someone, the first thing to do is to ask what they need. The postcolonial approach identifies structural inequalities and relations of subordination as key features of poverty and focuses on building power and agency as solutions.[10]

Drawing on global perspectives can provide tools for thinking critically about some of the answers proposed in the global justice literature.[11] Some scholars have proposed to remedy global inequality by challenging the sovereignty of "authoritarian predators" who rule poor countries.[12]

---

[8] Charles Mills, "'Ideal Theory' as Ideology," *Hypatia*, 20/3 (2005), 165–184; Mills, "White Ignorance" in Shannon Sullivan and Nancy Tuana (eds.), *Race and Epistemologies of Ignorance* (Albany: SUNY Press, 2007), 11–38.

[9] Carol Gould, *Globalizing Democracy and Human Rights* (Cambridge: Cambridge University Press, 2004).

[10] Monique Deveaux, "Beyond the Redistributive Paradigm: What Philosophers Can Learn from Poor-Led Politics" in Helmut Gaisbauer, Gottfried Schweiger, and Clemens Sedmak (eds.), *Ethical Issues in Poverty Alleviation* (Leuven: Springer, 2016), 225–245.

[11] Boaventura de Sousa Santos, *Epistemologies of the South: Justice against Epistemicide* (Abingdon: Routledge, 2015).

[12] Thomas Pogge, *World Poverty and Human Rights*, 2nd edn. (Cambridge: Polity, 2008); Jan Narveson, "Welfare and Wealth, Poverty and Justice in Today's World," *Journal of Ethics*, 8/4 (2004), 305–348.

These solutions rely on a social imaginary that juxtaposes idealized images of Westerners and realistic or negative portrayals of non-Westerners. By making this social imaginary visible and rendering it problematic, more critical accounts can contribute to the search for better solutions.

Subaltern Standpoint Theory

The term "standpoint theory" describes the feminist reworking of the Marxian view that ideology is the product of class interests. According to Marxists, the free market looks free from the perspective of the bourgeoisie, but it may feel like coercion to the worker who is forced to sell his labor at any price or starve. As Marx and Engels famously put it in the *Communist Manifesto*, "Your very ideas (the ideas of the bourgeoisie) are but the outgrowth of the conditions of your bourgeois production and bourgeois property, just as your jurisprudence is but the will of your class made into a law for all."[13] Nevertheless, actual workers did not necessarily evaluate capitalism from a proletarian standpoint, and Marx realized that it was not easy to penetrate bourgeois ideology. Widespread identification with the proletarian standpoint required both historical processes such as urbanization and industrialization as well as political mobilization. Marx's underlying analysis, however, rested on a distinction between appearance and essence. What looks like freedom and equality is actually exploitation and coercion. The concept of commodity fetishism also rests on this distinction; what looks like the circulation of things is actually the expression of social relations.[14]

Feminist standpoint theory suggests that women play a structural role similar to the role of the proletariat in Marxist theory. According to Nancy Hartsock, "Women's lives make available a particular and privileged vantage point on male supremacy."[15] This vantage point provides critical perspectives on patriarchal institutions and ideology. This version of feminist standpoint theory rests on the strong epistemological claim that insight into domination is the product of a determinate social position.

Feminist standpoint theory has been widely criticized over the past two decades. There are at least three main lines of criticism. First, "women's

[13] Karl Marx and Friedrich Engels, *The Communist Manifesto* in *The Marx–Engels Reader*, ed. Robert C. Tucker, 2nd edn. (New York: W. W. Norton, 1978), 487.
[14] *The Marx–Engels Reader*, 320.
[15] Nancy Hartsock, "The Feminist Standpoint: Developing the Ground for a Specifically Feminist Historical Materialism" in Sandra Harding and Merrill Hintikka (eds.), *Discovering Reality: Feminist Perspectives on Epistemology, Metaphysics, Methodology and Philosophy of Science* (Leuven: Springer, 2004), 284.

lives" cannot be the basis of the feminist standpoint because women's lives are extremely diverse. Given this heterogeneity, women's experiences of oppression are better understood through the lens of intersectionality, a framework that highlights the role of class, race, and sexual orientation, among other factors.[16] Second, standpoint theory may not be as emancipatory as its proponents suggest. In *States of Injury*, for example, Wendy Brown suggests that identity politics can be a form of *ressentiment* that instrumentalizes powerlessness or dispossession in an effort to assume a position of moral superiority.[17] She uses the term "wounded attachments" to describe a politics that is invested in its own marginality because it provides a coherent identity and privileged standpoint. In so far as these wounded attachments attain coherence by politicizing exclusion from an ostensible universal, they are reproducing rather than challenging the dominant political logic.[18] Third, feminist standpoint theory, like its Marxist forerunner, is premised on a contradiction. How can workers or women be both socially constructed by capitalism or patriarchy and simultaneously be the source of counterhegemonic truths? According to Brown, standpoint theory "requires suspending recognition that women's 'experience' is thoroughly constructed, historically and culturally varied, and interpreted without end."[19] In other words, the epistemic privilege of the disempowered (women, people living in peripheral countries, racial minorities, etc.) is based on the untenable assumption that their identities and insights are not constructed by dominant social structures.

These critiques of feminist standpoint theory are convincing and they cast doubt on the assumption that subject position can be an unproblematic basis of critique. Are they applicable to subaltern standpoint theory? Many of the intellectuals who participated in the decolonization movements of the twentieth century defended some version of standpoint theory. In *The Wretched of the Earth*, Frantz Fanon wrote, "When the native hears a speech about Western culture, he pulls out a knife."[20] This suggests that the colonized have a distinctive standpoint, one that penetrates the colonial ideology of Western superiority.[21] At times Fanon

[16] Kimberlé Crenshaw, "Mapping the Margins: Intersectionality, Identity Politics, and Violence against Women of Color," *Stanford Law Review*, 43/6 (1991), 1241–1299; A. M. Hancock, "Intersectionality as a Normative and Empirical Paradigm," *Politics & Gender*, 3/2 (2007), 248–254.
[17] Wendy Brown, *States of Injury: Power and Freedom in Late Modernity* (Princeton, NJ: Princeton University Press, 1995), 45.
[18] Brown, *States of Injury*, 65.   [19] Brown, *States of Injury*, 41.
[20] Fanon, *The Wretched of the Earth*, trans. Richard Philcox (New York: Grove Press, 2005), 43.
[21] Joan Tronto, "Frantz Fanon," *Contemporary Political Theory*, 3/3 (2004), 245–252.

implies that this perspective emerges directly out of the lived experience of the colonized. There is a contradiction between the native's certainty of his own humanity and the dehumanizing treatment that he receives from the colonizer. Fanon notes how the settlers describe the native in zoological terms ("breeding swarms," "reptilian movements"), but rather than accepting this characterization, the native laughs every time he spots such an allusion, because he "knows that he is not an animal."[22] At other points, however, Fanon suggests that the critique of the "universal" values of colonial society is the outcome of a historical and political process. He draws a contrast between the colonial period – when hegemony functions effectively – and decolonization – a process of "discovery" that "shakes the world" and forces a revaluation of values.[23]

Initially, *The Wretched of the Earth* seems to reinforce the Manicheanism of colonialism itself. The colonized and the colonizer appear as two stable, unified, and opposed groups starkly divided, in the same way that the native medina and the colonial town are divided.[24] Later in the text, however, Fanon complicates this picture. He explains how urban intellectuals initially identify with the ethical principles and culture of the colonizers. Yet, this view shifts when they come into sustained contact with the people during decolonization. According to Fanon, the process of struggle itself – not rational reflection[25] – provides the experiential basis for reconsidering Western ideas. For example, the forms of organization required to achieve decolonization are based on solidarity, and this leads the intellectuals to reconsider the value of individualism.[26] This mirrors the Marxist claim that proletarian consciousness emerges out of the class struggle.

Fanon's analysis of decolonization is a nuanced version of standpoint theory. Throughout his writing on both the struggle for decolonization and the process of postcolonial founding, Fanon is acutely aware of class differences among the colonized. He notes that the urban bourgeoisie and even the small working class benefit from the colonial system in some ways and tend to support compromise with the colonizer rather than independence. After independence, the native middle classes have little economic power and ensure their status by serving as intermediaries who protect the economic interests of the former colonial powers.[27] In order to secure political power and its concomitant economic benefits, this native elite tries to foster a shared sense of cultural identity. This national,

---

[22] Fanon, *The Wretched of the Earth*, 43.   [23] Fanon, *The Wretched of the Earth*, 45.
[24] Fanon, *The Wretched of the Earth*, 37–38.   [25] Fanon, *The Wretched of the Earth*, 41.
[26] Fanon, *The Wretched of the Earth*, 47.
[27] Fanon, *The Wretched of the Earth*, 151–155.

cultural, or group consciousness is the glue that holds the people and the elite together and secures the elite's power.

Fanon's account shows that it is possible to advance a form of standpoint theory that avoids the simplifications and distortions that Brown identifies in her analysis of feminist standpoint theory. Fanon is also very aware that the colonial subjects are positioned differently in relationship to class and gender. Moreover, he emphasizes that national consciousness and identity politics have both a positive and a negative dimension. The positive side is the way that solidarity helps overcome the tendency toward atomization (individual or familial), which is depoliticizing and disempowering. The political process of struggle and emancipation depended on and created solidarity. The negative side is the way that essentialized identities can obscure economic interests and possibly undermine more emancipatory class-based solidarity. Fanon worried that racial, ethnic, or national solidarity would function ideologically to ensure that the masses would give uncritical support to the new indigenous elites.

What about the argument that subaltern subjects cannot be both deeply embedded in the dominant social structures and yet still somehow outside of them? Here *The Wretched of the Earth* provides somewhat less guidance. Fanon suggests that colonial society, unlike capitalist society, is not based on hegemony. In capitalist society, the education system and paternalist workplace guarantee a high degree of consent that "lightens the task of policing considerably." In the colonial world, the order is secured primarily through coercion rather than consent. The intermediaries are the soldier and the policeman, and these intermediaries do not seek to hide the fact that power is based on domination.[28] The colonized are aware of this domination but do not have the ability to resist it, and therefore, at least initially, they express their frustration through internalized violence.

In *Black Skin, White Masks*, Fanon analyzes his own experience as a black from the Antilles and reaches a somewhat different conclusion about the position of the colonized subject.[29] He describes a divided self who identifies with French culture even while experiencing exclusion from the ideals of universalism, equality, and reason. In contrast to *The Wretched of the Earth*, this text describes the colonial world as governed by hegemony rather than sheer coercion, but Fanon also emphasizes the distinctive way that colonial hegemony functions through both

---

[28] Fanon, *The Wretched of the Earth*, 38.
[29] Fanon, *Black Skin, White Masks*, trans. Richard Philcox (New York: Grove Press, 2008), 188.

inclusion and exclusion. Fanon argues, "A normal negro child, having grown up within a normal family, will become abnormal on the slightest contact with the white world."[30] The encounter with the white world is a traumatic one that creates a racialized subject.[31] Fanon emphasizes that the trauma is not a personal experience of violence or hatred.[32] It is the traumatic confrontation between the black child's identity and his position in a symbolic order that valorizes whiteness and fears or hates blackness. The child is alienated when his sense of self is not confirmed and recognized by the other (white society). Fanon uses the example of children's novels and comic books to illustrate how this happens. In popular stories, the brave, heroic adventurer or missionary is always white, and the sly or cruel adversary is always a dark-skinned Indian or a cannibal. According to Fanon, both black and white children identify with the white hero, but for the black child this identification is precarious, and it is shattered when the white man's gaze confronts him with "the full weight of his blackness."[33]

Black Skin, White Masks explains how colonized subjects can be constructed by colonialism/racism and still be the source of counter-hegemonic perspectives. Fanon emphasizes that both blacks and whites internalize the "collective unconscious" that links whiteness to progress and civilization and blackness to savagery and physicality. For blacks, this experience of identification and exclusion creates a divided consciousness and sense of alienation. The psychic responses to this alienation are varied and can include denial, internalization, rage, revenge, or overcoming. This means that the experience of alienation does *not* manifest itself as a distinctive, unitary black or colonial point of view. For example, Fanon notes that literary works produced by black poets do not necessarily differ from the work of white poets because the Antillean poets "are white."[34] In the following sentence, however, Fanon states that "the Negro lives an ambiguity that is extraordinarily neurotic." I take this to mean that Antillean blacks inhabit a contradictory position, which can be resolved in different ways. Some "are white" insofar as they work within the dominant framework, and others promote negritude as a way of challenging the symbolic order. Fanon himself eventually chose political struggle in order to

[30] Fanon, *Black Skin, White Masks*, 143.
[31] Françoise Vergès, "Creole Skin, Black Mask: Fanon and Disavowal," *Critical Inquiry*, 23/3 (1997), 578–595.
[32] Fanon, *Black Skin, White Masks*, 143; Fanon also writes, "Did the little black child see his father beaten or lynched by a white man? Has there been a real trauma? To all this we have to answer *no*." Fanon, *Black Skin, White Masks*, 145.
[33] Fanon, *Black Skin, White Masks*, 150.   [34] Fanon, *Black Skin, White Masks*, 192.

undermine the economic and political structures that underpinned the colonial order.

After his involvement with the Algerian struggle for independence, Fanon began to emphasize that the solution to this alienation was collective and political. In *The Wretched of the Earth*, he argued that the native intellectuals and the people each have limited insight into the structures of domination, and he hopes that sustained contact between them will enable them to overcome these limitations and produce a higher synthesis. Education, which plays a key role in his understanding of decolonization, is not knowledge that is transmitted from above to below, but rather a process of building a more comprehensive understanding out of existing fragments of knowledge.

Fanon's analysis of black consciousness illuminates the possibilities and limits of a modified version of standpoint theory. His nuanced insight into human psychology enables us to see that you cannot simply deduce an individual point of view from the person's structural location. On the other hand, he insists that there is a powerful collective cultural unconscious that is invisible to privileged actors because they do not experience it as a source of tension. The people who are drawn in by its hegemony yet excluded by its hierarchies are forced to confront it.

Fanon's work shows us that standpoint theory does not have to incorporate the features that scholars have rightfully criticized. It does not necessarily rely on an essentialized, unitary identity or uncritically assert an unassailable truth. To summarize, there are two salient features that distinguish this version of standpoint theory. First, notwithstanding the awkward nomenclature, it should be called *standpoints* theory. This plural version of the term highlights the fact that there are multiple subaltern (or feminist or working class) subject positions and different insights and experiences associated with these positions. Second, the political ideas or arguments advanced from these perspectives are not immune from criticism or outside of power. Both Gayatri Spivak and Aijaz Ahmad have argued that promoting a subaltern perspective can intentionally or unintentionally be a way of advancing elite interests. Fanon too made this point when he argued that indigenous elites used ethnic and national identity in order to secure their positions and exploit the masses. In the final section of this chapter I will return to this issue and explicitly consider the questions raised in Spivak's influential essay "Can the Subaltern Speak?"

Standpoint Theory and Objectivity

This modified version of standpoint theory is one that I think many people would find plausible, but there is another line of criticism advanced by normative theorists. These scholars object to standpoint theory and claim that perspectivalism is antithetical to objectivity. According to Thomas Nagel, "A view or form of thought is more objective than another if it relies less on the specifics of the individual make-up and position in the world, or on the character of the particular type of creature he is."[35] Since standpoint theory explicitly draws on the insights gained from a determinate position in the world, it would seem to be subjective rather than objective. In this section I will argue that this conclusion rests on a mistaken understanding of how we come to know the social world.

My defense of standpoint theory is not based on the distinction between appearance and essence. I do not claim that scholars or citizens from the global south have access to truth or that they are necessarily able to penetrate the dominant ideology. Instead, my claim is the more modest one that political and normative issues are extremely complex, and therefore the best account of these phenomena must draw on multiple perspectives. In *Justice as Fairness*, John Rawls analyzed the sources of reasonable disagreement among reasonable people. These include the complexity of empirical evidence, disagreement about how to balance different factors, and indeterminacy.[36] He also emphasized the importance of perspective. According to Rawls, the way that we assess moral and political values is shaped by our experience. Since our experiences differ, so do our judgments, especially in complex situations.[37] Rawls describes these constraints as "the burdens of judgment" but we can also see these factors as the "benefits of judgment."

Alternative perspectives improve judgment because they do not rely on the same tools for filtering information. The views of dominant actors (including social classes, intellectuals, policy-makers) tend to be hegemonic, and this hegemony often renders alternative accounts or views invisible or incomprehensible. For example, Page, Bartels, and Seawright have found that the policy preferences of wealthy Americans diverge considerably from those of other citizens.[38] My version of standpoint theory rests on the claim that scholars should explicitly privilege the insights and views of subordinate actors in order to counteract this tendency. Standpoint theory does not provide a privileged access to

[35] Thomas Nagel, "The Limits of Objectivity," *The Tanner Lectures on Human Values* (1980), 75–139.

[36] John Rawls, *Justice as Fairness: A Restatement*, ed. Erin Kelly, 2nd edn. (Cambridge, MA: Harvard University Press, 2001), 35.

[37] Rawls, *Justice as Fairness*, 36.

[38] Benjamin Page, Larry Bartels, and Jason Seawright, "Democracy and the Policy Preferences of Wealthy Americans," *Perspectives on Politics*, 11/1 (2013), 51–73.

truth but can be a way of breaking the discursive lock of dominant ways of seeing.

According to Amartya Sen, "What we observe depends on our position vis-à-vis the objects of observation."[39] For example, during an eclipse, the sun appears to be approximately the same size as the moon. Anyone observing the eclipse from the same position would reach the same conclusion about the relative sizes and could give the same reason for reaching this conclusion, e.g., the fact that the moon totally blocked the sun. Yet, the sun and the moon are not the same size, and they only appear equivalent when viewed from the earth. Sen calls this "positional objectivity." At first, this example seems to highlight the problem with standpoint theory. Something may reasonably appear to be true from a particular perspective, even though it is actually false.[40] Sen's sociopolitical examples suggest that something can be "positionally objective" but still wrong. For example, he notes that the Indian state of Kerala has the longest life expectancy but the highest rate of self-perceived morbidity. Residents of Kerala have better access to medical assessment and treatment, and therefore they live longer. Their access to medical care means that they are also more knowledgeable about sickness and its consequences, and therefore they express greater fear of death. Their assessments of their own morbidity are not accurate, but they are neither subjective nor irrational. Both the examples of the eclipse and morbidity rates suggest the superiority of scientific or what Sen calls "trans-positional" assessment.

It would be a mistake, however, to conflate scientific knowledge with "trans-positional" assessment, especially when we are examining political, cultural, and normative issues. Scientific knowledge is one perspective that should be taken into account alongside others in order to perform trans-positional assessment. By scientific knowledge, I mean "normal science": the way in which a particular topic is analyzed according to methods that are recognized by academic experts. Take for example the study of morbidity rates in India. Sen takes it for granted that the morbidity rates reported by the Indian government are themselves accurate. He assumes that the inconsistency between the statistics and perceptions must be due to inaccurate perceptions by ordinary people, but it is possible that government statistics may be distorted and that this distortion is known to the people in the local community. In Katherine Boo's ethnography of an informal settlement in Mumbai, several informants

---

[39] Amartya Sen, "Positional Objectivity," *Philosophy & Public Affairs*, 22/2 (1993), 126.
[40] Jonathan Quong, "Political Liberalism without Scepticism," *Ratio*, 20/3 (2007), 320–340.

mention that death certificates are routinely falsified by government officials who record "death by natural causes" and underreport the number of people who are killed by traffic accidents and violence.[41] These statistics are subsequently used for scientific analysis, but the perspective of the people living in poor communities generates a different and possibly more accurate insight into the phenomenon.

The benefits of trans-positional assessment are even more obvious when we look at normative issues rather than empirical ones such as morbidity rates. Consider one issue that is particularly relevant to the topic of global inequality and poverty: free trade. Since Adam Smith, most economists have agreed that free trade is beneficial because it allows different areas to increase efficiency by specializing in the production of goods for which they have a comparative advantage such as wine in Spain and wool in Britain. Most international political economists support this view, and conclude that increasing levels of global trade have benefited both poor and rich countries by contributing to higher levels of economic growth. *Countries* may benefit from free trade in the sense that GDP per capita increases, but this tells us nothing about which *groups* within a country benefit from these additional resources. Statistics also show that inequalities *between* countries are beginning to decrease (after a long period of dramatic increase), but that inequalities *within* countries are increasing.[42] This suggests that the benefits of international trade are not shared by all, and some people, such as local producers who cannot compete with foreign manufactured goods, may even be worse off in absolute terms. Nor are the benefits of globalization shared by the farmers who lose their land when their government leases large parcels to multinational agricultural companies to grow crops for export.[43] Even if we assume that these deals are not motivated by corruption in the narrow sense of financial kickbacks to government officials, elites benefit and the poor are dispossessed. How do we decide if free trade is beneficial without asking for whom and in what way?

The main goal of standpoint theory is to insist that normative and sociopolitical issues be examined from the perspectives of those who are not in positions of privilege. The epistemic claim is that this will generate a deeper, more thorough understanding of the issue. This does not mean that any particular viewpoint is guaranteed to be more accurate or to advance justice. A worker may be thrilled by low-wage employment in an

[41] Katherine Boo, *Behind the Beautiful Forevers: Life, Death, and Hope in a Mumbai Undercity* (New York: Random House, 2012).

[42] Robert Wade, "Global Trends in Income Inequality," *Challenge*, 54/5 (2011), 54–75.

[43] Saskia Sassen, *Expulsions: Brutality and Complexity in the Global Economy* (Cambridge, MA: Harvard University Press, 2014).

export processing zone and be unable to see that her country is losing tax revenue and that the local river is being poisoned. Benefits and harms are also agent relative. In order to decide whether something advances the public good, or whether there even is a public good, it is necessary to consider it from diverse perspectives. Since the perspectives of the subaltern tend to be ignored or dismissed, they must be privileged. By privileged I do not mean that they trump others, but rather that they should be given especially careful consideration.

Global Justice at the World Social Forum

The global justice literature tries to answer the question "What do we owe to distant others?"[44] The problem with this formulation is that the term "we" conflates two positions: the normative theorist and the ethico-political agent. Consider how the question changes if posed like this: "What do distant others (e.g., the rich in wealthy countries) owe to us?" This formulation shifts the conversation about global justice and privileges perspectives from the global south. Even if wealthy people or wealthy countries are the ethico-political agents who have a duty to promote global justice, this does not mean that they are uniquely able to understand the determinate content of the duty. Another related question that needs to be asked is "what are the political strategies that might generate global solidarity and destabilize the categories of us versus them?" Are there works of political theory that address these questions?

There has been a growing interest in examining whether diverse cultural, religious, and intellectual traditions such as Confucianism and Islam endorse democracy and human rights.[45] There is a growing English language literature that draws on non-Western or postcolonial perspectives on global justice.[46] This diverse scholarship draws on a wider range of sources such as legal debates about social rights in India and South Africa, manifestos of the World Social Forum (WSF), writings published by or about the Zapatista movement and Porto Alegre participatory budgeting process,

---

[44] Wenar, "What We Owe to Distant Others"; Risse, "Do We Owe the Global Poor Assistance or Rectification?"

[45] Joanne Bauer and Daniel Bell, *The East Asian Challenge for Human Rights* (Cambridge: Cambridge University Press, 1999); Abdullahi Ahmed An-Na'im, *Human Rights in Cross-Cultural Perspectives: A Quest for Consensus* (Philadelphia: University of Pennsylvania Press, 2010).

[46] See for example Jomo Kwame Sundaram (ed.), *Islamic Economic Alternatives: Critical Perspectives and New Directions* (Berlin: Springer, 2016).

academic postcolonial theory, and ethnographies of global social movements.[47]

There is a tendency in the field of political theory to ignore these sources, and I suspect that there are three reasons for this. First, there are implicit understandings of what types of writing can be recognized as legitimate political theory. Manifestos, ethnographies, policy documents, and legal briefs may articulate a clear vision of how to advance global justice, but they seldom explain and defend this vision in the writing genre of normative theory. They do not always have the nuance, rigor, or theoretical richness of academic political theory. Second, some scholars may worry that drawing on these accounts involves "speaking for others," which entails the risk of distortion, orientalism, and possibly exploitation.[48] Finally, the range of sources and views is so heterogeneous and pluralistic that it can seem daunting to know where to begin.

In this chapter I start with the WSF because it was explicitly designed as a place to examine global justice from the perspective of less privileged actors. The WSF was created in January 2001 in Porto Alegre (Brazil) in order to bring together local, national, and transnational movements engaged in challenging neo-liberal globalization from below. It was conceived as an alternative to the globalism of international institutions such as the G20, the World Bank, and the International Monetary Fund (IMF). According to Boaventura de Sousa Santos, the WSF is an expression of the epistemology of the South and an attempt to generate and strengthen alternative solutions to the global inequalities.[49] These solutions are alternatives to the policies that are usually described as neo-liberalism, or the Washington consensus. The Washington consensus promotes economic growth through austerity and deregulation. By dismantling welfare state provisions, weakening unions, privatizing public companies, and deregulating, states can lower the cost of doing business and attract investment. According to this theory, the role of the state is not to promote the public good directly, but rather to create an environment that enables business to flourish. The governing assumption is that "a rising tide lifts all boats."

---

[47] Rahul Rao, *Third World Protest: Between Home and the World* (Oxford: Oxford University Press, 2012); Manfred Steger and Erin Wilson, "Anti-Globalization or Alter-Globalization? Mapping the Political Ideology of the Global Justice Movement," *International Studies Quarterly*, 56/3 (2012), 439–454; Boaventura de Sousa Santos, "The World Social Forum and the Global Left," *Politics & Society*, 36/2 (2008), 247–270.

[48] Thomas Pogge, "Responses to the Critics" in Alison Jaggar (ed.), *Thomas Pogge and His Critics* (Cambridge: Polity Press, 2010); Linda Alcoff, "The Problem of Speaking for Others," *Cultural Critique*, 20 (1991), 5–32.

[49] de Sousa Santos, "The World Social Forum and the Global Left."

The unifying idea that links many of the groups in the WSF is opposition to marketization. This opposition does not necessarily imply advocacy of direct state control of the economy, but it does involve promoting alternatives to the market and exploring other ways of distributing burdens and benefits. These alternatives include the following: strengthening local democracy to assert collective control over local resources; decommodification of key areas such as education and health care; protection of the environment; promotion of values such as solidarity and justice; control and regulation of multinational corporations. In a systematic study of the ideology of the WSF, Manfred Steger and Erin Wilson found that that groups affiliated with the WSF advanced a coherent vision of "justice globalism."[50] Justice globalism is one important perspective that emerges from the global south. The key features of justice globalism include universal rights (especially economic, social, and cultural rights), participatory democracy, global solidarity, and socioeconomic and environmental sustainability.

How do these solutions compare to the ones that are most prominent in the Anglo-American global justice literature? There are a number of similarities, most notably the shared emphasis on universal rights and justice. Nevertheless, the discourse of the WSF points toward some subtle but important differences between the two approaches. For example, the term solidarity could be construed as a way of describing the normative claim that moral obligation extends beyond national borders and implies obligations to distant others. Yet, in the standard "what do we owe them?" frame, distant others remain both distant and other. Solidarity, on the other hand, connotes acting *with* others and implies common responsibility among members of a group.[51] At least at the rhetorical level it suggests a relationship of mutuality and reciprocity rather than a hierarchical relationship of donor and beneficiary.[52]

Among the forty-five organizations studied by Wilson and Steger, there were five common political claims. All five of these claims pointed toward the market, financial institutions, or corporations as agents responsible for increased inequalities. For example, Focus on the Global South emphasized that promoting the well-being of people and the planet requires "democratic controls over financial institutions." The Bamako Appeal is another document that expresses some of the core ideas of justice globalism. The Bamako Appeal was issued at the conclusion of

---

[50] Steger and Wilson, "Anti-Globalization or Alter-Globalization?"
[51] Avery Kolers, "Dynamics of Solidarity," *Journal of Political Philosophy*, 20/4 (2012), 365–383.
[52] See also Ruth Lister, "Power, Not Pity: Poverty and Human Rights," *Ethics and Social Welfare*, 7 (2013), 109–123.

a meeting of nongovernmental organizations (NGOs) and think tanks that was organized by Samir Amin and held in Bamako, Mali. The meeting took place in 2006 on the fiftieth anniversary of the Bandung Conference. The Bamako Appeal emphasized the suffering caused by "the dictatorship of financial markets and by the uncontrolled global deployment of transnational firms" and called for democratic control over international organizations, environmental sustainability, international solidarity, and alternatives to neo-liberalism.

There are some similarities between these proposals and the ones promoted by Thomas Pogge in his influential book *World Poverty and Human Rights*. Pogge argues that wealthy countries are partially responsible for global economic inequality, because these inequalities were produced by colonialism and are reinforced by a shared institutional order. Pogge advances two specific proposals to modify international institutions in order to help ensure "that all human beings can meet their own basic needs with dignity"[53]: the global resources dividend (GRD) and the borrowing privilege. The GRD is a tax on extractive industries such as mining and oil drilling. This tax would have the dual benefit of encouraging conservation and also generating funds that could be redistributed to help poor people in developing countries. Pogge's second proposal is to end the "borrowing privilege of authoritarian predators."[54] He argues that many people are poor because of the actions of their own leaders, who extract resources, borrow money, and steal foreign aid in order to enrich themselves at the expense of the public. One way to weaken the power of these leaders would be to limit their ability to borrow money that must be repaid by the public. Pogge suggests that nations in the global south should adopt constitutional amendments stating that debts incurred by nondemocratic governments will not be repaid by the people.

These two proposals are broadly consistent with the theory of justice globalism outlined above. The first aims to use international institutions to promote environmental sustainability and fill basic human needs; the second mechanism promotes democracy and weakens authoritarian governments. Yet, there are also some subtle differences between Pogge's approach and justice globalism. First, Pogge insists that the design of the GRD "must draw upon the expertise of economists and international lawyers."[55] Instead of recognizing the value of both grassroots and "expert" perspectives, Pogge only incorporates the latter. Despite

---

[53] Pogge, *World Poverty and Human Rights*, 203.
[54] Pogge, *World Poverty and Human Rights*, 159.
[55] Pogge, *World Poverty and Human Rights*, 212.

decades of research in development studies that documents the ineffectiveness and destructiveness of projects designed entirely by outside experts,[56] Pogge embraces technocratic solutions. He positions the poor primarily as beneficiaries and not as agents of change.[57]

Second, in outlining the rationale for the GRD and restrictions on the borrowing privilege, Pogge depicts the leaders of poor countries in a negative light. He describes them as "predators" and writes, "In some poor countries, the rulers care more about keeping their subjects destitute, uneducated, docile, dependent, and hence exploitable."[58] In these cases, he proposes funneling aid through UN agencies or NGOs rather than domestic governments. He also considers the possibility of authorizing military intervention to depose authoritarian predators.[59] In a similar vein, Martha Nussbaum suggests that the mechanisms for promoting global justice include "global economic policies, agencies and agreements, including the World Bank, the IMF, and various trade agreements" and "multinational corporations, to which we shall assign certain responsibilities for promoting human capabilities in the nations in which they do business."[60] These texts depict multinational corporations and institutions in their ideal form and developing countries in an ambivalent or negative way. This rests on and reinforces a social imaginary composed of Western saviors and third world predators. This is problematic for two reasons. It functions ideologically to justify concentrating greater power in the hands of existing international institutions even though this power has been the cause of much global injustice. Second, it frames the problem in a way that delegitimizes other kinds of solutions.

Consider Nussbaum's suggestion that multinational corporations should do more to foster human capabilities in places where they do business. This involves a certain level of critique, since it implies that multinational corporations do not currently promote human capabilities to a sufficient degree. But, more importantly, it depicts multinational corporations as organizations that *could* be persuaded to become agents of capability promotion. This seems extremely unlikely, given that

---

[56] Jan Nederveen Pieterse, *Development Theory: Deconstructions/Reconstructions* (London: Sage, 2002); Arturo Escobar, *Encountering Development: The Making and Unmaking of the Third World* (Princeton, NJ: Princeton University Press, 2011); James Scott, *Seeing Like a State: How Certain Schemes to Improve the Human Condition Have Failed* (New Haven, CT: Yale University Press, 1999).

[57] Monique Deveaux, "The Global Poor as Agents of Justice," *Journal of Moral Philosophy*, 12/2 (2015), 125–150.

[58] Pogge, *World Poverty and Human Rights*, 161–162, 212.

[59] Pogge, *World Poverty and Human Rights*, 159.

[60] Nussbaum, *Frontiers of Justice*, 314.

multinational corporations are acting in a competitive environment and are legally required to maximize profit for shareholders. As Marx pointed out in *The Poverty of Philosophy*, the moral character and intentions of the factory owner matter very little given that his choices are structured by capitalism.

Similarly, from a subaltern standpoint, it seems unlikely that existing global institutions can become agents of redistribution. They emphasize the evidence that supports the view that the austerity measures promoted by the IMF and the World Bank have increased poverty in developing countries.[61] The governance structures of the World Bank and the IMF gave a disproportionate share of power to the United States and under-represent heavily indebted poor countries.[62] Carla Norloff concludes that even though international institutions would seem to limit the power of strong states, in reality, the strongest state is well positioned to gain more than other states.[63] Trade agreements often force poor agricultural countries to allow free access to imports without requiring wealthy countries to end farm subsidies. There is also research that highlights the ways that international institutions or agreements benefit poor countries. The point is not to resolve this dispute, which is too complex and multifaceted to have a single definitive resolution, but rather to point out how the radical critique of economic orthodoxy can generate new questions, different answers, and alternative approaches.[64]

Justice globalism is informed by a distinctive social imaginary. Rapacious domestic elites are only mentioned in a spectral fashion, haunting the calls for greater accountability through democratic participation and mobilization. Multinational corporations and international institutions are depicted as the agents of dispossession and sources of inequality. This perspective too undoubtedly has its limitations, but it challenges the ideological assumption that only the distribution of aid – and not the production of economic inequality through the market – is an ethico-political issue. It also has the important effect of disrupting the narrative that casts Westerners as saviors and people in developing countries as passive victims or predators. This is the first step in building transnational movements that address global inequality both from

---

[61] David Harvey, *The New Imperialism* (Oxford: Oxford University Press, 2005); Naomi Klein, *The Shock Doctrine: The Rise of Disaster Capitalism* (New York: Random House, 2008).

[62] Rao, *Third World Protest*. In 2008 the Board of Governors approved a package of reforms that increased the representation of poorer countries.

[63] Carla Norrlof, *America's Global Advantage: US Hegemony and International Cooperation* (Cambridge: Cambridge University Press, 2010).

[64] Thomas Pogge and Krishen Mehta (eds.), *Global Tax Fairness* (Oxford: Oxford University Press, 2016); Wenar, "What We Owe to Distant Others."

above and below.[65] One part of this coalition consists of citizens in wealthy countries who are demanding that their governments regulate multinational corporations and the financial sector in order to change the way that inequalities are *produced* through the economy. It also includes citizens in poor countries who are mobilizing to elect governments that promote social rights, sustainability, and growth strategies that benefit the least well off. Both must work together in order to democratize existing international institutions so that they become more responsive to the needs of poorer countries.

Conclusion

There is a final issue to consider. What are the distinctive challenges that emerge when scholars represent subaltern perspectives and employ them for their arguments? Linda Alcoff examined this question in her path-breaking essay "The Problem of Speaking for Others."[66] She identified two specific challenges. First, there is the epistemic point that a scholar drawing on the insights of others is engaged in representation and must be aware that she is not revealing a viewpoint but rather interpreting, translating, and constituting it. As Spivak put it, "the much-publicized critique of the sovereign subject ... actually produces a subject."[67] Second, there may be power relations that are reinforced through these representations. When a privileged person speaks for a less privileged one he may be strengthening preexisting hierarchical relations.[68] Furthermore, the less privileged person usually does not authorize the privileged person and the privileged person is not accountable to him.

One response is that the goal of global standpoint theory is not speaking for others but rather listening to others. Theorists, theologians, lawyers, writers, and activists from the global south have written texts that advance arguments about global justice, and these texts are often ignored because their writing genres are not recognized and their authors are not part of dominant academic networks. Interpreting, organizing, and presenting (and potentially misrepresenting) them involves certain kinds of power relations but so does ignoring them. Although the pitfalls of the former have gotten more attention, it is this latter move that Spivak questioned in her famous essay "Can the Subaltern Speak?" Spivak focuses her attention on the problems that emerge when scholars attempt to avoid the

---

[65] Gould, *Globalizing Democracy and Human Rights.*

[66] Alcoff, "The Problem of Speaking for Others."

[67] Gayatri Chakravorty Spivak, "Can the Subaltern Speak?" in Cary Nelson and Lawrence Grossberg (eds.), *Marxism and the Interpretation of Culture* (New York: Macmillan, 1988), 271–317.

[68] Alcoff, "The Problem of Speaking for Others," 7.

pitfalls of representation by, as she puts it, letting the subaltern speak for themselves. She argues that "listening to" is problematic because it treats subaltern speech as authentic and transparent, thereby obscuring the way that it is already constituted through knowledge/power.

Many readers took the term "subaltern" to describe a broad category largely synonymous with "marginalized" or "lower rank." In a more recent essay, however, Spivak explains, "Neither the groups celebrated by the early subalternists nor Bhubaneswari Bhaduri, in so far as they had burst their bonds into resistance, were in the position of subalternity. No one can say 'I am a subaltern' in whatever language."[69] This suggests that the term subaltern marks a social position that cannot be fully recognized within the dominant framework. If we follow Spivak, then subaltern should not be used to describe *categories* like colonial subjects, workers, or women, since these categories contain individuals who vary considerably in their political subjectivity and agency. This restricted definition, however, departs from the broader Gramscian sense of subaltern. He used the term to describe groups that were in a subordinate position in the hierarchy of power and did not exercise hegemony. In "Notes on Italian History," Gramsci emphasized that subaltern groups may reproduce dominant ideologies, assert partial autonomy, or begin to produce new institutional formations.[70] I use the term in the Gramscian sense, as a structural position that can generate different perspectives on dominant ideas and practices.

Subaltern perspectives may be marginalized within Anglo-American normative theory (or even academia more generally), but they have been articulated with a great deal of sophistication by thinkers drawing on both indigenous traditions and European and global theories such as Marxism, liberal rights, and theology. These intellectual traditions are not subaltern in Spivak's sense, but a great deal can be learned by reading them and drawing on their insights, while remaining attentive to the point that transparency and authenticity are impossible and power is ubiquitous. This means that the messy, political, critical, contested work of interpretation is necessary.

In her essay "Scattered Speculations on the Subaltern and the Popular," Spivak raises a concern that is particularly relevant to this chapter. She worries that "the leaders of counter-globalist resistances" may be "faking subaltern collective initiative" in order to advance their

---

[69] Gayatri Chakravorty Spivak, "Scattered Speculations on the Subaltern and the Popular," *Postcolonial Studies*, 8/4 (2005), 476.
[70] Antonio Gramsci, *Selections from the Prison Notebooks of Antonio Gramsci*, eds. Quintin Hoare and Geoffrey Smith (New York: International Publishers, 1971), 52.

political goals.[71] This may refer to organizations affiliated with the WSF, which organized meetings attended by activists from the global south and, perhaps, used their presence to legitimize a political strategy that was formulated with little input. It is beyond the scope of this chapter to evaluate whether this is an accurate criticism of the WSF, but I do think that it raises a valuable cautionary note. It is possible that a "counter-globalist resistance movement," could function like Fanon's "national consciousness" and be used to create a false solidarity that obscures important issues and voices. Authenticity, like objectivity, can also be used to close off consideration of heterodox ideas and arguments. The best solution is to recognize that the benefits of judgment are secured by paying particular attention to marginalized perspectives.

---

[71] Spivak, "Scattered Speculations on the Subaltern and the Popular," 484.

8   Challenging Liberal Belief
Edward Said and the Critical Practice of History

Jeanne Morefield

> Whether we are hurting or refusing to help these impoverished societies
> is itself not relevant in evaluating the moral quality of our actions ...
> (The causal story we tell might be relevant in the design of remedial
> instruments, of course, but that is a different matter ...) The key to
> understanding our moral failing here emerges from the simple fact that
> we could alter such poverty, and have chosen not to do so.
>
> (Michael Blake, 2013)[1]

> All these elisions and denials are, I believe, reproduced in the strident
> journalistic debates about decolonization, in which imperialism is repeatedly
> on record as saying, in effect, you are what you are because of us; when we
> left, you returned to your deplorable state ... For certainly there is little to be
> known about imperialism that might help either you or us in the present.
>
> (Edward Said, 1986)[2]

Introduction

Michael Blake's words above represent an approach to global justice
literature that is both particular to his work, and at the same time, deeply
representative of a larger trend. Blake's goal in *Justice and Foreign Policy*
is to develop what he finds normatively useful about Rawls's *Law of
Peoples* into a liberal approach to foreign policy grounded in something
other than what Michael Goodhart refers to as "ideal moral theory."[3]
Rather than imagine a universal theory of justice appropriate to all the
peoples of the world, Blake urges scholars of global justice and foreign
policy experts alike to refocus their efforts on understanding "what one
state might do" in order to justify its actions under "the terms of a liberal
theory of justice."[4] Blake, however, shares with ideal moral theorists not

---

[1] Blake, *Justice and Foreign Policy* (Oxford: Oxford University Press, 2013), 116.
[2] Said, "Intellectuals in the Post-Colonial World," *Salmagundi*, 70/71 (1986), 59.
[3] Goodhart, *Injustice: Political Theory for the Real World* (Oxford: Oxford University Press, 2018), 1.
[4] Blake, *Justice and Foreign Policy*, 44.

184

only a belief that liberal theory is beyond philosophical scrutiny, but also, a proud dismissal of American and European imperial history as a factor relevant to theorizing justice in today's world. In Blake's words, despite its limitations, ideal moral global justice scholarship is correct in "its rejection of our history of imperialism and cultural disrespect." Thus, while his book occasionally gestures toward "a historical pattern of colonization and empire," Blake always returns to the same conclusion: that the "causal story" tying colonial exploitation to contemporary global inequality has no bearing on the larger questions of moral choice that confront self-defined liberal states in the present.[5] This conclusion ultimately provides the ideological terrain upon which Blake's argument then unfolds, an argument which, Michael Ignatieff raves, provides readers with a "bracing, rigorous and highly realistic account of how we could begin to believe in a liberal foreign policy again."[6]

Edward Said's argument above loosely mirrors Blake's intellectual endeavor: how should scholars interested in global politics *orient* themselves toward the world? In contrast to Blake, however, Said made his observations whilst articulating an approach that assumes the continuing presence of imperialism in contemporary culture and politics. While it is largely true, he maintained, that direct colonization ended in the middle of the twentieth century, "the meaning of colonial rule was by no means transformed into a settled question."[7] Rather, imperialism is still evident in the grotesque inequality of resources between the Global North and the South, the permanent political assignation of some states as "developed" and others as "developing," widespread poverty, dependency, and peripherality. Imperialism's tentacular presence is also evident in the same postwar, American-led, liberal foreign policy agenda that Ignatieff encourages us to "believe in"; a policy agenda historically grounded in the overt and covert dismantling of democracies in the Global South. Finally, Said argued, we see the influence of imperialism in the vital intellectual and political debates that still rage within formerly colonized societies over colonialist practices and the ideologies that sustain them. Speaking back to the seeming common sense of intellectuals like Blake who insist that "there is little to be known about imperialism that might help either you or us in the present" entailed, Said argued, not a "politics of blame" but a politics grounded in the critical, interpretive practice of what he called counterpoint.

---

[5] Blake, *Justice and Foreign Policy*, 1.
[6] See Michael Ignatieff's endorsement on the jacket of *Justice and Foreign Policy*.
[7] Said, "Intellectuals and the Postcolonial World," 44.

This chapter utilizes Said's contrapuntal methodology to counter the "belief" of both global justice scholars and liberal internationalists in the transformative power of an ahistorical liberalism. I do this by first arguing that their dismissal of imperial history makes it difficult for global justice scholars to see how aspects of their theorizing replicate the cultural and ideological practices of imperialism. In particular, their amnesia regarding the historical and ongoing relationship between liberalism and imperial politics obscures alternative understandings of justice that might bubble up from sites of former and current colonial occupation and violence rather than trickle down from the heights of a perennially well-intentioned liberal theory. More troubling, the unwillingness of most global justice scholars to call the imperial history of liberalism into question provides succor to a school of liberal internationalism that is interventionist, presentist, crisis-driven, and imperialist in all but name and which continues to exercise an outsized influence on American foreign policy. Blake's work, I argue, best captures the line of argument – grounded on an explicit need to *believe* in liberalism – that tethers these two approaches. In the second half of this chapter, I explore an antidote to this ahistorical vision that I locate in Said's contrapuntal disruption of dominant narratives about global politics. Rather than focusing on the need to theorize better liberal solutions to global poverty or international crises, a Saidian approach concentrates on "worlding" these issues by marrying the search for solutions to the complexity of historical context while, at the same time, understanding the search for solutions itself to be a product of imperial history. A Saidian approach to global justice thus requires intellectuals to slow down and actively reflect on that history even as it demands sustained political and scholarly engagement with the most pressing forms of injustice in the world today.

Global Justice, Liberal Internationalism, and the Dismissal of History

The emergence of global justice as a legitimate area of concern for philosophers and political theorists occurred in the 1970s and has largely been attributed to the work of a number of John Rawls's students who because increasingly dissatisfied with the way Rawls bound his theory of justice to the state. While some more sympathetic readers of this nation-oriented imaginary, such as Blake, have sought to recast Rawlsian liberalism as a model for how liberal states ought to act in an unjust world, others like Charles Beitz, Thomas Nagel, Onora Nell, and Martha Nussbaum took Rawls's vision and expanded it, in Nussbaum's words, "beyond the frontiers of justice," in ways that explicitly challenged Rawls's own disappointing attempt to do just this in *The Law of Peoples*.[8] And yet, as Goodhart points out, both the "statist" views of thinkers like Blake, the cosmopolitan approach of "global Rawlsians" like Beitz and Nussbaum, as well as the "overwhelming majority of theorists and philosophers working on problems of global justice today," remain committed to Rawls's "social liberalism" and to his methodological attachment to developing an ideal moral theory capable of guiding the just behavior of states and individuals in an unjust world.[9]

Scholars have given different explanations for *why* so many philosophers and political theorists would suddenly become interested in broad questions about global justice during the 1970s. According to Thomas Pogge, philosophical debates about these issues were driven by the increasing impossibility of avoiding the starkness of world poverty, an issue which had "overtaken war as the greatest source of avoidable human misery."[10] Samuel Moyn, by contrast, complicates this story considerably by asking us to consider the coincidence that a global justice debate that took place largely at the level of abstract moral theory would become so popular precisely at a moment when scholars, activists, and political leaders closely associated with the United Nations Conference on Trade and Development (many from the Global South) were championing a more radical and redistributive form of global justice, the "New International Economic Order" (NIEO).[11] Coincidence or not, exactly at a moment when scholars and activists from the former colonized world were asking for a major re-engagement with the material impact of modern imperialism's four-hundred-year history, a remarkably ahistorical form of global justice scholarship surged in popularity. Onora Nell's insistence, in 1975, on using a six-person-in-a-lifeboat thought experiment to address an issue as deeply structural, historical, and power-ridden as global poverty and resource distribution offers only one stark example of this philosophical flight toward abstract normative questions of morality, right, desert, and "global basic structure."[12] These questions shift the political gaze away from the problems of global capitalism and shear "developed" liberal states of their historical complicity in creating the very inequality that now kept Nell up at night.

---

[8] Nussbaum, *The Frontiers of Justice: Disability, Nationality, Species Membership* (Cambridge, MA: Harvard University Press, 2006).

[9] Goodhart, *Injustice*, 6.

[10] Pogge, *Global Justice, Seminal Essays* (St. Paul, MN: Parragon House, 2008), xiv.

[11] Moyn, "The Political Origins of Global Justice" in Joel Isaac et al. (eds.), *The Worlds of American Intellectual History* (Oxford: Oxford University Press, 2016), 133–153. See also the chapters by Moyn and Forrester in this volume.

[12] Nell, "Lifeboat Earth," *Philosophy and Public Affairs*, 4/3 (1975), 273–292.

This tendency to assume history has no bearing on the practice of theorizing global justice today remains so deeply embedded in global justice scholarship that even when thinkers like Pogge explicitly address the injustices of the past, they can only do so in a manner that provides deep background to a current problem whose *solution* must still be sought at the level of ideal moral theory. Pogge responds to the self-serving rhetoric of economists who insist that poorer states are entirely to blame for their current situation by "invoking the common and very violent history through which the present radical inequality accumulated."[13] He continues by arguing that the wealthy nations of the world still benefit from the inequalities that were generated over centuries through the economically and politically rapacious practices of imperialism. Thus, when richer states fail to help poorer states in the present, these states fail not only in their abstract duty to others, they also actively perpetuate the abusive, historically grounded, economic order from which citizens of the Global North continue to directly benefit. And yet, while Pogge's "invocation" of imperial history and his attention to its continuing effects is laudable, it remains just that; an "invocation." The rest of his approach is seemingly untouched by the *details* of that history; the specific practices of extraction, dispossession, slavery, and underdevelopment that took place in the different colonized regions of the world.[14] Moreover, the actual voices of the colonized and formerly colonized are almost entirely absent in Pogge's account of what must be done to right the wrongs of the past, as if their specific cosmopolitan innovations (e.g., the NIEO) never existed.

The fact that the majority of scholars interested in theorizing global justice today are so unable/unwilling to acknowledge the diversity of historical experience and, instead, prefer to rely heavily on ideal moral solutions that are primarily liberal in orientation to address contemporary global problems, has had a spillover effect in political theory. In other words, ahistorical, ideal moral theorizing has become the dominant mode through which political theorists approach urgent international issues despite the diversity of interpretive strategies that characterize the sub-discipline more generally – strategies that include (but are obviously not limited to) insights drawn from: psychoanalysis, critical race theory, feminist theory, the history of political thought, radical political economy, comparative political theory, postcolonial scholarship, ethnography,

---

[13] Pogge, "World Poverty and Human Rights," *Ethics International Affairs*, 19/1 (2005), 2.
[14] Pogge, "Priorities of Global Justice," *Metaphilosophy*, 32/1–2 (2001), 6–24; Pogge, *World Poverty and Human Rights* (Cambridge: Polity Press, 2008).

etc.[15] The predominance of this historically forgetful orientation has troubling implications for both global justice theorizing itself and for politics more generally.

First, this approach is troubling because of what it *occludes*. In other words, ahistorical, ideal moral theorizing constrains normative theory itself by inadvertently participating in an imperialist idiom that suppresses alternative ethical responses to contemporary examples of injustice, responses that might be identified if one took imperial history seriously. For instance, when political theorists concerned with justice and multi-culturalism have tried their hand at imagining ethical solutions to the Israel/Palestinian question, they have tended to do so through the application of abstract principles that are developed elsewhere but are considered both universally germane and entirely modular. Iris Marion Young, for instance, addresses the situation by carefully thinking through the ways a model of "self-determination as non-domination" might offer conceptual resources for Jews and Palestinians alike that go beyond the political limitations of statehood.[16] Reimagining self-determination in these terms, she suggests, opens up our political horizons to alternatives other than the current order (grounded in separation, alienation, and apartheid) and takes seriously the "dense interrelation" of Jews and Arabs in the land of Palestine/Israel. Young is deeply concerned with the experiences of the two communities while at the same time acknowledging that the "unequal relations of interdependence" between them "result from histories of unjust domination that should be recognized, but cannot be completely undone."[17] But, that is as far as history impinges on her thinking. Missing is any engagement with the way the culture discourse of imperial domination in Mandated Palestine specifically constructed Palestinians as either "other" (e.g., lazy natives, inscrutable Orientals) or a people passing out of history. Young's importation of "self-determination as non-domination" thus inadvertently replicates the rhetorical move by which colonial administrators and Zionists were/ are able to occupy not only land but the ideological space necessary to represent Palestinians as a people to the world; a people to be studied and ordered, a people incapable of generating their own political and cultural stories, a people, in Said's words, who have historically been denied "permission to narrate."[18] This move runs counter to Young's desire to

---

[15] See Andrew March's useful description of the "organizational fiction" that is political theory in "What Is Comparative Political Theory?" *Review of Politics*, 71/4 (2009), 533.

[16] Young, "Self Determination as Non-Domination," *Ethnicities*, 5/2 (2005), 139–159.

[17] Young, "Self Determination as Non-Domination," 156.

[18] Said, "Permission to Narrate," (1984), reprinted in *The Politics of Dispossession* (New York: Pantheon Books, 1994), 247–268.

treat the Palestinians as a discrete community who deserve some measure of self-determination while obscuring other potentially just and ethical forms of political coexistence that might be found in the actual multicultural, multiethnic, multireligious history of Palestine itself. This does *not* mean that the application of "self-determination as non-domination" is a useless exercise or that it is necessarily imperialist. Rather, it means that the threads of imperial history run through the application of ideal, modular theories like Young's in ways that deserve intentional scrutiny. Simultaneously, it means that the very act of "applying" this model can, without concerted reflection, proactively occlude other normative resources for reimagining the "interrelation" between Palestinians and Jews that are specific to their shared history.

Second, the heavy reliance of so many global justice scholars on the moral resources of liberal theory – shorn of all historical entanglements – is troubling because of what it inadvertently *produces*: a discourse about liberal identity that is then used by foreign policy pundits to justify political practices that are essentially imperial. This is the case despite the fact that the last thing most of these liberal theorists want is to reinforce the injustices of the current global order. Consider, by way of example, Joseph Carens's philosophically rich arguments about immigration. In Carens's view, just because liberal principles were developed within the context of the modern state, and just because the modern liberal state has historically excluded immigrants and aliens, does not mean we ought to reject the possibility that "liberal democratic principles entail a commitment to open borders."[19] For Carens and other liberal ideal moral theorists, the solutions to global problems like the refugee crisis can almost always be found within liberal theory despite the contradictions generated by liberalism itself. Such contradictions include, for instance, the fact that: (a) liberal societies have historically insisted upon closed borders while liberal theory ostensibly remains committed to freedom of movement; (b) contemporary humanitarian crises created by the military excesses of liberal democratic states continue to unfold in the face of a liberal, moral obligation to protect human rights; (c) liberal Great Powers who insist they approach foreign policy in the name of equality, democracy, and sovereign autonomy have historically denied the benefits of equality, democracy, and sovereign autonomy to much of the world.

I am not arguing here that this liberalism-all-the-way-down orientation is a problem for political theory simply because it elides these

---

[19] Carens, *The Ethics of Immigration* (Oxford: Oxford University Press, 2013), x.

contradictions and avoids the increasing body of scholarship concerned with the historical co-constitution of liberalism and imperialism as ideologies. Nor do I maintain, with Uday Mehta, that there is necessarily something deeply exclusionary about liberalism as a political theory and practice that is then made explicit through the practices of imperialism.[20] I am also not suggesting that a liberal theory of open borders is wrong, unhelpful, or philosophically unjustifiable on its face just because liberalism has historically evolved alongside, and in the service of, imperial practices that have ultimately solidified into a state system that now makes immigration such a problem for theorists like Carens. Finally, I do not doubt Carens's intentions for a minute and understand that he and other thinkers influenced by the possibilities of liberal theory are sincerely committed to harnessing its tenets to emancipatory ends. Rather, what concerns me here is the way this philosophical/political gesture – this insistent turning toward a liberal, ideal moral theory to solve the global problems created by liberal states – contributes to a discursive environment in which liberal societies appear always to be just waking up to problems of global politics and always striving innocently to wrangle liberalism's pristine principles in response. Moreover, this gesture enables a deflective rhetoric about the liberal state (a rhetoric with a long and ignoble imperial history), which constantly draws our attention away from the state's illiberal actions by dragging the conversation back to its liberal pedigree.[21] Finally, the assumed integrity of a liberal, ideal moral theory – so omnipresent in the language of global justice – can and has been weaponized by liberal internationalists for imperial ends.

Blake's argument in *Justice and Foreign Policy* exemplifies a rhetorical bridge of sorts between the ahistorical language of much global justice scholarship and the goals of a crisis-driven, liberal internationalist foreign policy agenda. In contrast to most global justice scholars, Blake does not focus his analysis on the need to change anything about a global order that is assumed to be currently unjust, nor is he interested in developing ideal moral solutions to problems generated by this unjust order. Rather, he assumes that the injustices of the current global system will be with us for the foreseeable future and that "some states will continue to be significantly wealthier than other states."[22] Blake, therefore, concentrates his efforts on theorizing how – in the face of this ongoing global injustice and

---

[20] Mehta, *Liberalism and Empire: A Study in Nineteenth-Century British Liberal Thought* (Chicago: University of Chicago Press, 1999), 6–8.
[21] Jeanne Morefield, *Empires without Imperialism: Anglo-American Decline and the Politics of Deflection* (New York: Oxford University Press, 2014).
[22] Blake, *Justice and Foreign Policy*, 46, 116.

inequality – "already committed" liberal states can develop moral approaches to foreign policy out of their state-oriented, but universally rationalized, conceptions of justice and what he elsewhere refers to as the "limited and faulty tools" of liberalism.[23] This looks, on its face, like a species of realism and, indeed, to emphasize the realistic nature of his ideal suggestions, Blake turns to the same kind of thin historical precedent that Rawls used in *The Law of Peoples*. Thus, just as Rawls maintains that the "familiar and largely traditional principles I took from the history and usages of international law and practice" justify what he describes as his "realistically utopian" approach to global justice, Blake asserts that the history of international law not only provides deep background for his approach but ought also to be "part" of the liberal foreign policy story even as he rejects it as the "primary source of moral duties," notes its unenforceability, and promotes its regular violation.[24] Thus, for Blake, because history proves that international law is limited and because the world is unfair and populated by states with anti-liberal values, "already committed" liberal states will sadly be forced to make hard choices about foreign policy measures that entail coercion, or the "use of dangerous tools."[25] Blake's intervention is to develop an approach to foreign policy that allows liberal states to rationalize the use of such dangerous tools from a self-satisfied position of justice.

And yet, despite the fact that this approach seems to depart significantly from much global justice scholarship, Blake shares with these thinkers a sense that, at the end of the day, the "communities and agents that are already committed to liberalism" (states almost exclusively associated with the Global North) are actually committed to liberalism. In other words, states which have historically *called* themselves liberal can safely be assumed *to be* liberal at heart for Blake and for global justice scholars despite these states' extensive histories of illiberal behavior both within their own borders (e.g., slavery, settler colonial dispossession, Jim Crow politics) and beyond (e.g., imperial exploitation, resource extraction, the undermining of nascent democracies throughout the world). Likewise, with most global justice scholars, while he accepts that the imperialist practices of wealthy states in the past might be "causally" related to the

---

[23] Blake, *Justice and Foreign Policy*, 3, 5. Blake referred to liberalism's "limited and faulty tools" at a round table on Catherin Lu's *Justice and Reconciliation in World Politics* at the International Studies Association annual conference, San Francisco, April 4–7, 2018.

[24] John Rawls, *The Law of Peoples* (Cambridge, MA: Harvard University Press, 1999), 57. This is similar to *Political Liberalism* where Rawls argues that the "wars of religion" provide deep historical background for his largely ahistorical theory. See Rawls, *Political Liberalism* (New York: Columbia University Press, 2005), 303; Blake, *Justice and Foreign Policy*, 43.

[25] Blake, *Justice and Foreign Policy*, 84.

unequal shape of the global order today, Blake doesn't see the necessity of integrating this history into his theory of justice and foreign policy. Finally, Blake and global justice scholars both assume that, despite its historical attachment to slavery, settler colonialism, and imperialism, liberalism is a bottomless resource, an untroubled philosophical well from which scholars might continually drink without fear of contamination. In sum, Blake's theory tethers what appears to be a reluctant realism with a blind faith in the salvageability of liberal theory and states that call themselves liberal.

In politico-spatial terms, this means that, for Blake, self-identified liberal states ought to approach their foreign policy as a mode of sometimes coercive action that issues forth from a place of unquestioned integrity, even when it doesn't. In other words, he acknowledges that the United States has historically acted in ways that were obviously illiberal and that willfully violated international law by dressing up the state's imperial acts of aggression as humanitarian intervention.[26] And yet, throughout *Justice and Foreign Policy*, he breezily sets this history aside and continues to theorize *as if* the American state's illiberal actions have no bearing on his model, *as if* the only question perennially before us is the need to frame foreign policy going forward in line with the demands of a liberal theory of justice that is both universally valid, specific to America and its liberal allies, and endlessly available as a source of moral guidance. This supposedly future-looking foreign policy vision is deeply tautological. First, it assumes that self-identified, "already committed" liberal states ought to draw upon their endlessly well-intentioned liberal principles to make moral choices about foreign policy. Second, it assumes that these self-identified liberal states live in an unequal, dangerous, and unfair world occupied by illiberal states which sometimes requires them to use coercion or "dangerous tools" in their foreign policies. Third, in making such foreign policy choices, "already committed" liberal states are not required to reflect on the ways their historical use of "dangerous tools" might have contributed to making the world unequal, dangerous, and unfair in the first place. Finally, this lack of reflection is acceptable because we know these states to be "already committed" to liberalism. And we know this, because they tell us they are.

Given the linkages Blake forges – between an ahistorical conception of liberal identity, a liberal theory that is always the answer to its own problems, and a "realistic" foreign policy agenda that must sometimes (feet dragging) use coercion against nonliberal states – it is hardly surprising that a liberal internationalist like Michael Ignatieff would endorse the

---

[26] Blake, *Justice and Foreign Policy*, 54.

book. Blake's "realistic" argument aligns beautifully with the combination of rhetorical ingredients that liberal internationalists have historically used to confect a global vision that leans heavily on the need to "believe" in a liberalism that is, in Ignatieff's words, a "fighting creed" able to strategically violate its own principles when necessary.[27]

Liberal internationalists like Ignatieff, John Ikenberry, and Anne-Marie Slaughter – self-identified adherents to a school of thought that claims historical origins in the international vision of Woodrow Wilson and who came to prominence following Obama's election in 2008 – believe that the strength of their approach lies in its unique combination of abstract, liberal principles and practical, foreign policy sensibilities, what Ignatieff describes as a fusion of the "view from nowhere" with the "view from somewhere."[28] The confidence expressed by liberal internationalists that they speak more directly and realistically to global politics than do liberal theorists and global justice scholars no doubt emerges, in part, from the fact that these thinkers are often public intellectuals who straddle the worlds of academia, popular media, and the "foreign policy establishment." Whatever their origins, the "realist" impulses of the liberal internationalists lead them to explicitly embrace – in a way that most global justice scholars do not – the permanent necessity of American military, political, and economic domination; an ideal of international order that Ikenberry describes as "liberal hegemony."[29] At base, these thinkers understand themselves as balancing between the soft realm of "professional ethicists" and the hard zone of "realist" policy-making.

Thus, while both liberal internationalists and most global justice scholars dismiss the impact of imperialism on contemporary politics, they frame that dismissal differently. In contrast to many global justice scholars, liberal internationalists usually admit that most of the existing international norms, traditions, and institutions associated with the current global order are the product of former imperial relations and the triumph of Western powers after World Wars I and II. At the same time, they insist that these norms were never, in Ignatieff's words, "imposed from the top down by an international

---

[27] Ignatieff, "Liberal Values in Tough Times" (2009). www.macleans.ca/politics/ottawa/liberalism-is-not-a-bloodless-breviary-for-rootless-cosmopolitans/.

[28] For the clearest articulation of contemporary liberal internationalism see the final paper of the Princeton Project on National Security, *Forging a World of Liberty Under Law*, eds. John Ikenberry and Anne-Marie Slaughter (Princeton, NJ: Princeton University Press, 2006). See also Ignatieff, "Reimagining a Global Ethic," *Ethics and International Affairs*, 26/1 (2012), 12, 18.

[29] Ikenberry, *Liberal Leviathan: The Origins, Crisis, and Transformation of the American World Order* (Princeton, NJ: Princeton University Press, 2012).

elite."[30] Rather, as Ikenberry puts it, after 1945, "other countries, particularly in Western Europe and later in East Asia, handed the reins of power to Washington just as Hobbes' individuals in the state of nature first construct and then hand over power to the Leviathan."[31] In an odd torqueing of the global justice argument that history has no bearing on the constructions of ideal moral solutions to the problems of the contemporary world, liberal internationalists acknowledge the imperial and coercive origins of today's American-led order but insist that this order is liberal nonetheless and, even when it isn't, it is the best we can get. Moreover, their intense belief in "the idea" of America as the indispensable nation without whom "nothing gets done" compels liberal internationalists to obsessively fixate on maintaining the status quo of American power because they are convinced that this power is always the only thing standing between stability and utter chaos.[32]

Liberal internationalists thus share with Blake (and much global justice scholarship) both a fascination with international crises that threaten American hegemony and a fixation on the need to address these crises as quickly as possible (with no reference to history) in order to shore up global peace and security. Ignatieff's response to the crisis in Syria is particularly illustrative of this fascination/fixation. Co-author of the R2P doctrine, Ignatieff has always insisted that the United States and Canada ought to intervene militarily in Syria for humanitarian reasons.[33] By the summer of 2014, however, Ignatieff's rhetorical urging had shifted from mild fear to the kind of full-on panic that he experienced just before the war with Iraq in 2003 when he insisted that our "contemporary situation in global politics has no precedent since the age of the later Roman emperors."[34] For Ignatieff, this was a "new world" in which, "the proclamation of a terrorist caliphate in the borderlands of Syria and Iraq" indicated that "the dissolution of the state order created by Mr. Sykes and Monsieur Picot in their treaty of 1916 is proceeding to a fiery denouement."[35]

[30] Ignatieff, *Human Rights as Politics and Idolatry* (Princeton, NJ: Princeton University Press, 2003), 143.
[31] Ikenberry, *Liberal Leviathan*, 10.
[32] Slaughter, *The Idea That Is America* (New York: Basic Books, 2008), xvi, 233.
[33] Ignatieff, "The Duty to Protect Is Still Urgent," *The New York Times*, September 13, 2013, www.nytimes.com/2013/09/14/opinion/the-duty-to-protect-still-urgent.html.
[34] Ignatieff, "Barbarians at the Gate?" *New York Review of Books*, February 28, 2002, www.nybooks.com/articles/archives/2002/feb/28/barbarians-at-the-gate/.
[35] Ignatieff, "The New World Disorder," www.nybooks.com/articles/2014/09/25/new-world-disorder/.

The Sykes–Picot Agreement was, of course, a secret treaty brokered by Britain and France during World War I in which these two imperial powers divided up the former Ottoman territory of the Middle East between themselves after having promised independence to the Arabs who fought with them against the Axis powers. Sykes–Picot, and eventually the Mandated territories that resulted from it, transformed this corner of the Ottoman empire into one of most volatile regions of the world through the creation of new borders, the installation of puppet leaders, the rampant extraction of oil, the violent repression of civilian populations – sometimes, as with the British Mandate in Iraq, through the use of chemical weapons – and the promotion of religious and ethnic distinctions and hierarchies that remain to this day. The states it created were never stable and were often purposely destabilized by France, Britain, and the United States throughout the coming century.[36] The order it secured served no one's purpose aside from those global world powers intent on oil extraction and the anti-democratic leaders they supported, and the kind of Arab Nationalism it engendered was often state-centered and militaristic. Ignatieff's conviction that this "order" was preferable to anything else speaks volumes. His is an international vision rooted in a reactive attachment to an American-led status quo that is imperial in all but name, that is always the only thing standing between stability and chaos, and that must be protected through urgent intervention in the sovereign politics of putatively nonliberal states.

This presentist fixation with preserving order because the alternative to American hegemony is always worse stops inquiry in its tracts and demands action, action that, in Said's words, usually entails "more destruction and death for distant civilizations."[37] There is never time in a disordered world on the brink of catastrophe to reflect on the nature of Sykes–Picot, to stop and think seriously about the history of power lurking behind the looming crisis. Rather, in the minds of liberal internationalists, America is both the hegemonic power that sews together the strands of liberal civilization in a disordered world *and* perennially in peril.[38] This temporally compressed vision reduces the aspirations of all the people in a region as fraught with recent imperial history as the Middle East to a feedback loop of order versus disorder that inadvertently strips

---

[36] Syria, for instance, was the site of the first CIA-sponsored coup in 1949. Douglas Little, "Cold War and Covert Action: The United States and Syria, 1945–1958," *Middle East Journal*, 44/1 (1990), 51–75.

[37] Said, *Humanism and Democratic Criticism* (New York: Columbia University Press, 2003).

[38] See Ikenberry on how "America's tradition of civic nationalism" provides the necessary "background support" for a multilateral foreign policy. Ikenberry, "Is American Multilateralism in Decline?," *Perspectives on Politics*, 1/3 (2003), 543.

democratic protestors, rebel fighters, stateless civilians, children, ethnic minorities, soldiers, and refugees alike of historical context and lived experience. By this logic, if the end of American hegemony signifies the end of the world, any narrative that calls the good intentions of that hegemon into question – whether that narrative issues from anti-colonial theorists, "hostile revisionist powers," or Donald Trump himself – becomes complicit in a project that can only end in Armageddon.[39]

Speaking History to Power: Said and Contrapuntal Critique

Scholars of comparative literature, cultural studies, postcolonial theory, anthropology, and history have long been drawn to Said's approach to texts and politics. And yet, despite his far-reaching influence, international relations scholars and political theorists have largely ignored Said's body of work, a lacunae that seems particularly strange given what Jennifer Pitts has termed the recent "turn to empire" in the history of political thought.[40] This neglect may, in part, be explained by disagreements over genre and Said's use of the novel as a site for textual analysis in much of his work. More likely, for a field used to throwing in its lot with the conceptual parsimony of philosophy, it is the unsettled quality of Said's mode of critique – the way it explodes conventional distinctions between genre, rhetoric, culture, and politics and between literary, historical, and political analyses – that has proven so difficult for theorists to embrace. Said's intellectual orientation is also explicitly political insofar as it links this crossing of disciplinary boundaries to a "clarified political and methodological commitment to the dismantling of systems of domination."[41] While partisan, however, his writings reject political practices that lasso themselves too tightly to national identities or to narratives associated with colonial "sites of intensity."[42] Rather, Said's writings embrace a *contrapuntal* approach to critique that takes aim at both the violence and injustice of imperialism while simultaneously engaging the history of anti-colonial resistance and shared experience. This perspective understands "Western and non-Western experiences as belonging together" because, according to Said, "they are connected

---

[39] Ikenberry, "The Plot against American Foreign Policy," *Foreign Affairs*, May/June 2017, 1.
[40] Pitts, "Political Theory of Empire and Imperialism," *Annual Review of Political Science*, 13 (2010), 211–235.
[41] Said, "Orientalism Reconsidered," *Cultural Critique*, 1 (1985), 107. See also Said, "Representing the Colonized: Anthropology's Interlocutors," *Critical Inquiry*, 15/2 (1989).
[42] Said, "Intellectuals in the Post-Colonial World," 45.

by imperialism."[43] As such, his work rejects any critical orientation that assumes "one overarching theoretical principle governs the whole imperialist ensemble" and focuses instead on first wresting Western cultural forms from "the autonomous enclosures" in which they are usually analyzed and then placing them back into the polyphonous, "dynamic global environment" created by imperialism.[44]

Said's work thus resists the systematizing impulses of much academic political theory. More particularly, it resists the impulses of both global justice scholars and liberal internationalists to theorize world politics through ideal philosophical lenses hewn largely from the European tradition and/or found within the conceptual promise of liberal theory. It thus provides an exceptionally sharp form of critique to wield against the tendency of these same theorists to excise history, power, and culture from international relations and to reduce contemporary crises either to natural disasters or problems in search of liberal solutions. Finally, Said's insistence on a "much sharpened sense of the intellectual's role both in defining the context and in changing it" provides a response to the baseline hubris of scholars who dismiss the possibility that historical context matters (Blake), or who don't consider that scholars and activists from the colonial world could possibly alter the shape of theory (Pogge), or who imagine their own forms of intellectual intervention as the only conceivable alternatives to the ineffable postulates of "professional ethicists" on the one hand, and global chaos on the other (Ignatieff).[45]

Said referred to the intellectual disposition that he both theorized and modeled as worldliness.[46] A worldly approach to history and politics requires that we understand cultural and political artifacts (novels, poetry, textbooks, training manuals, geographic surveys, policy documents, maps, political treatises) as always situated in the world, in the ideological push and pull of local, national, regional, imperial, and anti-imperial relationships. For Said, imperialism was/is a dynamic process that orders the world spatially through the discursive and political constructions of what he famously refers to as "imagined geographies," forms of knowledge and cartographic common sense that inscribe, reinscribe, and naturalize fundamental differences between the East and West, the Global North and the Global South, the colonized and the colonizing, the developing and the developed.[47] The novelty of *Orientalism* lay in its assertion that understanding how the West came to dominate the East politically requires a deeper understanding of this geographic thinking

---

[43] Said, *Culture and Imperialism*, 279.   [44] Said, *Culture and Imperialism*, 51.
[45] Said, "Orientalism Reconsidered," 107.
[46] See Said on "worldliness" in "Representing the Colonized," 205–225.
[47] Said, *Orientalism* (New York: Vintage, 1979), 49–72.

and of the ways the West studied, imagined, quantified, divided, and described the Orient. More than anything else, worldly critique aims to destabilize the "permanence of vision" so central to imperialist narratives through a granular reading of history's "disruptive detail," those tension-filled, human-created moments that Said found, for instance, in the deeply conflicted narrative visions of metropolitan authors such as Joseph Conrad and T. H. Lawrence and in the work of anti-colonial writers like C. L. R James and Franz Fanon.

Again, Said understood the process of interrogating history's disruptive detail as inherently political and his writings frequently illuminate densely woven interconnections between the rhetorical and intellectual complexities of imperial history and contemporary politics and culture. Said sometimes describes this open, secular, political orientation as a form of "democratic humanism" that cannot not be engaged "without a sense of being someone whose place it is publicly to raise embarrassing questions, to confront orthodoxy and dogma ... to represent all those people and issues that are routinely forgotten or swept under the rug."[48] Implicit in the humanist endeavor, for Said, is a commitment on the part of the public intellectual to remain attentive to the forgotten and the marginalized and to cast a wary eye on anything that calls too shrilly for order (intellectual or political) over justice.

Said was all too aware of the tension between, on the one hand, his invocation of humanism, his turn to universal ideas like justice and freedom, and his refusal to dismiss human rights as "cultural or grammatical things," and on the other, his equally deep attachment to the critical tools of poststructural discourse analysis.[49] Some critics have argued that Said's commitment to both dispositions means that his work is plagued throughout by a basic, unsettling irreconcilability.[50] Other detractors have insisted that Said's use of Foucault in *Orientalism* was purely situational or banally symptomatic of a larger turn toward poststructural analysis in the late 1970s and early 1980s.[51] Said, however, was never an uncritical consumer of Foucault and his attitude toward poststructuralist approaches to power transformed in the years following the publication of *Orientalism*. In response to critics of that text who felt he ignored not only the agency of the colonized but also the historical fact of resistance, Said further developed a form of critique that challenged the

[48] Said, *Humanism and Democratic Criticism*, 22; Said, *Representations of the Intellectual* (New York: Vintage Books, 1994), 11.

[49] Said, *Humanism and Democratic Criticism*, 136.

[50] Aijaz Ahmad, *In Theory: Classes, Nations, and Literatures* (London: Verso, 1994), 168.

[51] See Leela Gandhi's summary of this argument in *Postcolonial Theory: A Critical Introduction* (New York: Columbia University Press, 1998), 69, 72.

"univocal" movement of culture and power, from the metropole to the colonies. He described this fugal approach as an "integrative or contrapuntal orientation in history."[52] In the context of the imperial encounter, such an orientation focused on the way cultural products – the nineteenth-century English novel, for instance – were shot through with, overlapping references to both the colonies and the ongoing reality of anti-colonial resistance. Moreover, Said's inquiry revealed that the "anti-imperialist intellectual and scholarly work done by writers from the periphery" (e.g., Fanon, C. L. R. James) reflected not merely the influence of a metropolitan education but, also, "an extension into the metropolis of large-scale mass movements."[53] In other words, for Said, throughout the empire, "there was *always* some form of active resistance."[54] And, he argued, not only did this resistance ultimately win out; it also shaped the development of culture, philosophy, and politics in the West.

This expansive, contrapuntal reading of history *as* imperial history had a profound impact on Said's interpretation of power. By his lights, any theory of power focused exclusively on its metastasizing *symptoms* that ignored the brutality of its practices and the reality of resistance movements was ultimately unable to avoid mimicking precisely those univocal, universalizing metaphysics against which it emerged in protest. Thus, Said not only rejected the "unworldly" quality of high literary analysis but also any orthodox embrace of poststructuralism that draws "a circle around itself, constituting a unique territory," imprisoning the critic in a pen of political detachment rather than enabling a worldly engagement that opened up the discursive imagination to protest.[55] Said's "homemade resolution of the antitheses between involvement and theory," as he put it, rests on a wholesale refusal to choose one or the other but, rather, to demand a contrapuntal interrogation of their entanglements.[56]

Thus, by necessity, Said's contrapuntal practice of worldly, humanist engagement entails keeping a variety of theoretical and political balls up in the air at the same time; embracing "the essential untidiness, the essential unmasterable presence that constitutes a large part of historical and social situations" while attending to both disciplinary power *and* resistance.[57] In other words, engaged, contrapuntal critique interrogates both the proliferating, justifying technologies and ideologies that sustain

---

[52] Said, *Culture and Imperialism* (New York: Random House, 1993), 279. Bill Ashcroft and Pal Ahluwalia, *Edward Said* (New York: Routledge, 2001), 92.

[53] Said, *Culture and Imperialism*, 244.   [54] Said, *Culture and Imperialism*, xii.

[55] Said, "Traveling Theory" (1982), *The Edward Said Reader* (New York: Vintage, 2000), 215.

[56] Said, *Culture and Imperialism*, 194.   [57] Said, "Traveling Theory," 210.

power *and* those movements and experiences that have historically existed "beyond the reach of dominating systems, no matter how deeply they saturate society" and whose influence can be felt in contemporary culture.[58] Contrapuntality thus challenges Foucault's notion of a subject always already bamboozled by discourse and discipline, insisting rather that history "does not get made without work, intention, resistance, effort, or conflict," none of which is "silently absorbable into micronetworks of power."[59]

Said's approach to the role of public intellectuals in an unjust world was similarly attentive to power and resistance and similarly two-pronged. On the one hand, his insistence upon the final unabsorbability of the thinking subject profoundly influenced his belief that public intellectuals ought to "remain outside the mainstream, unaccommodated, uncoopted, resistant" to the unifying discourses of the day.[60] At the same time, Said maintained that these same intellectuals should routinely reflect upon their own relationships to contemporary forms of power and community. The model of intellectual life he developed for negotiating these dual requirements emerged out of his own experience as a Palestinian living in exile and the critically generative qualities of this experience. On the one hand, the intellectual "who considers him or herself to be part of a more general condition affecting the displaced national community is ... likely to be a source not of acculturation and adjustment, but rather of volatility and instability." In this mode, Said's exilic critic was often a tenacious provocateur, a "ranting Thersites," standing before domination and insistently calling its logic into question, a disposition that Said described as "curmudgeonly disagreeableness" sometimes "bordering on dyspepsia."[61] Importantly, he did not limit this understanding of exile to those who had experienced expulsion from a home country but, instead, argued that anyone could adopt an exilic perspective by aligning themselves with outsiders rather than insiders. Exile in this "metaphysical sense" thus implied an intellectual disposition toward restlessness and movement, toward "constantly being unsettled and unsettling others."[62] On the other hand, Said was also acutely aware that despite the interpretive and political importance of remaining "marginal and undomesticated," no one "is ever free of attachments and sentiments." Exiles, he maintained, are never entirely loosed from connections to other human beings, longed-for and lost homelands, family, and complicated social/

[58] Said, "Traveling Theory," 216.
[59] Said, *Humanism and Democratic Criticism*, 49; Said, "Traveling Theory," 215.
[60] Said, *Representations of the Intellectual*, 53.
[61] Said, *Representations of the Intellectual*, 53.
[62] Said, *Representations of the Intellectual*, 53.

political/cultural communities. Thus, the job of the exilic, public intellectual must be to remain both attentive to these attachments and also "unusually responsive to the traveler rather than the potentate, to the provisional and risky rather than the habitual."[63]

Said modeled this intellectual self-reflection in his writing not only by explicitly wrestling with the relationship between his scholarship, his politics, and his experiences as an exile, but also by bringing a fine-grained, philological sensibility to bear on those limpet-like assumptions that cling to seemingly innocuous pronouns.[64] "An American columnist," he argued in *Representations of the Intellectual*, "writing during the Vietnam War, for example, using the word 'us' and 'our,' has appropriated neutral pronouns and affiliated them consciously either with that criminal invasion of a distant Southeast Asian nation, or, a much more difficult alternative, with those lonely voices of dissent for whom the American war was both unwise and unjust."[65] It is the intellectual's task, Said continued, to be attentive to the way the subtleties of language mask some identities and construct others. The national "we," he insisted, is "not a natural or god given entity but is a constructed manufactured, even in some cases invented object, with a history of struggle and conquest behind it that is important to analyze and, sometimes, to represent."[66] Thinking in complicated ways about all that lurks behind the effortless assertion of a "we" then pushes the critic to think more expansively about, and sympathetically toward, those who are *not* "us." Turning to Vico to help him make his point, Said maintained that this kind of subjective generosity entails a willingness on the part of the exilic intellectual to approach the object of critique – the text, the political narrative – "from the point of view of the maker."[67]

This form of critique opens up both our critical and empathetic horizons in precisely the opposite way from that of most global justice scholars and liberal internationalists who speak in a remarkably consistent "we" voice throughout their work, although the presumptions and intentions behind this voice vary from author to author. Pogge's work is written for, and aimed squarely at, citizens of the Global North who ought to be concerned about world poverty.[68] Blake's "we" is of the far more internally conflicted (but externally serene) variety evoked by foreign policy commentators when they talk about "our" invasion of Iraq or how "we"

[63] Said, *Representations of the Intellectual*, 64.
[64] Said, *Humanism and Democratic Criticism*, 61.
[65] Said, *Representations of the Intellectual*, 33.
[66] Said, *Representations of the Intellectual*, 33.
[67] Said, *Humanism and Democratic Criticism*, 92.
[68] Pogge, *World Poverty and Human Rights*, 4.

might do things differently in the Middle East the next time. This subject position remains remarkably consistent regardless of the fact that the vast majority of "us" have little to no impact on what "our" states do in the world. Blake, however, betrays no discomfort with this disconnect between fact and reality, noting blithely that the mere fact of living in a democracy in no way requires "us" to engage "in stupid or counter-productive interventions in the name of democracy; we are, in the most cases, severely limited in the forms of policy options available to us by which we might directly work for domestic government abroad."[69] Ignatieff and Ikenberry flit between Blake's "we" (overdetermined by sovereignty) and a "we" that refers more generally to liberal peoples of good faith who represent the interests of the international community and its rhetorical cocktail of universal human rights, democracy, and free trade. This liberal "we" is not necessarily Western and is expansive and tolerant enough, they argue, to accommodate a variety of different per-spectives and cultures. However, as soon as an international crisis pre-sents itself – the war in Syria, the Israeli bombing of Palestine, the crash of a passenger jet over the Ukraine, Donald Trump's handling of North Korea – the veneer of generosity implicit in the liberal "we" falls away, replaced by a much more brittle, explicitly aligned "we": the beleaguered citizen of liberal democracies, pressed reluctantly into action by our better natures and a world that requires intervention.

Despite their differences, however, at the very core of all of these invocations of "we" lies a basic conviction that the ground upon which the theorist stands is completely solid, that it enables and legitimates the construction of theories, and calls for actions aimed at saving/disciplining/bombing a "them" whose lives, experiences, needs, and desires are always infinitely accessible to "us." Indeed, these authors exude a sense they are at home with themselves and their societies – even when America is betrayed by Trump's failure to believe in America's leadership – and they know that the best intentions and possibilities of liberalism embolden them to speak about the rest of the world with the same calm, unreflective surety as the nineteenth-century Orientalist scholars observed, diag-nosed, schematized, and ultimately *knew* the East.

By contrast, the kind of critical, exilic, unsettled and unsettling subject that Said calls for is driven to consider those voices and perspectives obscured by the sheer tonnage of the "we" behind the liberal status quo. In 1984's "Permission to Narrate," for instance, Said examined precisely this phenomenon by focusing on the discursive/cultural econ-omy that made it so impossible for the suffering of the Palestinian people

[69] Blake, *Justice and Foreign Policy*, 3.

to break through the ideological bulwark of a US and Israeli narrative that insists; "since Israel is in effect a civilized, democratic country constitutionally incapable of barbaric practices against Palestinians . . . its invasion of Lebanon was ipso facto justified."[70] This dominant presumption relies on the long-standing, imperial narrative that effectively erases the Palestinian people from history by denying them "permission to narrate" their own experience in the present. In the absence of political institutions that both recognize their existence and legitimate their concerns, Palestinians are faced with choosing between political possibilities that are completely divorced from their lived experiences. As Said put it in *After the Last Sky*, "we lead our lives under a sword of Damocles, whose dry rhetorical form is the query 'When are you Palestinians going to accept a solution?' – the implication being that if we don't, we'll disappear."[71] For Said, engaging the question of "peace" in Israel/Palestine requires thinking explicitly about the *absence* of a Palestinian narrative in these debates. As the media's refusal to cover the peaceful Palestinian "Walk of Return" in 2018 as anything other than a terrorist onslaught demonstrates, this absence is only aided and abetted by the unwillingness of policy-makers and liberal public intellectuals "to make necessary connections, draw different, more nuanced conclusions, and at base, to acknowledge reality."[72]

The focus of Said's criticism here is not merely "policy makers, the media, and the liberal intelligentsia" but also leftists who believe that research, exposure, and an encyclopedic recitation of the facts on their own can make a difference. For instance, while tremendously sympathetic to Noam Chomsky's careful documentation of the long, complicated relationship between Israel, the United States, and the Palestinians, Said was not convinced that this compiled mass of evidence would, on its own, have any impact on the Western publics who must be convinced in order to demand change from the Israeli state. In his words, "Facts do not speak for themselves, but require a socially acceptable narrative to absorb, sustain, and circulate them." In the absence of that narrative, bombings, apartheid, displacement, the struggle for water, the struggle to move freely, and the struggle to survive – the stuff of historical/everyday Palestinian life – simply cannot stick to the edifice of a state "incapable of barbaric practices." Moving beyond the deflective edifice of this iron-clad gridlock between facts and meaning required, for Said, "a theory of perception, a theory of intellectual activity" that he identified as the very

[70] Said, "Permission to Narrate," 247–248.
[71] Said, *After the Last Sky* (New York: Columbia University Press, 1998), 46.
[72] Said, "Permission to Narrate," 250.

essence of humanist practice. This critical practice is hyper-attentive to power, history, and language, grounded in an "oppositional analysis between the space of words and their various origins and deployments in physical and social place ... from silence to explication and utterance."[73]

An excellent example of the way Said applied this sensibility to his political writing can be found in a 1989 article in which he looked closely at emerging plans to hold elections in Palestine as an alternative to the *intifada* and Israel's violent response. The Israeli Prime Minister and Bush administration officials alike, argued Said, refused to discuss "whatever might give substance" to the idea of elections, what leaders from both countries dismissed as "details" to be worked out later. Behind this caginess, Said identified an Israeli and American rhetorical desire to have their cake and eat it too; to engage in a political performance that looked and sounded like democracy but never actually acknowledged the existence of the *demos* behind the election – the Palestinian people. Said went on to interrogate this phenomenon through a careful exegesis of an interview Prime Minister Shamir gave to the *Jerusalem Post* that year which went largely ignored by the US media. In the interview, Shamir made it clear that he had no interest in discussing the "details" of the election itself. The reporter continually pressed him on this:

What if, after elections, the Palestinian representatives declare themselves a government? No, answers Shamir, there has to be prior agreement on the process as a whole. Q: But agreement by whom? A: By the body with whom we will negotiate before the election. Q: So the agreement won't come before the elections? A: It must come before the elections. Q: But before the elections no one has been elected. So who will agree? A: ... Elections will be held only after agreement with a body which is going with us to the negotiations. Q: But who is this body? A: It will have to be a Palestinian body ... [74]

Said's analysis here guides us toward those things being left out of Shamir's discursive response, specifically, any recognition of the Palestinian people as a discrete nation, forged under conditions of imperialism, exile, apartheid, and dispossession, who could neither be seen nor heard by those state, media, and intellectual actors now insisting that elections *must* replace uprising.

At the same time, Said's commitment to understanding the world contrapuntally in terms of the dynamic, polyphonous global environment created by imperialism meant that his deep sympathy toward postcolonial nationalism and the lived experiences of the Palestinian people was

[73] Said, *Humanism and Democratic Criticism*, 83.
[74] Said, "Sanctum of the Strong," *The Politics of Dispossession*, 275.

always tempered by a wariness regarding nationalism and all essentialized forms of identity politics. The real challenge for anyone engaged in an analysis of imperial history and its relationship to contemporary politics, Said argued in 2002, "is to keep in mind two ideas that are in many ways antithetical – the fact of the imperial divide, on the one hand, and the notion of shared experiences, on the other – without diminishing the force of either."[75] The promise of counterpoint, for Said, lay in its capacity to take multiple visions, voices, identities, and political desires and just "hold them together" without "the need to reconcile them."[76] A contrapuntal response to global injustice thus resists calling for singular political, national, philosophical, or economic solutions to world problems and, instead, focuses on the critical process of writing "counter-narratives" that both illuminate the present and disclose different political possibilities for the future.

To elucidate this explicitly political rendering of counterpoint, I again turn to Said's writings on Palestine. Committed to tying the imperial foundation of the state of Israel – and the Orientalist discourse that supported it – to the current oppression of the Palestinians, these writings collectively paint a picture of the Palestinian people as a discrete nation without essentializing nationalism. For instance, in *The Question of Palestine*, Said focused much of his analysis on the period of most intense Zionist planning for what would become the state of Israel (during and after World War I) and on the emergence of an increasingly popular discourse in Europe that imagined this future society as emerging from the all but empty ruins of an older, Arab Palestine. Said examined the way this discourse mirrored and combined conceptions crucial to European imperialism; the idea of the lazy native who was also passing into obscurity, the need for Western ingenuity to make an otherwise unused desert bloom, the descriptions of an all but empty landscape dotted with a few villages that nearly resembled a *terra nullius*, the rise of a Zionist discourse that took it upon itself "to explain the Oriental Arab to the West."[77] The Balfour Declaration of 1917, in which the British (soon to be the Mandatory power in Palestine) declared that they "view with favor the establishment in Palestine of a national home for the Jewish people" was, Said argued, similarly imperialist in its logic and execution.[78] In this book and elsewhere, Said braided the past with the present in ways that

[75] Said, "Always on Top," *The London Review of Books*, March 20, 2002, www.lrb.co.uk/v25/n06/edward-said/always-on-top.
[76] Said, "Criticism, Culture, and Performance," *Power, Politics, and Culture: Interviews with Edward W. Said* (New York: Vintage, 2002), 99.
[77] Said, *The Question of Palestine* (New York: Vintage Books, 1992), 26, 13–15.
[78] Said, *The Question of Palestine*, 15.

linked the continuing absence of Palestinian voices to early twentieth-century imperialist narratives about Palestinians aimed at "expressing what the Arab were really like and about."

Said's approach to the current conditions of injustice in Israel–Palestine thus looked distinctly different from the way either global justice scholars or liberal internationalists assess the situation. With Young, Said most desired a political solution to the conflict that avoided separation and apartheid because, as he noted, "everywhere one looks in the territory of historical Palestine, Jews and Palestinians live together."[79] Unlike Young, however, who observed this same problem and then offered a model of "self-determination as non-domination" as a solution, Said articulated his response as a form of "binational" citizenship (that required neither "a diminishing of Jewish life as Jewish life or a surrendering of Palestinian Arabs") through two, contextually oriented, critical moves. First, he coupled counternarratives about imperial culture in twentieth-century Palestine – narratives that both exposed the erasure of the Palestinians as a people and took seriously the historical experience of Jewish suffering – with a deep analysis of the current forms of settler dispossession, occupation, and apartheid that structure every-day life for the Palestinians today. A binational solution to the current conflict, he maintained, must ensure reciprocal recognition and equality between Palestinians and Jews and that can only happen when all parties attend to the specificities of history and the texture of each other's experiences. In the absence of that, he argued, there can be no reconciliation.[80]

Next, said shifted his analysis toward the longer, multicultural history that prefigured the British imperial moment and the creation of Israel as a settler colonial state.[81] Here, Said's reading of Palestinian history stands in opposition to that of Michael Walzer who famously attempted to "capture" the political meaning of the Exodus narrative by arguing that "it is possible to trace a continuous history from Exodus to the radical politics of our own time."[82] Rather than funneling history through "its end," Said employs a contrapuntal – or "Canaanite" – reading of Palestine that draws attention to both the "severe excisions and restrictions" implicit in Walzer's "strategy of *decoupage*" as well as to the noisy, fractious, diverse history of Palestine foreclosed by this

[79] Said, "Invention, Memory, and Place," *Critical Inquiry*, 26/2 (2000), 191–192.
[80] Said, "The One State Solution," *The New York Times Magazine*, January 10, 1999, www.nytimes.com/1999/01/10/magazine/the-one-state-solution.html?_r=0.
[81] Said, "The One State Solution."
[82] Walzer, *Exodus and Revolution* (New York: Basic Books, 1985), 25.

curating of the past.[83] In later works, Said found inspiration in the multiplicities of this uncurated past for a more just solution to the Israeli-Palestinian conflict, noting in 1999:

> Palestine is and has always been a land of many histories; it is a radical simplification to think of it as principally or exclusively Jewish or Arab. While the Jewish presence is longstanding, it is by no means the main one ... There is as little historical justification for homogeneity as there is for notions of national or ethnic and religious purity today.[84]

By approaching Palestinian history in a manner that seeks out multiple groups and identities and "holds them together," Said thus imagined the outlines of a fair, binational state for Palestinians and Jews in the present that opened up a world of possibilities for shared political life necessarily foreclosed by expurgated readings of history and the application of ideal moral theories.

Said's interpretive and political commitment to "protect against and forestall the disappearance of the past" also directly challenges the relentless presentism of both global justice scholars and liberal internationalists by demanding that inquiry *take the time* necessary to reintegrate texts and events that have been "forcibly excluded" from the mainstream of history.[85] What Homi Bhabha describes as Said's practice of "slow reflection" resists the process of totalization whereby aesthetic schools and universalizing philosophies dispense with ambiguity, polyphony, and multiplicity and, instead, move immediately from the event/text to the realm of transcendental value, a move all too apparent in the ideal moral theorizing preferred by global justice scholarship.[86] Moreover, Said's demand that inquiry pause, refuse to belch out solutions to "acts of terror" or "escalating violence," and, instead, engage in the time-consuming work of filling in the discursive holes left by the linguistic bulldozer of the powerful, stands in stark contrast to the crisis-driven approach liberal internationalists take as they throw history to the wind in their headlong rush to shore up the liberal world order.

Ignatieff's truncated reflections on America's role in the 2003 Iraq war offer a particularly stark example of the relentless forward press of the liberal internationalist imaginary. Because he can only imagine the world in totalizing terms that pit liberal order against chaos, even Ignatieff's

---

[83] Said, "Michael Walzer's Exodus and Revolution; A Canaanite Reading," in Said and Christopher Hitchens (eds.), *Blaming the Victims: Spurious Scholarship and the Palestinian Question* (London: Verso, 1988), 161.

[84] Said, "The One State Solution."

[85] Said, *Humanism and Democratic Criticism*, 141; Said, *Culture and Imperialism*, 671.

[86] Bhabha, "Adagio," in Bhabha and W. J. T. Mitchell (eds.), *Edward Said: Continuing the Conversation* (Chicago: University of Chicago Press, 2005), 12.

musings on the recent past necessarily reduce the idea of reflection to pointless dithering. "Part of the challenge of thinking about the Middle East is to learn from the lessons of failure," Ignatieff noted at a panel discussion at Harvard in the summer of 2014. "Clearly," he continued, "invading a large and proud Arab country with a lot of troops and trying in a very short period of time to build stable institutions and then coming home didn't work very well at all. But the alternative, which is to give a lot of speeches and walk away, seems to me to draw the wrong lesson from failure."[87] Hence, even in the very moment of "re-evaluation," Ignatieff's attachment to liberal order annihilates any possibility for reflection grounded in "slow but rational" analysis that engages the complexities of the past, makes visible American power, and clears a space for alternatives other than invasion or inaction, war, or empty speeches.

Said spoke directly to this narrow foreign policy impulse in the concluding chapter of *Humanism and Democratic Criticism*. "It takes a good deal more courage, work, and knowledge," he argued,

to dissolve words like "war" and "peace" into their elements, recovering what has been left out of peace processes that have been determined by the powerful, and then placing that missing actuality back in the center of things, than it does to write prescriptive articles for "liberals," à la Michael Ignatieff, that urge more destruction and death for distant civilians under the banner of a benign imperialism.[88]

The role of the exilic intellectual in these moments, Said argued, was to take the time necessary to forge historical countermemories and counterdiscourses that "will not allow conscience to look away or fall asleep." Retelling a history of the present through those moments, political events, and discourses that have been suppressed and withheld by the victors holds public intellectuals like Ignatieff to account by slowing down their rush to diagnose and contain the world. As such, it reveals Ignatieff's elaborate narratives about political necessity and good intentions for what they really are: bedtime stories to help liberals "begin to believe" in their empire. All over again.

Conclusion

At the end of the day, a Saidian approach to contrapuntal critique resists both the presentism of global justice scholarship and the liberal

---

[87] See Ignatieff's comments on this panel in Christina Pazzanese's "Cruel Summer: Violence in the Middle East and What it Means for the Future," *Harvard Gazette*, September 11, 2014, http://news.harvard.edu/gazette/story/2014/09/cruel-summer/.

[88] Said, *Humanism and Democratic Criticism*, 143.

internationalist fixation with crisis by sewing history and imperial history to politics and, in so doing, revealing what has been left out of political processes "determined by the powerful." Placing such missing actualities "back into the center of things" both contextualizes the current unjust order while gesturing toward alternative visions of political life that arise from history's disruptive detail. A contrapuntal reading of history thus resists the tendency of global justice scholars to ignore the potentially generative possibilities of the past while simultaneously pulling the brakes on a fast-moving foreign policy discourse that responds to perceived crises with calls for rapid-fire intervention, drone strikes, or "boots on the ground," all in the service of a theological liberalism. Instead, a Saidian critique demands that foreign policy pundits and public intellectuals alike set aside their preconceived understandings of who "we" are as a liberal people in order to "imagine the person whom you are discussing – in this case, the person on whom the bombs will fall – reading in your presence."[89] This generous disposition toward the other demands that global justice scholars and liberal internationalists alike approach the subjects of analysis not merely as victims or enemies but, rather, as readers, thinkers, and makers of politics and history. As such, a Saidian disposition resists the tendency to ignore the agency and history of precisely those individuals and communities in the Global South at whom these scholars aim both their ideal moral theories and their foreign policy recommendations. Such an approach also requires time for concerted reflection on the historical complexities of imperial context, time to dig into the nature of the "we" and the "them," and time to identify those subjects who have been denied permission to narrate.

The contrapuntal insistence on slow critique, however, should not be confused for a lack of urgency. Critical inquiry, for Said, must remain worldly and committed to a politics of justice. At the same time, contrapuntal engagement never elevates urgency over analysis, or the search for solutions over the kind of deconstructive practice necessary to expose the powerful discursive histories behind imperialist constructions of contemporary culture, politics, and global order. Moreover, Said's slow critique rejects the bifurcation of the world into idealized liberal theorizing and *real politic* – Ignatieff's "view from nowhere" and the "view from somewhere." Rather, a contrapuntal disposition urges us to "just hold" multiple, potentially conflicting, perspectives together without reconciling them. The point then is to strive, in Said's words, to "grasp the difficulty of what cannot be grasped" and to "go forth to try anyway."

---

[89] Said, *Humanism and Democratic Criticism*, 143.

9   Cosmopolitan Just War and Coloniality

Kimberley Hutchings

Introduction

The wars that captured the imagination of western scholarship about war in the twentieth century were the wars of great powers. Both the First and Second World Wars continue to inspire a massive amount of attention in the broader literature on war, and it is still in only a minority of cases that these wars are also understood as colonial and imperial wars. This pattern has been reflected in western inspired ethics and laws of war since the end of the Second World War. Within this context the ways in which colonial wars have been specifically legitimated has been treated as irrelevant to theoretical questions about justice in war. The concept of war in which both ethicists and lawyers have anchored their arguments and rules has been one derived from the Clausewitzean model of duelling great powers, taking a rough symmetry, rather than an essential asymmetry between parties to conflict, as the norm. Michael Walzer's *Just and Unjust Wars*, which dominated much Anglophone scholarship on just war from the late 1970s until the last decade, insisted on drawing a sharp distinction between determination of justice *ad bellum* and *in bello* in order to preserve the moral parity of states as actors in world politics and the equal moral status of soldiers fighting on different sides, regardless of the justice of their cause.[1]

In recent years, however, the theory and practice of colonial warfare has regained attention, because of the way in which a legacy of colonial unilateralism appeared to have been revived in the military operations of western, liberal states. The nature of this colonial legacy has been well-explored by postcolonial and decolonial scholars examining practices of humanitarian intervention and military operations in the so-called 'war on terror'. These military operations and doctrines replay colonial tropes, from the point of view of the coloniser, in three ways in particular. First, in

---

[1] Michael Walzer, *Just and Unjust Wars: A Moral Argument with Historical Illustrations* (New York: Basic Books, 1977).

colonial warfare, the conduct and fate of communities in the world at large are constructed as peculiarly the remit of a sub-set of world-political actors with the authority to use violence for good ends. Second, in colonial warfare, the notion of war is expansive, so that a whole range of policing and pre-emptive military action across borders can become subsumed under the concept of war. This position reflects the first assumption in which the world is already characterised as belonging to the coloniser, whose just violence has to be imagined as a permanent possibility. Third, in colonial warfare, military action is legitimised in civilizational terms. Ideas such as humanitarian intervention and the successor doctrine of 'Responsibility to Protect', clearly construct the world as the business of powerful actors as forces for good. Various practices of counter-insurgency in Iraq and Afghanistan, and ongoing use of drone strikes and special operations in Yemen and Pakistan have been conceptualised in hybrid terms, somewhere between war and policing, as well as being justified in largely pre-emptive or preventive terms. And it has been shown repeatedly that the gendered, legitimising narratives for contemporary liberal wars echo the claims of nineteenth-century colonial wars, to be wars with a civilising mission.[2] These operations have been presented as wars that will protect the innocent against barbarous violation and enable the education of backward populations into a world of civilised conduct. Within this imaginary, there is a clear asymmetry between the moral status of the humanitarian/liberal actor on the one hand, and the objects of their policies on the other. The only fully agentic player in this imaginary is the humanitarian/liberal. In keeping with the moral universe of colonial warfare from the perspective of the coloniser, others involved in practices of civilising violence, as parties to conflict or objects of rescue, are either morally or practically incapable, in need of protection, education or punishment.

The coming to prominence of these types of warfare, along with the high profile of violent action by non-state actors following the 9/11 attacks, has posed problems for the statist and symmetrical assumptions on which Walzerian ethics of war, and most existing international

---

[2] Robert Belloni, 'The Trouble with Humanitarianism', *Review of International Studies*, 33/3 (2007), 451–74; Krista Hunt and Kim Rygiel (eds.) *EnGendering the War on Terror, War Stories and Camouflaged Politics* (Abingdon: Routledge, 2016); Anne Orford, *Reading Humanitarian Intervention: Human Rights and the Use of Force in International Law* (Cambridge: Cambridge University Press, 2003); Orford, *International Authority and the Responsibility to Protect* (Cambridge: Cambridge University Press, 2011); Patricia Owens, *Economy of Force: Counterinsurgency and the Historical Rise of the Social* (Cambridge: Cambridge University Press, 2015); Robin Riley and Naeem Inayatullah (eds.), *Interrogating Imperialism: Conversations on Gender, Race and War* (New York: Palgrave, 2006).

regulation of war are based. And this may be one reason why an alternative strand for thinking about justice in war has gained greater purchase in Anglophone philosophical debates in just war theory in the past decade. This strand of thinking is internally connected to broader debates about global justice. It is an explicitly *cosmopolitan* argument, which claims continuity between questions of justice inside and outside the context of war.[3] This chapter examines this development in just war theory and suggests that, in spite of its explicit moral egalitarianism, cosmopolitan just war theory replays and reinforces the colonial and neocolonial imaginary of war in the three respects outlined above. It recreates a script in which a sub-set of moral agents holds the global remit to conduct just violence, in which the line between war and other uses of violence becomes blurred, and in which wars are subsumed under a higher civilizational purpose.

The chapter will begin by spelling out the ways in which the arguments of cosmopolitan just war theory are formulated, and the audiences to whom they are implicitly directed. It will then look at two specific arguments made by different proponents of cosmopolitan just war: first about the differential moral status of combatants; and second, about the possibility of severe economic deprivation as a justification for war. It will argue that in both cases the way in which theory distributes moral knowledge and agency, and the distinction it draws between ideal and non-ideal worlds, confirms an imagined global order that is colonial in form. It suggests that the message of cosmopolitan arguments, even when that message is explicitly directed against contemporary global injustice, reflects the shifting of the boundaries of what counts as legitimate military action and the civilizational terms in which military interventions on the part of liberal states have been legitimated in the post-Cold War period.

The Practice of Cosmopolitan Just War Theory

Scholars in applied ethics have long used deontological and utilitarian moral theories to address the ethics of killing in war.[4] Such arguments have recently been extensively developed by philosophers such as David Rodin and Jeff McMahan to ground a methodologically individualist,

---

[3] Laura Valentini, 'Just War and Global Justice' in David Held and Pietro Maffetone (eds.), *Global Political Theory* (Cambridge: Polity, 2016), 143–57.

[4] Jonathan Glover, *Causing Death and Saving Lives* (Harmondsworth: Penguin Books, 1977); Richard Norman, *Ethics, Killing and War* (Cambridge: Cambridge University Press, 1995).

rights-based account of the ethics of war.[5] Within political philosophy,
building on cosmopolitan, post-Rawlsian theories of global justice, theorists such as Caney and Fabre have also developed individualist, rights-
based accounts of just war.[6] All these theories are cosmopolitan in that
they operate on the assumption of continuity between the normative
principles governing human interaction inside and outside the context
of war, across domestic and international boundaries, and in their commitment to fundamental, universal principles of equal moral worth for all
human beings, and the fundamental moral priority of individuals.[7]

   The above forms of cosmopolitan just war theory, as with other cosmopolitan theories of global justice, operate with a clear distinction
between the ideal world in which the meaning of true justice can be
revealed, and the non-ideal world in which justice will have to be adapted
to conditions of partial rather than full compliance with the order of the
ideal. McMahan and Fabre both differentiate between a realm of deep
morality and the actual world, and both note the difficulties of institutio-
nalising some of the implications of their arguments in international law
or the regulation of military conduct.[8] There is a flourishing literature
explaining, attacking and defending the ideal/non-ideal distinction.[9]
What is significant from the point of view of the coloniality of cosmopolitan just war theory is how the relation between the moral theorist and his
or her privileged realm of operation – the world of deep morality – is
constructed. The essential moral universe (deep morality) is not one in
which there is or could be any fundamental contestation, since it is
grounded in a certain set of premises about what justice means. As we

[5] David Rodin, *War and Self-Defence* (Oxford: Clarendon, 2002). Jeff McMahan, 'Just
   Cause for War', *Ethics and International Affairs*, 19 (2005), 1–21; McMahan,
   'The Ethics of Killing in War', *Philosophia*, 34 (2006), 23–41; McMahan, *Killing in War*
   (Oxford: Clarendon, 2009).
[6] Simon Caney, *Justice Beyond Borders: A Global Political Theory* (Oxford: Oxford University
   Press, 2005), 189–225; Cécile Fabre, *Cosmopolitan War* (Oxford: Oxford University Press,
   2012), 18–23.
[7] Fabre, *Cosmopolitan War*, 2. Fabre uses 'Cosmopolitan' to describe her approach to the
   ethics of war. In this chapter I am extending it to encompass the work of thinkers such as
   Rodin and McMahan, who operate on similar universal and individualist assumptions.
   This is a particular, narrow usage of the term 'cosmopolitan' for the purposes of this
   chapter, it does not presume to cover all of the various meanings that the term 'cosmopolitanism' carries in ethical and political theory.
[8] McMahan, 'The Morality of War and the Law of War'; Fabre, 'Guns, Food and Liability
   to Attack in War', *Ethics*, 120 (2009), 39.
[9] Charles W. Mills, '"Ideal Theory" as Ideology', *Hypatia*, 20/3 (2005), 165–84;
   David Miller, 'Political Philosophy for Earthlings' in David Leopold and Marc Stears
   (eds.), *Political Theory: Methods and Approaches* (Oxford: Oxford University Press, 2008),
   29–48; John Simmons, 'Ideal and Non-Ideal Theory', *Philosophy & Public Affairs*, 38/1
   (2010), 5–36; Valentini, 'Ideal vs Non-Ideal Theory: A Conceptual Map', *Philosophy
   Compass*, 7/9 (2012), 654–64.

will see, not only is the theorist positioned within that realm as having unilateral powers, there is a sense in which the theorist occupies all of the ethical space. In the imagination of ideal theorising, the theorist encompasses the world as a whole.

In keeping with other strands of 'ideal theory' in the global justice literature, cosmopolitan just war theory works through the construction of a simplified, theoretical reality in which various assumptions are given, and moral principles, moral agency and moral dilemmas are specified as clearly and carefully as possible. This theoretical world operates as a laboratory, in which the implications of cosmopolitan justice are elaborated, and also tested in terms of the accordance of the outcomes of argument with the principled starting point. In order for this to happen the moral *principles* that make up the first element of the theoretical world of the cosmopolitan just war theorist are operationalised through being brought into relation to imagined *agents* and *situations*.

The choosing *agents* in the theoretical world are *rational, knowledgeable* and *effective*. They are rational and knowledgeable in the sense that they fully understand the meaning and implications of the values and first principles they enact, in the sense that they can correctly weigh up the implications of alternative pathways for action, and in the sense that they have full information about the nature of the situation in which they are placed. For example, they may be combatants that endorse deontological first principles and have to decide whether it is morally justifiable to foreseeably but unintentionally kill a certain number of non-combatants, as opposed to intentionally killing a lesser number of non-combatants in the context of an overall just war. Such moral agents are effective in the sense that they are able to be fully compliant with the requirements of the principles by which they are animated, their actions *matter* in their world. The theorist is also a choosing moral agent, peering into the test tube of her experimental world and adjusting either her experiment or her claims in relation to the results.

The positive agency of idealised moral actors and moral theorists is typically accompanied by the presence of less than ideal moral agents in the theoretical world. The focus in the world's scenarios is on the entitlements and liabilities of moral agents and therefore on the question of what it would be right in certain situations for moral agents to do. But in order for this question to be both raised and answered, the theoretical world needs to be peopled by competent moral agents and by others who are not competent moral agents in the fullest sense, as for instance the shadowy non-combatants that the just warrior may or may not foreseeably but unintentionally or intentionally kill. The latter are actors that fail one or more of the requirements of *rationality*, *knowledge* or *effectiveness*. They are the mistaken, the wicked, the ignorant and the helpless.

The *situations* in which inhabitants of the simplified world are placed are abstractions from situations one encounters in the actual world. Very often, the theorist begins with references to actual *ad bellum* and *in bello* historical instances of war, humanitarian intervention or terrorism.[10] The process of abstraction is designed to illuminate the general point at issue, regardless of the specificities of any actual case. This involves a process of selective mirroring of elements of the actual world so as to produce a simplified context for thought. These situations are further illuminated using thought experiments, fictional and historical analogies, examples and facts, the latter drawn from histories with which theorists assume their audiences will be familiar. For example, when discussing the ethics of assassination *in bello*, Altman and Wellman draw on the example of the assassination of J. F. Kennedy rather than, for example, Gandhi. Which not only locates their reader in one history rather than another, but also supports claims about the proportionality of assassination as a tactic, which would stand up much less well to scrutiny if confronted by alternative histories.[11]

Within cosmopolitan just war theory the model for authoritative moral judgment is epistemic, which implies a series of relationships between the theorist, herself and various object/ audience others. The aspiration of the theorist is to live up to the demands of reason, regardless of interests, feeling or the counter-intuitive results of her reasoning that may follow. The authority of the cosmopolitan theorist is secured through a self-effacing relation to self, but also through her relation to different others, the occupants of the theoretical worlds of ethical experimentation, the actual populations that they (the occupants of the theoretical world) stand in place of and in some sense represent, and the putative addressees of moral theory. In terms of the first set of relations, the theorist relates differently to different actors in the theoretical world (some are like the theorist and some are not), and different actors in the theoretical world are asymmetrically positioned in relation to each other. The markers of difference are truth and competence, the theorist and the competent moral agents in the theoretical world know and can act on moral truths that, for one reason or another, other actors in that world do not know and/or cannot act on. The relations set up between the theorist and the morally defective inhabitants of theoretical worlds are imagined in

---

[10] Andrew Altman and Christopher Heath Wellman, 'From Humanitarian Intervention to Assassination: Human Rights and Political Violence', *Ethics*, 118/2 (2008), 228–32; McMahan, *Killing in War*, 153.

[11] Altmann and Wellman, 'From Humanitarian Intervention to Assassination', 252 n43.

different asymmetrical ways. Three kinds of relation are particularly common: *protective*, for those that are unable to act for themselves; *educative*, for those that are ignorant or mistaken about what is the right thing to do; *punitive*, for those characters that know the right but refuse to act on it.

Occupants of the theoretical world stand in for real people, in the sense that they model the kinds of issues and dilemmas that actual participants in war are going to be faced with. In this respect, the cosmopolitan theorist relates herself not only to theoretical agents but to categories of actual moral agents: soldiers fighting for just and unjust causes, military leaders, civilians who support or contest war directly or indirectly, prisoners of war, politicians, terrorists, oppressed minorities or peoples and so on. In one respect this may be a highly indirect relation. Because of the distinction between ideal and non-ideal theorising, much of what the cosmopolitan theorist concludes may have little prescriptive purchase on what any of these categories of moral agents should actually do in the world as it is. However, to the extent that the findings of deep morality may be able to be operationalised in a non-ideal world, the relation between the theorist and the moral actor is one of action-guidance. And even when such action-guidance is impossible in the short term, deep morality provides an authority for judgement in the actual world that is global in reach, and an orientation towards which moral actors should strive in the long term.

The identification of the theorist with those who act as full moral agents within the theoretical and actual worlds is carried through into her relation to her audiences. These are potentially twofold: the epistemic community of other just war or cosmopolitan theorists, perhaps other moral and political philosophers more generally; and broader publics, which may include members of other epistemic communities (foreign policy analysts, historians, teachers of military ethics), and collective as well as individual actors, such as militaries, states, non-governmental advocacy groups. The capacity of audiences to identify with, and learn from, the narratives of theoretical worlds relies on their capacity to follow lines of argumentation, which means being open to the theorist's moral starting points and being able to reason logically. But this capacity also relies on being able to recognise themselves as competent moral agents within the theoretical world, that is to say, to identify with the real and hypothetical illustrations being deployed, which means identifying with the moral/political position, choices and dilemmas of the protector, the teacher and the law enforcer. In this respect, the homology between theoretical and actual worlds, in terms of asymmetrical distributions of power and moral agency, oils the wheels of the process of identification for those

audiences already positioned in the actual world as presumptively competent moral agents and representative of forces for good. The complex
theoretical and actual relations set up in the practice of cosmopolitan just
war theorising, I suggest, endow the ethical theorist and the addressees of
her arguments with a position of ethical privilege, one that empowers both
theorist and audience, within the moral imaginary of the theoretical
world, to act unilaterally because of their grasp of moral and empirical
truth. Within the terms of this imagined justice the world is permanently
open to the question of just violence and the adjudication of the question
of just violence is located in idealised or actual liberal actors. Moreover,
the theorist of justice is empowered to re-work and expand the categories
of war to underpin the use of just violence as a permanent possibility. And
because war is ultimately justified in terms of particular moral ideals of
justice, it cannot be detached from a programmatic commitment to make
the world a better place in the terms laid down by idealised or actual
liberal actors.

Justified Killers and Their Others

I do not suggest that it is any way the *intention* of cosmopolitan thinkers to
reproduce or reinforce colonial imaginaries when it comes to the theory
and practice of war. In general leading cosmopolitan theorists have been
critical of western interventionism in the Cold War period. Nevertheless,
this section aims to elaborate on claims made in the previous section
through an examination of two novel arguments that have emerged
from cosmopolitan just war theory, and which have very different kinds
of political implication. These are McMahan's claim as to the differential
in bello liabilities of just as opposed to unjust combatants, and Fabre's
claim as to the possibility of justifying subsistence wars *ad bellum*.
McMahan's argument is quite explicit in its aim to read just war as
a form of law enforcement and is very readily interpreted as reproducing
colonial tropes of civilised and barbaric actors and as excluding large
swathes of the world's population from the capacity to grasp or do justice.
Fabre's argument, in contrast, self-consciously aims to grant moral
agency in relation to just violence to the poor and oppressed.
Nevertheless, in spite of the radically different directions in which the
substantive conclusions of these arguments can develop, I aim to show
that the upshot of cosmopolitan just war theory is a mode of imagining
justice characterised by the ethical privilege of ideal and real liberal actors,
the opening up of discretion over the practice of just violence to ideal and
real liberal actors, and the identification of just ends of war with
a civilizational mission.

McMahan's most famous innovation in just war theory is his rejection of the claim that combatants *in bello* should be seen as having equal moral status, regardless of whether they are fighting for a just or an unjust cause. Following through the cosmopolitan insight that justice is the same regardless of context, McMahan argues that we need to treat the morality of killing in war in the same way as we treat it in all other contexts. In all other contexts we see the liability of an actor to be killed as indissociable from his own actions and intentions. McMahan's book *Killing in War* unpacks the implications of this central insight in considerable detail. I will focus on three aspects of the argument: first, the key tropes through which the justified killer is figured in McMahan's arguments; second, McMahan's argument for what the moral asymmetry of combatants means for soldiers' individual responsibility when assenting to fight; third, the way McMahan invokes the ideal/non-ideal theory distinction in order to manage the practical implications of his own argument. In all cases, I will suggest, we find confirmed the identification of full moral agency with liberal military and civilian actors, the identification of archetypal just war with a form of civilizational practice in which enlightened moral actors are pitched against the ignorant and the evil in defence of the helpless, and the identification of the appropriate audience of just war theory with what we might call the beneficent powerful.

McMahan, arguing on the basis that the morality of killing is the same inside and outside the context of war, claims that the moral status and liabilities of justified as opposed to unjustified killers cannot be the same.[12] The example he uses repeatedly to express and elaborate on this claim is that of the policeman killing an armed criminal in order to stop or prevent a lethal attack on an innocent victim. If we take this example, on McMahan's account, although we think the criminal, threatening an innocent person and being targeted by a policeman, is liable to be killed by the policemen, if there is no other way of stopping him, we don't think the policeman is liable to be killed by the criminal, even if the criminal shoots at the policeman in self-defence. McMahan argues the key to justice *in bello* is whether combatants are acting for a just cause or not, if they are then they are like the policeman, if they are not then they are like the criminal. The use of this example reinforces a clear moral asymmetry between just and unjust killers and binds the figure of the justified killer in war to the policeman and the unjustified killer to the criminal. These figures are defined by their different relation to an innocent victim, protected by the justified killer and violated by the unjustified one. It not only identifies justified war with law enforcement, thereby

[12] McMahan, *Killing in War*, 38–103.

blurring the boundary between war and policing, but also the justified warrior with a particular kind of chivalrous, regulated heroism.

The other figure McMahan uses to exemplify a just killer is the anti-Nazi fighter in the Second World War.[13] In this case, the example speaks to an established Western civilizational order of values in which Nazism is known to be the most evil thing that there can be. The Second World War is frequently cited in order to show that there can be such a thing as a just war in moral philosophy and political theory. Its iteration positions the theorist, and the cosmopolitan moral and political values he or she argues for, as the antithesis of what is evil. It situates rightfulness historically and geographically in a way that occludes any temporal or spatial overlap between cosmopolitanism and the systematic oppression of others. And it enables those who were positioned on the anti-Nazi side of the Second World War to be reassured that they can be justified killers.

McMahan's distinction between just and unjust combatants has radical implications for *in bello* justice. It puts the idea of the equal rights of combatants qua combatants into question, and also puts much more emphasis on the moral responsibility of individual soldiers to avoid fighting in an unjust war than is found in contemporary international law. Broadly speaking, current norms of war do not hold soldiers to account for the justice or injustice of the cause for which they are fighting, but only for whether they uphold standards of justice *in bello*. McMahan's argument, in contrast, implies that any soldier with an inadequate *ad bellum* justification is acting unjustly and has effectively forfeited his or her right not to be attacked.[14] It also implies that such soldiers could be held to account for unjustified killing in the aftermath of war. In spelling out the implications of his argument, we find McMahan reinforcing distinctions between illiberal and liberal militaries in ways that differentially distribute moral competencies between them.

For example, in McMahan's case the position of soldiers in illiberal states and militaries, though morally the same as that of soldiers in liberal states and militaries, is such as to render it excessively unlikely that they would be able to benefit from the moral knowledge he is conveying about the moral status of soldiers fighting for an unjust cause. This is because of the range of ways in which the actions of such soldiers are constrained and limited by authoritarian power and ignorance.[15] Although these soldiers are morally responsible for what they do, they are very largely excused from culpability, and from any very high level of moral expectation. In contrast, soldiers in contexts that allow for information, deliberation

---

[13] McMahan, *Killing in War*, 153.   [14] McMahan, *Killing in War*, 32–37.
[15] McMahan, *Killing in War*, 115–22.

and choice may be able to act on their duty to work out whether the war they are being asked to fight is just or not and to refuse to fight if the war is unjust. In other words, they may be able to act according to their responsibilities and be expected to do so.[16]

Even if it is not currently the case that liberal militaries and states enable soldiers to exercise proper discretion *ad bellum*, it is within liberal states and militaries that the legal and regulatory reforms that would enable this possibility are most likely to be established. Here the theorist is the privileged source of the knowledge on which the soldier ought to act, but relates differentially to soldiers in different kinds of militaries. The moral agency of a member of an illiberal military is significantly constrained in terms of knowledge and effectiveness; the member of a liberal military is, at least potentially, like the theorist, an unconstrained, knowledgeable and effective moral agent capable of working out, and acting on, what it is right to do. In addition, then, to setting up a general relation of epistemic authority in relation to actual moral actors, cosmopolitan ethics of war also constructs categories of actual moral agents in ways that reflect existing centre/periphery hierarchies, and self-consciously addresses itself to the 'people who might read this book'.[17] Where soldiers of non-liberal militaries are presented as having something closer to full moral agency, on McMahan's account, they shift from the category of the 'ignorant' to that of the 'evil'. So that, for instance, elite soldiers in the Iraqi Republican Guard in the 1990 Gulf War are to be held to account for the injustice of their actions, in a way not appropriate for that of poor conscripts in the Iraqi army.[18] Thus, what appears to be a radical and democratising development in thinking about the ethics of war, seems in practice to reaffirm civilisation hierarchies that underpin moral and political unilateralism when it comes to the use of military action.

McMahan's argument about the differential moral status of those fighting for a just as opposed to an unjust cause imply a radical revision of the existing laws of armed conflict. He acknowledges, however, that in the world as it is, any such revision would be likely to licence more harm than good. The ideal or deep morality of war cannot be institutionalised because of the lack of the right kind of institutions, within militaries, states or at the global level, to make judgements about the justice or otherwise of causes.[19] In effect, fully just war could only be possible in a world in which international conflict resembled the law-enforcement model of the

---

[16] McMahan, *Killing in War*, 137–54.   [17] McMahan, *Killing in War*, 147.
[18] McMahan, *Killing in War*, 194.
[19] McMahan, 'The Morality of War and the Law of War'.

policeman/criminal. As in other branches of global justice literature, the invocation of the ideal/non-ideal theory distinction reinforces the identi-fication of justice with being like a world of idealised liberal actors, or perhaps like the theorist himself. It does more than imply that the world at large is morally second best, it removes justice doubly from those actors who do not approximate to the model of the armed policeman or the western anti-Nazi fighter to begin with. And it confirms that morality is a matter of privileged access.

Fabre shares McMahan's views that we need to think about the justice of killing in war in relation to the same criteria of justice that we would use in relation to killing in other contexts.[20] And, like him, she accepts that the liability to attack of combatants is different depending on whether they are or are not fighting for an unjust cause.[21] She also, like McMahan, acknowledges that it may not be possible to institutionalise the implica-tions of the deep morality of war. However, Fabre's development of cosmopolitan just war theory takes it in much more radical directions than McMahan, providing arguments for how different kinds of war may be justified from the point of view of weaker parties in world politics, including for example those who are 'very deprived', those who are having their rights systematically violated or those who are fighting for a just cause in situations of radical power asymmetry. In effect, she follows through the logic of making individual rights the cornerstone of just cause, and just cause the cornerstone of justice *in bello*. The challenge to the moral exceptionalism of war, characteristic of cosmopolitan just war theory because of its identification of just war with just violence in general, opens up questions of what counts as war, and enables various kinds of violent conflict to be subsumed within the ethics of war.

One of Fabre's more controversial arguments is that, in principle, severe material deprivation may provide a just cause for war where responsibility for that deprivation, in terms of acts or omissions, can be located.[22] She makes this argument through the right to self-defence, which comes into play where lethal harms are being done because of actions taken or not taken by other parties. This argument is particularly interesting because of how it puts the figure of the global poor in the frame as moral agents, in contrast to the ways they are persistently excluded or marginalised in McMahan's account. However, on examination, the mode in which Fabre's cosmopolitan just war speaks truth to power presents certain problems for the moral agency of the 'very deprived' and the justice of their violence. From the beginning, Fabre's account

---

[20] Fabre, *Cosmopolitan War*, 55–64.   [21] Fabre, *Cosmopolitan War*, 71–81.
[22] Fabre, *Cosmopolitan War*, 97–129.

of the moral agency and status of the 'very deprived' is compromised. The justice of subsistence wars in terms of just cause is countered and constrained by other elements of just war theory, which reflect issues around the competence of the poor as moral agents in terms of what they can do and how they can do it, but also the nature of the moral liability of the affluent. On the one hand, the 'very deprived' lack effectiveness as moral agents; they do not have the material capability to hold the affluent to account in practice, even when they are justified in principle. In addition, the capabilities they do have are liable to be unjust *in bello*, since they will be obliged to use the indiscriminate weapons of the weak, targeting civilians. On the other hand, the degree of liability to attack of affluent populations is very difficult to calculate, and it is likely that no single individual in such population in general will bear sufficient responsibility for lethal deprivation to be a legitimate target in a war against the rich. The individualist premises of cosmopolitan just war theory requires individual perpetrators and victims, and issues of structural injustice have a tendency to dissipate into the never entirely enough responsibility of any one of many individual actors.[23] Fabre suggests that some individuals, perhaps senior officials working for the World Bank or the International Monetary Fund might carry sufficient responsibility to be liable to attack, though the discussion is not entirely conclusive.[24] The key point, however, is that such war could only be just if the individuals deliberately targeted had forfeited their liability not to be attacked through having a major and direct effect on the situation of the 'very deprived' (126).[25] The 'very deprived', in turn, would have to be in a position both to identify those actors with a reasonably high degree of certainty and attack them without violating principles of proportionality and discrimination.

[A]lthough such wars might usually succeed only at the cost of a non-negotiable principle of a just conflict, such as the principle of non-combatant immunity, the door remains open, on principle, for deeming just a subsistence war fought in accordance with that principle. Likewise, although the very poor usually might not be in a position to persuade the affluent to reverse their policies, the door remains open, on principle, for deeming just a war which would succeed on that count.[26]

The issue of the legitimacy of a just war by the poor against the rich reveals the significance within Fabre's cosmopolitan just war theory of the connection between the moral and material competence of justified killers at the level of the ideal. The starting point of cosmopolitan ethics of war in

---

[23] Fabre, *Cosmopolitan War*, 124.   [24] Fabre, *Cosmopolitan War*, 124–5.
[25] Fabre, *Cosmopolitan War*, 126.   [26] Fabre, *Cosmopolitan War*, 118.

idealised conditions always assumes the capacity of the moral agent facing particular moral dilemmas; it is a world in which ought implies can. When it is difficult, even at the level of ideal theory, to assume the effectiveness of the moral actor then their equal status as a moral actor becomes hard to maintain. The self-evident material weakness of the 'very deprived' in the theoretical world of cosmopolitan judgement raises the question, which is echoed in Fabre's treatment of military humanitarian intervention, of the circumstances in which the right to kill should be transferred to a third party who does have the material power to address the wrong that has been done. Here, Fabre is clear, that this is legitimate when those with just cause for lethal resistance, which include those suffering severe violations of their social and economic rights, have either explicitly transferred their right to self-defence to a third party, or can be presumed to have done so. She points out that the notion of presumptive consent poses problems for potential interveners: 'though not to such an extent as to undermine the claim that there is a *prima facie* right to intervene'.[27] Given appropriate conditions, the positioning of weak actors on the world stage as moral agents merges into their positioning as objects of legitimate rescue.[28]

Fabre's argument asserts the moral agency of peripheral actors in world politics in a way that McMahan's does not. Nevertheless, the epistemic and individualist requirements of her cosmopolitan just war theory make it difficult for that agency to be sustained in any meaningful way, outside of an 'in principle' deep morality in which the kind of power and competence available to the poor would require a world that was already very differently ordered. Effectively, the kind of world that the liberal moral theorist already inhabits, in which moral knowledge and efficacy belong together. This is the imagined world in which the world is genuinely amenable to righteous violence, and the righteous are already idealised liberal/humanitarian actors. In the meantime, the possibility of the transfer of the right to self-defence to a third party reintroduces the three-way split between victims, perpetrators and justified killers that is the hallmark of just war for McMahan. As with McMahan, the identification of the morally authoritative actor in the ideal world of principle as combining rationality, knowledge and effectiveness, implies an ideal of just war as fundamentally asymmetrical in ways that set mutually reinforcing moral authority and effective power to work on behalf of the powerless against the wicked. When the audience of such arguments are already those self-identified as potentially just killers in contemporary world politics, then it is far easier for powerful actors to read themselves into the heroic role than for the global poor, even when they should, in principle, be able to do so.

---

[27] Fabre, *Cosmopolitan War*, 178.   [28] Fabre, *Cosmopolitan War*, 172–3, 175.

Decolonising Just War Theory?

Colonial war was expressly justified in terms of its purpose of bringing civilisation into benighted areas of the world. This justificatory discourse rested on a principle of pre-emptive possession, in which the moral claim of civilisation rendered war as a kind of law enforcement, even outside of any existing lawful relation. It rested also on hierarchies between the ideal and real, the just and the unjust, the competent and the incompetent, which colonial civilisations were projected to overcome. The real world had to be made to conform to the ideal conditions of Christian and European civilisation, the just had to prevail over and punish the unjust, the incompetent had to be protected and educated by the competent. In being based on assumptions about fundamental individual rights, cosmopolitanism is necessarily global in its reach, extending the parameters of just cause in more permissive ways. In its moral emphasis on the issue of just cause being linked to individual responsibility for harm, it blurs the boundary between justified killing inside and outside of the context of war, confusing the line between war and policing, adding to the range of what might count as theatres of war, and extending the realm of potential legitimate targets to include wrongdoers who may not be fighters. In this respect, although cosmopolitan just war theory is not equivalent to the civilizational discourse of imperial warfare, it replays analogous moves in a world in which those moves resonate very clearly with colonial and neo-colonial global relations of power. As noted above, it seems unlikely to be entirely coincidental that at a time in which liberal great powers have wanted to conceptualise the world as always pre-emptively the object of its just violence, to legitimise the blurring of distinctions between what is and isn't war, and to figure its military projects in civilizational terms, that a strand of just war theory developed that echoes those themes in its own imagined world.

From the point of view of cosmopolitan justice, the context of its theoretical development and reception as a starting point for thinking about just war is irrelevant to its meaning. Justice must be thought at the level of the universal and in relation to the equal moral status of all human beings. And it is tempting to locate the coloniality of cosmopolitan just war theory solely in its commitment to this universalism and individualism. However, this is, I would argue, too simple. The contrast between the political implications of McMahan's arguments as opposed to Fabre's speak to the variable potential of this mode of theorising in terms of its substantive implications for the powerful as opposed to the powerless. This potential, however, is liberated not only by the rigour of the arguments involved but also by the permissive conditions in which they are made. In a world in which liberal states retrench into the language of national interest and realpolitik the extent to which liberal hegemonic actors, and their others, are able to identify themselves with a moral language grounded on universal human rights may shift. This raises the question of what rejecting cosmopolitan approaches to thinking about just war might mean. One response, represented in Walzer's objection to McMahan's reduction of war to a type of law enforcement, would be to return to other strands of just war theory that treat war as a moral exception and entrench symmetrical relations into ideal type determinations about justice *ad bellum* and *in bello*.[29] However, from a decolonial perspective, the statism of much of this just war thinking reflects another hegemonic moral imagination, which problematises possibilities of counting various kinds of anti-colonial violence as just. As the world turns back to the moralisation of national identity and a white supremacy made explicit, this might incline decolonial critics to favour some forms of cosmopolitan argument over other aspects of the just war tradition.[30] The asymmetries of cosmopolitan just war thinking do, after all, speak to features of most actual wars and other uses of collective violence, in the sense that conflicts in which the strength of competing parties is roughly equal are rare, and almost all warring parties everywhere inhabit a world of moral asymmetry in which just fighters are opposed to unjust ones. Anti-colonial struggles have drawn on both statist and individualist moral imaginaries in justifying their own uses of violence.

To challenge the coloniality of cosmopolitan just war theory cannot advance a project of decolonising just war theory without a much deeper consideration of in what that coloniality consists. And this is never a matter of thinking about modes of theorising about justice in isolation, or even of identifying what kinds of justificatory discourses have characterised anti-colonial violence, but rather of thinking about to whom those modes of theorising are or could be addressed, and how they are received by, and their effects on, the world into which they are released. At the theoretical level a combination of moral certainty and moral unilateralism all too easily opens up the world to the righteous violence of righteous moral agents, whether the basis of this deep morality is the fundamental value of individuals or of states. In this respect it is not clear that traditions of just war theory more closely aligned with the current norms and laws of war are any less colonial in their imagination of justice than cosmopolitan just war theory.

---

[29] McMahan, 'Just Cause for War'; Walzer, 'Response to McMahan's Paper', *Philosophia*, 34 (2006), 43–5.

[30] Christopher J. Finlay, *Terrorism and the Right to Resist: A Theory of Just Revolutionary War* (Cambridge: Cambridge University Press, 2015).

Conclusion

In more venerable strands of Christian just war theory, one condition of just war *ad bellum* is the principle of 'comparative justice'. This is premised on the assumption of the fundamental partiality and incompleteness of human judgement, and requires a recognition that those that are identified as unjust combatants may have some justice on their side. It asks that those engaged in war acknowledge that they are not God and that they may be wrong. This suggests one pathway for thinking about justice, in which to do justice is about embedding the possibility of one's own injustice in how wars are justified and regulated, as opposed to focusing on what is permitted if one's violence is righteous. However, even if there are ways of theorising justice that have a different relationship to coloniality than existing strands of just war theory, they may still find themselves reproducing a colonial imagination, depending on both the imagined and the real relation between the subject positions of knower/theorizer and those about whom and to whom they speak. The imagination of justice may shift but if only at the level of theory, or of 'deep morality', then power relations are likely to continue to shape the meaning of justice in ways that block a more radical understanding of what the decolonisation of 'just war' might mean.

A particular feature of cosmopolitan just war theory is that, given its rejection of the idea of the moral specificity of war, it is entirely driven by a concept of justice. As in the colonial imagination, war is simply a tool to bring about the ends of justice and is not itself interrogated as an ethical or political practice. In this context all of the ways in which practices of war, whether understood in more or less expansive senses, produce and reinforce hierarchies of identity and power is rendered irrelevant to the question of justice. This suggests that in order to engage with the possibility of decolonising the idea of just war one has to think about just war theory less as a set of claims about the moral truth of just violence and more as ethos and practice, including its effects on and resonances with practices of war. If we think of cosmopolitan just war theory as a way of producing and reproducing identities and relations between people in a world that is always both imagined and real, rather than as the establishment of moral truth and the inferences that follow, then we can begin to address the question of what kind of ethos and practice of justice might be less imperial in its implications.

10 Indigenous Peoples, Settler Colonialism, and Global Justice in Anglo-America

Robert Nichols

Justice at Standing Rock

In the past several decades, conflicts over land use in North America have accelerated and intensified, no more so than in relation to the natural resource extraction and transportation industries. The building of a network of new oil and gas pipelines best typifies this process. These pipelines bring together a complex set of concerns regarding the environment, energy policy, labor, land use, and national security. Most interestingly perhaps, they have also sparked a new wave of Native American political mobilization. As I write, a unique and nearly unprecedented gathering is taking place: thousands of indigenous peoples from across the North American continent are gathering at the Sacred Stone Camp in joint opposition to the Dakota Access Pipeline. An estimated $3.8 billion project, the pipeline is scheduled to transport between 470,000 and 570,000 barrels of crude oil per day over 1,200 miles, traversing the Missouri river immediately upstream of the Standing Rock Sioux reservation.[1] On October 23rd, 2016, indigenous activists declared they were enacting *eminent domain* on the contested lands, claiming rights from the 1851 Treaty of Fort Laramie.[2] As Joye Braun, organizer with the Indigenous Environmental Network, stated: "If [Dakota Access Pipeline] can go through and claim eminent domain on landowners and Native peoples on their own land, then we as sovereign nations can declare eminent domain on our own aboriginal homeland."[3]

To truly understand the struggle at Standing Rock, we need to situate it in a longer historical trajectory. For, although rare, this is not the only such major gathering. In 1851, 10–15,000 Great Plains indigenous

---

[1] A point of clarification on terminology and naming: "The *Sioux* are a confederacy of several tribes that speak three different dialects, the *Lakota, Dakota*, and *Nakota*. The Dakota are the largest and most western of the three groups, occupying lands in both North and South Dakota." www.legendsofamerica.com/na-sioux.html.

[2] http://sacredstonecamp.org/blog/2016/10/23/citing-1851-treaty-water-protectors-establish-road-blockade-and-expand-frontline-nodapl-camp.

[3] http://ca.reuters.com/article/topNews/idCAKCN12O2FN.

peoples met nearby with representatives of the United States.[4] Amongst other agreements, this historic gathering produced the Treaty of Traverse des Sioux and the first Fort Laramie Treaty, securing lands for the Dakota peoples in what was then the Minnesota Territory, as well as safe passage through "Indian country" for settlers on their way to California. By 1862, however, the United States was already beginning to abrogate its responsibilities. The *Homestead Act* of that year effectively opened up some 270 million acres of land west of the Mississippi for settlement by providing incentives for squatter-settlers. Subsequent encroachment on Dakota land quickly led to the 1862–64 Great Sioux Uprising. In this conflict, thousands of Dakota civilians were held in an internment camp at Fort Snelling (in present-day Minneapolis-St. Paul), where hundreds perished of cold and starvation and thirty-eight Dakota men were sentenced to death in the single largest penal execution in US history.[5]

In 1868, a second Fort Laramie Treaty set aside large sections of Montana, Wyoming, and South Dakota for the Sioux Nation, including the sacred Black Hills (one of the last official treaties made before the 1871 *Indian Appropriation Act* declared a formal end to the process). After gold was discovered in the area, however, thousands of settlers streamed into the Black Hills in direct violation of the Treaty, sparking a second Great Sioux War (1876–77), during which Colonel Custer and the 7th Cavalry were famously defeated at the Battle of Greasy Grass (Little Bighorn). In response to this defeat, the US Army undertook the mass killing of buffalo as a means of undermining the subsistence economy of the Plains nations. The conflict ended with the *Black Hills Acts* of 1877 (known colloquially as the "Sell or Starve Act"), which demanded the Sioux relinquish control of the Black Hills in exchange for government rations to mitigate starvation.[6]

In 1887, the *Dawes Act* once more opened up tribal and reservation lands for sale by the federal government to settlers and, two years after that, the United States again violated the Fort Laramie Treaty when it unilaterally broke up the Great Sioux Reservation into five smaller units and imposed private property ownership as a means of rendering the land more alienable. In response, the Lakota Sioux took up the Ghost Dance, a religious movement aimed at reviving the spiritual foundations of the society. The US Bureau of Indian Affairs called in the Army to suppress

---

[4] https://nycstandswithstandingrock.wordpress.com/standingrocksyllabus/.

[5] On controversies over use of the terms "genocide" and "concentration camp" in this context, see Waziyatawin, *What Does Justice Look Like? The Struggle for Justice in Dakota Homeland* (St. Paul, MN: Living Justice Press, 2008), esp. ch. 1.

[6] James Daschuk, *Clearing the Plains: Disease, Politics of Starvation, and the Loss of Aboriginal Life* (Regina: University of Regina Press, 2013).

the movement, leading to the 1890 assassination of Crazy Horse and Sitting Bull, followed by the Wounded Knee Massacre, at which the 7th Cavalry killed hundreds of Dakota civilians, mostly women and children.[7]

In 1924, American Indians were unilaterally declared citizens of the United States, ushering in a long period of "termination."[8] From 1945 to 1960, more than one hundred tribes and bands were officially dissolved and incorporated into the United States without their consent. During this same time, the Army Corps of Engineers built the Lake Oahe dam, blocking the Missouri River on Cheyenne and Standing Rock Sioux reservation lands and submerging more Native land than any other water project in the United States.

In the 1960s and 1970s, a new wave of indigenous activism emerged, led by the American Indian Movement (AIM). AIM was involved in the 1969 occupation of Alcatraz, and the 1973 standoff of the Pine Ridge Sioux Reservation. Purposefully chosen as the symbolically charged site of the Wounded Knee massacre nearly one hundred years earlier, the latter conflict lasted seventy-one days until forcibly broken up by US Marshalls, FBI agents, and other law enforcement officers.[9] In 1980, the US government admitted to having illegally seized the Black Hills and offered $120 million in compensation. The Lakota rejected the monetary offer and to this day insist on the return of their land.[10] In 1999, Bill Clinton became the first sitting US President since Calvin Coolidge to meet with the Sioux when he made a stop at the Pine Ridge Reservation. President Obama followed suit in 2014 with a visit to Standing Rock. One year later, the US Army Corps of Engineers began work on the Dakota Access Pipeline. A collection of Indigenous Nations, including the Lakota, Dakota, Osage, and Iowa nations, voiced their concerns with the project at that time, saying "We have not been consulted in an appropriate manner about the presence of traditional cultural properties, sites, or landscapes vital to our identity and spiritual well-being." In August of 2016, the Standing Rock Sioux filed an injunction against further work. The parent company of Dakota Access LLC, Energy Transfer Partners, sued the Standing Rock Sioux chairman and other leaders for blocking construction, leading to the current standoff.

---

[7] James Mooney, *The Ghost Dance: Religion and Wounded Knee* (New York: Dover, 1973).

[8] On "compulsory enfranchisement" as a colonial tool, see Robert Nichols, "Contract and Usurpation" in A. Simpson and A. Smith (eds.), *Theorizing Native Studies* (Durham, NC: Duke University Press, 2014).

[9] Paul Chaat Smith and Robert Allen Warrior, *Like a Hurricane: The Indian Movement from Alcatraz to Wounded Knee* (New York: New Press, 1997).

[10] Jeffrey Ostler, *The Lakotas and the Black Hills: The Struggle for Sacred Ground* (New York: Penguin, 2010).

One of the first acts of the new Trump administration was to give a green light to the project, setting the stage for renewed battles.

The Lakota scholar Waziyatawin asks: In such a context, what does justice look like?[11] In the terms of this volume, we can ask more specifically: Is the conflict at Standing Rock a matter of *Global Justice*? A survey of the available literature would suggest not. One searches in vain for relevant analysis in the leading monographs, journals, and anthologies of the field.[12] What is at stake in this question? What difference does it make to frame the conflict in these terms? What kind of knowledge is required to make this determination? In what follows, I should like to use this conflict as something of a test case for Global Justice as a framework of analysis.[13] I will argue that Global Justice theory is not especially well equipped to respond to the deeper challenges posed by indigenous struggles of this sort and, moreover, that attending to these limitations draws us into deeper questions regarding history, narrative, method, and critique.

For several decades, debates within Global Justice theory proceeded without comment on how centuries of European and Euro-American imperialism had shaped the transnational economic and political order. References to empire were peripheral, marginal, and defensive. Although more systematic inquiry into the imperial foundations of global politics has expanded of late, it remains haunted by the specter of settler colonialism. Settler colonialism challenges established narratives of Global Justice in uniquely demanding ways. It presses upon conventional and taken-for-granted distinctions, such as between the domestic and foreign, internal and external, the Global North and Global South, the West and "the rest." It moreover forces consideration of the *constitutive power* of colonization. Most advocates of Global Justice view wealthy, Western states – as well as the international organizations they control and fund – as the primary agents of justice. In effect, these scholars view imperialism as a normatively problematic form of foreign policy, i.e., the outward projection of power beyond the extant boundaries of the polity. It is extremely rare to find any reflection on colonization in its specificity, that is, a complex set of historical processes that have constituted the very polities and corporate agents now taken to be the primary bearers of a Global Justice agenda. One symptom of this elision is the near total

---

[11] Waziyatawin, *What Does Justice Look Like?*

[12] Thom Brooks (ed.), *The Global Justice Reader* (Malden, MA: Blackwell, 2008).

[13] "Global Justice theory" comprises an admittedly loose and baggy collection of thinkers and set of debates, broadly liberal and "Anglo-American" in character, populated by libertarians, liberal nationalists, cosmopolitans of various kinds, all of whom nevertheless share a common conceptual vocabulary. Two recent surveys include: https://plato .stanford.edu/entries/justice-global/ and www.oxfordbibliographies.com/view/docu ment/obo-9780199743292/obo-9780199743292–0114.xml.

silence on what decolonization might look like in the context of settler colonial societies. For that, I will suggest, we need to reorient our basic frame of reference.

The argument proceeds as follows. Narrative I provides a general survey of the standard narrative concerning the emergence and theoretical preoccupations of Global Justice, with a particular focus on the uneasy relation this field has to its Anglo-American heritage. I consider how in this context "Anglo-American" signals a curious conflation of language, style, geography, and ethnonational belonging, in a manner that betrays some of the blind spots and limitations of the field. Drawing on the work of Sheldon Wolin, I consider how commitment to an ideal, analytic, contractualist mode of argumentation may block critical analysis of the contested histories of Anglo-America as an ethnonationalist and geospatial marker. In Narrative II, we turn to an altogether different perspective on "Anglo-America," one provided by indigenous peoples and scholars of settler colonialism. I focus specifically on the manner in which colonial power in the Anglo-American world has operated, in part, precisely by subordinating and incorporating indigenous political life so as to render it a matter of "domestic" (rather than international or global) concern. The conclusion considers the implications of this for the methodological and political commitments of Global Justice theory.

Narrative I: Global Justice as "Anglo-American" Political Philosophy

Despite the rather lofty and abstract nature of most treatments of Global Justice, this tradition of thought – like all such traditions – is embedded in a set of historical narratives. Some are self-consciously integrated into the received tradition itself; others are implicit and subsurface. Together, these narratives (official and unofficial, explicit and implicit) function to stabilize a tradition, serving as the relatively unquestioned background field of shared meaning upon which secondary, internal debates may unfold. They constitute a kind of *common sense*.[14] In this section, I should like to explore some of the gaps and tensions between the official and unofficial scripts that form the background understanding of debates in Global Justice, before juxtaposing these against indigenous narratives of colonialism in Anglo-America.

---

[14] I am indebted to the work of Mark Rifkin in helping me think through the notion of *settler common sense*, which I discuss below in relation to "Anglo-American" theories of justice. See Mark Rifkin, *Settler Common Sense: Queerness and Everyday Colonialism in the American Renaissance* (Minneapolis: University of Minnesota Press, 2014).

As a point of departure, let us consider a passage from a recent introductory book on the topic of Global Justice:

After many years of neglect, Anglo-American philosophers have begun to turn
their attention to issues of global justice. Discussions of domestic justice flour-
ished following the publication of *A Theory of Justice* by John Rawls in 1971
(Rawls, 1999a). Until the 1990s, however, these discussions usually put aside
questions of how a just society should relate to other societies and to non-
citizens ... One important explanation of this recent flourishing is the collapse
of Soviet communism. The Cold War was such a pervasive and overwhelming fact
that for Anglo-American political theorists, at least, it tended to crowd out other
topics in international relations ... A second explanation for the increased interest
in global justice relates to the process of globalization.[15]

This is just one short selection, but it is, I believe, representative of the
generally accepted, official narrative. Let me highlight a few features of
this script before turning to some of its lesser-noted features.

The standard narrative has it that, prior to the 1970s there was very
little systematic work done in political philosophy that was worthy of the
name. As George Klosko argues, although there were a number of important works written over the course of the twentieth century by such figures
as Adorno, Arendt, Berlin, and Marcuse, these were not *political philosophy*, at least not "according to what we now mean by the term." Klosko
suggests that they are better described as "social theory," since they are
characterized by a "deep intermixture of normative and empirical
concerns."[16] By this definition at least, there were no "classic works" of
political philosophy produced in the first three quarters of the twentieth
century, nothing on par with Mill's *On Liberty*, or Hobbes's *Leviathan*. All
this changed with the 1971 publication of John Rawls's *A Theory of Justice*
(*TJ*). Whatever objections critics may have raised to some of its substantive claims and conclusions, *TJ* set the model for political philosophy to
come. It did so by bracketing most empirical-descriptive questions in
favor of a purer form of ideal, normative inquiry; it moreover reactivated
"contract theory" as a central idiom of political philosophy and established that such work could be systematic, analytic, and programmatic or
action-guiding.

We can only say that Rawls bracketed *most* empirical-descriptive questions because, by his own account, the scope of *TJ* was confined to
a specific historical and sociological context. As Rawls was forced to
explain repeatedly to his critics, the principles of justice found in *TJ*

---

[15] Jon Mandle, *Global Justice: An Introduction* (Cambridge: Polity, 2006), 1–2.
[16] Klosko, "Contemporary Anglo-American Political Philosophy" in Klosko (ed.),
The Oxford Handbook of the History of Political Philosophy (Oxford: Oxford University
Press, 2011).

were never intended to apply "universally," but only obtain under certain circumstances. First, they speak only to "the basic structure of society"[17] in the domestic sphere. Second, although it was not made fully explicit until later debates – particularly those surrounding *The Law of Peoples* (1999) – the domestic orientation of *TJ* was further qualified by the liberal character of the society in question. "Peoples" in their internal or domestic relations must already share a common system of government and a shared set of basic moral intuitions (what John Stuart Mill called "common sympathies").[18] The principles of justice were not merely intended to apply to *any* domestic sphere then, but to a relatively unified *liberal* one. What made these peoples liberal in a sociological sense was that they demonstrated the requisite balance between a plurality of world-views (comprehensive moral doctrines) set within a sufficiently coherent and cohesive set of political institutions (e.g., rule of law, system of rights, etc.).

The originally "domestic orientation" of *TJ* reflects a long-standing traditional view in Western political philosophy, one that has held that questions of justice to obtain only *within* relatively bounded communities that share a sociocultural context, a system of law, and a mechanism for the enforcement of that law; in the absence of such institutions we cannot speak of justice. Under pressure by such thinkers as Charles Beitz, Thomas Pogge, and Onara O'Neill, that view has slowly given way to more systematic inquiry into the principles of justice that might obtain between individuals in different political associations and between those political associations themselves (typically states). As Mandle hints in the passage with which we began Narrative I, this largely took the form of an extension of Rawls's work to the global realm, driven by developments internal to the academic field, as well as externally by international politics (e.g., the fall of the USSR, processes of globalization, etc.). The field is now populated by a range of positions regarding the normative distinctiveness of domestic versus transnational political relations, as well as the moral standing of states and borders themselves. Responses to this set of problems include those who think, for instance, that (a) domestic relations within states are the only proper context of justice, (b) states are irrelevant to the proper context of justice – we can simply extend the

---

[17] "[T]he primary subject of justice is the basic structure of society, or more exactly the way in which the major social institutions distribute fundamental rights and duties and determine the division of advantages from social cooperation" (Rawls, *Theory of Justice*, 7–6).

[18] "A portion of mankind may be said to constitute a nationality if they are united by common sympathies which do not exist between them and any others," Mill, *Considerations on Representative Government* (New York: Prometheus Books, [1862] 1991), 308.

principles of domestic justice – and (c) states are relevant but in restricted ways, or in a manner that requires modification from the way they were originally framed by Rawls and other theorists of "domestic justice."[19] As a field of analysis concerned with such questions then, Global Justice emerged as Rawlsian political philosophy shed its domestic orientation.

One additional feature of Global Justice is also worth remarking upon, although it typically goes unnoted. Rawlsian political philosophy and, by extension Global Justice theory more generally, is generally described as *Anglo-American* in character. Although Global Justice is commonly labeled in this way (as it is by Mandle above), rarely do thinkers working within this field stop to reflect on what precisely the descriptor is meant to signal. Most often, it is used in a loose and shifting manner to refer to the primary natural language in which it is most often written (i.e., English); its style or mode of reasoning; its geographical origins, current primary location, and/or primary object of study. In this way, an ethnonationalist designation is used variously and somewhat interchangeably with "English-speaking"; "analytic" or "contractualist"; from, based in, or best pertaining to the Anglophone world.

To recapitulate then, theories of Global Justice have been largely wedded to this specific standard or official narrative: A mode of political philosophy originating in, or at least reactivated in modern times by Rawls, initially intended to apply only to the domestic realm of liberal societies, has been gradually if unevenly and controversially extended outward to consider matters on the international plane. The revival and formalization of an "Anglo-American" (or analytic) style of reasoning appropriate to liberal (but especially "Anglo-American") societies in their domestic relations has been increasingly pressed into service to confront questions of international relations by the processes of globalization that have driven liberal societies into increased proximity to their nonliberal neighbors. The new field of Global Justice retains an "Anglo-American" character, designating its historical emergence as a field, its primary object of study, and its mode of analysis.

Despite the fact that theorists of global justice regularly speak of this intellectual tradition in this way, they have remained remarkably uncurious about Anglo-America itself, about what this designator is supposed to mean, what work it does in constituting the settled norms and conventions of the field. What does it mean to adopt this ethnonational predicate? What is it for a body of thought to pride itself on its Anglo-American character when it lacks any substantive engagement with the idea of

---

[19] For an extended overview and critical analysis of these debates, see Mathias Risse, *On Global Justice* (Princeton, NJ: Princeton University Press, 2012), esp. Part I.

Anglo-America, historically and in the present? What significance (if any) can be attached to the fact that the term slides so easily between these different uses and meanings?

I submit that the relative paucity of thought regarding the scope and character of "Anglo-America" from within the Global Justice literature is indicative of larger concerns. That "Anglo-American" signals confusing imbrications of language, style, geography, and ethnonational forms of belonging (and thus also exclusion) is symptomatic here of deeper questions that drive to the heart of any quest for justice (however framed). Ultimately, I want to suggest, Global Justice's commitment to an Anglo-American *style of reasoning* – one juxtaposed against and fearful of sliding backwards into that "deep intermixture of normative and empirical concerns" Klosko warns against – ultimately blocks its ability to interrogate some of the basic terms and frames of reference that thinkers in this vein typically try to hold constant and fixed, including "Anglo-America" as a geographical and ethnonational placeholder, not to mention the more general distinction between the domestic and global spheres of justice. This is brought to light in a distinctive way by indigenous struggles in and against "Anglo-America," or so I shall argue.

Work by the political theorist Sheldon Wolin is useful in helping us first flesh out the theoretical stakes of this concern. Responding to the revival of ideal "social contract" theory in the contemporary Anglo-American political philosophy of Rawls and Nozick, Wolin concedes that these contemporaries employ contractualist language in a more idealized sense than one finds in earlier thinkers (such as Hobbes or Locke). Newer work tends to deploy the "contract" merely as a heuristic device in prescribing the "principles of a rights-oriented society," rather than an empirical-descriptive account of how such societies "have actually come into existence." Despite this reorientation, Wolin presses forward with an important critique. Contractualism, even as an idealized model of reasoning, all the same proceeds on the assumption "that it is possible to talk intelligently about the most fundamental principles of a political society as though neither the society nor the individuals in it had a history."[20] He attacks on these latter grounds. For Wolin, the language of contractualism has the effect of eroding our capacity to grasp ourselves as fundamentally political creatures, that is, to understand and illuminate what he terms our essential "politicalness." Politicalness requires grasping oneself as situated within a historical tradition, as a subject constituted by forces that precede and exceed oneself and that shape the tenor and tone of one's

---

[20] Wolin, *The Presence of the Past: Essays on the State and the Constitution* (Baltimore, MD: Johns Hopkins University Press, 1989), 139.

own choices. Echoing Hegel before him, Wolin suggests that to speak of political membership, authority, and obligation as grounded in individual choice and discretion is fundamentally to misidentify these phenomena.[21] Truly wrestling with them requires some measure of reconciliation to their necessarily unchosen and imposed forms. Politicalness therefore makes demands upon us. It "calls for a citizen who can become an interpreting being, one who can interpret the present experience of the collectivity, reconnect it to past symbols, and carry it forward."[22] Contractualism erodes this quality, supplanting it with an abstract, analytic, and ultimately denuded conception of political membership. For, in a contract, citizens are related to one another in a relation of equality precisely because, and insofar as, they have no prior history. When juxtaposed with our true historical situation – the fact of a bloody inheritance that cannot be redeemed and yet cannot be evaded – "the function of social contract thinking becomes clear: to relieve individuals and society of the burden of the past by erasing the ambiguities."[23]

All of this is to say that, as a model of reasoning and as a political allegory, the analytic of contractualism is a means of binding citizens together in a specific way, namely, as formally equal individuals whose medium of interaction is that of exchange. By the same token, however, it also *unbinds* us. A society of individuals who imagine their relations to be ideally oriented around contractualism is a society that can make little sense, let alone effective use, of ideas of collective memory, responsibility, obligation, and identity. If my political subjectivity is constituted in and through acts of contract, if the entirety of society is imagined to be the product of a contract, then talk of inherited and historically constituted identities and responsibilities will appear incoherent, even dysfunctional. By historical constitution, I mean the manner in which political form is handed down to us by the past, that we all come into the world already invested with a set of relations and institutions that are not ours to choose – indeed, whatever mythologies of "founding fathers" might suggest, political form is never the product of a wholesale decision at any particular point in time. Such moments are more the product of ideological construction in the present, retrospectively imposed upon the past so as to authorize a certain kind of future. This fact of *political thrownness* is distorted by the allegory of the contract, rendering us ill-equipped to deal with the vagaries, tensions, and ambivalences of our own inheritance. From the standpoint of contractualism, such demands can

---

[21] Hegel famously offered an extended critique of "contractualism" in political philosophy along these lines in *The Philosophy of Right*.
[22] Wolin, *The Presence of the Past*, 141.   [23] Wolin, *The Presence of the Past*, 138.

only be experienced as unjust impositions, as violations of the fundamental principle that political responsibilities flow from individual consent. Such a contract politics lives in an eternal present. When attempting to work through questions of historically structured injustice, contractualist models of reasoning appear therefore at a distinct disadvantage. They lack the tools to express the historical constitution of the present, and thus tend to confuse these inherited structures of collective domination and oppression as individualistic, moral failures. Even as we attempt to critique the negative features of society, we repeat and replicate the contractualist mode of reasoning.

One appeal of Wolin's critique of contractualism is that it aspires to move beyond purely formal concerns (that is, with the idea of contract in the abstract) toward an investigation of the historical function of contract thinking within a particular intellectual and political tradition. The event that occasioned Wolin's reflections on contract theory was the bicentennial of the US Constitution of 1787. The central aim of his "essays in retrieval" on that occasion was therefore not merely to grasp the *form* of contractualist reasoning, but rather to apprehend its *function* within the US context.[24] For, as Wolin repeatedly points out, this "function assumes practical importance because contractualism is not solely an academic philosophy. It is part of American political mythology, of the collective belief that define our identity and help shape our political attitudes and opinions."[25] His concern then is not exclusively with what contract *means* (to political philosophy), but rather what it *does*, that is, with the practical effects this archetypal metaphor can have in the specific context of the contemporary United States. The function of contract theory in this context, Wolin suggests, is to reinforce the peculiar ahistoricism of the US political imaginary. For, in his estimation, the United States is an essentially *post-mnemonic society*, a place where citizens are either uncomprehending or indifferent to the idea of historical constitution, and where collective memory is "at best ritualistic and, more likely, treated as dysfunctional."[26]

Wolin's cautionary mediation on the deleterious effects of contractualist thinking remains, in my view, relevant and salutary. Nevertheless, in his move from formal to functionalist critique, his rendering of the problem is haunted by a certain ironic limitation. For although suggestive, Wolin's critique remains – despite itself – paradoxically rather ahistorical. His concern remains primarily with the idea of political order as based on the model of a contract, and on revealing the ultimate incoherence of this

---

[24] Wolin, *The Presence of the Past*, 4.   [25] Wolin, *The Presence of the Past*, 144.
[26] Wolin, *The Presence of the Past*, 32.

framework. As a result, little attention is given to demonstrating the specific historical operation of contractualism, its genealogy or its effects. Put more concretely, if Wolin is correct to suggest that contract thinking is a part of American political mythology – "nowhere has this idiom been more influential than in America"[27] – making good on such a claim requires an account of *why* this might be the case. We need a historical analysis of the contract's mechanism of articulation. Instead, we are left only with fragments and traces of a historical reconstruction. And, in those moments when Wolin does pause to consider the matter, he tends rather disappointingly to fall back upon another set of myths. Citing Louis Hartz's influential narrative of American political development, Wolin examines the peculiar hold that contractualism has had on the USA as a function of lacking a feudal past. For Wolin, as for Hartz (and indeed for Tocqueville before them both), to "have no feudal past means to have a politics without history." Feudalism, on this rendering, is a system in which inheritance is "the master notion" and archetypal metaphor for historicized politics. It thus imagines politics as a process that "over time inevitably produces inherited privileges and unequal powers. The result is a social space crowded with prior claims to unequal ownership and status and the transformation of a manifold of injustices (unlawful conquest and forcible seizures) from the dim past into vested rights of the present." In juxtaposition to this "postlapsarian" vision of politics, stands the "New World of America." This latter "New World" appears as "fresh land":

seemingly without limits or boundaries and innocent of past inequalities. Land was easily available, and opportunities for wealth and higher status seemed endless. Accordingly, America's politics was natural rather than historical. America's political practices developed as though written on a *tablua rasa* much as the contract theorists of the seventeenth century had imagined men imposing a civil association upon a state of nature. Inscribing politics upon nature rather than history was the essence of what was modern about America ... To have no history is to face only natural obstacles and one's own limitations.

Lacking the traditions and customary institutions of a feudal society, America is future-oriented and unbounded *will*. While this may appear utopic to some, for Wolin it portends doom: "Unrelieved newness is the stuff of despotism."[28]

Sheldon Wolin is not the first (or last) thinker to suggest "America" is contract theory's natural home, nor that this is explainable in terms of political culture. A long lineage of thought holds up the United States as exemplary in this regard, as the site of the purest instance of any society to begin *de novo*. Wolin can cite Thomas Paine's boast, to the effect that

---

[27] Wolin, *The Presence of the Past*, 138.   [28] Wolin, *The Presence of the Past*, 74–75.

newly independent Americans had it in their power "to begin the world over again." He can reach back as easily to Locke, Tocqueville, and Hartz.[29] Such a conception of "America" can be found in more recent commentators as well. It is, for instance, quite evident in Hannah Arendt's ruinous veneration of the *pathos* of novelty supposedly embodied in the US revolutionary moment,[30] just as we find it in Francis Fukuyama's *The End of History*, where it is decidedly more prideful of its "Anglo-Saxon" heritage (and all the more ominous for that reason).[31]

So, perhaps Wolin is correct to suggest that contractualism is rooted deeply in the political mythology of (Anglo) America, that the metaphor serves in this context as a "device to incorporate social amnesia into the foundation of society." As Wolin elaborates, "If men could forget, mutual absolution was possible, allowing society to start afresh without inherited resentments. A necessary condition of social amnesia was, therefore, that men dehistoricize themselves."[32] It is no coincidence that the phrase *Novus ordo seclorum* ("New Order of the Ages") appears on the reverse of the Great Seal of the United States (since 1782) and, since 1935, on the back of the one-dollar bill. And, yet, to make good on this concern, we require something more. Does reference to America as timeless, as fresh land, as *tabula rasa*, really serve to *explain* the uptake of contractualism in its historical development? Or, does it merely push us backward one step to the necessity of explaining these other tropes? Without an analysis of how these different elements hang together, each metaphor appears explainable only in terms of the others. The threat of empty tautology looms.

---

[29] Louis Hartz, *The Founding of New Societies: Studies in the History of the United States, Latin America, South Africa, Canada, and Australia* (New York: Harcourt, Brace and World, 1964). On Hartz and settler colonialism, see Kevin Bruyneel, "The American Liberal Colonial Tradition," *Settler Colonial Studies*, 3 (2013), 311–321.

[30] Hannah Arendt, *On Revolution* (New York: Viking, 1963), 207, 219. For two critiques of Arendt in this context, see Aziz Rana, *The Two Faces of American Freedom* (Cambridge, MA: Harvard University Press, 2010) and Jason Frank, *Constituent Moments: Enacting the People in Postrevolutionary America* (Durham, NC: Duke University Press, 2010).

[31] In a chapter of the latter text titled "The First Man," Fukuyama spins a tale in which liberal democracies

were deliberately created by human beings at a definite point in time, on the basis of a certain theoretical understanding of man and of the appropriate political institutions that should govern human society ... The principles underlying American democracy, codified in the Declaration of Independence and the Constitution, were based on the writings of Jefferson, Madison, Hamilton, and the other American Founding Fathers, who in turn derived many of their ideas from the English liberal tradition of Thomas Hobbes and John Locke.

(Fukuyama, *The End of History*, revised edition [New York: Free Press, 2006] 153)

[32] Wolin, *The Presence of the Past*, 38.

To break out of this ahistorical and circular explanation, we require an account that introduces an independent explanatory device, one that can make sense of contractualism's resonance in this context without simply reintroducing it in another guise. The concern I am pursuing here is that grasping the political function of a mode of reasoning in this context requires expanding our frame of reference, repudiating American exceptionalism (in both its critical and laudatory registers), and foregrounding the deep resonance of this political vocabulary across "Anglo-America." As I have argued elsewhere, *settler colonial dispossession* is the explanatory device that best makes sense of this function, of this resonance. It is my sense that this form of thought has been so powerful and successful in the English-speaking world because it has been so politically useful for those in the so-called "new world" colonies. A certain form of analytic contractualism has a deep resonance with the ethnonational ideal of "Anglo-America" – to the point that, even today, the two are commonly conflated – because the former has played a role in the historical constitution and ahistorical exculpation of the latter. I don't claim that contractualism has *only* been useful in this context, nor that it has always or even predominantly been deployed in a purposeful or conscious way to evade and avoid questions of the historical constitution of those societies in conquest, genocide, and dispossession. But, this effect is a part of its specific function within the Anglo settler world, and part of its appeal. Let me expand and explain.

Narrative II: Settler Colonialism and "Anglo-America"

Since the 1990s, a subfield of interdisciplinary research has emerged under the banner of *Settler Colonial Studies*. Traversing history, anthropology, sociology, comparative literature, law, and political science, this field of study has been unified and animated by an investigation into settler colonialism as "a distinct social and historical formation" (in the words of the editorial board of the newly founded journal of *Settler Colonial Studies*). Work in this vein commonly takes as its point of departure a simple, yet powerful and productive distinction. In the long, complex, and multitudinous history of reflection upon empire, a distinction has emerged between two "family languages" of colonization. *Extraction colonies* have tended to operate through the subordination and domination of racialized underclass populations, with the primary aim being the exploitation of their labor. By contrast, *settler colonization* involves the large-scale transplantation of foreign populations who seek to displace indigenous inhabitants with the aim of forming a wholly new society, one that mimics or replicates the settlers' mother-country. In this latter case, it is not labor, but land that colonizers seek from the colonized. Accordingly, native populations are frequently viewed as obstacles or obstructions to colonial aims, rather than resources to be exploited.

Use of settler colonialism as an analytic with which we might read the historical archive and its contemporary traces emerged in a new way in the 1990s due to leading work by the comparative historian Patrick Wolfe. In the groundbreaking book *Settler Colonialism and the Transformation of Anthropology*, the oft-cited essay "Settler Colonialism and the Elimination of the Native," and more recently published *Traces of History: Elementary Structures of Race*, Wolfe has done more to establish the parameters of settler colonial studies than perhaps any other single scholar.[33] He has since been joined by a bevy of major scholars from across a diverse range of fields, including Joanne Barker, James Belich, Jodi Byrd, Lisa Ford, Alyosha Goldstein, J. Kehaulani Kauanui, Audra Simpson, and Lorenzo Veracini.[34] Although newer work in this field of study has taken on a distinctly comparative and transnational tenor, many of the leading thinkers in the field specialize first and foremost in the *Anglo settler world*. Accordingly, while Francophone, Hispanic, Germanic, and Israeli forms of settler colonization are increasingly taking stage as key alternative cases, they are most often situated in relation to the Anglophone model, which remains in some ways the "classic form." Paralleling the role that they play in the debates over liberalism, analytic philosophy, and Global Justice, Anglophone societies function here as *primus inter pares*. The objective of this body of work has never been to assert that these societies are uniquely or exhaustively determined by their historical constitution as settler colonies. It has, rather, been to ask what

---

[33] Patrick Wolfe, *Settler Colonialism and the Transformation of Anthropology* (London: Cassell, 1999); Patrick Wolfe, "Settler Colonialism and the Elimination of the Native," *Journal of Genocide Research*, 8/4 (2006), 387–409; Patrick Wolfe, *Traces of History: Elementary Structures of Race* (London: Verso, 2016).

[34] Joanne Barker, *Native Acts: Law, Recognition, and Cultural Authenticity* (Durham, NC: Duke University Press, 2011); James Belich, *Replenishing the Earth: The Settler Revolution and the Rise of the Anglo-World, 1783–1939* (Oxford: Oxford University Press, 2009); Jodi Byrd, *The Transit of Empire: Indigenous Critiques of Colonialism* (Minneapolis: University of Minnesota Press, 2011); Lisa Ford, *Settler Sovereignty: Jurisdiction and Indigenous People in America and Australia, 1788–1836* (Cambridge, MA: Harvard University Press, 2010); Alyosha Goldstein and Alex Lubin, eds., "Settler Colonialism," Special Issue Edition of *The South Atlantic Quarterly*, 107/4 (2008); J. Kehaulani Kauanui, *Hawaiian Blood: Colonialism and the Politics of Sovereignty and Indigeneity* (Durham, NC: Duke University Press, 2008); Audra Simpson, *Mohawk Interruptus: Political Life across the Borders of Settler States* (Durham, NC: Duke University Press, 2014); Lorenzo Veracini, *Settler Colonialism: A Theoretical Introduction* (New York: Palgrave Macmillan, 2010); Veracini, *The Settler Colonial Present* (New York: Palgrave Macmillan, 2015).

comparative difference it makes to study them in this manner, to ask after the relative merits of analyzing the societies of the "Anglo settler world" within a unified conceptual frame. This has allowed for the common, yet distinguishing features of "Anglo settler colonialism" in particular to emerge, despite its differentiated articulation across Australia, Canada, New Zealand, and the United States.

Three such features stand out. The first is a distinctive *orientation to land*. Armed with a unique commitment to agrarian improvement and small-scale private landholding, Anglo colonizers sought first and foremost to dispossess indigenous peoples of their ancestral lands so that these lands could become the territorial foundation for "neo-European" societies populated predominately by white settlers. To paraphrase Patrick Wolfe, this orientation to land is Anglo settler colonization's "specific, irreducible element." Second, indigenous peoples who survived this territorial dispossession process were "incorporated" or "domesticated" into the emergent Anglo settler societies. That is, indigenous peoples in this part of the world have been subjected to a particular *internal colonization process*, such that they now exist, and are largely treated by both domestic and international legal orders, as relatively small "minority populations" situated within larger polities. In (at least) these two respects (*territoriality* and *internal colonization*), Anglo settler societies are seen as distinct from other kinds of imperial formations (most particularly the kinds of overseas dependencies typically envisioned by work on empire). The third component is what Wolfe terms the "logic of elimination." In extraction colonies, imperial administrators seek to harness the labor power of a racialized underclass. By contrast, because settler colonizers seek access to *land*, this commonly renders indigenous labor power superfluous. Accordingly, indigenous peoples within such settler colonies become highly vulnerable to total elimination. Rather than attempt to maintain a large and distinct racialized underclass, settlers typically seek to eliminate, absorb, and co-opt the position of the "native" in the expansion and consolidation of their neo-European societies. As Wolfe puts it,

settler colonialism has both negative and positive dimensions. Negatively, it strives for the dissolution of native societies. Positively, it erects a new colonial society on the expropriated land base – as I put it, settler colonizers come to stay: invasion is a structure not an event. In its positive aspect, elimination is an organizing principal [*sic*] of settler-colonial society rather than a one-off (and superseded) occurrence. The positive outcomes of the logic of elimination can include officially encouraged miscegenation, the breaking-down of native title into alienable individual freeholds, native citizenship, child abduction, religious conversion, resocialization in total institutions such as missions or boarding schools, and a whole range of cognate biocultural assimilations. All these strate-gies, including frontier homicide, are characteristic of settler colonialism.[35]

In some ways, the contemporary interest in settler colonialism – as well as its ambiguous relation to the Anglophone world as a paradigmatic case – is actually a revival of an older idiom of empire. At the turn of the twentieth century, for instance, it was commonplace to divide the study of empire into its two exemplary forms. It was taken for granted that the "world of empire" could be analytically partitioned into the imperial dependencies and the white settler colonies, a fact reflected in the orga-nizational structure of two such differently oriented works as J. R. Seeley's *The Expansion of England* (1883) and J. A. Hobson's *Imperialism: A Study* (1903).[36]

To illustrate the convergence of the conceptual and practical implica-tions of this view, consider briefly the life and work of Theodore Roosevelt.[37] Roosevelt is well known as an ardent defender of US imperial ambitions overseas at the turn of the twentieth century, having defended and celebrated annexations and conquests in Hawaii, Guam, Puerto Rico, and the Philippines, as well as overseeing the build-ing of the Panama Canal. At the same time, Roosevelt was central to the process by which settler expansion in the white, Anglo-Saxon colonies was reframed and consolidated. As he explained in an 1889 speech, the "English-speaking peoples" of the world had been fortunate enough to discover and peacefully settle the "world's waste spaces."[38] At one point, Roosevelt even envisioned the white settler world might be restructured into a single Anglo-American Union.[39] Roosevelt's defense of US empire had, therefore, as Aziz Rana argues, two faces.[40] It posited a strong distinction between internal and external relations, combining a vigorous defense of external expansionism with an exculpatory and

---

[35] Wolfe, "Settler Colonialism and the Elimination of the Native," 388.
[36] See here Duncan Bell, *Reordering the World: Essays on Liberalism and Empire* (Princeton, NJ: Princeton University Press, 2016), ch. 2.
[37] David Temin, *Remapping the World: Vine Deloria, Jr. and the Ends of Settler Sovereignty.* PhD Dissertation (University of Minnesota), October 2016.
[38] Theodore Roosevelt, *The Winning of the West* (New York: Hastings House, 1963 (1889)), quoted in Aziz Rana, "Colonialism and Constitutional Memory," *UC Irvine Law Review*, 5/2 (2014), 266.
[39] On transnational intellectual exchanges about Reconstruction and racially restrictive immigration, especially among the United States, South Africa, and Australia, see Marilyn Lake and Henry Reynolds, *Drawing the Global Colour Line: White Man's Countries and the International Challenge of Racial Equality* (New York: Cambridge University Press, 2008), 49–74; 310–334. On the politics of Anglo-American Union, see Duncan Bell, "Beyond the Sovereign State: Isopolitan Citizenship, Race, and Anglo-American Union," *Political Studies*, 62/2 (2014), 418–434.
[40] Rana, *The Two Faces of American Freedom*.

decidedly counterfactual narrative of US domestic state formation as pacific. Accordingly, for Roosevelt, as wrong-headed as anti-imperial sentiment was in cases such as the Spanish-American War and its aftermath, it was a conceptual absurdity when applied to the domestic state formation process of the United States itself. Framing Indian policy in imperial terms, "would make it incumbent upon us to leave the Apaches of Arizona to work out their own salvation, and to decline to interfere in a single Indian reservation. Their doctrines condemn your forefathers and mine for ever having settled in these United States."[41] Criticizing the rightness and fitness of the white settler populations in the Anglophone world to rule these "waste spaces" was tantamount to a betrayal of one's ethnoracial and nationalist allegiances. Despite this, Roosevelt was of course aware that these spaces were not literally empty or unclaimed. The self-stylized "Cowboy of the Dakotas," Roosevelt spent considerable stretches of his life on a ranch built on the Little Missouri River, near Medora, North Dakota. Now found in a national park that bears his name, Roosevelt's ranch is fewer than 200 miles from the Standing Rock Sioux Reservation. In 1941, his likeness was dynamited into the sacred Sioux Black Hills, now known as Mount Rushmore.

Over the course of the twentieth century, in response to mounting immigration pressures and the general delegitimizing effect that Nazism had on overtly white supremacist ideologies within the "Allied nations," Anglophone settler societies sought to rebrand themselves. No longer would they be bastions of an imagined family of Anglo-Saxon societies; they would now be exemplary postnational, cosmopolitan liberalism.[42] Indigenous peoples living within these societies tell a different story. The celebratory postnational, cosmopolitan liberalism of these (formerly?) white settler societies is alternatively rendered as one more turn of the screw, as an invitation for a wider swath of humanity to partake in the plunder reaped through dispossession and ongoing occupation of indigenous lands. As Glen Coulthard (Dene) and Elizabeth Povinelli have extensively argued, multicultural liberalism has effectively worked to erode indigenous collective self-determination. Thus, as Audra Simpson (Mohawk) points out, indigenous peoples in the English-speaking world continue to reject the "gift" of liberal citizenship, and persist in enacting alternative political forms that sit uncomfortably

---

[41] Theodore Roosevelt, *The Strenuous Life: Essays and Addresses* (New York: Dover, [1889] 2009), 9.

[42] For an argument to the effect that liberalism has stretched and expanded in such a way as to now effectively incorporate the claims of indigenous peoples, see Duncan Ivison, *Postcolonial Liberalism* (Cambridge: Cambridge University Press, 2002).

within settler states that can neither fully incorporate nor expunge them.[43]

Attending to the constitutive force of settler colonialism in the emergence and continued sustenance of "Anglo-America" (as an idea, an ideal, as well as a geographic location) enables a number of its distinctive features to come sharply into view. We can now better comprehend the imbrications of contractualism and the peculiar, endemic antipathy to history that one finds in Anglo-American social and political thought. Rather than explain this in terms of *a lack* (as Wolin does, for instance, by way of an absent feudal past), we can now more properly view the "new world begun anew" myth as a politically productive fantasy in a specific operation of power. As decades of research into Locke and the early modern emergence of contract theory has now demonstrated, contractualism was, from its very inception, a discourse of colonial justification and ideation.[44] Moreover, as I have endeavored to show elsewhere (working alongside such thinkers as Carole Pateman and K-Sue Park), as the language of contractualist societies came across the Atlantic, later circulating to the Anglophone South Pacific, it was pressed into service as a tool of indigenous dispossession.[45] This cannot be understood without foregrounding the specific form of settler colonialism.

Second, the analytic of settler colonialism permits us to reframe another major topic, central to this volume as a whole: race. Under the influence of the linguistic and discursive idealism of early waves of postcolonial studies literature, one prevailing way of thinking through the relationship between race (or, more precisely, white supremacy) and imperialism has been to posit that the latter operated through the construction of a binary opposition between the white, European world and its racialized, non-European "other." One persistent difficulty with this approach, however, lay with accounting for the immense heterodoxy and dynamic mutability of racial taxonomies. Accordingly, as the field developed postcolonial theorists gradually came to concede that white

---

[43] Glen Coulthard, *Red Skin, White Masks: Rejecting the Colonial Politics of Recognition* (Minneapolis: University of Minnesota Press, 2014); Elizabeth Povinelli, *The Cunning of Recognition: Indigenous Alterities and the Making of Australian Multiculturalism* (Durham, NC: Duke University Press, 2002); Simpson, *Mohawk Interruptus*.

[44] See, for example, Barbara Arneil, *John Locke and America: The Defence of English Colonialism* (Oxford: Clarendon, 1996); James Tully, *An Approach to Political Philosophy: Locke in Context* (Cambridge: Cambridge University Press, 1993), esp. ch. 5.

[45] I have extensively discussed Pateman, Mills, and the "critical contract" literature in a number of other pieces. See Robert Nichols, "Contract and Usurpation": "Indigeneity and the Settler Contract Today," *Philosophy & Social Criticism*, 39/2 (2013), 161–182; "Of First and Last Men: Contract and Colonial Historicality in Foucault" in A. Swiffen and J. Nichols (eds.), *The End(s) of History: Questioning the Stakes of Historical Reason* (Abingdon: Routledge, 2012).

supremacist ideology operated along a spectrum, rather than a strict dichotomy, along which racial difference could be plotted according to its proximity to whiteness.[46] In the terrain with which we are concerned, this led to a highly problematic and suspect way of locating indigenous peoples alongside and in relation to other "nonwhite" peoples, but especially African-Americans.[47]

Using settler colonialism as a framework of analysis has aided in the reorientation of this debate. Settler colonialism was, and is, structured through a commitment to white supremacy. Attention to its specificity also enables us to better explain the complexity and variability of white supremacist technologies of governance across space and time. Here, we are aided by Wolfe's encyclopedic study, *Traces of History*. In that work, Wolfe points out that while "Blackness" and "nativeness" were both racialized categories in Anglo-America, they were not so in interchangeable ways. In fact, contrary to common assertion, their externality relative to whiteness is not only different, it was often contrasting. This is starkly dramatized in the example of anti-miscegenation policy in nineteenth-century America. As Wolfe points out, whereas "one drop" of Black lineage rendered one fully Black, "one-drop" of white blood was enough to compromise Indian authenticity. Thus, "whilst the one-drop rule has meant that the category 'black' can withstand unlimited admixture, the category 'red' has been highly venerable to dilution."[48] Explaining these divergent practices requires shifting away from the critique of white supremacy as an ideology, toward a political economy of racial colonialism. Under this alternative mode of inquiry, the political construction of Blackness can be better apprehended as a specific project whereby certain bodies are rendered into property for the purposes of exploitation as free, highly mobile, and vulnerable labor. In this case, anti-miscegenation laws reflect the need to maintain a large reserve pool of labor, immune to reduction through intergenerational admixture and racial dilution. On the other hand, however, the existence of an available and easily exploitable labor pool renders indigenous bodies highly vulnerable to elimination and/or assimilation. Where indigenous labor is largely superfluous, indigenous difference (comprehended in racial, cultural, or political terms) can only function as an obstacle to settler expansion and

---

[46] For a detailed, edifying overview of these debates, see Robert Young, *Postcolonialism: An Historical Introduction* (London: Blackwell, 2001), esp. Part V.

[47] On the (sometimes fraught) relation between Postcolonial and Indigenous studies, see Kevin Bruyneel, *The Third Space of Sovereignty: The Postcolonial Politics of U.S.-Indigenous Relations* (Minneapolis: University of Minnesota Press, 2007); Jodi Byrd, *The Transit of Empire: Indigenous Critiques of Colonialism* (Minneapolis: University of Minnesota Press, 2011).

[48] Wolfe, *Settler Colonialism and the Transformation of Anthropology*, 2.

solidification. Put most starkly then, whereas African Americans were primarily targeted for their *labor*, Native Americans were primarily targeted for their *land*. These two imperatives for a burgeoning settler society such as the United States of the early nineteenth century serve as the single most important explanatory devices for understanding the contrasting character tropes of "Blacks" and "Indians" of the period (in particular, their relative proximity to, and capacity for absorption into, whiteness).[49] A synoptic analysis of colonialism, capitalism, and racialization is required to bring these different diverse threads together while, at the same time, expressing their underlying functional similarities.

Conclusion

Where does this leave us with regard to the question of indigenous struggles and Global Justice today? What relations of obligation, responsibility, and mutual recognition bind us (variously positioned actors) to the Sioux Nation? I do not know how to achieve justice at Standing Rock, but I do know that this question is *deeply historical.* By this, I do not mean of course that it exists in the past. As the battle at Standing Rock reveals, these issues are urgently contemporary. Rather, they are historical in the sense that we inherit the meaning and significance of such struggles from structures, systems, and narratives that predate the present, which we cannot choose but must nevertheless own. Recovering some sense of these rich and complex histories is part of our "politicalness," as Wolin put it.[50] Thus, it is not that we can reach for some interpretative framework that stands "outside" of history as a means of adjudicating a conflict that stands "within" it. Rather, there is a recursive relation between historical struggles and the languages we draw upon to make sense of them.

The kind of ideal, analytic, and contractualist mode of analysis that travels somewhat ironically under the heading "Anglo-American" does not equip us with the requisite tools for apprehending such problems. For

---

[49] This analysis is also indebted to, *inter alia*, Andrea Smith, "Heteropatriarchy and the Three Pillars of White Supremacy," in A. Smith, B. Richie, and J. Sudbury (eds.), *Color of Violence: The INCITE! Anthology* (Cambridge, MA: SouthEnd Press, 2006), 66–73. For further work on miscegenation and the "one-drop" rule, see F. J. Davis, *Who Is Black? One Nation's Definition* (University Park: Pennsylvania State University Press, 1991) and I. F. Haney Lopez, *White by Law: The Legal Construction of Race* (New York: New York University Press, 1996). On the centrality of racial constructs to the project of colonial expansion in nineteenth-century America, see Reginald Horsman, *Race and Manifest Destiny: The Origins of American Racial Anglo-Saxonism* (Cambridge, MA: Harvard University Press, 1986).

[50] For an alternative rendering of the relationship between historical sensibility and politicalness, see the chapter by Jeanne Morefield in this volume.

to model political relations as grounded in individual choice and discretion is already to misidentify the nature of the historically constituted relations of obligation and responsibility that bind us "Anglo-Americans" to the Great Sioux Nation.[51] Lacking any historical sensibility, Global Justice frames of reference deprive us of the thick interpretative tools required to make sense of these struggles as something other than contestations over a fixed set of resources and identities, missing the degree to which they are also *meaning-making activities*, contests over the historical narratives that structure our "common sense" understandings of politics. In suggesting that the struggles of indigenous peoples press hard upon the methodological presuppositions of the field, what I am ultimately arguing then is not only that the "Anglo-American" presuppositions and preoccupations of Global Justice disable its capacity to grapple with indigenous challenges, but more pointedly, this also undermines its own self-understanding as an intellectual traditional that is always already enmeshed in a set of colonial narratives.

The struggles of indigenous peoples are, in part, struggles over particular, concrete objects of concern – a pipeline, dam, burial site, or mountain range. More abstractly, they are also struggles over property, ownership, rights, nationhood, and sovereignty. Perhaps most important of all, however, they are *interpretive struggles*, challenging and unsettling the very terms of global political order. These do not map neatly onto the familiar terms of reference that orient "Anglo-American" political philosophy. The political life of the Standing Rock Sioux is neither fully "domestic" nor wholly "foreign" to the United States. It does not sit comfortably within the paradigms of internal/external, the "Global North" and the "Global South," or the West and "the rest," that so often serve to structure debates within the prevailing literature. Moreover, truly attending to these conflicts requires seeing how we are already located within them. Speaking explicitly now as a nonindigenous settler myself, I think that our self-conception as "Anglo-Americans" – with all the range of meanings lodged within the term – is itself indebted to the same past that haunts us in these contemporary struggles. Thus, to grapple with the Sioux uprising to is grapple with *ourselves*, with our historical inheritance as much as theirs, with our essential politicalness. If it is the case that these are struggles over the very terms of political discourse, then we need more than a normative theory that holds the messy matter of history at bay, for instance, by juxtaposing the domestic and global faces of justice as if these terms of reference make sense

---

[51] Here, I speak specifically as an Anglophone European-descendant settler, born and raised in Canada but currently residing in the United States.

without hermeneutic work. What is required, rather, is an account that analyzes the processes that constitute such distinctions in the first place, how they are enacted, narrated, and contested over time. In short, it requires an account of settler colonization as a transnational phenomenon that comprised the corporate entities in question (i.e., the United States, the Great Sioux Nation). That account will however unavoidably require the "deep intermixture of normative and empirical concerns" that Global Justice so prides itself on circumventing.

11 Decolonizing Borders, Self-Determination, and Global Justice

Catherine Lu

Introduction: The Case of the Legally Extinct Sinixt First Nation's Rights

In 2010, Rick Desautel hunted and killed a cow elk about sixty-five kilometers north of the US–Canada border, near Castlegar, British Columbia, and was charged by conservation officers for hunting without a license and hunting as a nonresident. Desautel lives on the Colville reservation in Washington state and is a member of the Sinixt or Arrow Lakes First Nation, but this particular indigenous group was declared legally extinct in the Indian Act of 1956 in Canada.[1] Although the traditional territories of the migratory Sinixt traversed the international boundary between Canada and the United States, pressures of settler colonization in Canada led members of the Sinixt eventually to move southward to the Colville reservation. In the British Columbia court case in March 2017, Desautel argued that given his aboriginal right to hunt in the traditional territory of his ancestors, which extends into Canada, the conservation officer was wrong to penalize him for hunting in Canada without a licence. The BC court acquitted Desautel of all charges, and

The author thanks Duncan Bell for editing this volume and organizing the conference at Cambridge University in April 2016 that stimulated the writing of this chapter. Versions of this chapter were subsequently presented at the "On Global Inequality" conference organized by the Center for Ethics and Human Values at Ohio State University (April 2017), the "Territorial Rights" conference, held at the Université du Quebec à Montreal (UQAM) in Montreal (April 2017), the "International Rule of Law" conference at the University of Richmond, Virginia (October 2017), the Research Group on Constitutional Studies Works-in-Progress series at McGill University (November 2017), and the Centro de Investigación y Docencia Económicas (CIDE) in Mexico City (April 2018). The author is grateful to the organizers of these conferences and workshops, as well as to Arash Abizadeh, Samuel Bagg, Amandine Catala, Paulina Ochoa Espejo, Evan Fox-Decent, Hoi Kong, Pablo Kalmanovitz, David Lefkowitz, Jacob Levy, Claudio Lopez-Guerra, Margaret Moore, Colleen Murphy, William Clare Roberts, Christa Scholtz, Mohamed Sesay, Hasana Sharp, Anna Stilz, Yves Winter, and others for their constructive comments and criticisms.

[1] For a chronology of dates relating to the legal status of the Sinixt in Canada, see "Schedule A" of *R. v. Desautel*, 2017 BCSC 2389, Supreme Court of British Columbia: www.courts.gov.bc.ca/jdb-txt/sc/17/23/2017BCSC2389.htm.

recognized that the Sinixt still enjoyed rights in Canada.[2] The BC government, however, is appealing the acquittal decision, arguing that aboriginal rights recognized in Canada cannot be extended to nonresident aboriginals, and that an indigenous group located in the United States cannot be recognized as a "rights-bearing aboriginal collective" entitled to aboriginal and treaty rights in Canada.[3]

This curious case about the transboundary claims of an "extinct" indigenous group helps to illuminate some of the challenges confronting any theory of global justice that aims to respond to an international order built upon a history marked by colonialism, settler colonialism, and empire. In my recent work, I have focused on two main critiques of contemporary international order.[4] One is that the state-centric institutions and practices of global governance reflect deep structural injustices that emanate from the colonial origins of the modern international order. The other is that the contemporary interstate order is alienating to many peoples and groups that were forcibly and arbitrarily incorporated into conditions of settler colonialism or postcolonial states. These avenues of critique reveal that the project of constructing a just global order is inseparable from the project of decolonizing contemporary international order.

This line of thinking allows us to raise the following kinds of normative questions regarding the transboundary claims of indigenous peoples, such as the Sinixt First Nation. First, what does decolonization entail with regard to the self-determination claims of such indigenous peoples as well as other peoples who were not only forcibly incorporated into settler colonial and postcolonial states, but also divided jurisdictionally and territorially by the establishment of such states? Second, how should such self-determination claims inform or condition the rights of states to assert sovereignty over their territorial boundaries, and their rights to control the movement of people, goods, and services across such boundaries? Third, under what conditions might peoples or groups with transboundary claims be reconciled with or nonalienated from a state-centric world order?

---

[2] Ashifa Kassam, "Sinixt First Nation Wins Recognition in Canada Decades after 'Extinction'," *The Guardian*, March 30, 2017, www.theguardian.com/world/2017/mar/3 0/canada-sinixt-first-nation-extinct-recognition.

[3] Bill Metcalfe, "Province Appeals Sinixt Hunting Case," *The Nelson Star*, May 1, 2017, www.nelsonstar.com/news/sinixt-hunting-trial-goes-to-appeal/. The Supreme Court of BC dismissed the appeal in December 2017. See *R. v. Desautel*, 2017 BCSC 2389. The Crown's appeal of that decision was granted in April 2018. See *R. v. Desautel*, 2018 BCCA 131: www.courts.gov.bc.ca/jdb-txt/ca/18/01/2018BCCA0131.htm.

[4] See my *Justice and Reconciliation in World Politics* (Cambridge: Cambridge University Press, 2017).

In the following section, I briefly consider the statist turn in cosmopolitan theories of global justice, and argue that this reliance on states as agents of global justice can obscure the extent to which the expansion and entrenchment of a state-centric international society has generated a structural legacy of injustice and alienation for those who continue to experience subjection to the state and international system as a colonizing project. One task of a theory of global justice must be to halt the contemporary reproduction of morally objectionable political and social relations that have their roots in practices of colonialism and settler colonialism. In the third section, this task of decolonizing international order leads to an examination of the international structure of state sovereign control over territorial boundaries. The international territorial boundaries of states are physical markers of state sovereignty that signify the limits of a state's jurisdiction. I argue that indigenous peoples experience structural injustice and alienation when forced into a sovereign state and interstate system that continues to deny their status as self-determining associative groups. The 2007 United Nations Declaration on the Rights of Indigenous Peoples (UNDRIP) constitutes some recognition of this structural injustice, and marks an extension of the decolonization process to indigenous peoples.

In the fourth section, I argue that this extension is not as straightforward as it appears, and that the self-determination claims of indigenous peoples force us to rethink the traditional prerogatives of a state's jurisdictional authority. Political theorists have pursued two broad strategies for accommodating the self-determination claims of substate groups within an order of sovereign states: redrawing boundaries (such as in cases of secession) and reforming internal governance structures (toward great intrastate autonomy or federalism). I argue, however, that these strategies still involve an underlying premise that ties claims of group self-determination to the justification of a state's authority to use coercion to enforce exclusive territorial rights, such as its rights to control borders.

In addition to sometimes requiring a redrawing of lines or reform of internal state structures, I argue that what the self-determination claims of transboundary (indigenous and other) groups may require is a revised international structure that places limits on the authority of states to control unilaterally or restrict coercively their social relations across international borders. My argument to untie the value of self-determination from statist models of instantiating group self-determination derives from considerations of both justice and reconciliation. First, if self-determination is constitutive of political justice, then the self-determination of transboundary indigenous peoples requires making international state boundaries more porous, in order to develop a states system that facilitates rather than hinders the legitimate self-determination claims of substate and transnational agents. An international order that facilitates indigenous self-determination in these respects is one that is more basically just than one that does not. Second, if existential alienation is the legacy of acts and practices of genocide, dispossession, and cultural destruction that have marked the interaction of indigenous peoples with the modern interstate order, overcoming such existential alienation requires the states system to accommodate the self-determination claims of indigenous peoples in ways that do not reproduce conditions of alienated agency. The good of nonalienation is an essential supporting condition for indigenous peoples to engage meaningfully in struggles for global justice in modern conditions.

Statism and Global Justice

We live in a world of states, and states have overseen the development of international institutions, law, norms, and practices – "global governance" – that govern, organize, and mediate the agency and activities of various actors in world politics.[5] Global justice theorists have been at the forefront of analyzing a variety of challenges to such a system, questioning whether it is desirable, legitimate, effective, or sustainable as a basic structure of global governance.[6] Debates between cosmopolitans and statists have focused on questioning in particular the moral grounds for favoring compatriots over noncompatriots on matters of distributive justice, and institutionally on whether the realization of global justice can be achieved through a reformed society of states or peoples, or requires the development of a world state.[7] In these contributions, cosmopolitan theorists of global justice have mounted deep moral critiques and institutional challenges to the current sovereign states system.

---

[5] As institutions and processes of globalization continue to develop, scholars of international relations have noted that the international context is increasingly characterized by "multiple authorities," and the "growing importance of nonstate or supra-state actors," including international organizations, nongovernmental organizations, professional associations, corporations, and advocacy groups. See Deborah D. Avant, Martha Finnemore, and Susan Sell (eds.), *Who Governs the Globe?* (Cambridge: Cambridge University Press, 2010), 356.

[6] See, for example, Gillian Brock, *Global Justice: A Cosmopolitan Account* (Oxford: Oxford University Press, 2009); Laura Valentini, *Justice in a Globalized World: A Normative Framework* (Oxford: Oxford University Press, 2011); Lea Ypi, *Global Justice and Avant-Garde Political Agency* (Oxford: Oxford University Press, 2011); Mathias Risse, *On Global Justice* (Princeton, NJ: Princeton University Press, 2012); David Miller, *National Responsibility and Global Justice* (Oxford: Oxford University Press, 2012).

[7] See my "Cosmopolitan Justice, Democracy, and the World State" in Luis Cabrera (ed.), *Institutional Cosmopolitanism* (Oxford: Oxford University Press, 2018), 232–52.

At the same time, even theorists with a cosmopolitan orientation have come to embrace the state institutionally, or at least accommodate the sovereign state as a legitimate form of political organization. This strategic move derives from an understanding that abstract cosmopolitan principles of global justice need to be combined with an account of agency in order to be effective and sustainable.[8] Martha Nussbaum, for example, despite her misgivings about patriotism,[9] has acknowledged the instrumental significance of the nation-state in her account of global justice, citing it as "the largest and most foundational unit that still has any chance of being decently accountable to the people who live there."[10] Lea Ypi's "statist cosmopolitanism" bridges cosmopolitan principles with an account of states as the relevant available agents that can effectively institutionalize such principles. Although Ypi has subsequently also gone beyond statist cosmopolitanism, and argued that cosmopolitanism "entails committing politically to the establishment of a global political authority representing all *states* and enforcing cosmopolitan obligations in a fair, impartial, and consistent manner,"[11] her account of global political authority still presupposes a statist structure of political representation and agency at the global level.[12]

Showing the plausibility of realizing cosmopolitan principles of global justice in a statist world order renders such principles relevant and feasible for here and now, rather than for some remote and utopian future. This reliance on states as instrumentally efficacious agents of global justice, however, tends to obscure the contentious development of the contemporary interstate order, and fails to consider its structural legacy for those who continue to experience subjection to the state and international system as a colonizing project. Acknowledging that the forcible incorporation of indigenous peoples in postcolonial and settler colonial contexts is not only a historic injustice, but a contemporary or ongoing structural injustice, should raise fundamental challenges to the legal and political authority and

[8] Lea Ypi, *Global Justice and Avant-Garde Political Agency* (Oxford: Oxford University Press, 2012).
[9] Martha Nussbaum, "Patriotism and Cosmopolitanism" in Joshua Cohen (ed.), *For Love of Country: Debating the Limits of Patriotism* (Boston, MA: Beacon, 1996), 2–20.
[10] Martha Nussbaum, *Frontiers of Justice: Disability, Nationality, Species Membership* (Cambridge, MA: Harvard University Press, 2006), 257.
[11] Lea Ypi, "Cosmopolitanism without if and without but," in Gillian Brock (ed.), *Cosmopolitanism versus Non-cosmopolitanism: Critiques, Defences, Reconceptualizations* (Oxford: Oxford University Press, 2013), 75–91, emphasis mine.
[12] It is unclear in her account how such a global political authority would accommodate claims to representation by nonstate groups, such as indigenous peoples.

legitimacy of postcolonial and settler colonial states as well as of the international order of sovereign states.[13]

Following Iris Marion Young, I understand social structural injustices to place individuals and groups in social positions or socially produced categories that entail their vulnerability to unjust treatment, structural indignity, or morally objectionable social relations or conditions.[14] These vulnerabilities and injustices can include marginalization from the structures and benefits of social cooperation, exclusion from universes of moral obligation and the social bases of dignity and respect, exploitation of productive labor, denial or distortion of social and political appropriative agency, and unjustified regulatory coercion and arbitrary violence.[15] In social and political contexts, structural injustices work to condition in morally objectionable ways the social positions, identities, agency, roles, aspirations, and potential and actual achievements of persons and groups. When structural injustices inform laws and norms, shape the design and purposes of institutions and social practices, and produce material effects, they enable, legitimize, normalize, and entrench conditions under which structural and interactional injustice may persist on a regular and predictable basis.[16]

In settler colonial and postcolonial contexts, it may be the configuration of international legal and political structures of state sovereignty itself, as well as processes of colonial and postcolonial state formation, that are causally fundamental in reproducing structural injustice and oppression. Such social conditions make some groups disproportionately more vulnerable to usurpation of decisional agency, dispossession, severe human rights violations, as well as poverty. For example, as the Colombian civil war ends, the Nasa (Cxhab Wala Kiwe) Indians of the Cauca Valley in Colombia, along with twenty other indigenous groups in the area, have experienced renewed conflict stemming from land disputes. While the indigenous groups seek acknowledgment of their ancestral land claims, and to grow subsistence crops in environmentally sustainable ways, the Colombian government faces pressures on land access and use by

---

[13] See Glen Coulthard, *Red Skin, White Masks: Rejecting the Colonial Politics of Recognition* (Minneapolis: University of Minnesota Press, 2014); Jennifer Balint, Julie Evans, and Nesam McMillan, "Rethinking Transitional Justice, Redressing Indigenous Harm: A New Conceptual Approach," *International Journal of Transitional Justice*, 8 (2014), 194–216.

[14] For her posthumous book that provides the most comprehensive account of her view of social structures and structural injustice, see Iris Marion Young, *Responsibility for Justice* (Oxford: Oxford University Press, 2011), 53–74.

[15] See also Iris Marion Young, *Justice and the Politics of Difference* (Princeton, NJ: Princeton University Press, 1990), 39–65.

[16] This description of structural injustice is drawn from my *Justice and Reconciliation in World Politics*, 35.

nonindigenous and commercial interests in property development, mining, and global sugar production.[17] To make progress on overcoming the structural and interactional injustices that disproportionately afflict indigenous peoples, global justice theorists should be especially concerned with the task of decolonizing global order. One task of global justice must be to halt the reproduction of such objectionable political and social relations that have their roots in practices of colonialism and settler colonialism. In general, for theories of global justice to be complementary to the task of decolonization, they should be more critical of statist frameworks and premises for conceptualizing a globally just order.

Decolonizing Borders and Territorial Rights

One aspect of international order that a decolonizing agenda should interrogate relates to the international structure of state sovereign control over territorial boundaries. The international territorial boundaries of states are physical markers of state sovereignty that signify the limits of a state's jurisdiction, or "its plenary authority to prescribe, adjudicate, and enforce its laws and policies."[18] Through their control of territorial borders, states enable and constrain the agency of people to move and travel, to trade and exchange, and to engage in various sorts of social relations across borders.[19] The territorial rights of states constitute a pillar of international law, which affirms the right of states to exclusive jurisdictional authority over their territory, and prohibits violations of a state's territorial integrity and political independence as grave injustices that undermine the principles of the equality and self-determination of states.

At the same time, it is commonly acknowledged that most if not all political boundaries are arbitrary constructs, typically resulting from natural contingency, war, conquest, and other historically and morally arbitrary and even unjust actions, events, or conditions. The boundaries of African states, for example, are results of negotiations between European powers at the Berlin Conference of 1884–85, to fix their various spheres of influence. Historically, one can say that boundary-drawing was an imperial activity, and there was no self-determination of the people affected by these boundaries at their inception. While "rival European

---

[17] See Jonathan Watts, "Battle for the Mother Land: Indigenous People of Colombia Fighting for Their Lands," *The Guardian*, October 29, 2017. www.theguardian.com/environment/2017/oct/28/nasa-colombia-cauca-valley-battle-mother-land.

[18] Steven R. Ratner, "Land Feuds and Their Solutions: Finding International Law Beyond the Tribunal Chamber," *The American Journal of International Law*, 100/4 (2006), 809.

[19] A. John Simmons, "On the Territorial Rights of States," *Philosophical Issues*, 11 (2001), 306.

claims to territory were frequently supported by treaties made with local rulers," such treaties were made relevant to territorial settlements "only when a European power concerned decided so."[20] The limited knowledge of European powers at the time about existing patterns of human settlement or even physical geography translated into the use of straight lines or astronomical lines, with the result that almost 30 percent of boundary lines in Africa are straight lines. As geographers have noted, boundaries were "dehumanized" on the African continent: there are 177 "partitioned culture areas," with all African states incorporating several distinct culture areas as well as several partitioned culture areas.[21] Colonial legacies also appear in boundary disputes between and within states in many parts of the world, including between China and India, between China and Taiwan and Tibet, between Ethiopia and Eritrea, Nigeria and Cameroon, Israel and Palestine, Saudi Arabia and Yemen, as well as Thailand and Cambodia. In the context of settler colonial states such as Canada and the United States, as the case of the Sinixt First Nations shows, interstate territorial borders also pose a particular problem for those indigenous peoples whose traditional social relations and practices traverse international boundaries.

Despite any normative concerns arising from such arbitrariness, the dominant principle at work in settling international disputes over territorial boundaries has traditionally been based on the "stability and continuity of boundaries," mainly due to concerns about the destabilizing effects of attempting to redraw boundaries. The principle of stability has also conditioned how new claims of justice in international politics have come to be institutionalized with the repudiation of colonialism as a legitimate form of political relation. Decolonization as a historical process entailed the recognition of the self-determination claims of formerly colonized peoples. In theory, the principle of self-determination grounded the rights of colonized peoples to political independence and jurisdictional authority over their territories.[22] In practice, the self-

---

[20] Ieuan Griffiths, "The Scramble for Africa: Inherited Political Boundaries," *The Geographical Journal*, 152/2 (1986), 207.

[21] Griffiths, "The Scramble for Africa," 204. On culturally partitioned areas, see A. I. Asiwaju (ed.), *Partitioned Africans: Ethnic Relations across Africa's International Boundaries 1884–1984* (London: Hurst, 1985).

[22] See Anna Stilz, "Decolonization and Self-Determination," *Social Philosophy and Policy*, 32/1 (2015), 1–24. In this article, Stilz constructs an "associative account" of the value of self-determination to explain why historical decolonization was morally required. She then considers how such an account of self-determination can be applied to other cases, including that of indigenous peoples. I would argue, however, that the case of indigenous self-determination should be characterized as a further extension of the decolonization process, which entails acknowledging that the 1960s era of decolonization was far from sufficient to realize the moral requirements of decolonization.

determination of the colonized translated into a "presumptive inheritance of colonial era boundaries by new states." Concerns for maintaining stability motivated the nearly strict application of the doctrine of *uti possidetis de jure* in cases such as the dissolution of empires as well as decolonization of states from colonial political relations. Thus, as Steven Ratner and others have observed, "the stability of boundaries remains a core norm of the international legal system."[23]

Although the boundaries of African states have colonial origins, and their entrenchment in the process of decolonization was motivated mainly by considerations of stability, one might argue that in that process of decolonization, African states have legitimized these boundaries. Paragraph 3 of Article III of the 1963 Charter of the Organization of African Union (OAU) contains a pledge by all member states to respect "the sovereignty and territorial integrity of each State and for its alienable right to independent existence."[24] Furthermore, in a clarificatory statement in 1964, the OAU states, "Considering that border problems constitute a grave and permanent factor of dissention ... all Member States pledge themselves to respect the borders existing on their achievement of national independence."[25] Although arbitrary or contingent in their origins, then, international boundaries have also been legitimated, typically through international treaties or adjudication. The arbitrariness of boundaries thus does not necessarily translate into their injustice. The principles of stability and self-determination have combined to produce an interstate order that has universalized the equal rights of states to jurisdictional authority over their territories, with the implication that, "once a boundary has been established, it is extremely difficult to challenge or revise it without the consent of all the bordering states."[26]

It is important to acknowledge that the contemporary system of equal sovereign states, which covers practically the entire habited world, required the transformation of colonial international order, through the destruction of the institutional divide between those (largely European) states that were "civilized" and therefore entitled to independence and equal toleration, and those (largely non-European states) that were in need of "civilization"

---

[23] Ratner, "Land Feuds and Their Solutions," 809.

[24] Organization of African Union Charter, May 1963, https://au.int/en/treaties/oau-charter-addis-ababa-25-may-1963.

[25] Organization of African Union AHG, Resolution 17(1) Border Disputes among African States, Adopted by the First Ordinary Session of the Assembly of Heads of State and Government Held in Cairo, UAR, July 1964, https://au.int/sites/default/files/decisions/9514-1964_ahg_res_1-24_i_e.pdf.

[26] Michal Saliternik, "Expanding the Boundaries of Boundary Dispute Settlement: International Law and Critical Geography at the Crossroads," *Vanderbilt Journal of Transnational Law*, 40 (2017), 120.

and therefore subject to colonization or international supervision by European "civilized" powers.[27] The universalization of sovereign equality constitutes a repudiation of the unequal status of peoples that was a defining feature of colonial international order. The United Nations General Assembly, in its 1960 "Declaration on the Granting of Independence to Colonial Countries and Peoples," equated the "subjection of peoples to alien subjugation, domination and exploitation" to "a denial of fundamental human rights"; affirmed the principle of self-determination for all peoples in their political status and economic, social, and cultural development; and condemned the "standard of civilization" rationale for colonial rule by asserting that "inadequacy of political, economic, social or educational preparedness should never serve as a pretext for delaying independence."[28]

I want to argue, however, that the unequal status of peoples is still a feature of contemporary international order, and that further decolonization is still required. The continued subjection of indigenous peoples within postcolonial and settler colonial states reflects their subordination in the international order of states. In this sense, the decolonization movement in the mid-twentieth century was a bittersweet development for those whose claims to self-determination were not accommodated in the decolonization process. As Steven Ratner has observed, the repudiation of colonialism involved the declaration that "colonialism in all its forms is an affront to basic human rights," however, while "colonial peoples and indigenous peoples both suffered from conquest by settlers from far away," international law's use of the principle of *uti possidetis de jure* "gives only the former a right to independence, simply by virtue of their physical separation from the colonizing state."[29] In fact, even this division between "colonial peoples" and "indigenous peoples" is misleading, since indigenous or precolonial peoples also exist in many postcolonial settings, as well as in settler colonial contexts. Furthermore, in both cases, they may experience structural injustice and alienation when forced into a sovereign state and interstate system that continues to deny their self-determination.

Claims by indigenous peoples for international recognition of their status as self-determining agents have appeared since the advent of

---

[27] Edward Keene, *Beyond the Anarchical Society: Grotius, Colonialism and Order in World Politics* (Cambridge: Cambridge University Press, 2002).

[28] United Nations General Assembly resolution 1514 (XV), "Declaration on the Granting of Independence to Colonial Countries and Peoples," December 14, 1960, www.un.org /en/decolonization/declaration.shtml.

[29] Steven R. Ratner, *The Thin Justice of International Law: A Moral Reckoning of the Law of Nations* (Oxford: Oxford University Press, 2015), 155.

modern international organization in the early twentieth century. In 1923, among the representatives of the colonized and subjugated who sought an international audience at the League of Nations in Geneva was Chief Levi General (Deskaheh), leader of the Six Nations. His petition to League members sought to rectify treaty violations and erosions of indigenous sovereignty by the Government of Canada, wrongs that constituted, to the Six Nations, "an act of war" and "a menace to international peace."[30] In the nascent international order still dominated by a league of colonial nations, however, the petition was never heard. Canada blocked the petition by asserting that the Six Nations suffered from incapacity to assume the responsibilities of statehood, and Great Britain endorsed Canada's position by casting the dispute as a domestic matter within the British Empire. This international denial of indigenous self-determination followed and entrenched the forcible incorporation of indigenous groups into settler colonial states. In the United States in the mid-1800s, this process culminated in the transfer of relations between the federal government and Indian tribes from the Department of War, which handled relations between the federal government and "domestic dependent nations" or "weak states," to the Department of the Interior, a department that manages natural resources and wildlife.[31]

The 2007 United Nations Declaration on the Rights of Indigenous Peoples (UNDRIP) constitutes some recognition of this structural injustice, and marks an extension of the decolonization process to indigenous peoples within states. Thus, Article 3 of that Declaration mirrors Article 2 of the 1960 Declaration on the Granting of Independence to Colonial Countries and Peoples: "Indigenous peoples have the right to self-determination. By virtue of that right they freely determine their political status and freely pursue their economic, social and cultural development." While such a direct translation from the 1960 Declaration to the 2007 UNDRIP makes the extension of self-determination rights to indigenous peoples seem like a straightforward development of the earlier process of decolonization, in fact, full implementation of the 2007 Declaration would entail great challenges to the conventional claim of states to exclusive jurisdictional and territorial rights.

---

[30] See Mark Pearcey, "Sovereignty, Identity, and Indigenous-State Relations at the Beginning of the Twentieth Century: A Case of Exclusion by Inclusion," *International Studies Review*, 17 (2015), 449, 451–2.

[31] See N. Bruce Duthu, *American Indians and the Law* (New York: Penguin, 2008), xxviii–xxix; Duthu, *Shadow Nations: Tribal Sovereignty and the Limits of Legal Pluralism* (Oxford: Oxford University Press, 2013), 12–14.

According to Article 43, the Declaration constitutes "the minimum standards for the survival, dignity and well-being of the indigenous peoples of the world." These standards include domestic and international political and financial support for indigenous self-government (Article 4); control over relevant political boundaries and territories (Articles 10 and 26–8); natural resource exploitation and environmental protection (Articles 29 and 32), and social, economic, educational, and cultural development. In addition, the Declaration explicitly asserts transboundary rights of indigenous peoples divided by international borders, thus it provides for such indigenous peoples to "have the right to maintain and develop contacts, relations and cooperation, including activities for spiritual, cultural, political, economic and social purposes, with their own members as well as other peoples across borders" (Article 36). For example, the peoples of the Iroquois Confederacy traverse the US–Canada border, and recognition of their self-determination would impose various kinds of limits on the scope of the regulatory powers of Canada and the United States to control the movement of people, goods and services across their international borders.[32] The self-determination claims of the Tohono O'odham Nation, which occupies a reservation that traverses the US–Mexican border, would also challenge the legitimacy of any US plan to build a 1,954-mile border wall in the name of national security.[33]

Decolonization and Self-Determination

While the appeal to collective self-determination as an ordering principle of global justice has become pervasive, Anna Stilz is right to note that the concept "has proved enduringly difficult to theorize."[34] In the contemporary context, Steven Ratner has identified four categories of "peoples" whose self-determination claims are accommodated in some way by international law. First, the "people of an existing state" have a right to self-determination in the form of maintaining their "status of statehood against external and internal coercion." Thus, the people of an existing state enjoy a right to self-determination or nonviolation of the norm of nonintervention by other states, as well as a right against attempts to divide the state internally. The people of an existing state also have

[32] See Audra Simpson, *Mohawk Interruptus: Political Life across the Borders of Settler States* (Durham, NC: Duke University Press, 2014).
[33] Fernanda Santos, "Border Wall Would Cleave Tribe, and Its Connection to Ancestral Land," *The New York Times*, February 20, 2017, www.nytimes.com/2017/02/20/us/border-wall-tribe.html.
[34] Stilz, "Decolonization and Self-Determination," 2.

a right to self-determination in "the form of a government that represents the whole of the people in the territory (without distinction as to race, creed or colour)."[35] Second, people of a "non-self-governing territory," in the form of a colony or in the form of a "people subject to foreign occupation following a use of force," are entitled to self-determination. Third, although peoples are not defined in international law, there is also some provision of the right of peoples "within" states to a representative government, although there is disagreement about the cultural, religious, and linguistic rights any subset of peoples within a state, such as a national minority, may claim, short of sovereignty. Finally, Ratner notes that indigenous peoples have "rights to autonomy and self-government, rights to practice and protect their culture in robust ways, and the right to set up their own education systems, as well as the right against forced removal from their land."[36]

While contemporary international law has not resolved tensions and conflicts that can arise between these different types of self-determination claims, Ratner observes that international practice has fairly consistently favored the equation of sovereign right with the unrestricted freedom to determine political boundaries and allegiances without consultation of the populations affected or regard for their interests. Thus, "despite the evolution of the norm of self-determination of peoples, states are still under no general duty to consult or act according to the wishes of the population of a disputed territory with respect to its future status."[37]

Anyone who seeks to reorder the world based on the principle of self-determination of peoples also needs to be mindful of the dangers of previous political attempts to use self-determination as a basis for reforming international order. These dangers have been highlighted by historians who have studied the politics of self-determination in the early twentieth century, and their devastating consequences in issuing in forced migration, ethnic cleansing, and genocide. Eric Weitz has detailed the transformation from the Vienna system to the Paris system of international order, showing that historically, the term "self-determination" did not exist in isolation, but was a key component in a political shift in international relations toward "population politics."[38]

Such politics asserted the rights of "civilized" populations to their own state as a foundation for world peace, but in practice, this logic "justified

---

[35] Ratner, *The Thin Justice of International Law*, 145. An outlier was apartheid South Africa.
[36] Ratner, *The Thin Justice of International Law*, 147.
[37] Ratner, "Land Feuds and Their Solution," 811.
[38] Eric D. Weitz, "From Vienna to the Paris System: International Politics and the Entangled Histories of Human Rights, Forced Deportations, and Civilizing Missions," *American Historical Review*, 113/5 (2008), 1328.

imperial and colonial rule over Africans and even genocide in accordance with racial hierarchies, as well as forced deportations in accordance with visions of sovereignty based on national or ethnic homogeneity." According to Weitz, the principle of self-determination, mixed with the rise of ethnonationalist politics in a context of the dissolution of multi-ethnic empires (Habsburg, Ottoman, and Russian), wrought much blood and grief. Thus, the Lausanne Treaty that concluded the peace settlement after World War I marked the first international legitimation of forced deportations. While many Greek refugees had fled Anatolia, the treaty made the removal of the remaining Greeks as well as Muslims compulsory, forcing "the 'exchange' of 1.5 million people in the name of creating states that were nationally homogenous."[39] The historical development of a society of self-determining nations has thus meant the systematic transfer of populations according to ethnic lines. We witnessed this version of the politics of self-determination haunt the immediate post-Cold War world, and we see a revival of such exclusionary movements in Europe and settler colonial states in response to increased migration from the formerly colonized world.[40]

While human rights treaties, as well as the UNDRIP, assert the "right of self-determination" for "all peoples" so that they can "freely determine their political status and freely pursue their economic, social and cultural development," Weitz argues that the United Nations has still to wrestle with the question – "self-determination for whom?" – and has not yet resolved conflicts and tensions between individual human rights and collective rights to self-determination.[41]

Anna Stilz has provided one of the most compelling accounts of self-determination and its value as a basis for states' political legitimacy and territorial claims. She argues that people have an interest not only in good or just government, but also in "being the authors or 'makers' of their political institutions."[42] A legitimate state or political structure of governance should not only protect basic rights of its citizens, but also be subjectively affirmed by them: "If citizens attain subjective freedom, they will see their state as a creation of their own free cooperation, not

[39] Weitz, "From Vienna to the Paris System," 1328. Weitz's historical analysis makes a plausible case that the politics of self-determination at the beginning of the twentieth century supported the development of both the rights of minority groups, *and* practices of forced deportation and genocide.
[40] See Lucy Mayblin, *Asylum after Empire: Colonial Legacies in the Politics of Asylum Seeking* (London: Rowman & Littlefield, 2017).
[41] Weitz, "From Vienna to the Paris System," 1342.
[42] Anna Stilz, "The Value of Self-Determination" in David Sobel, Peter Vallentyne, and Steven Wall (eds.), *Oxford Studies in Political Philosophy*, *Vol. II* (Oxford: Oxford University Press, 2016), 101.

as an institution of subjugation."[43] The value of self-determination consists in citizens being coauthors of the institutions that govern their lives. When some group of citizens fails to relate to their political institutions in this way, their self-determination claims may translate into an alteration of political boundaries: "Where their priorities (a) are consistent with the provision of basic justice, and (b) can be feasibly addressed through institutional reconfiguration, I believe we may be required to redraw political boundaries to afford them greater self-determination. On my approach, the boundaries of the people are always up for renegotiation." She also acknowledges that accommodating a subgroup's self-determination "may be adequately guaranteed through federalism or internal autonomy,"[44] as well as special representation rights or devolution.[45]

Political theorists have generally pursued two broad strategies for accommodating the self-determination claims of substate groups within an order of sovereign states: redrawing boundaries (in cases of secession) and reforming internal governance structures. Those concerned with the internal political legitimacy of states have argued that secession (involving the redrawing of international boundaries as well as the creation of new states) may be justified as a remedial practice in response to grave injustice by the larger state.[46] Some theorists have also argued that the principle of self-determination may generate a nonremedial right of groups to political independence (and with that, changes to territorial jurisdictions).[47] Stilz argues that when a persistently alienated group is "territorially organized" and possesses "broadly representative practices," the existing state's failure to meet the criterion of subjective legitimacy may provide such subgroups with "*pro tanto* claims to create new political units."[48]

Postcolonial states have resisted such arguments, preferring a principle of self-determination that translates into a principle of protection from any foreign or international interference, rather than one that entails any positive commitment on their part "to representative government, human rights, minority rights, or indigenous peoples' rights." As Ratner has explained, "developing states are still far more reluctant to link the right

---

[43] Stilz, "Decolonization and Self-Determination," 12.
[44] Stilz, "The Value of Self-Determination," 119–20.
[45] Stilz, "Decolonization and Self-Determination," 4.
[46] See Allen Buchanan, *Justice, Legitimacy, and Self-Determination: Moral Foundations for International Law* (Oxford: Oxford University Press, 2007).
[47] For a critique of remedial theories of secession and an argument for nonremedial grounds for secession, see Amandine Catala, "Remedial Theories of Secession and Territorial Justification," *Journal of Social Philosophy*, 44/1 (2013), 74–94.
[48] Stilz, "Decolonization and Self-Determination," 20.

to self-determination of peoples to a particular form of government" (such as a human rights respecting democracy).[49] Postcolonial states may argue that redrawing boundaries to accommodate the self-determination claims of substate groups, including indigenous peoples, conflicts with postcolonial states' right to equal recognition as self-determining peoples. Stilz's account, however, may still normatively prevail over such arguments, given substantial evidence that "self-determination as non-interference" has not generally translated into a nondominating social or political order.[50]

At the same time, the strategies envisaged by Stilz subscribe to an underlying premise that ties claims of group self-determination to the justification of a state's authority to use coercion to enforce exclusive territorial rights, such as its rights to control borders. Thus, while Stilz's account of the value of self-determination makes her supportive of accommodating indigenous self-determination, the types of accommodation she mentions, such as secession, internal autonomy, federalism, and devolution, fit into a fairly conventional statist framework. The self-determination claims of indigenous peoples, including transboundary peoples, however, may requiring going beyond these forms, and positing more radical transformation of conceptions of legitimate political authority and the jurisdictional rights of states.

To see why this might be the case, consider that Stilz rejects as infeasible the self-determination claims of "dispersed minorities" without the capacity for "territorial organization in representative institutions."[51] It is not clear how her Kantian-based account of the state as a shared political project subjectively affirmed by its citizens can accommodate the self-determination of transboundary peoples or small groups of indigenous peoples who are dispersed over a large geographical area that the small group could not feasibly control. In practice, if the principle of self-determination were to be applied to every "culture area," or even to those "partitioned culture areas," on the continent of Africa, this could involve over a hundred claims to redraw existing international

---

[49] Ratner, *The Thin Justice of International Law*, 159. On the challenges of state-building in Africa, see Jeffrey Herbst, *States and Power in Africa: Comparative Lessons in Authority and Control*, rev. ed. (Princeton, NJ: Princeton University Press, 2014).
[50] Two concepts of self-determination, as noninterference and as nondomination, were developed by Iris Marion Young, *Global Challenges: War, Self-Determination and Responsibility for Justice* (Cambridge: Polity, 2007), 15–38. For a partial defence of self-determination as noninterference, see Jacob T. Levy, "Self-Determination, Non-Domination, and Federalism," *Hypatia*, 23/3 (2008), 60–78. I am broadly sympathetic to Young embedding the concept and value of self-determination within a republican theory of justice and freedom as nondomination.
[51] Stilz, "The Value of Self-Determination," 123.

boundaries. It is also difficult to redraw territorial boundaries or create new political units in the case of indigenous peoples forcibly incorporated into settler colonial states, given that many indigenous peoples typically had overlapping traditional territories, and did not conceive of their relationship with the natural world in ways easily reconcilable with the practice of drawing sovereign boundaries at all.[52]

In both cases, the arbitrariness of current boundaries represent a source of structural alienation of groups from the modern interstate order. They also can constitute sources of structural injustice, to the extent that such boundaries entail "social processes" that "put large categories of persons under a systematic threat of domination or deprivation of the means to develop and exercise their capacities, at the same time as these processes enable others to dominate or have a wide range of opportunities for developing and exercising their capacities."[53] While Stilz is right to note that self-determination claims are not absolute, and can be overridden by "countervailing considerations," such as "avoiding conflict or instability," the structural impossibility of accommodating the self-determination claims of some marginalized groups, such as transboundary or geographically dispersed peoples, may constitute a persistent pattern of structural injustice that disproportionately affects indigenous peoples.

My argument is that it is misguided to think that the principle of self-determination can generate more appropriate redrawings of boundaries. The problem is not (mostly) that the boundaries are drawn in the wrong places. To a large extent, there will be a degree of arbitrariness of where any international boundary is drawn or redrawn. I am arguing that it is not their arbitrariness that makes them unjust, but states' exclusive and coercive jurisdictional and territorial rights that makes such boundaries sources of structural injustice. Redressing the structural injustice of colonial boundaries requires transformations of sovereign rights over cross-border activities and relations. The way to decolonize territorial borders, then, is not to redraw the lines. While theorists have aimed to determine the conditions under which the principle of self-determination may justify how political boundaries should be redrawn or internal governance structures reconfigured, these strategies are insufficient, and sometimes inappropriate.[54]

Just as others have argued that requirements of global justice affecting resource use and migration should qualify states' territorial

---

[52] The territorial claims of the Sinixt to a large area of southeastern British Columbia, for example, overlap with claims made by the Ktunaxa Nation.
[53] Young, *Responsibility for Justice*, 52.
[54] See my *Justice and Reconciliation in World Politics*, 268.

rights,[55] I would argue that the claims of individuals and collectives to self-determination encompass their engagement in meaningful social relationships, including marriage and family relations, as well as those derived from religious and cultural community, and that these claims to self-determination should constitute another set of qualifications on states' territorial rights. As Alan Patten has put it in his discussion of the value of self-determination, "there are some areas of life where it seems especially important that a person enjoy the opportunity to conduct her life on the basis of her own values and purposes." These areas include "developing and pursuing one's own religious and moral outlook," as well as the realms of intimacy, "sexuality, friendship, and basic relations of community with others" with whom one has a meaningful connection.[56] States may be instrumental in providing the regulatory structure for facilitating such self-determined social relations across international boundaries, but their authority to control borders is constrained by a duty not to undermine nonstatist and transnational forms of individual and collective self-determination. Furthermore, as Young argued, "the self-determination of peoples requires that the peoples have the right to participate *as peoples* in designing and implementing intergovernmental institutions aimed at minimizing domination."[57]

I am also arguing that decolonizing the territorial rights of states is not just a matter of justice, but also of reconciliation. In a large number of cases, where the territorial borders that have been drawn are largely arbitrary, they are not so much unjust as alienating. This is to say that there is no truth to the matter, and no right answer, about where state boundaries in many postcolonial contexts should be drawn – any boundary is admittedly arbitrary. The fact that existing borders were drawn arbitrarily, largely without regard for existing patterns of human social relations, makes such borders a source of structural alienation that generates a need for reconciliation of contemporary agents.

To understand the distinct additional challenge of reconciliation, I draw on the work of Rahel Jaeggi, who has developed a conception of alienation that refers to experiences of disconnection, disruption, or

[55] See Lea Ypi, "A Permissive Theory of Territorial Rights," *European Journal of Philosophy*, 22/2 (2014), 288–312; Mathias Risse, "The Right to Relocation: Disappearing Island Nations and Common Ownership of the Earth," *Ethics and International Affairs*, 22/1 (2008), 25–33. For a comprehensive overview of the relevant literature, see Amandine Catala, "Territorial Rights," *Routledge Encyclopedia of Philosophy* (London: Routledge, 2017).
[56] Alan Patten, *Equal Recognition: The Moral Foundation of Minority Rights* (Princeton, NJ: Princeton University Press, 2014), 133.
[57] Young, "Two Concepts of Self-Determination," 51.

distortion in "the structure of human relations to self and world" and "the relations agents have to themselves, to their own actions, and to the social and natural worlds." Jaeggi conceives of alienation as a "particular form of the loss of freedom" that involves "a relation of disturbed or inhibited appropriation of world and self." Successful appropriation by an agent "can be explicated as the capacity to make the life one leads, or what one wills and does, one's own; as the capacity to identify with oneself and with what one does; in other words, as the ability to realize oneself in what one does."[58] This activity of self-realization in the world is typically disrupted or distorted in individuals and societies that have experienced colonial injustice. Jonathan Lear also captures this form of what I have termed "*existential* alienation" in the experience of indigenous peoples whose particular social and moral frames have been disrupted, and even rendered inoperable or unintelligible, through colonial settlement, exploitation, genocide, and dispossession.[59]

With respect to such colonial legacies, the challenge of agents *becoming* free, equal, and nonalienated authors of their social structures is not resolved by recognizing their rights to be participants within a social structural framework that is itself a product of colonial injustice, or their rights to reproduce such structures through creating a new or reformed state. As Glen Coulthard has argued, following Frantz Fanon, dominated agents need to struggle to create new decolonized terms of self-determination that they can call their own, and not only seek equal status based on structures of colonial domination, otherwise "the colonized will have failed to reestablish themselves as truly self-determining: as creators of the terms, values, and conditions by which they are to be recognized."[60]

Under what conditions might indigenous peoples be reconciled or nonalienated from a world of territorially bordered states? In addition to greater devolution of governing powers, or the redrawing of lines, in many cases, what agents may require is internationally recognized limits on the authority of states to control unilaterally or restrict coercively transboundary social relations of indigenous and other groups. According to geographers in critical border studies, international law is changing. The International Court of Justice (ICJ) is starting to deviate from the principles of continuity and stability in determining boundary

---

[58] Rahel Jaeggi, *Alienation*, trans. F. Neuhouse and A. E. Smith (New York: Columbia University Press, 2014), xxi, 22, 2, 36, 37.

[59] See Jonathan Lear, *Radical Hope: Ethics in the Face of Cultural Devastation* (Cambridge, MA: Harvard University Press, 2006). On existential alienation, see my *Justice and Reconciliation in World Politics*, 182–216.

[60] Coulthard, *Red Skin, White Masks*, 39.

disputes. In some recent judgments, it has explicitly departed from historical boundaries and justified the departures based on "[substate] collective self-determination, peacemaking, utilization of water resources, protection of pasture rights, and access to heritage sites." The needs of local populations, for example, to resources such as water, can limit what any state can do in terms of claiming a territorial boundary or asserting a right to territorial control with implications for resource use.[61] Such considerations are pertinent not only to determining the *location* of where state boundaries are drawn or redrawn, but also in outlining conditions on states' internal and external authority to control or inhibit the development and fulfillment of social relations that traverse their borders.

Conclusion

A decade after the adoption of the United Nations Declaration on the Rights of Indigenous Peoples, the political struggles of indigenous peoples all over the world continue, as they face challenges consisting of the distortion and usurpation of their self-determination, continued dispossession from their traditional territories, deep deprivation, and the assimilationist policies that attend state-building projects. Such vulnerabilities are hallmarks of colonial structural injustice and intricately associated with the position of "structural indignity" accorded to indigenous peoples within contemporary international order.[62] In response to these structural injustices produced in postcolonial and settler colonial conditions, the project of global justice must entail establishing limits on the authority of states to engage in forced incorporation or collectivization projects of assimilation that adversely affect indigenous peoples and other transboundary social groups. Theories of self-determination that are wedded to political projects that entail state-building or nation-building along the lines of modern states, and do not problematize the exclusive and comprehensive political and territorial rights of state authorities to control people, land, and borders, cannot redress such structural injustices.

An anti-colonial theory of global justice needs to dethrone the bounded territorial sovereign state as the primary site of collective self-determination, and open institutional space that can accommodate a greater pluralism of self-determining communities both above and below the traditional sovereign state, for peoples "who dream of creating

[61] Saliternik, "Expanding the Boundaries," 132 and 135.
[62] On "structural indignity," see Duthu, *Shadow Nations,* 12–14.

their own forms of political association and governing themselves in their own ways."[63] Ultimately, the quest for global justice may entail truly revolutionary structural transformations of world order that involve pluralizing the agents that can have political standing in domestic, international, and transnational institutions and structures. In addition, decolonizing global order may entail fundamental modifications of the constitutive political and territorial rights of states, and the coercive architecture of the modern sovereign states system that enforces such rights.

More immediately, the argument for transboundary rights for transboundary peoples is focused on rectifying colonial-based international structural injustice, and is distinct from an argument that endorses a universal or general right to freedom of movement for all individuals, or a world with open borders.[64] But, the necessity of international rather than bilateral or domestic rules of recognition for state obligations to recognize transboundary rights of transboundary peoples points to a compatibility of this argument with great transformations of the modern interstate system, even toward world state formation. Whether or not such developments transpire, for the here and now, my argument about decolonizing the territorial rights of states may be one way that the traditional prerogatives of state sovereignty may transform in a more emancipatory direction.

I have argued that to take the project of decolonizing global order seriously, political theorists of global justice need to examine the institutional implications that follow from recognizing the right of indigenous groups to self-determination. Specifically, such normative claims have the potential to challenge, in quite radical ways, the current international presumption of states' exclusive jurisdictional authority and territorial rights. In contemporary international order, there exist international mechanisms of adjudication for states to settle disputes among themselves over jurisdictional issues that affect their territorial claims. But, Yet states have the ultimate authority to decide whether or not to take their boundary disputes to international tribunals or the ICJ. While the ICJ can recommend post-adjudicatory processes to take into account human and other considerations in how states exercise their territorial and jurisdictional rights, the court's willingness to introduce such restrictions on states' authority and power may also propel

---

[63] James Tully, *Public Philosophy in a New Key, Vol. II* (Cambridge: Cambridge University Press, 2013), 140. See also my "Cosmopolitan Justice, Democracy, and the World State."

[64] See Joseph Carens, "Aliens and Citizens: The Case for Open Borders," *Review of Politics*, 49/2 (1987), 251–73.

some to eschew adjudication and resolve their conflicts with force. Indigenous peoples have understood this lesson well, and their continued subjection to the threat and actual use of state coercive power to determine whose claims prevail should be a somber reminder of how far we have yet to go to decolonize global order and justice.

Index

CPSIA information can be obtained
at www.ICGtesting.com
Printed in the USA
LVHW090140180720
661032LV00010B/95